COLORADO PIONEERS

IN
PICTURE AND STORY

Alice Polk Hill

HERITAGE BOOKS
2008

HERITAGE BOOKS
AN IMPRINT OF HERITAGE BOOKS, INC.

Books, CDs, and more—Worldwide

For our listing of thousands of titles see our website
at
www.HeritageBooks.com

A Facsimile Reprint
Published 2008 by
HERITAGE BOOKS, INC.
Publishing Division
100 Railroad Ave. #104
Westminster, Maryland 21157

Copyright © 1915 Alice Polk Hill

Copyright © 2002 Heritage Books, Inc.

— Publisher's Notice —
In reprints such as this, it is often not possible to remove blemishes from the original. We feel the contents of this book warrant its reissue despite these blemishes and hope you will agree and read it with pleasure.

International Standard Book Number: 978-0-7884-2224-9

TO

JOSEPH ADDISON THATCHER

*Colorado's Oldest Banker
and a Prominent Figure
in the History of the State*

THE AUTHOR

Private Subscription Edition

OF

Colorado Pioneers

IN

Picture and Story

LIMITED TO TWO THOUSAND COPIES, OF WHICH THIS IS

No. __39__

Alice Polk Hill

Author

PREFACE

In presenting this revised edition of my book, entitled "TALES OF THE COLORADO PIONEERS," I have given it the title of "COLORADO PIONEERS IN PICTURE AND STORY."

It has been my effort to weave around a thread of history the legends, traditions and reminiscences of the Pioneers, which accentuate the great phases in the development of Colorado, from its earliest history to the time it became a State in 1876.

Ever since I journeyed into Denver in a Pullman car, in 1872, I have been interested in the people who "blazed the way." I have listened to their tales of how they "won the West," and have found in the real incidents in the lives of real people a charm to which fiction can never attain.

The labor of the Pioneers involved the highest type of moral as well as physical courage, and by placing their brave deeds in an historical setting I hope to preserve their intensely interesting human side and show how the isolated settlement, in a dreary desert, found its way into the sisterhood of states.

My first book had a favorable reception. Its success encouraged me to write this larger work, in which most of the earlier features are included.

In preparing the thread of history, I found help in Frank Hall's "History of Colorado;" Fossett's "Colorado;" Hollister's "Mines of Colorado;" Parson's "Making of Colorado;" J. C. Smiley's "Story of Denver;" William L. Visscher's story of "The Pony Express," and to A. E. Pierce for many pioneer stories.

I am especially indebted to Judge Wilbur F. Stone—a scholarly pioneer who has been a part of every phase of Colorado to the present time—for his careful reading and helpful criticism of the manuscript.

I wish also to express my obligations to Mr. Chalmers Hadley, of the Denver Public Library; Mr. E. B. Morgan, for use of his valuable collection of books in the "State Historical Society;" Hugh Steele, secretary of the "Colorado Pioneers' Society;" Mr. Will C. Bishop, of the "Trail;" Mr. A. E. Carson's "Colorado, Top o' the World," and Harry Ruffner, secretary of the "Sons of Colorado," through his big "scrap book." I have drawn heavily from "The Rocky Mountain News," "The Denver Republican," "The Times" and "The Post."

I have given facts about people, some tinged with humor, some filled with pathos; I have given incidents relating to the organized beginnings of Denver in 1858-'59-'60, so that my readers may understand the dangers and difficulties the Pioneers had to meet and overcome in order to carve a state out of the wilderness and establish good government.

The last part of the book is devoted to the pioneer state builders of today. I make no attempt to treat in detail the recent phases of our social, political and industrial history, but merely emphasize the factors in our development which appeal to me as most vital from the standpoint of today.

ALICE POLK HILL.

CONTENTS

PART I

THE WILDERNESS OF THE WEST

	Page
CHAPTER I—THREE MYSTERIES	3
The Cliff Dwellers	3
The Indian	9
The Buffalo	13
CHAPTER II—ENTERING THE GREAT AMERICAN DESERT	16
Coronado's Expedition	16
The Purchase of Louisiana	18
The Explorers	20

Captain Zebulon M. Pike, Stephen H. Long, John C. Fremont, John W. Gunnison.

CHAPTER III—TRAPPERS, TRADERS AND HUNTERS	27

The Bent Brothers, Ceran St. Vrain, Christopher ("Kit") Carson, Richens L. Wooton, Jim Bridger, Jim Baker, Scout Wiggins.

PART II

THE ARGONAUTS

CHAPTER IV—THE FOUNDING OF DENVER	39
Montana City	41
Auraria	41
St. Charles	46
Denver	47

	Page
CHAPTER V—HAPPENINGS AT THE CAMP	53
Rush for Gold	53
Stampeders	58
CHAPTER VI—IMPORTANT EVENTS	61
Changes from Cottonwood to Lumber and Brick	61
The State Convention	65
Horace Greeley	66

PART III
THE PROVISIONAL GOVERNMENT

CHAPTER VII—THE CRITICAL PERIOD	71
The First Legislature	71
The People's Court	79
The Attack on the News	79
The Fourth of July	85
The Unwritten Law	87
CHAPTER VIII—CLOSE OF PROVISIONAL GOVERNMENT	93
Permanent Population in 1860	93
Auraria and Denver United	96
How Colorado Territory Was Created	99
CHAPTER IX—SOME PIONEERS OF THAT DAY	103

Henry M. Porter, J. F. Brown, Rodney Curtis, Dennis Sheedy, John Good, Wilbur F. Stone, James M. Wilson, Daniel Witter, George Tritch, Wolfe Londoner, Joseph B. Donavan, Dr. O. D. Cass, Cyrus H. McLaughlin, O. P. Baur, Captain Richard Sopris.

PART IV
THE DEVELOPMENT OF PIONEER ENTERPRISES

CHAPTER X—ESTABLISHING FORCES OF CIVILIZATION	131
Churches	131
Schools	139
Newspapers	146

Contents xi

	Page
CHAPTER XI—SOCIAL AND ECONOMIC CONDITIONS	153
Denver a Culture Center	153
The Society of Colorado Pioneers	156
Pioneer Ladies' Aid Society	159
The Pioneers' Picnic	159
Real Estate's Rise in Value	164
Wheat	166
Banks	169
Boulder	175
Colorado State University	178

PART V

THE TERRITORY OF COLORADO

CHAPTER XII—ESTABLISHING LAW AND ORDER	181
The Migratory Legislature	181
H. C. Brown's Gift	184
The Civil War	188
The Removal of Gilpin	189
CHAPTER XIII—UNDER EVANS' ADMINISTRATION	193
Fire	193
Denver's Volunteer Fire Department	194
Cherry Creek Flood	197
CHAPTER XIV—THE INDIAN WAR	202
The Reign of Terror	202
Capturing Spotted Horse	205
Taking the Baby to His Father	208
Battle of Sand Creek	212
Treaty With the Indians	215
CHAPTER XV—THE GROWTH OF DENVER	218
The Lot Question	218
How Broadway Was Laid Out	218
Early Day Amusements	222
Society	223
Founding of Daniels & Fisher's Stores	228

	Page
Equal Suffrage	232
Women's Clubs	234
The Territorial Governors	239
Territorial Representatives in Congress	241
Early Mayors of Denver	241

PART VI

THE PIONEER STATE BUILDERS

CHAPTER XVI—CHANGES IN MEANS OF COMMUNICATION....... 243
    Freighters 243
    The Pony Express.. 247
    Telegraph 251
    Telephone 252

CHAPTER XVII—THE PIONEERS FACED QUESTION OF SUPPLY.... 256
    Water 256
    Walter Scott Cheesman... 257
    The Pioneer Cattle Growers.................................. 262
    Agriculture 266
    Irrigation 270
    Nathaniel P. Hill... 274

CHAPTER XVIII—RAILROADS... 280
    How Denver Was Kept on the Map...................... 280
        Governor Evans, General Bela M. Hughes, David C. Dodge, D. H. Moffat.

CHAPTER XIX—SETTLEMENT BY COLONIES......................... 302
    The Union Colony... 302
    The Fate of Mr. Meeker.. 305
    Growth of State Teachers' College....................... 310
    Industries of Northern Colorado........................... 313

CHAPTER XX—STATEHOOD CONSUMMATED......................... 315
    Jerome B. Chaffee.. 315
    T. M. Patterson.. 324
    The "Centennial" State... 328

PART VII

THE MOUNTAIN TOWNS

	Page
CHAPTER XXI—PROSPERITY OF THE COUNTRY	330
The Ranchman's Story	330
Golden	332
George West, W. A. H. Loveland, Captain E. L. Berthoud, John Gregory.	
Mining Laws	338
Central City	345
Henry M. Teller, James B. Belford, Joseph Standley, Henry R. Wolcott, W. A. Clark, George M. Pullman, Eben Smith, Major Hal Sayre, E. O. Wolcott, Joseph A. Thatcher, Frank C. Young, Judge E. T. Wells, Mrs. James B. Belford.	
CHAPTER XXII—SCENERY AND STORIES	371
Clear Creek Canon	371
Idaho Springs	371
Georgetown	376
Gray's Peak	379
Legend of Mount of the Holy Cross	381

◘

PART VIII

THE WESTERN SLOPE

CHAPTER XXIII—OVER THE MAIN RANGE	388
Platte Canyon	388
How Fairplay Was Named	396
Breckenridge	399
Duels	402
The Stage Ride	403
Ouray	413
Grand Junction	414
CHAPTER XXIV—LEADVILLE	420
How the Mining Excitement Started	420
William R. Owen's Reminiscences	422
Starting a Western Paper	432
The Alpine Tunnel	435

Contents

	Page
CHAPTER XXV—GUNNISON	437
Frontier Banking	437
The Royal Gorge	442

◘

PART IX

THE TOWNS OF THE PLAINS

CHAPTER XXVI—THE GARDEN SPOT OF COLORADO 444
    Canon City 444
    The Religious War.. 446
    The Hunt 449

CHAPTER XXVII—MANUFACTURES AND EARLY SETTLERS........ 454
    Pueblo 454
        John A. Thatcher, Mahlon D. Thatcher, Governor Alva Adams.
    Colorado Springs 462
        Colorado College, Irving Howbert, William J. Palmer, The Cog Road.
    Colorado City ....
    Manitou 471
    Landmarks Knocked Away........................... 473
        476

◘

PART X

THE GREAT STATE BUILDING EPOCH

CHAPTER XXVIII—PERSONAL GLIMPSES OF STATE BUILDERS... 479
    The Queen City of the Plains......................... 479
        H. A. W. Tabor, John C. Mitchell, William H. James, David May, Dennis Sullivan, J. J. Brown, Thomas F. Daly, Henry Bohm, Judge Luther M. Goddard, O. E. Le Fevre, James B. Grant, Mrs. James B. Grant, John F. Campion, Charles Boettcher, Dr. Lewis Lemen, Charles S. Thomas, Isaac N. Stevens, John W. Springer.

	Page
Denver's Clubs	505
How Denver Was Made City of Lights	506
Dr. Pfeiffer's Prophecy	510
CHAPTER XXIX—A GREATER COLORADO	512
Chamber of Commerce and Board of Trade	512
The Moffat Tunnel	515
Library	519
CHAPTER XXX—PIONEER WORK OF TODAY	524
Present Day Pioneers	524

Chester S. Morey, Verner Z. Reed, Tyson S. Dines, Lawrence C. Phipps, John F. Shafroth, Mrs. John F. Shafroth.

Some Present Day Activities	534
Denver's Mountain Parks	539
Estes Park	541
Good Roads	543
Motoring in Colorado	543

PART I
THE WILDERNESS OF THE WEST

CHAPTER I

THREE MYSTERIES

THE CLIFF DWELLERS

An interesting story of Colorado's "first settlers" is told by the ruined homes of an extinct race in the southwestern part of the state.

America is called the "New World," yet some antiquarians believe that these laboriously built dwellings, with roofs, doors and windows, were abandoned long before the time of Columbus. There is every indication of great age in what remains of that bygone people. They were not savages, as were our American Indians; they farmed by irrigation and their reservoirs were high up near the mountain tops.

The cliff dwellings were discovered by accident. The Wetherill boys were wintering their cattle in this region, and one day, following their herd, they found themselves among the lofty cliffs of Cliff Canyon. Looking up, they saw what seemed to their surprised vision a palace in the sky.

The cowboys left their cattle grazing in the valley and went to explore this strange building. They found one hundred and twenty-four rooms on the ground floor —three hundred and fifty rooms in all—with the remains of twenty round and square towers. The discoverers named it Cliff Palace, because this wonderful structure, with its towers, ramparts, and strong walls, had the appearance of a palace-fortress, where might have dwelt the ruler of a powerful nation. When seen from the top of the opposite cliff on a bright morning, with the sunshine flooding its recesses and bringing out the lines of the ruined building, it presents a picture of marvelous beauty. For a long time the Wetherills acted as guides to this land of the past.

In the valley of the Mancos, and on the Mesa, many ruins have been found in groups, in isolated and barren places, along ridges, and some are perched five hundred to eight hundred feet above the bottom of the canyon, reached by steps cut or built in the cliff, hence the name "Cliff Dwellings."

In these ruins have been found cotton thread, fragments of blankets, robes made of feathers which are singular pieces of handiwork; cloth made of milkweed fiber; sandals plaited from various fibers; mats made of coarse grass and reeds; hampers and other wicker work, and pottery of various kinds. Much of their pottery bears geometric figures, put on in colors, some of their decorative patterns being artistic in design and execution.

The perfect absence of metallic substance from the relics of these people convinced me that the dwellings were abandoned before the coming of the explorer in 1492, for had they lived at that time they certainly would have known of metals.

A German antiquarian who visited Denver several years ago said that in our Historical Society's collection of pottery from the cliff dwellings are vases and bowls ornamented with designs identical with those upon similar objects found in India and attributed to the Aryan people, in which case their antiquity reaches back to the dawn of the history of the human race.

Since the discovery of these ruins carloads of treasure have been taken away by people who cared little or nothing for scientific knowledge and were led on simply by a desire for relics.

At a meeting of the State Federation of Women's Clubs in Pueblo, October, 1897, Mrs. Mahlon D. Thatcher of Pueblo, president of the federation, appointed a committee of fourteen women to act in whatever way would best serve the interest of this cause. The ladies appointed were: Mrs. Gilbert McClurg, Colorado Springs; Mrs. William F. Slocum, Colorado Springs; Mrs. C. A. Eldredge, Colorado Springs; Mrs. W. S. Peabody, Denver; Mrs. John L. McNeil, Denver; Mrs. Frederic J. Bancroft, Denver; Mrs. Henry B. Van Kleeck, Denver; Mrs. E. G. Stoiber, Denver; Mrs. J. J. Burns, Denver; Mrs. B. Austin Taft, Denver; Mrs. Gordon Kimball, Ouray; Mrs. C. B. Rich, Denver; Mrs. J. S. Gale, Greeley; Mrs. Thomas A. Lewis, Pueblo. This committee was afterwards increased to twenty by Mrs. James A. Baker when president of the State Federation.

In May, 1900, it was felt that more effective work could be done if there was an organization for that sole purpose; accordingly, the Cliff Dwellings Association was incorporated. A legislative committee was appointed, with Mrs. W. S. Peabody, chairman.

Through the untiring efforts of Mrs. W. S. Peabody the plea of science reached the heart of the United States government. For six years she gave of her time, her strength and her money in the work of securing the preservation of the prehistoric relics for the state and for the country.

Congressman Shafroth was the first to lend a helping hand. He came to Denver long after Colorado was admitted into the Union and has devoted his remarkable energies to the service of the State. He has been Congressman, Governor twice, and is now United States Senator. When Mrs. Peabody was pushing forward her

work, he was in Congress, and gave his fine ability to help her carry out her ideas. Against the most violent opposition he introduced the measure to Congress session after session to have the Mesa Verde placed under government control. Finally he educated his fellow members sufficiently to secure its passage.

Senator T. M. Patterson then interested himself in the bill in the Senate. He pushed it at once to the public lands committee. The opposition in the Senate was overcome and January 15, 1906, Colorado stood possessed of a great national park containing 38,966 acres. By the establishment of a national park the tortuous trail to this marvelous mystery will be changed to a system of good roads dotted with modern, comfortable hotels. Then the Mesa Verde National Park will be second to none in this country, not even the far-famed Yellowstone Park.

In appreciation of Mrs. Peabody's valuable service in securing the passage by Congress of the bill creating the park, the American Anthropological Association passed the first public vote of thanks which has ever been tendered to anyone by that noted scientific organization. Colorado is proud of her and she has aptly been named the "Mother of Mesa Verde National Park."

The "Peabody House" is a magnificent cliff ruin which Edgar L. Hewitt, director of the School of American Archaeology of the Archaeological Institute of America, named for her.

Through the shadows of many years has come to us a glimmering light of this old race, but no record of any kind has ever been found that might suggest who they were, where they came from, how long they stayed, and when they vanished. There are theories in plenty—some think they see reasons for associating the Lost Tribes of Israel with the race which erected and used these buildings. There is an old tradition of the Utes that the Moquis had the Cliff Dwellers for ancestors. and they have a superstition that evil will follow the disturbance of the homes and bones of the ancient race.

It would not be in keeping with my purpose to take

up this subject with any attempt at detail. I am seeking legends and stories, and, with this in view, I found myself conversing with Mrs. Helen M. Wixson, a pioneer of the San Juan country.

"Are you interested in the Cliff Dwellers?" I asked.

"Indeed I am," she quickly replied. "Surely all the inhabitants of Colorado are interested in the first settlers of their state. The study of these queer people so fascinated me that some years ago I joined a party on a trip to this land of the past. We had with us the usual archaeologist, who assured us that the early inhabitants of these ruined homes had been of a dark race. I think we were quite agreed upon that point, but one day we found a mummy in a secluded, remote room of a cliff house. We hastened to the light with our treasure and carefully removed the outer wrapping of matting, then a wrapping of soft feather cloth, and lo, we had before us a red-headed mummy. So much for the theory of a dark race—and our archaeologist!" She laughed, and continued:

"We went there fully determined to ascertain something of the origin, progress and disappearance of these people, and what relation they were to the Toltecs, Aztecs, the Mokis and Zuni. We saw for ourselves the ruined homes of this extinct race; we looked upon a spruce tree, fully a hundred feet high and nearly ten feet in circumference, that we found growing in one of the deserted homes; we dug into the accumulated dust of ages and found relics of value, but we returned with our question still unanswered. Those long-departed people seem to have been without any record-making intelligence, for, as yet, no recording picture writing has been found."

There is a legend which tells us that the Toltecs, with a civilization older than the pyramids, came from a remote country to our own; that theirs was followed

The Wilderness of the West

by an Aztec dynasty which, in turn, was overthrown by a fairer, larger people. The overthrow occurred about 900 A. D., when a primitive civilization extending from the lakes of the North to the Gulf was wiped out and the stricken survivors fled to establish homes and defenses among the cliffs.

Such may be the story of the people who were making American history before the time of Columbus. But it is only a legend, and some scientific excavation in the future may reveal the secrets of this early chapter in our history.

The Indian

A strange contrast to that earlier and unknown people, the Cliff Dwellers, was the Indian, for he constructed no permanent habitation. The wild untrammeled life seemed to him the only one worth living. He had magnificent ideas as to his rights, and wanted the vast plains for his buffalo range and the whole mountain region for his deer park. His vigorous resistance to boundary lines defined by the white man was one cause of his swift downfall.

The old school books taught that the red man and his descendants were the aborigines, but modern investigation reveals the fact that the Indian came upon the stage in the world's drama centuries after the actors in the earlier scenes had made a final exit.

Columbus supposed he had reached India when he landed on the American shore and gave the inhabitants the name of Indians; ever since they have been known by that inappropriate name. The Indian's peculiar copper color made him one of the distinctive races of the world.

In 1879 our government established a Bureau of Ethnology for the careful study of the Indian. But his origin is still a mystery; as yet there is nothing to tell where he came from and why he migrated; even his language betrays no affinity to any other tongue.

Indians

In his native state he was thoroughly a savage—a cruel, unrelenting foe and a merciless captor. He subsisted almost entirely upon the result of the chase; the successful hunter and the great warrior were the big men of the tribe. He knew little of agriculture; indeed, any and all kind of manual labor was, in the opinion of an Indian brave, positively degrading and only to be done by squaws. The squaws strung the "wampum," took care of the children and did all of the hard work, while the men basked idly in the sun, unless when in council or occupied with war or the chase.

A tribe included a number of families or clans and a totem was the coat-of-arms of the family or clan to which the individual belonged; out of this a curious and complicated system of totems was formed.

The Indian's religious belief included many superstitions that centered around a vaguely defined theory of a Great Spirit. They lived in teepees, and an Indian village, when viewed from a distance, was picturesque. It held the eye by the charm of being unlike the habitation of any other race.

The Utes occupied all the mountain region of what is now Colorado. They were the enemies of the tribes of the plains and often dashed down upon them in fierce war. They were brave, crafty and cruel fighters, and their wicked deeds fill many bloody chapters in the history of Colorado, which I will touch upon later.

Was the Indian an intruder in the sense that the white man later became one, or was he an indigenous product of the country? These are questions the ethnologist has not yet been able to answer.

According to Smiley, the New England colonists, in their effort to account for the origin of the Indian, decided, according to their serious way of thinking, that he was a descendant of the Lost Tribes of Israel. This theoretical association with the religion of these straight-laced folks was no advantage to the red man, for when he interfered with their practical plans and purposes they went bravely to work to exterminate Israel's alleged descendants. An old chronicler said the New England pioneers first fell on their knees and then on the aborigines.

A legend of the origin of the red man is found in the report of Lewis and Clark's exploring expedition, made nearly a hundred years ago. Lewis and Clark say: "Their belief in a future state is connected with this theory of their origin: The whole nation resided in one large village, underground near a subterranean lake. A grapevine extended its roots down to their habitation and gave them a view of the light. Some of the most adventurous climbed up the vine and were delighted with the sight of the earth, which they found covered with buffalo and rich with every kind of fruit. Returning with the grapes they had gathered, their countrymen were so pleased with the taste of them that the whole nation resolved to leave their dull residences for the charm of the upper region. Men, women and children ascended by means of the vine, but, when about half the nation reached the surface of the earth, a corpulent woman, who was clambering up the vine, broke it with her weight, and closed upon herself and the rest of the nation the light of the sun."

That is an amusing variation of the old story that woman brought trouble into the world.

Among the Tabeguache Utes, as related by Governor Lafayette Head, their agent, there was a deluge legend which landed the ark near Palmer Lake. Their tale was to the effect that when their ancestors found a landing place for their big canoe on a mountain eminence near Palmer Lake, and got the various animals they had undertaken to save from the all-pervading freshet safely on the ground again, the men went to look over the country, leaving the disembarked menagerie in charge of the squaws. The animals becoming hungry and restive made the women so much trouble that they got angry, and, with brandished sticks and waving blankets, attempted to make the unruly creatures behave. But, instead of this, the animals were so badly frightened by the fearless and menacing squaws that they all turned tail and fled. From that time they have so feared mankind that they have remained wild and must be hunted by all who want any of them for food or other purposes—a consequence much deplored by the braves, and, by them, held to be sufficient cause for their general bad opinion of womankind and for the harsh treatment they bestow upon the squaws.

For a long time the power in handwriting was a mystery to the Indians. In later years they often obtained a "talking paper" introducing them to white men with whom they desired social recognition. And, sometimes, the "talking paper" entered into truthful particulars not in keeping with the desire of the red man. Richardson relates that when he and Greeley were nearing Denver in 1859 a Cheyenne brave approached him and complacently presented a document probably procured at Denver which conveyed the following frank bit of compact information: "This Indian is a drunkard, a liar, a notorious old thief; look out for him."

The Wilderness of the West

In the museum at the State Capitol can be found a variety of skulls. There are "long heads," "round heads," "short heads," and "flat heads," but whether round, long or short they tell no story of the origin of the Indian.

THE BUFFALO

In the early part of the nineteenth century the prairies of what is now Colorado were literally covered with buffalo. Their large, shaggy heads presented an exag-

R. R. Fuller's Narrow Escape

gerated appearance of ferocity, but they were not combative animals, and at the first intimation of danger the clumsy, lumbering creatures would start off in a slow bumping gallop, often tumbling in a blind sort of way over a precipice, crushing and trampling to death many of their numbers.

A stampeded herd of buffalo meant destruction to the unfortunate man or beast in the way. R. R. Fuller, a division superintendent of the Leavenworth and Pike's

Peak Stage Company, made a narrow escape. While riding the route of the stages the plains became suddenly black with a stampeded herd of buffalo; the surging mass bore down upon him; his mule, with the beastly stubbornness peculiar to his kind, refused to move. A buffalo gave the balking animal a ripping blow with his short horns and he fell dead, Fuller still astride him. Fuller quickly drew his revolver and fired in rapid succession at the buffalo jumping over him. Scared by the report and the smoke, the herd divided and passed on each side, leaving him unharmed.

The destruction of these animals commenced with the fur companies. Long before the founding of Denver they shipped to the East buffalo hides by tens of thousands every year; the California emigrants destroyed many thousands, and when the hide hunters appeared on the scene the fate of the buffalo was sealed. These pitiless butchers would attack a herd and never leave one alive. Then it became a fashionable sport to hunt buffalo; hundreds of would-be sportsmen, who killed for the wicked love of killing, came from distant parts of our country, from England and other foreign lands to engage in the brutal sport of killing inoffensive, noncombative buffalo. In the history of the world, there is no record of such slaughter of harmless, useful animals.

At the present time there can be found a small bunch in Northwestern Colorado, and another on the headwaters of the South Platte River; in the Yellowstone Park there is a small number, a small herd in our City Park, and a few can be seen in zoological collections.

The Indian and buffalo disappeared from this broad land at the coming of the white man, and their passing marks a closing era.

When and from where came the buffalo?

The Indians believed that God gave them the buffalo for a constant and unfailing supply. Their flesh fed

The Wilderness of the West

and nourished them and their hides served them for clothing, beds and covering for teepees.

William F. Cody ("Buffalo Bill") says: "Every plains Indian firmly believed that the buffalo were produced in countless numbers in a country underground; that every spring the surplus swarmed like bees from a hive out of the immense cave-like openings in the region of the Llano Estacado, or Staked Plains of Texas. In 1869, Stone Calf, a celebrated chief, assured me that he knew exactly where the caves were, though he had never seen them; that the good God had provided this means for the constant supply of food for the Indians, and, however recklessly the white man might slaughter, they could never exterminate them."

CHAPTER II

ENTERING THE GREAT AMERICAN DESERT

Coronado's Expedition

The romantic, gold-seeking Spaniards were pioneering in the Great West, near the foothills of the Rocky Mountains, almost a century before the Pilgrims landed at Plymouth Rock. They circulated stories embellished with verbal art of the vast wealth of the region, dwelling particularly upon the Seven Cities of Cibola, which they reported to be situated in a peaceful, luxurious valley enclosed by huge mountains of solid gold.

Francisco Vasquez De Coronado, a young man of fine character and great courage, was inspired by these stories to organize an expedition to go in search of the cities of fabulous splendor. His plans met with the approval of Mendoza, the Viceroy of Mexico, who was anxious to extend the domain of New Spain, as Mexico was then called, and, to that end, heartily encouraged northern explorations.

Coronado's company was composed of eight hundred Indians, drawn from the adjacent country, and three hundred and fifty Spaniards; among them were a number of Franciscan Friars. This period of the world's history was one of intense religious belief, and so we find mingled with the Spaniard's thirst for gold a fervent missionary zeal. The Franciscan Friars were eager to carry their faith to the benighted and plant the cross whenever and wherever the opportunity was given.

Coronado was full of the spirit of adventure and had high hopes of winning fame and wealth. With his band of enthusiastic explorers he moved off on Easter Monday, 1540, amid the shouting of people and the sounding of trumpets.

After reaching the Gila River, they proceeded northward over the great desert, lured by the gold of the Seven Cities of Cibola. He was bitterly disappointed to find that the anticipated magnificent Seven Cities were only pueblos of hostile natives living in barbarism. The Spaniards heaped maledictions on the heads of those who had so grossly deceived them with their fanciful stories of the cities of splendor.

They heard from the natives of a place far away to the north which was called Quivera. At this time an Indian united himself with the Spaniards whom they called El Turco (The Turk), from his resemblance in dress and manner to the subjects of the Sultan. He told Coronado that he was a native of that region, a thousand miles to the northeast, in which Quivera, roofed and paved with gold and silver, was situated. It was easy for El Turco to find other Indians to corroborate his story. Only one had the boldness to contradict him. But El Turco's story appealed to the romantic Spaniards and they scorned the man who made the contradictory statement.

It then became the further object of Coronado to find Quivera. His company divided, the main part returned to New Spain, and Coronado, with a few chosen followers, proceeded on the long march in search of Quivera.

Quivera, which afterwards was called Kansas, proved to be a village of Indian wigwams, thought by some writers to have been a Pawnee town.

This deception threw the Spaniards into a furious rage and they seized El Turco. In shivering alarm he confessed that the people of his tribe feared the mailed invaders, and, to save his people, he was leading the army away in hope that they would never return. After his confession he was condemned to be strangled. They did not stop to consider the heroism and unselfishness of El Turco in risking his life to save his people, and his death was the quick work of the infuriated Spaniards.

Coronado had chased the golden mirage of the western desert until he was broken in spirit; he had found savages and buffalo, but the cities of gold he had not found. Discouraged and disillusioned, he took up the long march back to the Mexican towns. On the journey he was thrown from his horse and received injuries from which he died a year later. He, with his little army, were the first white men to tread the soil of Colorado. He went and returned through Colorado when he was wandering around on his get-rich-quick scheme more than three hundred years ago, but did not leave in this country a trace of his expedition. The Spaniards were not colonizers; they were gold seekers, yet they failed to find gold in the rich lands through which they had so painfully toiled. If Coronado could ride into Denver today and stop long enough to see the gold in the Denver mint, what would he think of himself as an explorer?

The Purchase of Louisiana

This portion of our continent was a sealed book for nearly three centuries after Coronado, and was generally designated the Great American Desert.

France, by a treaty with Spain in 1800, came into possession of all Louisiana west of the Mississippi.

President Jefferson, with remarkable foresight, realized the necessity of the United States owning and controlling the Mississippi. He sent James Monroe to Paris to aid Livingston—our minister in Paris—in negotiating the purchase of Louisiana. At first Napoleon rejected any offer, but owing to the strong naval power of Eng-

The Wilderness of the West

land and the threatening clouds of war that hung over England and France, he became impressed with the idea that if he did not at once sell the country he would lose it to Great Britain. For this reason he authorized his foreign minister, Talleyrand, to take the offer of the American commissioners. And, April 30th, 1803, the United States purchased from France the immense territory known as Louisiana, the price being fifteen million dollars—one of the largest real estate deals on record.

Thomas Jefferson

When Napoleon was informed that the treaty had been concluded, he said: "This accession of territory strengthens forever the power of the United States, and I have given to England a maritime rival that will sooner or later humble her pride." Upon signing the ratification of the treaty he threw down his pen with the exclamation: "I have signed away an empire!"

The boundary lines of the Territory were not clearly defined in the ideas of either party; Jefferson's one purpose was to get possession of the Mississippi and give the citizens of the United States the navigation of the river from its source to the ocean.

The most important event of American history in the first half of the nineteenth century was this purchase of Louisiana. The negotiations were initiated, carried forward and consummated under the direction of President Thomas Jefferson, for which abuse was heaped upon him by the New England Federalists. From the standpoint of today no act of any executive of our nation has been followed by such wonderful results.

The Explorers

Captain Zebulon M. Pike

In 1806 Captain Zebulon Montgomery Pike was sent with a party of government explorers to ascertain the resources of this new acquisition. He was chosen for this difficult and daring enterprise because he possessed the superior qualities of courage and bravery which would enable him to endure hardships and privations in the service of his country.

Captain Zebulon M. Pike

The little band traveled along near the line of what is now the Santa Fe Railway, and they built a fort on the present site of Pueblo. Pike ran up his flag, and this was the first Star Spangled Banner that waved in the limits of what is now Colorado.

He had gazed with admiration on the "Grand Peak," as he called it, and one morning he, with a few of his company, started out with the idea of climbing it and returning the same day. When night closed around them they found themselves, as they supposed, at the foot of the "Grand Peak," and the next day they climbed to the top of it. On reaching the summit the "Grand Peak" appeared to be as far away as when they first began. They had climbed Cheyenne Mountain.

Their mistake in the distance, caused by the rarefied atmosphere, probably originated the story of the two men who started to walk to the mountains from Denver before breakfast. After tramping what seemed to them an unconscionable distance, one suggested to the other to proceed slowly, while he returned to Denver for a carriage. When overtaken by the friend in the carriage the pedestrian was sitting on the bank of a clear running brook, scarcely more than a step in breadth, deliberately taking off his clothes. On being asked why he did not step across, he replied: "I've got the deadwood on this thing now; you don't catch me making a fool of myself by trying to straddle this stream. It looks but a step, but it might be a mile for all I know, so I shall just take off my clothes and prepare for swimming."

When Pike and his company returned to their camp they were almost famished, the snow was deep and their feet were frozen, thereby possibly adding to the vernacular of the West the term "tenderfoot."

Pike subsequently indulged in a kind of appropriation peculiar to the West called "land grabbing." He crossed the Sangre de Cristo Range into the San Luis valley and built a fort on the Rio Grande del Norte. He ran up his flag, claiming the land in the name of the United States. The Spaniards heard of Pike's expedition and sent a squad of cavalry to arrest him. Suddenly the Spanish force appeared at the fort. Pike was on their ground, so they claimed; he was taken prisoner and politely escorted to Santa Fe, where he was treated with kindness and consideration until his release.

He did not take to himself the credit of being the first explorer of Western Louisiana, but gave the honor to one James Pursley of Bardstown, Ky. Pursley, with amazing generosity, credited it to Pike. The politeness of these gentlemen is without a parallel in history. Had they known the importance the country was destined to assume half a century later, it would, no doubt, have taken coffee and pistols to decide the question of precedence.

There were other white men in this country before Pike, but Pike had a passion for the pen. He left a full account of his expedition, and, for that reason, we may say that Colorado history begins with Pike's expedition.

The great monarch of the mountains was named for him and Pike's Peak and Colorado became synonymous terms in the vocabulary of travel.

Stephen H. Long

Stephen H. Long was sent out with another exploring party June 6th, 1820. This party was larger than Pike's and better equipped in every way. They were instructed to learn more of the vegetable and animal life; the agricultural possibilities of the plains, and ascertain the number and character of the savage tribes.

Stephen H. Long

On the fifth of July they camped near the present site of Denver and were the first to leave any record of their rovings near the place where the city now stands.

Dr. James, the historian of the party, in company with three men, climbed to the summit of Pike's Peak. In honor of this achievement Major Long named the peak for him, but the trappers and traders of 1840 fastened Pike's name upon it.

The Wilderness of the West

These explorers gathered columbine on the Divide, which has since become the State flower. They passed over the present site of Colorado Springs and camped near the boiling springs of Manitou.

Long's geographical and scientific report delayed for years the settlement and development of this country. The mountains were represented as being grand and beautiful, but without any desirable qualities, and the Arkansas Valley, now famous for farming and fruit-growing, they reported as arid and sterile and must forever remain desolate.

A magnificent mountain bearing the name of Long looks down over the region which he said was worthless. Another mountain in the front range bears the name of James.

The supply of biscuits ran out and Major Long thought it was necessary for the expedition to return. That was about the middle of summer, when the plains were swarming with animals that were good to eat. What a striking contrast to Pike and his freezing, starving men, pushing bravely forward amid the blasts of winter.

John C. Fremont

John Charles Fremont led five expeditions through this western country and made known routes of travel across the plains to the Pacific coast. For this reason he was called the "Pathfinder." Kit Carson, a noted frontiersman, was his guide on two expeditions.

Fremont's expeditions were in the interest of expansion. Long's report had given such a false impression of the character and resources of the country that the expenditure of public funds to find out whether a railroad could be built through such a country was considered reckless extravagance by many sincere and patriotic citizens.

When a bill providing for a mail route from Independence, Missouri, to the mouth of the Columbia River came before the United States Senate in 1838, Daniel Webster voiced the general beliefs of the time when he said:

John C. Fremont

"What do we want with this vast worthless area? This region of savages and wild beasts, of deserts, shifting sands and whirlwinds, of dust, of cactus and prairie dogs? To what use could we ever hope to put the western coast, a coast of three thousand miles, rock-bound, cheerless, uninviting, and not a harbor on it? What use have we for such a country? Mr. President, I will never vote one cent from the public treasury to place the Pacific coast one inch nearer to Boston than it now is."

The character of the country was practically settled in the minds of the people, and Fremont's first expedition was considered a useless and daring undertaking. At this time he was Lieutenant of Engineers in the United States army. The vast plains, the majestic mountains and the grand canyons fired him with enthusiasm and colored the reports of his explorations which gave to the people an enlarged knowledge of the western world. He was a careful observer; he noticed that the soil was good, and the barrenness of the country, he rightly concluded, was due almost entirely to the extreme dryness of the climate.

In 1845, the Pathfinder, whose name had become known in two continents through his services to geography, was promoted to a captaincy.

He married Jessie Benton, the daughter of Senator Thomas H. Benton of Missouri, whose pet scheme was a highway across the continent to the Pacific coast.

Fremont's fourth expedition, in 1848, was financed by himself and his father-in-law, Benton. On this expedition he entered the Sacramento valley. After his arrival in California he became identified with political affairs. Two years after the discovery of gold, California was admitted to the Union as a State without going through the form of a Territory, and Fremont was chosen United States Senator.

In 1853 he led an organization in the interest of a Pacific railway and succeeded in finding passes where he believed steel tracks could be laid. He met with numerous disasters during his five expeditions, but he had been cast in a Spartan mold and his spirit was never crushed. He threw wide open the gates of our Pacific empire and became one of the most picturesque characters in the annals of Rocky Mountain exploration.

John W. Gunnison

In the spring of 1853, Captain John W. Gunnison was sent by the Secretary of War at the head of an expedition for the purpose of finding a route for a railroad from St. Louis to the Pacific coast. In the exploring party, besides Captain Gunnison, were Lieutenant E. G. Beckwith and several scientists and topographers. They left St. Louis in June and traveled by stage to the Kansas frontier, where they were joined by Captain Norris with a detachment of thirty soldiers from Fort Leavenworth. They followed the Kansas river and Smoky Hill route until they came to Bent's Fort in Eastern Colorado. Gunnison passed through the Sangre de Cristo pass on the old Spanish military wagon road, near where the Denver and Rio Grande Railway is constructed, known as La Veta Pass.

The explorers worked their way through the country that has been named Gunnison County in honor of the explorer. It was anything but easy to drive over some of the steep mountains, where never a white man had been before, yet they continually found great pelasure in the wild beauty of the Rockies. They traveled for some distance through the valley of the river that has been named for Gunnison, but they did not enter the "Black Canyon" which the Indians said was inaccessible to man. It is now considered the grandest canyon in Colorado. The Denver and Rio Grande Railroad runs through it.

Gunnison followed the Spanish trail westward as far as the Sevier River in Utah, where he was murdered by the Indians. No braver man than Captain Gunnison ever gave up his life in exploring the western country.

With these explorers commenced the forward movement that has girdled the earth.

CHAPTER III

TRAPPERS, TRADERS AND HUNTERS

THE BENT BROTHERS

In the world's drama, the scenes are continually shifting. The curtain goes up now on the American frontiersman—rough, daring, fearless—without a parallel in history.

In the early part of the nineteenth century the Missouri Fur Company, Astor's Northwest Fur Company, and the American Fur Company were organized, and, in the service of these companies, a large number of trappers, traders and frontiersmen wandered over the West.

They were the pioneers of the great plains and mountains. Most of them were illiterate, reckless and improvident, often squandered the earnings of a season in a night, but they were true to each other in times of hardship and danger.

Several hundred of them were in this western country, but I will mention only those who were in some degree identified with the making of Colorado.

The Bent brothers and Ceran St. Vrain were the first traders who established themselves within the limits of what is now Colorado. They built a trading post in 1826 on the Arkansas river, about half way between the present cities of Pueblo and Canon City, and, owing to their large trade with the Mexicans and Indians, they soon became men of distinction and influence. This region was the common ground of several of the most warlike tribes of Indians, and Bent's Fort was a place of safety. Travelers of every distinction and rank were entertained there.

Colonel William Bent abandoned the old fort in 1829 and built a new one on the north bank of the Arkansas River, near the location of the present United States Fort Lyon. This was a pretentious building of adobe walls five or six feet thick, enclosing an open area large enough in which to corral an entire wagon train driven in through an enormous portal, made secure with double doors. The fort had a high tower on one

corner as a lookout, surmounted by a flagpole on which floated the Stars and Stripes for more than a quarter of a century. It became a stage station in 1865 and continued as such until the Santa Fe Railroad was built to Pueblo.

For more than twenty years this trading post was the most active and historic place between the Missouri River and the Pacific coast. Here, all the "free trappers" sold their furs, and the surrounding Indian tribes bartered their buffalo robes and deer pelts for blankets, ammunition and food. Explorers and travelers stopped and bought supplies, the stranded were employed, the poor fed. Long wagon trains of merchandise from the Missouri River came and went in a ceaseless stream, while pack-trains made their rounds to and from the mountains, supplying trappers, camps and small trading posts hundreds of miles north and west. In fact, Bent's Fort was then the center of the romance and adventure of the "trapper age" of America. A motley crowd of divers races and languages made this spot the emporium and babel of the plains and mountains.

The Bent brothers were gentlemen of family and education. One of them, Charles, was the first American Governor of New Mexico after its acquisition by the United States. His dramatic life was ended during his governorship by his murder in the Mexican revolt at Taos. These men, with Colonel Ceran St. Vrain, George Simpson, Dick Wooton, Jim Bridger and their associates, were the earliest pioneers when the rude foundations were laid for this prosperous and happy home land of ours.

In 1838 the Bent brothers and Ceran St. Vrain built a fort on the Platte, about forty miles north of the site of Denver. It was named St. Vrain, and soon became famous as the favorite resort of hunters and trappers who roamed in this part of the country. Within the high adobe walls surrounding the fort were storehouses and dwellings and a corral to protect horses and mules from theft at night. The people assembled there formed the connecting link between Indian savagery and the pioneer settlements of 1858-59.

A weekly express was established between Fort St. Vrain and Fort Bent, and R. L. Wooton was the courier on this line for several years. This probably originated the idea of the pony express in the Rocky Mountain region.

CHRISTOPHER CARSON

Christopher ("Kit") Carson was a conspicuous figure in the frontier days. He was a native of Kentucky, and, at the age of seventeen, left his home and entered upon his career of adventure in the far West. His service to Fremont as guide on two exploring expeditions first brought him prominently before the public and made him famous. Upon the breaking out of the Civil War he joined the Union army and rose to the rank of Brigadier-General. He served as Indian agent and won renown for his honest dealings with the government and the Indians.

He was small in stature, with a fair complexion and quiet, intelligent features. Though his education was limited, he possessed fine natural ability; was quick and shrewd in business, and acquired orally French, Spanish and several Indian tongues. His wonderful escapes from what appeared to be impending death led his associates and many Indian tribes to believe that he bore a charmed life, and made him the hero of numerous stories of adventure.

He married a handsome Mexican woman of varied accomplishments and made his home at Taos, New Mexico. His devotion to his wife was very beautiful, and shortly after her death he passed away with an affection of the heart. His last public service was rendered in the winter of 1867-68. He, with Hiram P. Bennet, D. C. Oakes and Lafayette Head, escorted Ouray and several other Ute chieftains to Washington on a visit to the President.

Kit Carson was one of nature's noblemen. When the western end of civilization was fringed with drunkards, horse thieves and cut-throats, Kit Carson, the little mild-mannered, blue-eyed scout, Indian fighter and trailblazer, was honest, sober, kind and courageous. This hero

The Wilderness of the West

of the mountains and plains, by his achievements, placed himself in line with men who blazed trails in science and literature.

PIONEER MONUMENT AND CAPITOL

KIT CARSON

A magnificent monument commemorating the pioneers of Colorado was erected under the direction of the public improvement committee of the Denver Real Estate Exchange, with J. S. Flower as chairman. The monument epitomizes truly the sacrifices, sufferings and victory of the pioneers, and is surmounted by an equestrian figure of Kit Carson.

One of America's greatest sculptors, MacMonnies, did the work, which so ably represents fine art dedicated to a heroic cause.

RICHENS L. WOOTON

Richens L. Wooton was a contemporary of Carson and his comrade in many encounters with Indians. He was born in Virginia and made his way to the West when about twenty years old. He had a good education, was far above the average frontiersman, and his ability, force of character and kind heart made him many lasting friends, among whom he was familiarly known as "Uncle Dick." He had a long and adventurous career as trapper, trader, merchant and ranchman.

Inman, in "The Old Santa Fe Trail," tells this story of Wooton. In the caravan, in which he was employed as teamster, on this initial trip across the plains, every man had to take his turn in standing guard. Wooton's post comprised the whole length of one side of the corral, and his instructions were to shoot anything he saw moving outside of the line of mules farthest from the wagons. The young sentry was very vigilant. He did not feel at all sleepy, but eagerly watched for something that might possibly come within the prescribed distance. About two o'clock he heard a slight noise and saw something moving about. Of course, his first thoughts were of Indians, and the more he peered through the darkness at the slowly moving object the more convinced he was that it must be a bloodthirsty savage. He rose to his feet and blazed away. The shot roused everybody and all came rushing with their guns to learn of the cause.

R. L. Wooton

Wooton told the wagon master that he had seen what he supposed was an Indian trying to slip up to the mules, and that he had killed him. Some of the men crept very cautiously to the spot where the supposed dead savage was lying, while young Wooton remained at his post eagerly awaiting their report. Presently he heard a voice cry out with a customary oath: "If he haint killed Old Jack!" Old Jack was a lead mule of one of the wagons. He had torn up his picket pin and strayed outside of the

The Wilderness of the West

lines, and the faithful brute met his death at the hands of the sentry.

Wooton declared that he was not to be blamed, for the animal had disobeyed orders, while he had strictly observed them.*

As one of the pioneer business men of Denver I will speak of him later on.

JIM BRIDGER

Jim Bridger was also a comrade of Kit Carson, and a leader among the mountain men. He was born in Washington, D. C., and came to the West when a boy. He discovered the way through the mountains known as Bridger Pass, and acted as guide for the engineers who made surveys for a railroad to the Pacific. Later on he decided, in a few minutes, the route for the Union Pacific Railroad across the mountains, a problem that the engineers had worked over for a whole season.

The engineers of the Union Pacific Railway, while in Denver in the early 60's, became confused as to the most practicable point in the range over which to run their line. After debating the question they determined, upon a suggestion from some of the old settlers, to send for Jim Bridger, who was then visiting in St. Louis.

When the old man arrived he asked why he had been sent for from such a distance. The engineers explained their dilemma. The old mountaineer waited patiently until they had finished, when, with a look of disgust on

Jim Bridger

---
*Kit Carson, ten years before, while on his first journey, met with a similar adventure.

his withered countenance, he demanded a large piece of paper, remarking: "I could a told you fellers all that in St. Louis and saved you the expense of bringing me out here."

He was handed a sheet of manila paper, used for drawing the details of bridge plans. The veteran pathfinder spread it on the ground before him, took a dead coal from the ashes of the fire, drew a rough outline map, and, pointing to a certain peak, just visible on the serrated horizon, said: "There's where you fellers can cross with your road, and nowhere else, without more diggin' an' cuttin' than you think of." The crude map is preserved in the archives of the great corporation.

Jim Bridger had an interesting experience with Sir George Gore, a distinguished Irish sportsman, who abandoned luxurious European life in 1855 and dwelt for over two years in the wilds of the Rocky Mountains. He had a train of thirty wagons, besides numerous saddle horses and dogs. His party consisted of fifty persons, comprising secretaries, stewards, cooks, fly makers, dog tenders, hunters and servants.

He camped first near Fort Laramie and there engaged Jim Bridger as interpreter, guide and companion in his excursion to the parks and forests for game. Middle and North Parks and the valleys of Routt County became familiar grounds to him and his attendants.

It is claimed that he was the first to visit Steamboat Springs, and, through difficult places in that rugged country, he built wagon roads and bridges for his convenience in hunting. There are traces of these works still visible, and Gore's Range was named for him.

Sir George had an income of $200,000 per annum and was one of those enthusiastic sportsmen who, like our own "Teddy," derived real satisfaction from successful hunting. The adventures of this titled nimrod were upon a most gigantic scale, exceeding anything of the kind ever attempted on this continent, and are compared with the extravagant performances of Gordon Cumming in Africa.

Byers says: "While in the wilderness among savages, he was exposed to all the perils and privations consequent upon such a life, but in camp he lived like a king. His after-dinner habit was to read from Shakespeare, Sir Walter Scott and other standards to the attentive, but not very appreciative Jim Bridger, who 'reckoned Shakespeare was a leetle too highfalutin' for him and rayther calkerlated that the big fat Dutchman "full-stuff" was a little too fond of beer.' He believed 'Baren Mountchawson to be a durned liar,' and assured Sir George that according to Sir Walter Scott's account of the battle of Waterloo that 'them Britishers must a fit better than they did down to Horleans, whar Old Hickory gin um the forkedest sort o' chain lightnin' that perhaps you ever seen in all your born days.'"

JIM BAKER

Jim Baker was, next to Kit Carson, Fremont's most trusted guide. He was employed by the government in many undertakings and always rendered faithful service. He came to the mountain from Illinois when he was eighteen years old. Following his calling, he had many hair-breadth escapes and thrilling adventures, and became noted for his fearlessness and unselfishness; often he risked his life to defend or save a friend. He married an Indian woman.

Many of the trappers deserted their Indian wives, but old Jim Baker was true to his, though he had a poor opinion of Indians as a people. He is quoted as saying: "They are the most onsartainest varmints in all creation, an' I reckon thar not more'n half human, for you never seed a human, arter you'd fed and treated him to the best fixin's in your lodge, jes turn 'round and steal all your horses, or any other thing he could lay hands on. No, not adzactly. He would feel kind o' grateful, and ask you to spread a blanket in his lodge ef you ever come his way. But the Injun don't care shucks for you and is ready to do you a lot of mischief as soon as he quits your feed."

After Denver was founded, Baker built a cabin a little to the north of it. He then moved to Clear Creek and built a bridge where the road to Boulder crosses that

stream. It was a toll-bridge in the 60's, and is still known as "Baker's Bridge."

I often talked with him in the early days, and, though he had a rough exterior and rough manners, he was a generous, noble-hearted man.

From a pioneer I gathered the following incident in the life of Jim Baker:

"Jim was a squaw man and was very fond of his family, especially his oldest daughter, Jane. It was while he kept a toll bridge on Clear Creek on the Boulder-

Greeley road that Jane became known to all the people 'round about' as a fine nurse. With patient kindness she nursed many an invalid back to health. Finally Jane sickened and died, and poor old Jim's cup of sorrow was full to the brim. Jane had kept his house and been his comfort in all his trying times, and her going left a deep wound in the old man's heart. He wandered over the hills day after day, perfectly inconsolable. He could not stand the house where the sound of her footsteps came back to him. His friends endeavored with consoling words to reconcile him to her loss, but it was of no avail. It was not until he left the house where Jane died that he became anything like himself. When advanced in years and feeble, he went back to the cabin with the queer 'lookout' which he built in the early 40's in the valley of the Little Snake river, in what is now Routt County, Colorado.

"An old organ was stored away in the loft of his barn. A traveling musician, whose business was the repairing and tuning of musical instruments, got hold of the instrument, put it together and tuned it. Old Jim was happy then. Often his cramped old fingers moved over the keys and low melodies, quivering with love and pain, filled the shadows of the cabin."

The fur trade of the Rockies had passed away, still he made his living hunting and trapping. He died in his eighty-eighth year—almost the last of that brave type of men who paved the way for civilization. His body was laid away a short distance from his cabin.

Jim Baker's cabin should be preserved as a landmark of Colorado. It is perhaps the oldest house in the State built by a white man, and is one of the few relics of the fur trade carried on by the brave men who dared the perils of the western wilderness. It was built for defense and for shelter; from its "lookout" Baker and other trappers kept watch for Utes when they were on the warpath, and the bullet marks on the heavy hewn logs still tell of the attacks made upon its occupants by the Indians.

Scout Wiggins

Wiggins ran away from his home in Canada when a young boy and drifted into the employment of hunter and scout, and early in life earned the title of "old scout," which was his for more than sixty years. His services were ever in demand by trader, explorer and hunter. As hunter and scout he wandered over the plains of Missouri, Kansas and Nebraska. From 1858 until the beginning of the Civil War he hunted near what is now Denver. He was with the Third Colorado cavalry, under the command of Colonel John M. Chivington, when it surprised the Indians at Sand Creek. For years after the close of the war he continued to scout.

The fur-bearing animals were exterminated; the fur business vanished, and in 1840 the old trappers considered the resources of the country were exhausted, their "occupation gone," and they dropped away, one by one, in search of "pastures new."

PART II
THE ARGONAUTS

CHAPTER IV

THE FOUNDING OF DENVER

W. Green Russell

A large proportion of the explorers, adventurers, pilgrims, prospectors and colonial tramps that, since the days of Noah, have marched away to establish settlements elsewhere have, to a great extent, been driven to it by some unpleasantness at home.

Colorado was, in a measure, an outgrowth of the great financial crash of 1857. Time-honored houses had reeled, tottered and gone down in the overwhelming business convulsion of that period, and men were ready for any venture which gave even faint promises of rebuilding their ruined fortunes.

W. Green Russell, a miner in Georgia, when returning from California where he had been mining, heard from some Cherokee Indians of gold in the Pike's Peak region. In the spring of 1858 he organized a party of white men and Cherokee Indians to go to Pike's Peak to search for gold. When the caravan moved away it consisted of sixty people, thirty yoke of cattle, fourteen wagons, one two-horse team and a dozen ponies. They came out by the Smoky Hill route and camped June 24 under the cottonwood trees on the west side of Cherry creek, at a point where it empties into the Platte. This was the first organized party that came to the Pike's Peak region in search for hidden treasure.

Closely following them was another party from Lawrence, Kansas, under the command of John Easter. They put in at the base of Pike's Peak and camped in the "Garden of the Gods." Three men of this party—Frank M. Cobb, John D. Miller and Gus Voorhees—climbed to the top of the peak. After they returned, other members of the party, including Mrs. Anna Archibald Holmes, also went to the top of the peak, which gives Mrs. Holmes the distinction of being the first woman to accomplish that arduous task, and, according to the chronicler, she bore the fatigue of climbing with as much fortitude as the men. She was afterwards the first school teacher in Pueblo.

John Easter

Meantime, the Russell party prospected up the east side of the

Platte with such scant success that the Cherokees began to show signs of waning enthusiasm. They lacked industry, patience and hope, which are so essential to the prospector, and, in less than ten days, were completely disillusioned of the charm of gold seeking. They argued that there would be trouble with the Indians, and the discontented white men added the argument that they had not found pay dirt and that they had all come out on a fool's errand.

Russell entreated them not to break up the party, but they refused to listen, and started on their long homeward journey. Nothing daunted by the desertion of the larger number of the party, Russell and his remaining associates—thirteen in all—continued prospecting, and, finding gold where Dry creek empties into the Platte near the present site of Englewood, they stopped there, and gave it the name of "Placer Camp."

Montana City

The Lawrence party pulled into Placer Camp on the fourth of September. They were more inspired by the spirit of real estate speculation than digging for gold, and, thinking that Placer Camp diggings would help to build up a town, they organized a town company and went to work in earnest. By the middle of September a number of cabins were built fronting on the streets in dignified town-like manner. To this settlement, a mile north of Placer Camp, they gave the name of Montana City. In the vocabulary of the West, a collection of houses was always a city.

Auraria

A fall of snow about the last of September set Dr. L. J. Russell and his brother, Green, thinking of winter quarters, and they decided that the mouth of Cherry creek would be a better place to winter than at Placer Camp or Montana City.

While their plans were being formed the old trader, John Simpson Smith, arrived at the camp. He proposed to unite with the Russell brothers and build a double cabin. W. Green Russell sanctioned the arrangement because Smith was married to a squaw and on friendly terms with the Indians, which might be of advantage should the Indians resent the location of a town on their land. They lost no time in building the double cabin which, being near an Indian tepee, was called "Indian Row." This formed the nucleus for the camp which was the actual beginning of Denver.

S. M. Rooker was the first man with a family to join the settlement. His house was a continuation of "Indian Row." McGaa came in with a number of Indians trooping after him and built a shack. A Frenchman named H. Murat drifted in with his wife. Murat was a queer genius and became commonly known as "Count," because he claimed to be related to Bonaparte, King of Naples. He shaved men's beards and his wife toiled at the washtub. Individuals and small groups drifted in from various directions. The fanciful stories told around the evening camp fires of what the Russell boys had done at "Placer Camp" had a wonderful power in exciting the hopes and ambitions of the more recently arrived people.

About the first of October a town company was organized, arrangements for surveys formed, and the christening of the settlement was left to Green Russell, who selected the name of Auraria, after his home town in Georgia. A few days later, W. Green Russell and his brother, J. O. Russell, started to their old home for the purpose of organizing a large company of gold seekers. They were convinced that rich deposits of gold existed somewhere in the Pike's Peak region and they were determined to find it.

The Argonauts

Cherry Creek, now risen to the dignity of a settlement, became the focus for gold seekers, and Pike's Peak continued to be the popular landmark for the whole region. Up to this time there had been neither glass nor nails in the country and many expedients were resorted to in order to give the rude habitations light, entrance and exit. However, the pioneer merchants were not far behind the gold seekers. October 27th, Blake and Williams

arrived with a large stock of mining merchandise. A week later Kinna and Nye came in with a stock of hardware, and other merchants soon followed.

A party under the command of D. C. Oakes reached the camp October 10th. Oakes was an energetic and forceful man. He saw the possibilities of a town near the mouth of Cherry creek, and returned East late that fall to remain through the winter. When he reached his home in Iowa, he published a pamphlet on Pike's Peak.

It was widely sold and had a potent influence in causing a great emigration to Pike's Peak.

E. P. Stout, with a small party, arrived in Auraria about the last of October. Mr. Stout became so prominent in founding Denver that a street was named for him. He gives the following experience: "We were met by Jack Jones and John Smith, traders with the Cheyenne and Arapahoe Indians, who were living in Auraria. That evening these two traders invited us to visit them and feast with them. We did so and were treated to a good meal provided by Jones' 'squaw wife.' It wound up with a hot whisky stew, made from whisky distilled from wheat and called 'Taos Lightning.' From the effect it produced on Jones and Smith, one would readily have concluded that it was a genuine article of fighting whisky. When it began to take effect those two gentlemen seemed to be seized with a fiendish desire to slaughter somebody, and, with their Colts revolvers, commenced a rapid fusillade upon each other. As that kind of entertainment was rather too vigorous for us tenderfeet, we managed to slide out through the darkness, making our way to our own tents, leaving our hosts to the tender mercies of each other and expecting to find next morning both of them riddled with bullets. On the contrary, before the sun was fairly up, both of these gentlemen came over to our tents to apologize in the most humble and contrite manner for the disgraceful and humiliating spectacle they had made of themselves before their invited guests. We came to the conclusion that it had been merely an effort on their part to impress us with their wonderful bravery."

Andrew Sagendorf and Oscar Lehow drove into Denver the first week in November and built a cabin, which was conspicuous because it had the first glass window in the whole Rocky Mountain region, but it had no door.

"What are we going to do for a door, Oscar?" asked Sagendorf.

Lehow was silent. Later he unstrapped some boards concealed under the wagon in which the two had crossed the plains. Sagendorf had not seen them before. He was surprised and also pleased with the prospect of a door for their cabin. "Why did you bring those boards, Oscar?" he asked.

"If you must know, Andy, I brought them to make a coffin for you," replied Lehow.

Sagendorf was a delicate man, but through the recuperative effects of the climate he outlived Lehow by eighteen years. He filled many important positions and was highly respected.

The first Masonic meeting was held in the Sagendorf and Lehow cabin, December 10, 1858. In January, 1859, a lodge was regularly instituted under the authority of the Grand Lodge of Kansas, and its meetings were held in the same cabin.

First Election

The politicians were busy even at that early day. An election was held in Auraria on the sixth day of November, 1858, about three weeks after the settlement of the town. H. J. Graham was elected a delegate to Congress and A. J. Smith was made representative to the Kansas legislature. In this election charges of fraud were openly made. Two days after this swift political action, Graham set out on his long journey to the national capital to deal with Congress. His instructions were to get Pike's Peak region set apart as an independent Territory to be called "Jefferson." He was a man of ability and earnestly endeavored to accomplish the wishes of his constituents. But he found himself without influence at Washington. The country was so far away from civilization that Congress refused to consider the scheme of its proposed permanent settlement, and doubtless regarded Graham as an escaped lunatic.

However, he had the honor of being our first representative in Congress, and his unselfish devotion to the public service was evident in the fact that he paid his own expenses, which makes him a unique character in politics.

Smith was more successful in Topeka. Arapahoe County had been created in 1855 by the first legislature of Kansas, so he was recognized in the legislature, and the region was launched into political existence as Arapahoe County, Kansas Territory.

St. Charles

The Montana real estate speculators were keeping their eyes open, and one fine day T. C. Dickson, Adnah French, Frank M. Cobb, John A. Churchill and Charles Nichols walked over to the mouth of Cherry creek with the view of founding another city. They fixed upon the land on the east side of the creek for their town. These promoters took Smith and McGaa into their company on account of their connection with the copper-colored people. They held a meeting and adopted the constitution of the St. Charles Town Association. Frank Cobb and Adnah French made and drove the first stake for the city of St. Charles.

All of these St. Charles men, except Trader Smith and McGaa, decided to go to Kansas to spend the winter. They had not built any kind of a structure on their townsite. When a short distance down the Platte, they met parties destined for the settlement at Cherry creek, and they became apprehensive that some of these people might locate on their unimproved townsite. Charles Nichols was at once sent back and instructed to put up a building on the land as evidence of the company's right to it.

Nichols offered to give lots to anyone who would build on them, but town lots "went a-begging." In eastern Kansas in those days all that was needed to establish

priority of claim was to cut four logs and lay them in the form of a square. He resorted to this expedient.

Denver

In 1858, James W. Denver of Ohio was governor of the Territory of Kansas. The reports from the western end of his dominion demanded his attention. He commissioned three county officers—H. P. A. Smith, probate judge; Hickory Rogers, chairman of the county board of supervisors; and E. W. Wyncoop, sheriff, to go to the new county as representatives of Kansas government. These officials fell in on the way with a company which had been organized at Leavenworth. They arrived at Cherry Creek November 16. The pioneers of 1858 were, as a rule, men of unusual force of character; these Leavenworth men were distinctively so; they didn't stand around whittling sticks and talking about what they were going to do; they immediately opened a new chapter of local history.

In less than a week after their arrival they had taken possession of the St. Charles townsite, which they declared was deserted, the only improvement on the land being Nichols' unfinished cabin. They named the new city Denver, in honor of J. W. Denver, Governor of the

Territory of Kansas. And St. Charles became an historical memory. The whole proceeding was an unceremonious jumping, highly theatrical and very effective.

The cabins of that time were in the prevailing style of round logs and dirt floor, so graphically pictured by the pioneer poet, Greenleaf:

"Inspect we this, built fifty-eight, by one of bluest blood;
  The logs are all square-hewn and chinked and plastered o'er with mud;
  The roof of poles o'erspread with brush and what you'd call dirt-shingles;
  Its chimney square-stones, sticks and mud artistically mingles.

"The earth had been well hardened down to constitute a floor;
They hadn't got to windows yet—'twas lighted from the door.
'Twas furnished in Auraria style, and that the very best,
Comprising four three-legged stools, a table and a chest;
The dishes—the prevailing style—were tin; when meals were o'er
What cared he for hot water? 'Twas a step beside the door,
To scoop of dirt a handful, and to pluck a wisp of grass,
Some skillful passes, lo! each plate would shame a looking-glass!
That's how he washed the dishes; next he seized each knife and fork,
And found the ground a substitute for rotten-stone and cork.
When, late at night, he stretched himself on skins of buffaloes
No couch of down held tenant yet who suffered such repose!"

In this Denver City Town Company were E. P. Stout, president; General William Larimer, R. E. Whitsitt, James Reed, J. H. Dudley, Charles Blake, Norman Welton, A. J. Williams, General John Clancy, Samuel Curtis, Ned Wyncoop, McGaa and Charles Nichols. Most of their names have been perpetuated in the names of the prominent streets of Denver.

The Denver men were great boosters. They claimed the advantages of the more eligible site, and interested the new arrivals at Cherry Creek in their city.

The aggressiveness of these wide-awake Denver people caused the Aurarians to lose their tempers. A bitter spirit of rivalry soon developed between the two towns, and they put in much time that winter throwing hard words at each other across Cherry creek.

Auraria's partisans boasted of her antiquity, claiming that she was a city three or four weeks before Denver was even down on paper.

The rivalry of these ragged little towns in the winter loneliness of the great plains may seem absurd to readers of this day and generation, but it goes to prove that human nature is the same the world over, in all times and places.

Richens L. Wooton

Richens L. Wooton and family arrived in Auraria on Christmas day, 1858. Wooton brought a large stock of merchandise, most of which was contained in barrels. He wanted to make a favorable impression and become popular among his new associates, so he knocked in the head of a barrel and invited his callers to help themselves with tin cups. No method could have been more effective in attaining the desired end than the one he adopted. All Auraria promptly called. News of the unusual liquid refreshments spread like wild fire through the city of Denver, and the inhabitants of that town exhibited their characteristic energy by a lively dash across Cherry creek. The rivalry and animosity between the two cities were forgotten for that day at least. Before the night closed down Richens Wooton was "Uncle Dick" to every man in both towns. He made that Christmas of 1858 a notable one in the annals of Auraria.

Richens Wooton soon began the erection of his famous business block. This was the most imposing and pretentious edifice in the town. It was a story and a half high, roofed with clapboards. The upper floor was made of boards sawed by hand with a whip-saw and was the first board floor laid in the country. This room was lighted by a four-light glass window, the only luxury of the kind in the city.

Auraria was named from Green Russell's home town in Georgia, but as time went on and new people came in there were many theories in regard to the name. One man suggested that it was derived from Aurora, the Roman goddess of the dawn; another had a vague theory that it was a contortion of the word auriferous, to indicate the gold-yielding country around the town. Uncle Dick Wooton, in his book, gives the following: "There must have been some classical scholars among the founders of the town, because I am told that the name has a Latin origin, the word 'aura' meaning a gentle breeze. I suppose Auraria was intended to mean the town of gentle breezes, and it was a rather pretty and appropriate name."

The pioneers at Montana lost faith in the future of their town and moved, cabins and all, to Denver or Auraria, leaving their townsite to revert to a state of nature.

DENVER 1859

The little band of pioneers camping beneath the cottonwoods on the banks of the South Platte and Cherry creek in '58-'59 did not realize that they were laying the foundation of a great State. From this little camp the hardy, courageous prospectors scattered, climbed the foothills, scaled the mountains, penetrated the wild gorges, stuck pick and shovel into the granite and quartz rocks and washed the sands of streams. The winter was open and the spring came early. While some prospected, others were busy platting new towns. They placed on the map, Central, Black Hawk, Idaho Springs, Georgetown, Golden, Boulder, Colorado City, Pueblo and Canon City.

The favorite pastime of the pioneers during the long winter day was writing letters to their friends in the States. These letters were filled with glowing accounts of the scenery and the richness of the land in gold, which as yet they had seen with the eye of faith only.

It was optimism like that and faith in the future of the country that inspired the pioneers in the midst of a lonely wilderness, where the only home lights at night were their camp fires and the camp fires of the Indians, to lay the foundation of this great "city of lights."

CHAPTER V

HAPPENINGS AT THE CAMP

Rush for Gold

While financial depression still ruled the land, and men were without money, credit or opportunity for business of any kind, fanciful fabrications of the discovery of gold at Pike's Peak caused a wild rush to the new Eldorado—good, bad and indifferent; the educated and illiterate; the merchant, the speculator, the mechanic, the farmer, the gambler, some of every kind, a sort of human mosaic, marshaled under a banner which bore the forceful, if inelegant, legend, "Pike's Peak or Bust."

An apparently interminable procession of white covered wagons, christened "prairie schooners," drawn by the contemplative ox and the patient mule, moved across the plains, and, at night their camp fires, like beacon lights, stretched along the Platte Valley route, the Smoky Hill route, and the Arkansas route from the Missouri river to the Rockies.

Nothing like this had ever been seen before; the flight of Mohammed was not a circumstance compared with this hegira. College graduates and city men were among the masters of ox-teams, cooks at camp fires, scullions and helpers in the drudgery of the long journey. Some of the white-topped wagons, moving at a snail's pace, bore the inscription, "Lightning Express," "Root, Hog or Die," "From Pike County to Pike's Peak." Strange vehicles of all sorts crawled on the trail to the golden shrine. One man pushed a wheelbarrow laden with supplies, and, it is said, took a boarder to help defray expenses; another packed an ox with tools and provision and trudged by the animal's side; many made the journey in pairs, with handcarts, alternately pushing and riding, and some cheerily walked the long way with their earthly possessions swung to a pole across their shoulders. Through the large majority of this patient, toiling host was the sanguine, buoyant, determined spirit characteristic of the American pioneer. The fact that they had the courage to face the hardships of the plains showed a trait in their "makeup" superior to those who remained at home.

It was not a holiday outing. A journey from the Missouri river in those days occupied from six to seven weeks. There were no settlements on the way, no opportunity to procure supplies for man or beasts, save at the occasional stations of the Hockaday stage line to California. It was genuine courage that prompted to such a journey through hot sun, fierce winds and drifting sands, across the wide, treeless plains, which, like the Clashing Islands that closed after the Argo and her crew of heroes, would cut them off from any communication with home and friends for months—years, perhaps, they knew not how long. It was by the help of Medea, who was found at the end of the road, that Jason captured the golden fleece. A few of the Argonauts of '59, thinking a bird in the hand worth two in the bush, took their helpmeets with them. They were not adorned society belles, or light-brained coquettes, but women of good, practical sense, of moral and physical strength.

What was the motive of this moving host? To find gold. It is the desire for what gold typifies that has settled every country on the globe.

The Old Testament, from Genesis to Malachi, makes frequent mention of gold and silver. "Abraham was very rich in cattle, in silver, and in gold." Solomon, the great king of the Hebrews, had portions of his temple "overlaid with gold." The followers of Moses made a golden calf and worshiped it. Even before the recital of the creation of woman the existence of gold is mentioned. Genesis 2:12 reads: "And the gold of that land was good." All people in all ages have found it to be a good thing to have in the house. It has a wonderful purchasing power.

While this wave of humanity was moving over the plains, a very different history was being enacted at Cherry Creek. About three hundred people had spent the winter here. Among them were five women—Mrs. S. M. Rooker and her daughter, Mrs. H. Murat, Mrs. Smoke and Mrs. Wooton.

A. J. Williams and C. H. Blake, for whom Blake street was named, put up the first hotel of the place. It was a log building one hundred feet long, thirty feet wide, and roofed with canvas, to which they gave the name of "Denver House."

Murat and Smoke opened the "Eldorado Hotel" on February 1st. It had a silk flag floating from the top of a lofty pine mast. The flag was made by Mrs. Murat, and so it came about that the first national emblem that waved in Denver was made by a woman.

On March 3, 1859, the first child was born on the site of Denver, the son of McGaa and an Arapahoe woman. The couple had married according to the frontier fashion, and McGaa named his son Denver.

Mrs. Catharine Murat

About this time Smith and McGaa received from the Kansas Territorial Legislature a charter to run a ferry across the Platte river at the mouth of Cherry creek. The boat was propelled by the current, and the expense of running it small. Its daily receipts were from two to three hundred dollars. The pioneers gave Smith and McGaa a liberal share of town lots and made them officers in the town organizations because they claimed, through their Indian associates, the right to all land here. They were both in many ways about as much Indian as white men—migratory in their nature, and having little or no identity with the settlement, they soon drifted away.

Rivalry between the towns ran high. Society was full of "envy, hatred, malice and all uncharitableness." "Are you a Denver man or an Aurarian?" was the one absorbing local question. This intense feeling indirectly gave rise to the quarrel which resulted in Bassett's death. One word led to another until, in his rage, Bassett seized a pickhandle and made at Scudder, who fired and mortally wounded him. Scudder left Denver and went to Salt Lake, where he remained nearly a year. In the spring of 1860 he returned to Denver and asked to be tried for his act. A People's Court was organized, with C. A. Lawrence as judge. The testimony presented proved that the killing was in self-defense and he was unanimously acquitted. H. P. Bennet and J. C. Moore defended him, and the prosecution was in the hands of W. P. McClure.

Bassett was the recorder of the Denver townsite and was succeeded by Richard E. Whitsitt. Stout, the president, resigned because of business affairs in the East demanding his presence. General Larimer, the secretary and treasurer, resigned and Whitsitt became the entire machine. He was a dominating fellow, vastly energetic, full of resources, and a gifted real estate man. He devised all sorts of schemes to make Denver grow. He maintained for twenty years the most extensive real estate agency in Denver, and was the first man to make a record for himself in that line. From the day of his arrival in the city in 1858 until the day of his death in

1882, he platted and surveyed, bought and sold lots and blocks. He took an active part in the long fight for statehood, helped to build up the board of trade, and contributed to the completion of the Denver Pacific Railroad.

Frank Hall said: "I have always regarded R. E. Whitsitt as the real founder of Denver. I knew him intimately. He was the aggressive and progressive head of the original Denver Town Company." It was in the fall of this year that he fought a duel with W. P. McClure. The fight came off in the presence of two hundred or more people about one mile above Cherry creek. McClure received a severe wound, from which he recovered.

While the first comers had been building cabins they had not forgotten the main thing that brought them here. They were not after town lots, but gold. And the failure to find it in paying quantities caused a gloom to settle down over the camp. This was the condition when the advance trains of "prairie schooners" arrived. In they came with a "hurrah." They were ignorant of the hard labor of mining; their calculations centered around a single purpose: Get-rich-quick and get back to civilization. But few of the many thousands who came cherished a thought of building a permanent home here.

A story is told of the Dutchman who was hanged for stealing. Before adjusting the noose he was asked what he had to say for himself. With a quavering voice he said: "I came out mit de spring to stay mit de summer and go back mit de fall, but now I tink I vill stay all de vile."

STAMPEDERS

Many of the new arrivals were mere "surface float," having come with Utopian ideas in regard to the wealth of the country, expecting to find great nuggets of yellow metal lying around loose and streams burdened with golden sand. These romantic fortune-seekers soon returned

OVER THE PLAINS 1859

A "BUSTED" EMIGRANT

East, anathematizing the country and declaring Pike's Peak to be an unmitigated swindle. Under the inscription, "Pike's Peak or Bust," was written in large black letters, "Busted, by Thunder."

The routes of travel for six hundred miles were a restless surging wave of humanity. D. C. Oakes' pamphlet describing and lauding the country was the means of inducing many to emigrate. He had returned to the "States" and was on his way back with a sawmill when he met the stampeders. They said he had "sworn deceitfully"—in other words, had told outrageous falsehoods, which they spelt with three letters, and they threatened to hang him and burn his mill. He met them bravely by stating the fact of his having invested every dollar he was worth in that mill, which ought to be proof conclusive of his faith in the country. They gave him his life, but had the satisfaction of pelting him with vicious epithets. A little farther on he came to a new-made grave, and on the headstone, which was the storm-polished shoulder blade of a buffalo, was written the following epitaph:

"Here lies the body of D. C. Oakes,
Killed for aiding the Pike's Peak hoax."

One of these returning pilgrims, a wag in his way, informed his friends at home that nothing but unpardonable ignorance stood in the way of his making a fortune in those days. If he had only given the subject a thought he would have known, of course, that domestic animals are always scarce in new countries; but he did not think, and it was another and a wiser man who was far-sighted enough to bring hither a cat which he had taught to follow him. The cat easily sold for five dollars, and then it followed its master and was sold again and again as the story goes. The returned pilgrim always insisted that if he had brought out a load of cats in his emigrant wagon, he would have made his fortune.

He also told a story of one of their party who was a man of family, and what is commonly termed a "great homebody," but he had a longing for wealth and started for the new Eldorado. It was not long before he became very homesick, and, one day, when they arrived at a town on the outskirts of civilization where it was hoped letters from home would be found waiting them; finding none, the poor man withdrew to a secluded spot and "lifted up his voice and wept" so loudly that his companions at a distance heard, and, hearing, were filled with great alarm. It sounded to them like the voice of some terrible monster of the plains. One of the party, gifted with more bravery than the rest, suggested that it might be a buffalo calf; whereupon they traced the noise to its source. By common consent the afflicted man was granted permission to leave the organization. He went at once, and remained at home, a very contented being, with no desire ever again to roam to the "far ends of the earth."

The army of "go backs" grew greater than the advancing host, and they did many a tale unfold declaring there was not a thimbleful of gold in the country; it was all a delusion and a snare. They warned the brave and bold who pushed forward to beware of the man who had buckskin patches on his pants; he was a thief, a liar and a villain; he was here, there and everywhere, like the Scriptural adversary, "seeking whom he might devour." The pilgrims harassed their minds devising how they would avoid this scoundrel of the Rockies. "Lo and behold," said my informer, "upon our arrival, every man in the mountains wore the confounded rogues' patches."

According to Smiley, one hundred and fifty thousand persons left the Missouri river for the Pike's Peak region in the spring and summer of '59, and, of these, not less than fifty thousand were turned back by the senseless panic that prevailed. It was thought that the new country was undesirable for any purpose save that of satisfying this love for gold.

If gold was the only allurement, the pioneers are entitled to larger credit for laying the foundation of a state where the initial environments were so forbidding.

CHAPTER VI

IMPORTANT EVENTS

Changes from Cottonwood to Lumber and Brick

Away up on the Divide were pine forests. Wyatt and Bennet soon found their way with their sawmill into this "forest reserve." D. C. Oakes, who was buried in effigy, placed his sawmill near Palmer Lake, and the first frame building in Denver was constructed of lumber sawed by Major Oakes. The changes from cottonwood logs to lumber and brick were kaleidoscopic.

Uncle Dick Wooton built the first two-story house, by long odds the most pretentious building in the town, and, as there was no ordinance at that time prohibiting skyscrapers, others soon followed his lead.

Mr. William N. Byers came in with his printing press April 19th. It was speedily placed in the second story of Uncle Dick Wooton's business block, which made this the first office building here and gave the Aurarians the glory of having the first newspaper. But their feathers fell when the first issue of the News ap-

William N. Byers

peared with the headline, Cherry Creek, K. T., instead of Auraria City.

The News office was subsequently removed to a frame building constructed expressly for the purpose, in the middle of the creek, on the dividing line between Auraria and Denver, to safely emphasize the neutrality of the press.

The quieting effect of Uncle Dick Wooton's whisky was lost before New Year's day, and the strife went on for ascendency in importance and population.

The very generous townsite companies, who had no legal title whatever themselves, graciously gave each person a lot who would build a house on it, and they were having trouble to find people willing to build on donated lots.

About the first of January, 1859, George A. Jackson discovered gold on the south fork of Clear creek, near Idaho Springs. The place is still known as Jackson's diggings, and a stone monument now marks the spot.

On May 6th, John H. Gregory, a Georgian, discovered gold on the north fork of Clear creek. This discovery occurred at a psychological moment. The news swept like wild-fire over the plains, and the little towns at the mouth of the historic creek gave way to boundless enthusiasm. The excited newcomers rushed through at the rate of five hundred a day to the mountains. The arrival of teams, the loud cracking of whips made "confusion worse confounded" of tongues and matter.

The majority of them were ignorant of mining, and the mountains were soon swarming with prospectors who did not know the indications of a true lode. Wherever "blossom rock" showed itself, or a streak of white quartz appeared, stakes were driven and prospect holes dug, with the extravagant expectation that they would soon dig up a fortune and return to "the States" to enjoy it.

On May 7, 1859, two Concord coaches, each drawn

by six galloping mules, rolled into Denver in a swirling mass of dust. A crowd of red-shirted miners assembled to greet this arrival with shouts and a lively firing of revolvers. The office was located on the East side; the alert Denver town company had arranged for that. Making Denver the terminus of the stage line was the vital move in establishing it as a commercial and financial center, for everyone had to go or send there for letters.

A Tale of Horror

"I was in the first coach of the Leavenworth and Pike's Peak Express Company," said Mr. Barney. "It arrived in Denver on the seventh of May, 1859. The supply wagons were sent on ahead, locating the stations, and every twenty-five miles they would drop a tent, a stove and a cook. At that season of the year the twilight is short, so when we drew up at one of the stations for supper it was quite dark. When I entered the tent I saw the most soul-sickening sight that my eyes ever rested upon, and the flickering light of the candle added intensity to the horror. At first I thought it was a 'spirit from the vasty deep'—a ghost or hobgoblin from the great unknown. I felt sick—it is real weakening to feel oneself in the presence of the—departed—no, the returned dead.

The poor man, from starvation, was reduced to a living skeleton. Rip Van Winkle himself could not have looked more ghastly. He was in the last stages of exhaustion when an Indian found him and brought him to the tent. After he was refreshed with food and stimulants he told us his sickening story:

"Three brothers set out from Illinois in a one-horse cart for the gold region. From Leavenworth they took the Smoky Hill route. Guided by incorrect ideas of the distance, they were poorly prepared for the hardships of the journey, and the provisions gave out before they were half way. They killed their horse for food and loaded their cart with it, taking turn about in the harness of the slaughtered animal. It was tedious and their strength was rapidly going. When the last piece of flesh was gone they sat down in despair to die, for they had wandered away from the trail in search of water and had no hope of being found by a human being. One sank faster than the others, and, when dying, requested the surviving brothers to live upon his flesh and try to get through. He died, and they commenced their cannibalistic feast—ate the body, and again saw starvation staring them in the face. Another died, which furnished food to the remaining brother. He said that he had even crushed the skull and eaten the brains.

"We took the miserable, famished creature in the coach to Denver. His body regained health and strength, but his mind was gone. He remained always an imbecile. The citizens of Denver made up a purse and sent him to his friends in 'the States.'"

Return of Russell

William Green Russell, the man who pushed the button and turned on the show, returned in May, 1859, bringing with him one hundred and seventy men. He proceeded to Gregory camp and, June 9th, made the third rich discovery in Gilpin County, which was given and still bears the name of Russell Gulch.

The Russell brothers, three in number, with long beards and long vision, organized the first company of goldseekers, directed the locating and building of the first cabin on the site of Denver and made the first shipment of gold out of the country. They took this gold to the mint at Dahlonaga, Georgia, and about five hundred dollars were coined out of it. While they did not remain here permanently, they linked their names with the progress of civilization and are entitled to rank as our first pioneers.

THE STATE CONVENTION

In the midst of all this confusion the pioneers found time for politics. They argued that they must have a government for the protection of the rights and property of the people pouring into the country. The Kansas jurisdiction was in theory only. Kansas was too remote and means of communication too slow for the people here to acknowledge any such allegiance; for all purposes of practical government and enforcement of the law, the country might as well be under the government of the man in the moon.

The pioneers had grand ideas. No "territorial government" for them. They determined to take steps looking to the organization of a State, and a jump right into the Union at the first bound was resolved upon.

In compliance with a call, a convention met June 6th to draft a constitution for a State. The first resolution adopted was: "Resolved, That the discussion of this convention shall have but one object, viz.: The formation of a new and independent State of the Union." Many names were proposed for the new State—Shoshone, Jefferson, Cibola, Pike's Peak, and one delegate made a strong appeal to call it "Bill Williams." He was deeply grieved when the convention gave "the laugh" to his proposition.

Bill Williams was one of the early frontiersmen. He was a Methodist preacher in Missouri before he wandered to the mountains. He often said that he was so well known in his circuit that the chickens recognized him as he went riding by the farm houses and the old rooster would crow: "Here comes Parson Williams. One of us must be made ready for dinner!" Upon leaving the States he lived among the various tribes of Indians on the plains and in the mountains. He possessed the faculty of easily acquiring languages, and could readily translate the Bible into several Indian dialects. He was at last killed by the Indians. His friends, who loved him because he was generous and warm hearted, gave his name to many peaks, rivers and passes discovered by him, chiefly in the region now embraced in Arizona.

The constitutional convention was duly held, a constitution submitted and adopted, the proposed State named Jefferson, and a full set of State officers elected, including a delegate to Congress, who went to Washington.

James Buchanan was president at that time and the approaching Civil war absorbed the energies of the administration at Washington. Congress was not in a mood to admit new states.

Horace Greeley

On the same day that this convention met, Horace Greeley of the New York Tribune arrived in Denver. Probably no paper in the country wielded a greater influence than the New York Tribune. The venerable editor's words of advice and wisdom were considered worth hearing and heeding. He addressed the convention and spoke strongly in favor of organizing a State without the preliminary form of a Territory.

Mr. Greeley was accompanied by two distinguished newspaper men—A. D. Richardson and Henry Villard. These men drew up and signed a statement about the discovery of gold in Colorado which was published in their respective papers. It was also published in an extra issue of the News and circulated on the various routes. The effect was immediate and a tide of immigration to the Pike's Peak gold fields set in which surpassed anything ever before witnessed in this country.

The Argonauts

Mr. Greeley and his distinguished friends stopped at the Denver House. The occupants of the drinking and gambling saloon demanded of him a speech. The tipplers silently sipped their grog, and the

gamblers respectfully suspended the shuffling of the cards while Mr. Greeley, standing in their midst, made a strong anti-drinking and anti-gambling speech which was received with many a sly and humorous wink.

The Cabin Greeley Jumped

The noise of the hotel was too great for literary work. Greeley "jumped" a cabin. His companion, Richardson, says: "A few days later the owner of the cabin came down from the mines and looked in upon us, quite unexpectedly, but observing that the nine points of the law were in our favor, he apologized humbly for his intrusion (most obsequious and marvelous of landlords), begged us to make ourselves entirely at home, and then withdrew, to jump the best vacant cabin he could find until the departure of his non-paying tenants—best specimen of the polite gentleman on the terrestrial globe!"

The old stage coach in which Mr. Greeley made his famous trip in 1859 was purchased by the Bent County Fair Association of Las Animas from Frank W. Nott, who drove it a number of years in Denver as a tally-ho. This stage ran in every famous route of the West, and was in more holdups than it has spokes in its wheels. It carries thirty people; has been in actual service sixty years, and is still in good condition—the most historic wagon on wheels today.

First Stage Coach
(Reproduced from an old print)

A pioneer said: When Mr. Greeley arrived in Denver he was received with all the honor the infant city could command. He stated that he did not intend to be deceived in this matter, that seeing was believing, and he wanted to wash out some of the dirt himself. So the men put their heads together to see "how they could come it over" the old gentleman. They themselves were satisfied as to the richness of Gregory Gulch—it was no intention to deceive, but Solomon says "there is a time for all things," and they wanted a "good one" on Horace Greeley. They sent a message to the camp that Horace was coming and to salt a mine. The boys cleaned up all the sluice boxes in the diggin's except one and emptied their contents into that one. They also scattered some of the richest into the "pit," or bottom, of the gulch where the "pay gravel" was then being taken out, and were then ready for the old man.

Bright and early the next morning a spanking team

was rigged up, and the distinguished gentleman started for the gulch, accompanied by some of the most plausible, entertaining and versatile talkers of the country. They escorted him over the diggings, related all the interesting events in the history of its discovery, showed him specimens of the dirt and the pure gold that had been washed out. Then they took him to the pit to let him test the dirt himself. Mr. Greeley was eager for the task. He called for a shovel and pan, rolled up his sleeves and went down into the pit. They gave him all the necessary instructions as to the process of panning and looked on with palpitating anxiety. Mr. Greeley was an apt scholar and put his dirt through like an adept in the art. It panned out big. All the bottom of the pan was covered with nuggets and gold particles. They slapped him on the shoulders in regular western style and told him to try it again, which he did, with the same success. Then they cleaned up the "salted sluice" before his eyes and let him see the output of one day's run. Mr. Greeley gathered up his gold dust in a bag and said: "Gentlemen, I have worked with my own hands and seen with my own eyes. The news of your rich discovery shall go all over the world as far as my paper can waft it."

As soon as he reached New York he devoted a whole side of the Tribune to an ecstatic description of the camp, headed with large, glaring type such as "bill-stickers" use. The report was read all over the country and caused a great rush to the land of promise. Those who had the fever took a relapse and had it bad. It was a raging epidemic and spread faster than the cholera in Egypt. He shouted into the ears of the overcrowded East until the welkin rang: "Young man, go West." It was his glowing articles and earnest advice about "going West" that caused the first great boom in Denver.

Count Murat, a barber, who, in honor of his royal blood, was dubbed "knight of the strop and razor," figured conspicuously in the editorial correspondence of the Tribune. While in Denver Mr. Greeley sat under the graceful manipulations of this tonsorial artist. The count, feeling he would be distinguished by a notice from the great journalist, and also wishing to impress him with the liberal product of the gold fields and the corresponding ability of the people to throw away money, accomplished it by charging the famous editor two dollars for a shave. It is said that ever after Mr. Greeley regarded barbers with suspicion and aversion and ceased to patronize them.

PART III
THE PROVISIONAL GOVERNMENT

CHAPTER VII
THE CRITICAL PERIOD

THE FIRST LEGISLATURE

The impending struggle between the North and the South absorbed the attention of Congress and nothing was done towards giving a form of government to the new region. The persistent pioneers decided to form a Territory independent of Congress and take it up with that body later. In October, 1859, they organized the Territory of Jefferson; a constitution was adopted by vote of the people, and on the twenty-fourth of October the following officers were elected: Robert W. Steele, governor; Lucien W. Bliss, secretary of state; Charles R. Bissell, auditor; G. W. Cook, treasurer; Samuel McLean, attorney general; A. J. Allison, chief justice of the supreme court; John M. Odell and E. Fitzgerald, associate justices; Oscar B. Totten, clerk; H. H. McAfee, superintendent of public instruction, and John L. Merrick, marshal. Beverly D. Williams was elected to Congress. He went, and remained there until the Territory of Colorado was created in 1861. A Legislature was elected consisting of eight members of the Senate and twenty-one in the House. Rev. Jacob Adriance was elected chaplain of the House.

The first Jefferson Legislature assembled in Denver

November 7, 1859, in the second story of a large frame building owned by the Leavenworth and Pike's Peak Express, which stood on the south side of Larimer street, nearly opposite the site of our city hall. Governor Steele presented his message. W. N. Byers says: "The message of Governor Steele was a well-considered document, defining the right of the position the people had taken for home government against the claim of sovereignty by Kansas." Committees were then appointed to prepare the framework of the various departments of the government and provisional laws deemed essential.

Robt. W. Steele,
Governor of Jefferson Territory

The Legislature adjourned to wait the readiness of the committees. On the tenth of November, three days after adjournment, the governor issued his proclamation calling the Legislature to meet in special session, in Denver, on January 23, 1860, to act upon the reports of the committee.

The law-makers assembled at the appointed time and proved to be a most industrious legislative body. An act was passed consolidating the three towns into one municipal organization under the name of "City of Denver, Auraria and Highlands." The town of Highlands existed only on paper at that time. Under the authority conferred by this act, an election was held to choose the first mayor and other city officers. John C. Moore, a former resident of Louisville, Ky., was elected the first mayor of Denver, and Arapahoe County, Kansas, became Jefferson Territory.

R. W. Steele's second proclamation was for the establishment and observance of the first Thanksgiving day.

> PROCLAMATION
>
> "I, Robert W. Steele, governor of the Territory of Jefferson, do hereby appoint Thursday, the twenty-ninth day of December, in the year of our Lord one thousand eight hundred and fifty-nine, as a day of thanksgiving and praise to the Supreme Ruler of the universe for our preservation, prosperity and happiness in this newly discovered land of gold, and recommend its appropriate observance by the citizens of the Territory."

The News was a loyal supporter of the new government. It at once discarded "Kansas Territory" as a headline and substituted "Jefferson Territory." Mr. Byers, the editor, wrote: "We hope and expect to see it stand until we can boast of a million people, and look upon a city of a hundred thousand souls, having all the comforts and luxuries of the most favored." I have quoted this because it shows the enthusiasm of the pioneer.

The adjourned sitting of the Jefferson Legislature met at Criterion Hall, in Denver, pursuant to the governor's proclamation, and adjourned to Golden for the reason that board was offered at $6 per week, wood, light and hall rent free. As these law-makers were serving without pay, such an offer was attractive. The people of Golden were so anxious to make their city the capital that they paid the traveling expenses of the legislators. One law-maker declared that they should not incur that expense for him—so he walked to Golden.

A Bloody Duel

"There occurred a most sanguinary encounter, or affair of 'honah,' between two citizens of the Territory," said Judge H. P. Bennet. "I remember it as though it were yesterday.

"The affair grew out of some personal language used by Dr. Stone against Secretary Bliss. Dr. Stone had drawn his pay as a member of the Jefferson Legislature. After having sold his pay warrants, the doctor publicly repudiated the Territorial organization. This action by a member of the Legislature was quite annoying to the other officers of the Territory, and particularly so to the sensitive secretary.

H. P. Bennet

"Bliss and Stone were together often, were jovial, free hearted, fond of a joke and a drink, and, up to this time, were the best of friends.

"On the evening before the seventh of March, 1860, the secretary, Lou Bliss, as he was familiarly called, had invited to his private rooms at the hotel a dozen or more gentlemen friends to break a few bottles of wine with him. While they were making themselves merry with the host and the generous wine, Dr. Stone, who had come down from Central that day, stepped into the room unbidden and took his seat among the convivial party. The call was inopportune, for the party had just been discussing his repudiation of the Territorial organization.

"Shortly after Stone came in, glasses were filled all around and Bliss, rising, said: 'Here's to the man who got his pay and then repudiated the government and left his friends.' Dr. Stone understood the remark to be aimed at him, as, in fact, it was. Fire shot from his eyes, and, without taking his wine, he and a friend who came in with him immediately withdrew.

"The friend who had retired with Dr. Stone soon returned with a note bearing a challenge to mortal combat. Bliss immediately accepted.

"Being the challenged party, according to the code he had the choice of weapons and chose double-barreled shotguns loaded with ounce balls; distance, thirty paces; time, afternoon of the next day.

"The place selected was on the west bank of the Platte river, opposite Denver.

"There was no secrecy, for there was no local law against duelling, and, for that matter, in the absence of statutes, the inhabitants of the western border of the Great American Desert were 'a law unto themselves' in all things.

"The town was full of excitement over the impending duel. People conversed in whispers and exchanged glances full of meaning. Some said Bliss would not fight, that he was a Northern man and hadn't the nerve. Others said Dr. Stone was from Harper's Ferry and would make Bliss fight or back squarely down. Others again averred that Bliss would fight and was sure to hit his man; that he was rehearsing for the combat and was a crack shot. He had, at the 'word,' shot the figure of a man at thirty paces distant full of holes from the crown of the head to the knees, hitting the figure every time where he said he would.

"And so the gossip went on, until the opinion became general that Bliss' superior skill would brace him up for the conflict.

"Not knowing the precise hour, I watched to see the crowd start, and then followed, thinking possibly I might stop the fight by reasoning with the parties on the ground.

"When I reached the appointed place Dr. Stone had just arrived, accompanied by his seconds and surgeon. Shortly after came Bliss, walking and carrying his shotgun carelessly on his shoulder. He was dressed in a dust-colored 'Raglan' coat, and impressed me at the time as though he was, as near as might be, following out his habit of bird hunting.

"He mingled in the crowd, talking and chatting with his friends and acquaintances with as much apparent ease and composure as though the occasion was but a Christmas shooting match. Dr. Stone walked with his surgeon, apart from the crowd, looking pale and highly wrought up.

"I began to counsel peace and compromise, but no one seemed to think a peaceful settlement could be effected. Some told me I had better keep still, or I might get hurt. 'They had come there to see a fight, and a fight it must be.' So, thinking prudence the better part of valor, I concluded to remain and witness, for the first time in my life, a duel.

"In about twenty minutes after the parties reached the place, the distance was measured off and guns loaded —one barrel each. The toss-up for the word was won by Stone's seconds. The belligerents were placed opposite, with left side presented each to the other, guns down in hand. The signal was one-two-fire-stop. The firing was to be done on or between the words fire and stop. Either principal firing before the word fire, or after the word stop, was, by the terms of the code, liable to be shot down by the seconds of his antagonist.

"The principals being ready, the seconds in their respective positions each armed with a Colt's navy revolver cocked and in hand, the word was given in a loud, clear tone, when, in quick but due time, Stone fired first, without raising his gun to his eye. Before the word stop was uttered Bliss fired and Stone fell to the ground with a heart-rending cry, 'Killed! O, my God.' He was pierced through the pelvis from hip to hip. Bliss, unharmed, except by the stain of murder on his soul, walked away, his face pallid and distorted with misery—it having been his intention not to kill, but to inflict a slight wound that would merely disable the doctor for a time.

"Stone was carried to his room and lingered for several months, wasting to a skeleton long before he expired. Bliss was never quite himself after the death of Stone, and soon drifted away."

This famous pioneer dinner which resulted in such a tragedy was held in the Broadwell hotel, which was a noted hotel in its time. It stood at the corner of Larimer and Sixteenth. While James Broadwell was building that house, he was told many times that he was throwing money away; some of the disappointed gold-seekers predicted that antelope would be grazing on the streets of Denver within three years.

It may not be amiss to contrast the prediction of those early Denver pioneers that the grass would yet grow in the streets of Denver with the facts of Denver's growth, and the proud position she now occupies among the great cities of the country. That

BROADWELL HOUSE

BROWN PALACE HOTEL

same Broadwell hotel has long since been torn down, and upon the site stands the splendid Tabor block. The palatial hotel costing $2,000,000, built by that optimistic pioneer, Henry C. Brown, and named in his honor. Its fame is world-wide. When we think of the Brown today, we think of the public-spirited and popular manager, Calvin H. Morse. The Albany hotel, which covers nearly a block in the heart of the city, and daily houses a good-sized colony of the traveling public. The Shirley hotel, the Savoy hotel, the Metropole, and a dozen other great hotels, with hundreds of apartment houses, that, in size and furnishings, rival the hotels of other cities. Denver's theaters and opera houses are in the list. The Denham, which is equal in size and artistic appointments to any of the great theaters of New York; the Broadway theater, the Tabor opera house, the moving picture theaters, rivalling in size and beauty the best of the metropolitan moving picture houses anywhere in the country, making Curtis street at night a great white way that is the wonder of strangers when they enter Denver's gates. Denver's church architecture, of which a number of the structures are replicas of the great churches of Europe. Its great department stores, which extort confessions from eastern visitors that they far surpass those of any city that is west of the Mississippi river and rival in variety and richness of their goods the best of the stores on the Atlantic coast. All of these are Denver's present boast! What of those early croakers who sought to discourage Jim Broadwell when

C. H. Morse

he planned, in the early 60's, the now defunct Broadwell hotel?

THE PEOPLE'S COURT

For a brief period in 1860 Denver was literally overrun with ruffians, thieves and gamblers; a series of murders was inaugurated by desperadoes. The various governments were unable to find ways and means of effectively enforcing laws for the preservation of public order.

The solons of the place were called together in the fall of '60 to draft a code of laws suitable to their needs. They organized a tribunal which they dignified with the title of People's Court. This was hastily called together when a murder occurred. It was speedily followed by retributive justice; there was no stay of proceedings, no appeal to a higher court, no imprisonment.

THE ATTACK ON THE NEWS

The News dealt vigorous blows against the desperadoes who infested Denver, and bravely condemned the killing of a negro named Starks by Charlie Harrison, one of the worst of the outlaws. Harrison sought the editorial sanctum to discuss the whys and wherefores, claiming that he killed Starks in self-defense, and exhibited his pistol covered with hacks which, he declared, were made by Starks' bowie-knife in the struggle between them. The subject was then dropped, to the mutual satisfaction of the News and Harrison.

Carl Wood, however, who delighted in bloodshed and violence, and who exercised a sort of despotic influence over his confederates, summoned them to his support, and one morning suddenly appeared in the News office and threatened to "clean it out." Approaching the senior editor, Mr. Byers, he seized him by the collar and commanded him to go at once to the Criterion saloon and apologize to the proprietor, Harrison, for the offensive editorial. He emphasized this order by flourishing a large navy revolver dangerously near to the editor's head.

Wood was informed that the difficulty with Harrison had been settled satisfactorily to all parties concerned and an apology at that time was uncalled for.

The appearance of these armed desperadoes in the News sanctum caused great uneasiness among the employes. A few printers in the composing room were for showing fight, but, unfortunately, they were not armed.

Mr. Byers stated his willingness to be escorted to the Criterion saloon by the ruffians, and so went with them. Wood walked close by his side, occasionally shoving his pistol under his nose, asking him how he liked the smell of gunpowder, and playfully threatening to blow his brains out "just for luck."

Arriving at the saloon, Harrison corroborated the statements made at the office, that all was quiet between himself and the editor, and urged that the matter be dropped. While Wood and his friends were filling themselves with liquor at the bar, Byers succeeded, by a ruse of Harrison's, in escaping through the back door, and returned to his office, which, during his absence, had assumed the appearance of a hastily improvised arsenal. The employes, apprehensive of another visit from the desperadoes, had armed themselves and prepared for a siege.

When the escape of the captive was made known, Wood and his riotous friends, armed with double-barreled shotguns, mounted their horses and drew up for consultation at an unoccupied log house a few rods away from the editor's office. They evidently realized the necessity of being cautious.

To George Steele, who was full of drunken bravery, was entrusted the honor of reconnoitering the enemy's camp. He advanced to the steps of the building and peered long and earnestly, but could see nothing—all was as still as the heart of the dead, yet at that very moment he was covered with a dozen rifles from within. Standing awhile, as if debating in his own mind the course to pursue, he returned to the log house, but soon appeared with a pair of heavy revolvers strapped around him. When in front of the building, he whipped out a pistol and fired into the office, but no one was wounded, nor was there any response. He then put spurs to his horse and sped like the wind over the foot-bridge that reeled and rocked under the clattering hoofs of his horse. Gaining the opposite bank, he rose in his stirrups and, turning, fired again, but the bullet passed through the building without harm.

A signal was then given to the News men, when they opened fire upon him from their windows. His coat was completely riddled with buckshot, and he reeled in his saddle, but did not fall. He rode rapidly to a brothel where his mistress lived, informed her of his wounded condition, and then dashed away to the Highland suburbs. A man by the name of Tom Pollock followed in his wake and shot him from his horse, but not fatally.

There were flying rumors that Byers had been killed, and in a few minutes the streets of Denver were filled with armed men. Search being instituted for Carl Wood, he was apprehended, just as he reached the door of his cabin, and compelled to throw down his arms and surrender.

The trial which ensued occupied three days. All business was suspended, and Judge H. P. Bennet, always a faithful and earnest advocate of the people's cause, did great credit to himself on this occasion.

It was decided that Carl Wood should be banished from the country on pain of death if he returned. He was provided with a fleet horse, led out on the prairie and given the word "go," which he obeyed without any unnecessary delay.

The Hanging of Gordon

The damp morning newspaper so often brought tales of blood that a "man for breakfast" became a common expression.

The killing of Jacob Gantz by James Gordon in July, 1860, created the most intense excitement that had ever agitated the public mind.

Gordon was subject to periodical sprees. On this occasion, it is said, he was crazy drunk. He entered a saloon, and, seeing Jacob Gantz seated on a keg in a corner, politely and pressingly urged him to take a drink. While standing at the bar, Gordon lifted his glass, sneeringly viewed Gantz from head to foot, threw the whisky in his face, struck him with his pistol and shot him dead. In the darkness, he made his escape to Fort Lupton. The fort was surrounded by his pursuers for twenty-four hours before he came out. At sundown the gate was thrown open and Gordon, mounted on a fleet-footed horse and a pistol in each hand, plunged through the crowd and disappeared in the gathering darkness.

Weeks passed before he was heard of again. He wrote a friend to sell some property and send the money to him at Kansas City. The letter fell into the hands of W. H. Middaugh, acting as the people's sheriff, and who undertook the dangerous mission of capturing him.

Taking the coach to Leavenworth, he intercepted Gordon on the high prairies, within sight of the line of the Indian Territory, when he was lying on the grass by the side of the trail, holding his horse by the bridle and allowing it to feed. When Middaugh read the warrant for his arrest, a deathlike paleness covered his face and every nerve seemed to tremble.

He was taken to Leavenworth, where a single half-hour's trial was held, and, in mockery of justice, he was acquitted, on the plea that the deed was committed outside the jurisdiction of that place, notwithstanding the long-asserted authority of Kansas to the contrary. A violent mob gathered around the house, however, with the avowed intention of hanging him. He placed himself under the protection of the mayor.

The wildest excitement prevailed. The seething, angry crowd surged to and fro, and, as night came on, bonfires were built, which threw their lurid light far out over a scene at once weird and fearful.

Infuriated men, armed with muskets, revolvers and knives, were sending up the fierce demand: "Hang him! Hang him!"

Mayor McDowell expostulated with the rioters and made several speeches, urging obedience to the law.

The ruling spirits at last agreed that Gordon should be delivered to Middaugh. The scene that ensued was indescribable. The brave officers gathered around the prisoner. They were forced by the frenzied crowd into a narrow rocky glen. Several times a halter was thrown around the neck of Gordon, and, as quickly, cut by an officer. Darkness closed about them, and the howls and oaths of the mob made a din that was fearful.

The prisoner begged to be hung, shot—anything to put him out of his misery.

He was bruised and lacerated; every shred of clothing torn from him; nothing left upon his body but clanking chains. Middaugh, at length, carried his prisoner away through the mob, and on the twenty-eighth of September they reached Denver.

Intense feeling began to manifest itself. The crowd which met them soon adjourned to a grove to organize a court, for they intended Gordon's trial to be in accordance with law and justice. Judge H. P. Bennet, who sat far off with his back to the crowd, was nominated as prosecutor for the people, but he declined, saying the judges appointed would control the jury. If they would appoint a new set of judges, he would prosecute. The request was acceded to, and the judge was chosen for the prosecution with a deafening yell. He arose and stated that it would require some time to collect his evidence, and requested the trial to be adjourned until the next morning at nine o'clock. He urged the people to let right be done, though the heavens fall. He said: "The trifling of one of the highest tribunals in the land with the life that is now in our hands has turned the eyes of tens of thousands in the States towards Denver, where no law of the great American Union claims jurisdiction. Let us temper justice with mercy, and let no mob or unlawful attempt interfere with the 'People's Court.'" Even after this ardent address, an attempt was made during the night to rescue Gordon.

The next morning they entered upon the trial. Gordon was allowed every advantage that could have been accorded him by the highest and best regulated court in the land. He was supported by able lawyers, who labored faithfully in his behalf. The verdict, "Guilty," was rendered by twelve of the most respectable and responsible citizens of the community, and the sentence of death passed by the court and endorsed by the assembled hundreds. He was given time to make temporal and spiritual preparation for his unhappy end. Petitions were circulated for a reprieve, but without success. If to be hanged was inevitable, he wished for no delay, for there was no reprieve from his conscience. From the depths of his misery thoughts came thick and fast of his misspent life, of the alluring woman who placed the red wine to his lips and led him to ruin; of the life he had taken; of the horrible death before him; of the hopes, prayers and tears of his gray-haired mother.

On the following Saturday—October 6th—as the sun was sinking behind mountains shrouded with mystic light, Gordon was led to the gallows. Rev. Dr. Rankin,

Sheriff Middaugh and a few others mounted the scaffold with him. Prayer for the doomed was offered, during which Gordon knelt and the vast assemblage stood with uncovered heads. At the close, he said in a faltering voice:

"Gentlemen, you who have been my friends and endeavored to obtain a reprieve for me in the hope of securing my banishment from the Territory, I thank you from the bottom of my heart; I thank the ladies and gentlemen who have visited me during my confinement and been so good to me. Speak of me kindly to my mother. Oh, if some good friend here would shoot me! But it is all well—good-by. Mr. Middaugh, remember to fix the knot so it will break my neck instantly. Oh, God have mercy!"

And thus ended the career of one who had many friends—but the people were inflexible in administering justice. Truly, the "way of the transgressor" is hard and his sins will find him out.

The foregoing stories illustrate the condition of affairs in the new settlement. The People's Court had a powerful influence in checking those inclined to deeds of violence.

THE FOURTH OF JULY

The great holiday event of 1860 was the celebration of the Fourth of July. The festivities opened with firing salutes and a grand procession. The crowd assembled in the cottonwood grove and listened to speeches by local orators that flashed with patriotism and expanded with predictions of the future greatness of this western country. A brass band was brought from Omaha, which enlivened the proceedings with the inspiring strains of the "Star Spangled Banner," "Yankee Doodle," "Hail Columbia" and other appropriate melodies. The pioneer women took an active part in the entertainment. They made a handsome silk flag, which they presented to the city, with the request that it be kept until Colorado should be admitted into the Union and then to be delivered to the Governor of the new State. Nineteen years later Mayor Sopris passed the flag to Governor Routt. It is now one of the State's historical banners in the capitol building.

A curious jumble of conflicting jurisdictions grew out of the ambition of the pioneers to have an independent State. In the history of the United States there is no parallel to the complicated political and legal conditions of 1859 and 1860. The Kansas Territorial government was asserting its jurisdiction. The Jefferson Territorial government was doing the best it could, but it was practically inoperative because it was without a source of revenue, and many of the settlers who adhered to the authority of the Governor of Kansas regarded it as illegal. The Miners' Courts and People's Courts scattered over the Territory, together with the Arapahoe County Claim Club, were recognized only by the local settlers who had established them.

The proceedings of the several governments became a "fearfully confused tangle." Many who desired to be law-abiding did not know where to bestow allegiance. These confused jurisdictions inevitably gave rise to novel complications. The following is an illustration:

DIVORCE—JUDGE HOWARD'S QUIT-CLAIM DEED TO HIS WIFE

MARY E. HOWARD,
      Plaintiff,
      vs.
JOHN HOWARD,
      Defendant.

In Court of Chancery, Denver City, Jefferson Territory.

PETITION FOR DIVORCE

To the Plaintiff in the above entitled action:

WHEREAS, having been cited through the press at Denver, to appear before one Judge Downing, of the above entitled Court, to show cause why your prayer to be divorced from me should not be granted;

I, the defendant, hereby state (waiving my own oath in the premises) that I don't know any such cause whatever, and, therefore, confess the corn. And said defendant, as Judge of the Canon City District Court, enters a decree in your favor accordingly; and in order to relieve you of any embarrassment in the matter, I have executed and send you herewith attached as part of this answer, a quit-claim deed of all my right, title and interest whatever in you. leaving a blank to be filled up by the name of the party ——— grantee, by whom you may in future be claimed under squatter title. Hoping you will fully appreciate my good feeling in the premises, I hereby attach the said deed, as follows, to wit:

Know all men (and one woman) by these presents, That I, John Howard, of Canon City, of the first part, do hereby give, grant, bargain, convey, and quit-claim, all my right, title and interest in and to the following (un) real estate, to wit: The undivided whole of that ancient estate known as Mary Howard, (the title to which I acquired by discovery, occupancy, possession and use,) situated at present in the town of Denver, Jefferson Territory, together with all the improvements made and erected by me thereon, with all the rents, profits, easements, enjoyments, long suffering and appurtenances thereto in anywise appertaining, unto ——— of the second part, to have and to hold unto the said ——— so long as he can keep her, without recourse upon the grantor or endorser.

In testimony whereof, I have hereunto set my hand and seal, this, the 24th day of Jan., 1861.

[SEAL]   Signed,   JOHN HOWARD.

Signed in the presence of A. Rudd, clerk of District Court.

Per WILBUR F. STONE, Deputy.

THE UNWRITTEN LAW

Mr. Hugh Steele is a son of R. W. Steele, who was at the head of the Provisional government. He is now Secretary of the Colorado Pioneer Society and likes to talk about the old times.

"My father and his family arrived in Denver on the twenty-fourth day of May, 1860," said Mr. Steele, "and we pitched our tent in a grove of cottonwood trees where the Colorado & Southern machine shops now stand. Many people were living in tents. I stepped out of our tent the next morning and the first thing that greeted my gaze was the body of a man swinging from the limb of a cottonwood tree. I was indeed shocked. I did not know but what it was a regular thing. If I remember correctly, the man was a murderer. The vigilance committee had been organized and had started out to show the people that law was going to be enforced, and one of the particular points was that indiscriminate killing must cease."

Hugh Steele

In response to my request for a story of the early days, Mr. Steele told me the following:

The heroic spirit of the pioneers was never more strongly exemplified than in their endeavor to rescue those lost and wandering in the mountains. Indeed, it was an unwritten law among them that one should imperil his own life in the defense or rescue of a pioneer in danger.

Mr. John W. Irion of Thomasville, Colorado, was one of a party that risked their lives to save others. This is the story, said Mr. Steele: In March, 1860, a party of men left Gregory Diggings for the purpose of prospecting the Middle Park country. They crossed the main range near James Peak. Thoughtless of the fact that they were going into a widely unsettled section, they carried a very slim allowance of provisions.

After crossing the range and going down the valley of Grand river, they camped at Hot Sulphur Springs, and prospected the surrounding country until their supply of provisions was gone. It became necessary to retrace their trail to Gregory Diggings.

In the meantime the weather had turned very cold,

and one of the party, Nathan Rowley, had his feet frozen and was unable to travel. After some discussion, it was decided to start at once and leave Rowley at the Hot Sulphur Springs, until assistance could be sent to him.

They had gone only a few miles on the return trail when Charles Tupper halted, with the remark that he had never abandoned a man in such a desperate condition and he never would. Taking with him his old-fashioned muzzle-loading rifle and blankets, he went back to Rowley, determined to stay with him to the bitter end.

The other men made their way to Gregory and scattered to other sections, leaving the rescue of Rowley and Tupper to a man by the name of Dorsey, who had been the leader of the expedition.

Dorsey was taken with a fever and lay for a month unable to do anything, yet he had not forgotten his companions and made strenuous efforts to get someone to go to the rescue.

Finally he induced two men, Heath and King, to make the effort. They went as far as James Peak, where a storm overtook them, and, worn out and discouraged, they returned to Gregory diggings. They said that no human being could get across the range at that season of the year.

Dorsey, undaunted by the failure of the first party sent out, went to Russell Gulch, where James F. Pierce, Harrison Dennis, Lyman G. Crippen and John W. Irion were engaged in whip-sawing lumber. Pierce and Rowley had camped together the previous winter and Dorsey thought he might be induced to assist in finding his former partner. Pierce said it would be absolutely impossible for him to leave, but he would pay wages to anyone who would volunteer to go.

Crippen at once declared himself ready to go, and Irion, with an emphatic exclamation, said he would accompany him. They started the following morning. Dorsey acted as guide, being too feeble from sickness to pack anything. From the pass of James Peak, Dorsey pointed out to them the route which his party had traversed to Hot Sulphur Springs. If Rowley and Tupper are still living, said he, they will be there waiting for the promised relief.

Crippen and Irion bade Dorsey farewell. From James Peak they proceeded north along the summit of the range about three miles, doubtless crossing the ground where the Moffat Road now runs. At one point they were confronted by an unsurmountable cliff of rock and were obliged to make a detour to the west slope and pick their way along the rough mountain side. Irion was in the lead, when suddenly he found himself being carried rapidly down the slope, accompanied by all the snow above and around him. Fortunately, he lodged against a ledge of rock, while the avalanche of snow deepened and widened until it looked to him about a quarter of a mile wide.

This was his first experience in snow slides. He had to climb one hundred and fifty feet to get back from where he started. Then they hurried along the ridge to the north, until they found a place where they could descend in safety to timber line. They built a fire, cooked supper and rolled up in their blankets for the night. An early start was made next morning and they expected to make a good advance in their search, but the snow was soft and treacherous and their snow-shoes were but makeshifts, being pieces of board about eight inches wide and thirty inches long, lashed on with pieces of cord. Threatened with snow blindness, they hastily melted snow, bathed their eyes, and were overjoyed to find it produced relief. The next morning they were up early and started on their journey. During the night the weather had changed, snow had fallen and it had softened the crust of the old snow, so that travel became extremely laborious. The crust would give way and down they would go to their arm-pits.

They became exhausted and went into camp. Irion climbed a tall tree, and from the top he could look down upon the country a few miles distant. This renewed their courage, and the next morning they started with the intention of reaching the open country that day. But their labors were to be brought to a conclusion much quicker than they dared to hope. They had proceeded about a mile when they heard a voice calling. Both of the men made answer to the call and fired their pistols several times, running as rapidly as possible towards the place whence the sound came. Irion called out, "Who are you?" A voice answered, "My name is Tupper." "Where is Rowley?" he asked. "He is only a short distance away," was the reply.

Tupper then stepped out from some thick undergrowth of timber which had concealed him, and in a few seconds he was joined by Rowley. Irion said they were two of the most unsightly human beings he had ever looked upon; they were unwashed, black with smoke, and veritable walking skeletons. It can be but faintly imagined with what intense emotions the rescuers grasped the hands of these poor fellows.

To each of them was given a small piece of bread, which was the first they had tasted in six weeks. Tupper, who had spent his time hunting and caring for Rowley, occasionally killed a duck, and was fortunate enough to kill one wild goose. They had been reduced to such straits that for nearly three weeks they subsisted on the carcass and skin of a ground hog. Feasting like this brought Tupper to a sick bed, and for a week he was unable to get up.

Together they went to where the rescuers had spent the previous night. They made a fire and prepared supper. To each of the poor, starving men was given tea, a piece of bread and a small piece of fried bacon. In their emaciated condition, had they been allowed to eat what they desired it might have proved fatal.

Around the camp fire the four men sat and talked. Tupper and Rowley asked what had brought two strangers on this fearful trip seeking for them. When the cause of the long delay was explained, the poor fellows broke down and cried like children, pledging, between sobs, everlasting friendship for Crippen and Irion.

After a rest of several hours they took up the march for Gregory Diggings. The unwritten law was obeyed, and when the boys were turned over to their friends, Crippen and Irion were given a real pioneer reception.

CHAPTER VIII

CLOSE OF PROVISIONAL GOVERNMENT

Permanent Population in 1860

When the grandeur of the scenery, the charm of the climate, and the resources of the country became fixed in the minds and hearts of the pioneers, they claimed this as their own land, and, in 1860, the permanent population of Denver rapidly increased.

The country was literally swarming with people; they crawled over the mountains, through the canyons and up the gulches, searching for gold. The yieldings of Gilpin, Boulder; the diggings in the South Park, on the Blue and the Arkansas, were immense. Fortunes were dug out in a day. California Gulch, the present site of Leadville, was producing astonishing wealth. Denver was the busy, surging headquarters for all the activity of the Pike's Peak region.

Real estate advanced; there were many new and important enterprises; a building boom was on—the sawmills could not meet the demand and carpenters commanded fabulous prices. Log cabins were pulled away to make room for frame buildings, and Denver commenced to assume city airs.

The fertility of the soil when properly irrigated had been demonstrated, and men turned their attention to agriculture. The grocery stores were supplied with home-grown vegetables. It was not unusual to see cabbages weighing twenty-eight pounds, beets thirteen pounds, and turnips fourteen pounds.

Women and children arrived in considerable numbers, and their presence meant the forming of homes and better social conditions.

First Philanthropic Society

In January of 1860, Mrs. William N. Byers organized a Ladies' Union Aid Society, which had for its purpose the aiding and assisting of the sick and unfortunate. The society held its meetings semi-monthly, and each person in attendance paid a mite of ten cents. This was the beginning of Mrs. Byers' charity, which has wound like a thread of gold through the development of Denver, until it culminated in the E. M. Byers Home for Boys.

To this institution she gave the land and the building, and today contributes largely to its support. The cause is a worthy one and places Mrs. Byers among the noted philanthropists of Denver. She came here in 1859, when there was scarcely half a dozen white women in the Rocky Mountain region—before Colorado was on the map.

"Someone always has to start things," she said, "and I am proud of being a pioneer; inexpressably proud of the city that the pioneers founded.

"Yet, being one of the first to enter a new country to

stay is an experience which I certainly would not care to undergo again. No one, without going through it, can understand the feeling of having to go without things, of knowing that even the necessities of life must be brought by wagon across the Great American Desert. During the years of the Indian uprisings, from 1864 to 1870, we were often not sure that our supplies would reach us, and many times I have seen flour sell for a dollar a pound. It was the constant anxiety of not knowing what would happen next, rather than any terrible things that actually did happen, that made life on the frontier so hard.

"We had many pleasures, too. My husband had a way of bringing people home to dinner unexpectedly. One day he came in with Judson Dudley, Dick Whitsitt and Lewis Tappan. I immediately set them to work— one ground the coffee, one went to the spring for a bucket of water, and one set the table. They enjoyed that meal, and so did I.

"Entertainments of various kinds were given," Mrs. Byers went on, "and, though in primitive style, were thoroughly enjoyed. Mr. Fred Salomon's dinners 'took the shine off of everything.' He was considered the most punctiliously polite man in the settlement, a reputation fairly won and well preserved, as the following story will attest:

"His was a bachelor's home, with a bona fide ground floor, and furnished with pine table and three-legged stools. On one occasion he gave a dinner to his lady friends, and it was a meal that would have delighted the most fastidious epicure.

"After the repast, the ladies, thinking it time to take their leave, requested Mr. Salomon to bring their wraps. Instead of protesting against the brevity of their stay, he instantly complied with their request, saying, 'Certainly, ladies, certainly I will, with the greatest of pleasure.' When the force of his speech dawned upon him, he hastened to apologize, at the same time nervously searching for his handkerchief to mop his perspiring brow. It was long before he heard the last of his after-dinner politeness."

Mrs. Byers does not show the signs of a life of struggle; she says she will never allow herself to be put on the shelf. She lives in her elegant home in South Denver, and is, at eighty, as interested in the problems of the day as she was in the early years of Denver's history.

One of her most treasured possessions is a framed copy of "The Rocky Mountain News." It is the first copy of the first paper issued in the Rocky Mountain region, and was taken from the press at ten o'clock on the night of April 22, 1859, forming part of the morning edition of April 23.

AURARIA AND DENVER UNITED

While the rival towns had been united by an act of the Legislature, there still existed a strong unpleasant feeling. During the last week in March, 1860, a mass meeting was held to decide the question. After considerable discussion, the following was submitted by Andrew Sagendorf:

> "Whereas, the towns at and near the mouth of Cherry creek are and ought to be one; therefore, be it Resolved, that from this time Auraria proper shall be known as Denver City, west division, and we hereby authorize the board of directors to change the name on the plat accordingly."

A short time before this, the first bridge across Cherry creek had been completed at Larimer street, which united the towns, and was then an important convenience. April 6th a public meeting of the citizens of both towns was held by moonlight on this bridge to rejoice over the

The Provisional Government

union of the cities and listen to speeches which are considered highly essential to the proper consummation of any event of a public character in this broad land of ours. Three big cheers for Denver City were given, and, while the pretty name of Auraria does not appear on the maps of today, its picturesque career of eighteen months makes an interesting chapter in Colorado's history. The inhab-

AURARIA 1860 NEAR MOUTH OF CHERRY CREEK

BLAKE BETWEEN 15TH AND 16TH 1860

G. W. CLAYTON

itants grew to be on such friendly terms that they constructed their dwellings in the creek's bed and the stream almost ceased to be a dividing line.

G. W. Clayton kept, at this time, a general supply store at the corner of Fifteenth and Larimer. He continually lamented the number of lots he had been compelled to take in settlement of accounts run by customers he trusted for goods. They had no money, but they had lots, and, in course of time, Clayton was loaded up with them. Many of these holdings he kept to the close of his life and they formed part of the basis of the large fortune which has been devoted to building and maintaining the George W. Clayton College—an institution for the care and education of white orphan boys born in Colorado. The purpose of the founder with reference to the training to be given to pupils of this institution is expressed in these words: "They shall be instructed in such various branches of sound education as will tend to make them useful citizens and honorable members of society." The college is located in the northeastern part of the city upon a tract of some three hundred acres of land. The college buildings—more than a dozen in number—are of permanent and substantial construction, the architecture being characterized by dignity and beauty. The chief buildings are constructed of stone and are roofed with red tiles.

Boys received into the college become its legal wards, and they are maintained there without charge or cost to their mothers or guardians until discharged by the board of trustees, at between fourteen and eighteen years of age. The boys are housed in dormitories, each dormitory having in charge a house master and a matron. The atmosphere of these dormitories is most pleasant and homelike.

The institution maintains its own school staff of teachers. As the boys grow older they are given vocational instruction. In this connection, the splendidly equipped farm is of the greatest importance in the teaching of agriculture, horticulture, dairying and poultry raising. It is the aim of the institution to turn out every boy so trained that he can support himself.

How Colorado Territory Was Created

The "Provisional" government was organized to provide laws for "Jefferson Territory" until a State or Territory could be legally established. When the thirty-sixth Congress met for its short and last session, December, 1860, Beverly D. Williams was still at Washington in the capacity of delegate from Jefferson. He labored under many difficulties—he was given no seat on the floor of the House, could not be heard there, and was only recognized as agent of the people in the Pike's Peak country. He was advised by the people of Jefferson to cease striving for statehood, and to concentrate his efforts to secure the passage of one of the two territorial bills that had been introduced in Congress.

The name for the new Territory caused much discussion in Congress. Jefferson was objected to, because of a decision not to name territories after presidents. Numerous names were presented and Idaho was accepted.

February 2, 1861, the Senate bill to organize the Territory under the name of Idaho was called from the table. Delegate B. D. Williams, at the suggestion of William Gilpin, moved to strike out the word Idaho and insert Colorado. This was agreed to, and the bill then passed the Senate. On February 28, 1861, President Buchanan signed the bill, and the organic act creating Colorado a Territory became a law. Beverly D. Williams proved, by the passing of this bill, that the pioneers had sent an able representative to Congress.

Beverly D. Williams

Receiving the New Governor

In 1844, William Gilpin, by special arrangements, made a report of his explorations. This report was read in the United States Senate and Gilpin was given the privilege of the floor, but his statements were received with almost unanimous incredulity, and his ideas concerning the settlement and agricultural development of the Great American Desert were scouted and denounced in the most vigorous and eloquent speeches, led by Daniel Webster, John C. Calhoun and other men of eminent ability. Gilpin, at that time, was a friend and favorite of President Polk, and the president was about the only important personage who paid any attention to his representation. Nearly a score of years later, February 26, 1861, the Territory of Colorado was organized. President Lincoln immediately appointed William Gilpin its first governor, in recognition of his services as an explorer of the great West.

The people of Denver set about to receive their distinguished executive with every manifestation of pleasure and respect in their power.

To Judge H. P. Bennet was assigned the honor of making the reception speech. In order to give greater tone to the affair, a platform was erected in front of the Tremont House, West Denver, where the reception was to be held, and a large anvil, in lieu of a cannon, was loaded for a welcome salute.

In due time, the governor and his escort, in a spring wagon, which was newly painted and decorated for the occasion, drew up in front of the orator. The governor thrust his hand in the breast of his closely buttoned coat and assumed, from force of habit, a dignified and striking attitude.

Bennet had prepared a real old-fashioned spread-eagle speech, full of solid rhapsodies on our Italian climate and exhilarating atmosphere. But, just as he had launched out with "Fellow Citizens," the cannon went off; whether by accident or in a spirit of mischief was never known, but it certainly did "spread itself" in the effort to make its presence known, and gave the speaker a mightier "send-off" than was expected or desired. The enthusiastic crowd scattered in every direction, and the orator was so stunned that he forgot what came next, or why he was there.

In June, 1861, R. W. Steele, in turning the governorship of the Territory over to Mr. Gilpin, issued the following:

Proclamation

By virtue of the authority in me vested, I, R. W. Steele, Governor of the Territory of Jefferson, under the provisional government, and in and by virtue of my election by the majority of the people of the then-called government of the people of the mining region, unrecognized by the general government, at the base of the Rocky Mountains on the east and at the center thereof, and placing our confidence in that Overruling Providence that has for so long a period of time steadied us as an American people through so many difficulties by foes, seen and unseen, I therefore issue this, my proclamation, in view of the arrival of Governor William Gilpin and other officers of the United States, whom I recognize as being duly in authority. I deem it but obligatory upon me, by virtue of my office, to "Yield unto Cæsar the things that are Cæsar's," and I hereby command and direct that all officers holding commissions under me, especially all judges, justices of the peace, etc., shall surrender the same, and from this date shall abstain from exercising the duties of all offices they may have held under me by virtue of said commission, and further, I advise and recommend to all law and order loving citizens to submit to the laws of the United States and restrain themselves from deeds of violence which so long have made our peculiar position almost a by-word in the eyes of the civilized world. Again I advise my fellow citizens who have known me "so long and so well" to yield obedience to the laws of the United States and do it by attending to your proper and legitimate avocations, whether agricultural or mining.

By the Governor.

R. W. STEELE,
Governor.

L. L. BOWEN,
Acting Secretary of the Territory of Jefferson.

Done at Denver this 6th day of June, A. D. 1861.

The Territory of Jefferson is a unique and picturesque effort that an isolated community made to establish a government, and will always fill a conspicuous place in the history of the United States.

Governor Steele lived to a ripe old age and witnessed the full fruition of everything in which he was a leader and a prophet concerning the wonderful possibilities of the region. He died at Colorado Springs February 7, 1901.

CHAPTER IX

SOME PIONEERS OF THAT DAY

HENRY M. PORTER

There are men here today who were here in the Denver of that day; men who saw a new page in history turned and Colorado written upon it. Their experiences are such as fall to the lot of few in the brief space set apart as man's lifetime.

It has been an age of progress, of advancement in every line of human endeavor. They have seen Denver grow from a little village of tents and log cabins to be the jeweled clasp in the girdle of the world's great achievements.

Henry M. Porter, in his quiet way, has been a vital factor in the upbuilding of the Denver of today. Upon his arrival in Denver he established the wholesale grocery house of Stebbins and Porter. He made money rapidly and became a rich man when there were few men of wealth in this part of the country. He did not lose his head, as many did, in the accumulation of wealth, but made wise investments, that grew and rewarded his good

H. M. Porter

judgment and industry. He became closely and actively identified with many public enterprises, including interests in the American Waterworks Company, Denver National Bank, Gas Company, The Denver Consolidated Electric Company, Colorado Fuel and Iron Company, Denver Stockyards Company, Denver Packing and Provision Company, and other local industries which place him in the forefront among the builders of the City and State. He married Miss Laura Smith, daughter of John W. Smith, a brave captain in Colorado's army of pioneers. Mr. Smith gave his children the advantages of education and travel. Mrs. Porter said: "My sisters and I went to Williamsport, Pennsylvania, to school, and when it became known that we were from the Rocky Mountain region we were looked at with great curiosity." Mrs. Porter is a cultured woman, and finds her chief pleasure in her home with her family. Mr. and Mrs. Porter have five children: Mrs. John Mason, Mrs. Harold Walker, Miss Ruth Porter, Mr. John Porter and Mr. W. E. Porter.

Mr. Porter is still a young man, and is a citizen much needed in present day enterprises. He looks with both a philosopher's and prophet's eye to legitimate investments, and is recognized as a clear-headed operator—not a speculator.

J. F. BROWN

J. F. Brown came to Denver in 1860, and, with his brother, J. S. Brown, established a wholesale grocery house. For fifty years it ranked among the firms transacting immense business.

The brothers gradually invested vast sums in their line, and, in the course of time, engaged in enterprises incident to the development of a new commonwealth, which will make them live in the history of the State.

They passed through some trying periods in the

growth of Denver; saw the town depleted in population; saw men become discouraged and leave to seek other locations, but they possessed determination and energy of purpose to a great degree; so they worked and waited till the clouds passed by.

J. F. Brown and Grand-children

MRS. BROWN

They accumulated an immense fortune, and Mr. Junius F. Brown retired from active business at the age of seventy, but not like the average American who retires from business—to die from lack of interest in living. Mr. Brown found an outlet for his energy in the study of art. He turned his quick intelligence which had been employed in the accumulation of wealth to the task of finding pleasure in the fortune which he had amassed. The strain of commerce was thrown off in time to cultivate the aesthetic side of his nature, and he became a fine judge of art.

He was never happier than when showing his pictures and talking about them.

One day I visited him in his art gallery, and he said frankly: "I bought pictures at first because they had bright bits of color in them, and, after studying them for a while, I outgrew them, so I exchanged them for others which I liked better. Continuing this study I found myself growing in taste, judgment and understanding.

"I became the despair of picture vendors," he laughed, and went on. "I knew what was good, and I insisted upon getting it. I persevered in this way until I have one of the best small collections of pictures in this country."

He said this without any feeling of pride, but with an expression of solid enjoyment in indulging his love for the beautiful.

"I have placed the work of young American artists beside the Barbizon masters, as you notice, and one does not detract from the other, which shows clearly that American art lacks nothing but recognition."

Measured by years, Mr. Brown might have been regarded as growing old, but the warmth of his greeting, his fondness for social life, his sympathy with humanity, all tended to keep his heart young.

He found his wife a great help in his study of art, and never bought a picture without her judgment upon it.

Mrs. Brown is refined and gracious, devoted to her family and her friends, deeply philanthropic, and finds her chief pleasure in helping others to carry out their ambitions. This beautiful characteristic of hers is fully evinced by the assistance she gave her husband in collecting pictures. Mrs. Brown is always busy with acts of practical charity. Her benevolence is the outcome of a sympathetic and generous heart, which considers the personal need of the individual.

Mr. Brown had a keen sense of humor and told me many amusing stories of picture dealers. I shall ever remember my pleasant visit with this interesting man, who spent the evening of life in such a beautiful way. Mr. Brown died in 1912.

Mr. Brown's daughters, Mrs. J. W. Douglas, Mrs. F. S. Titsworth and Mrs. J. J. B. Benedict, are prominent in the social life of Denver. His only son, Harry K. Brown, is occupied with affairs of importance. As a citizen he is generous, patriotic and progressive. In carrying forward his business activities he manifests the indomitable will and energy which was characteristic of his father, and which brought him success and fortune.

RODNEY CURTIS

Among the men who witnessed the majestic panorama of civilization unroll over the mountains from the Missouri to the Pacific was Mr. Rodney Curtis, and no one has more conspicuously participated in the development of Denver.

In 1860, he took up land near Denver and farmed to 1864. At that time he was appointed pay clerk in the United States mint; he was afterwards made chief clerk,

Rodney Curtis

and, in 1876, was appointed, by President Grant, melter and refiner. With Clarence J. Clarke, he platted Curtis and Clarke's addition to Denver.

He built many business blocks on Curtis, Larimer and other downtown streets.

FIRST STREET CAR BARN

S. H. FISHER

CAPT. L. C. ELLSWORTH

The first corporation to secure a street railway franchise in Colorado was the Denver Horse Railway Company. It was incorporated in 1867. Those interested in the franchise were Judge Moses Hallett, Judge Amos Steck, Freeman B. Crocker, Luther Kountze and Lewis N. Tappan. The charter was granted for a period of thirty-five years. In 1871 the franchise was sold to Colonel L. C. Ellsworth, who represented

Chicago capitalists. He immediately began the costruction of the pioneer street car line. The stables surrounded, in the shape of an L, what is now Scholtz's drug store. The entrances were on Sixteenth and on Curtis.

Mr. Ellsworth was the president and W. D. Todd was secretary. About 1881, the grasshoppers, for a period of four years, ate up every green thing in the western country, and Colorado suffered to such an extent that if people didn't actually pawn their clothing to buy food they had a hard time getting food for horses and cattle. Mr. Samuel H. Fisher was, at that time, financially interested in this first street car company in Denver, and during the grasshopper period, as it was called, he actually sold four lots which he owned at the corner of Tremont and Seventeenth streets for hay and grain to feed the horses that pulled the cars up and down the streets. The rattling old horse car was a potent factor in the prosperity of Denver.

Mr. Curtis was quick to see the possibilities for the street railway and promptly organized the Denver Tramway Company, then a cable line. Later, assisted by some of the most enterprising pioneers in the city, the system was made electric. The men who worked side by side with Mr. Curtis in this great enterprise were Governor Evans, David Moffat, F. A. Keener, William G. Evans, J. F. Brown, J. S. Brown, J. J. Riethman, Dr. McClellan and H. C. Brown.

Under the able management of these men the electric system was carried from its modest inception through the various changes and expansions to be a street railway system unsurpassed in its relative extent by that of any city in the world.

Mr. Curtis gave to the enterprise his untiring energy and far-sighted executive ability for seventeen years. After retiring from active business he gave time to travel and books. His library, well chosen, comprises many fine editions, and the magazines on his table showed that he kept in touch with the current thought of the day. He was liberal in his donations to charitable organizations. His wife and his daughters—Mrs. Charles Whitehead, Mrs. McDearmon and Mrs. Will Porter—are identified with many philanthropic movements of the city. Mrs. Curtis is a woman of fine character, energy and executive ability.

Mrs. Chas. Whitehead

In the death of Mr. Rodney Curtis, Denver lost an ideal man and a great citizen. He passed away April 26, 1915, in San Diego. Few lives have been so rich in acts of kindness as the life of Rodney Curtis.

Dennis Sheedy

Mr. Dennis Sheedy, who wields a power in finance today, is another high type of a self-made man.

He was born in Ireland, came to America as a boy, lived in New England until he was twelve years old, and, after his father's death, started out to make his way alone.

At the age of sixteen he crossed the plains to Denver and found employment in one of the general merchandise stores. He remained here a year and went to Montana, where he engaged in placer mining, and, after accumulating some money, he entered the mercantile business in Montana.

He afterward ran a store in Utah and one in Salmon City, Idaho. Later, at Helena, Montana, he opened a wholesale grocery store. From Utah he went to Nevada with a trainload of merchandise and a herd of beef cattle, which he drove across the desert and sold in the town of Hamilton, White Pine County, Nevada; then he went to California, and, afterward, to Old Mexico, with a view of living there, but after seeing the people and their social and political condition he left that country and went to Arizona, where he bought and sold droves of Texas cattle. Mr. Sheedy left Arizona and went to Texas, where he engaged extensively in the cattle business, traveling over six hundred miles on horseback on one occasion.

Dennis Sheedy

By 1883, Mr. Sheedy had accumulated several large herds of cattle, amounting, in the aggregate, to over thirty-two thousand head, and established ranches in the Indian Territory and Southern Kansas; then at the head of the Humboldt river in Nevada, and later in Western Nebraska and Eastern Wyoming on the North Platte river. In overlooking this large herd of cattle he braved the storms and blizzards of winter and the burning heat of summer. Many times he had narrow escapes from the Indians. On one occasion the Indians stampeded his cattle, and, as he was rounding them up, he was surrounded by a band of the redskins, who threatened to take him prisoner. Mr. Sheedy made his escape from them, and, after getting his twenty-six men together, remained in the neighborhood sufficiently long to gather up all the cattle and drive them through to the northern markets.

The death of his friend, A. B. Daniels, called him to Denver. In the management of the Daniels estate Mr. Sheedy proved himself a man of rare executive ability, for he doubled the value of the estate before handing it over to his ward, Mr. Daniels' son.

From the day of his arrival in Denver to the present time his genius has been visible in the forward movement of the city. He has been president of the Denver Dry Goods Company for twenty years, vice-president of the Colorado National Bank for thirty years, president and general manager of the Globe Smelting and Refining Company for fifteen years, and vice-president of the International Smelting Company of New York for the last ten years.

Mr. Sheedy remodeled and practically rebuilt the Globe smelter four times, adding a refining plant for refining gold, silver, copper and lead; an electrolytic plant for separating gold and silver; a filtering plant for filtering metallic fumes from the shaft furnaces, for which he used textile fabric bags. He also added a large furnace for gathering additional values by the precipitating process. In carrying forward this work Mr. Sheedy spent days and nights in ceaseless study of methods of handling the business, and made numerous inventions, for which he obtained United States patents.

His extensive investments have contributed largely to the industrial development and prosperity of the State. He is a man with a vision of the future and readjusts his business to meet the changing conditions. His success in the world of finance has not blunted his sensibili-

The Provisional Government

ties to the condition of the less fortunate. To many a friend he has rendered timely aid, and he has relieved suffering in numerous instances.

He has never cared for politics or publicity in any way. Through patient and persistent industry he has acquired wealth, and in the annals of his time has earned the name of empire builder.

Mr. Sheedy is a tall, dignified man, with broad shoulders, and blue eyes that flash with intelligence. He lives without pomp or worldly display. His wife is a beautiful woman, with a charm of manner that has drawn around her a large circle of friends.

Mr. Sheedy is a member of the Denver Club, the Denver Country Club, and the Denver Athletic Club.

John Good

John Good's life has been closely interwoven with the history of Denver from pioneer days to the present time. He came from Alsace to Colorado when a mere

MR. AND MRS. GOOD

boy, without money and without friends, but he had in his character all the qualities necessary for success and would have reached the top no matter to what line of endeavor he might have directed his energy. From the first he had a way of attending strictly to his own business; the comments and criticism of others made no impression upon him. He is honest and just in business and has acquired great wealth through no freak of fortune, but through his own steady, intelligent and persistent effort.

In the midst of luxury he has never become self-important, but has always a smile and cordial handclasp for old-time friends. His immense business demands much of his attention; he is fond of books and gives most of his leisure time to reading. His palatial residence, presided over by his wife and daughter, Mrs. J. E. Hasler, is often thrown open to friends, and every entertainment is marked by elegance and refined taste.

Mrs. J. E. Hasler

Mr. Good does not bestow large sums of money in public munificence to have his name blazoned abroad, but the needs of the poor or sick, or those in any kind of trouble, appeal to him, and, in his own way, he gives large sums of money.

Mr. Good is today a well-preserved, handsome man of seventy-five, commanding the respect and admiration of his friends and the devoted love of his family. His son, John E.

Good, a college man of fine characteristics, is associated with him in business. His grandson, John Hasler Good, is a student in Germany and is acquiring fame in the musical world.

WILBUR F. STONE

In the fall of 1859, Wilbur F. Stone, then twenty-six years old and finely educated, went to Omaha on legal business. He spent the winter there and was appointed assistant postmaster and incidentally edited the Omaha "Nebraskan" newspaper. During that winter he became acquainted with Robert W. Steele, governor of Jefferson Territory; William N. Byers, and other noted Pike's Peak fifty-niners, and was induced to join the rush to the new "gold diggin's," and, in the spring of 1860, Stone outfitted with a party of ox teamers and crossed the plains to Auraria and Denver, "at the mouth of Cherry creek," whence he went up into the gulch mines of Tarryall, in the South Park. In 1861, after the organization by Congress of Colorado Territory, Stone was elected a member of the Territorial Legislature from Park County, and afterwards served in the legislative session of 1864.

Wilbur F. Stone

In 1862 he was appointed assistant United States

attorney for Colorado and served until 1866, during the Civil war.

He was married in 1866 to Miss Sarah Sadler of Bloomington, Indiana, and settled at Pueblo, where he was president of the first town board and president of the school board, and editor of the Pueblo "Chieftain," Pueblo's first newspaper. He was the first general attorney of the Denver and Rio Grande Railroad Company, was one of the organizers and a director of the railway branch of the Kansas and Pacific.

In 1875-76 he was a member of the convention which framed the constitution under which Colorado was admitted as a State, and was chairman of the judiciary committee of that body.

Upon the admission of the State he was elected one of the judges of the first Supreme Court for the nine-year term, and in 1886 was appointed, by the governor, judge of the district criminal court of Denver and the then county of Arapahoe. In 1891 Judge Stone was appointed, by President Harrison, one of the five judges of the United States court of Spanish and Mexican land grant claims, and was reappointed by Presidents Cleveland, McKinley and Roosevelt, which court had jurisdiction in six States and Territories, and a term of service of nearly fourteen years.

Judge Stone has written much of the pioneer history of Colorado, especially its judicial history, and is now the oldest living member of the bar in length of service; has been president of the State Bar Association and is an honorary life member of the Denver Bar Association. He has traveled much abroad, and possesses a knowledge of the French, German, Spanish and Italian languages, and is an ardent student of literature and science.

Judge Stone now holds the office of United States commissioner of the federal district court of Colorado. His fund of humor keeps him young in spirit. He is one of the best preserved—mentally and physically—of the Colorado pioneers, and within the framework of this outline sketch he has had an eventful life since boyhood.

JAMES M. WILSON

Mr. James M. Wilson, a man by nature modest and retiring, came to Denver in 1860, a young country boy, with no stock in trade except his hands, good sense, and a strong determination to work out his own way.

Few figures in the history of this western State stand out with more distinctness than this man, who, from the first, has stood for high ideals in the world of finance, culture and humanity. In business, he demands all that is due him, but never reaches out for more than is justly his own. He is a friend to be relied upon, through prosperity or adversity, and, when once his word is given, he is sure to keep it.

James M. Wilson

He was active in every phase of Colorado's pioneer life, a freighter, a farmer, a cowboy, and, after years of hardships on the plains, developed into a "cattle king." Many positions of public trust have been filled by him, but he has always avoided the limelight.

In 1866, Mr. Wilson was elected county commissioner of Arapahoe County. In 1868, he went into the cattle business and was elected president of the Colorado Cattle Growers Association for three terms. With the late George Tritch and others, he organized the German National Bank, of which he was elected vice-president.

As a member of a committee named by the governor of the State, he selected the sites for the penitentiary at Canon City and the State reformatory at Buena Vista. As a member of the Denver Club, Mr. Wilson is known as a faithful friend and genial companion.

He has never gone into any wild speculations or schemes, but has acquired wealth along legitimate financial lines, and lives a quiet, unostentatious life. Still, back of this unassuming man there crowds a wealth of historical human incidents that are intimately woven with the development of Colorado.

"You have worked your own way to success," I said, when talking with him. "Can't you give a word of advice to young men who are starting in business?"

"No," he quickly replied. "What would be the use of it? The people of today are living under different conditions, and the young don't care to be bothered with advice."

"Then tell me a pioneer story," I said, knowing that he is an inimitable story-teller.

"Yes, I can do that. In 1860, I took up one hundred and sixty acres of land down on the Platte, and I put in the time that winter chopping and hauling wood to Denver. I was not living luxuriously and faring sumptuously at that time. One day I had sold my wood, and, with the money in my pocket, I felt rather opulent, so I decided to go to Riethman's bakery and get a dried apple pie (they were luxuries at that time)," he threw in parenthetically. "I seated myself at a table and cut my pie in four pieces. Just as I was about to help myself, a man rushed toward me, with a fine glow of happiness on his face.

"'Why, Bob!' he exclaimed. 'I am so glad to see you.' With this he drew his chair to the table and helped himself to a piece of pie. 'The last time I saw you,' the fellow continued, 'was over in camp Well. We had a high old time; I shall never forget it if I live to be a hundred. We were on the hunt for cattle, and at night we rolled ourselves up in our buffalo robes and slept, regardless of expense—no rent raised on us.' He laughed at his own humor, and helped himself to another piece of pie. 'Apples are fine fruit; Eve ate the first one, didn't she? But that is a theory in theology.'

"He ate pie and flitted from one subject to another, like a patent office report.

"I sat and looked on as dumb as a mummy in a pyramid. 'This is good pie, Bob.'

" 'My name is not Bob,' I remarked.

" 'What? Not Bob? I made sure you were my old friend Bob.'

" 'No, I am not.'

" 'I thank you for your hospitality,' he said, as he moved away, leaving me alone with my empty pie pan.

"The hungry fellow was out foraging," commented Mr. Wilson, in a humorous way, "and it was so neatly done that it aroused my admiration."

Daniel Witter

No pioneer of Colorado was more active in the enterprises of the formative days of the city and state than Daniel Witter. He established the first abstract of title office in Denver in the early '60's, which is still in existence. He was one of the incorporators and an officer of the Denver Safe Deposit and Savings Bank, established in 1874, which had connected with it the first safety deposit vaults between the Missouri river and the Pacific.

He was one of the organizers of the Platte Water Company. Its ditch, now known as the City ditch, supplies the lake at the City Park, and waters the farms between Denver and Littleton.

He was the leading land office attorney of the State

from the early '60's until his death. The business he established is still continued by his daughter, Miss Ellen C. Witter.

He was one of the resolute men in taking up the work of building the city and state, and he never faltered in it, even when prospects were most discouraging.

George Tritch

Mr. George Tritch was a man of quick wit, deep thought, and marked business ability. A short time before his death he said:

"We came to Denver because the tide of immigration was this way; the people heard of the Pike's Peak country and fabulous stories of gold. When we started out we had no idea where we were going, but I thought that towns had to spring up, and possibly I could make a living for my family. There is only one reason why we stopped in Denver. There was nothing here that was promising, but when we got this far our money had run out, and knowing that we could go no farther we were content to remain."

George Tritch

Mr. Tritch brought with him his tools, a small stock of goods, and at once began business in a cabin on Blake street near Cherry creek.

This picture was taken from an old paper. His business soon outgrew its quarters, and he built a large store room on Fifteenth and Blake. In 1884 his business again outgrew its quarters and he built a large block on Arapa-

The Provisional Government

hoe street and Seventeenth, in which he placed the present George Tritch Hardware Company, which is one of Denver's great commercial establishments.

He amassed a fortune by persistent industry and good judgment. All his interests were centered in Denver, which proved his faith in the city. Mr. Tritch died at his home on Grant street in 1899. He left a widow and eight children.

George Tritch's First Hardware Store—1859

Wolfe Londoner

Wolfe Londoner enjoyed the reputation of being Colorado's practical joker.

"I came out from Atchison," said Mr. Londoner, "with freighters, in 1860. I walked most of the way and had a terrible experience with a pair of hob-nail boots—regular miner's brogans, with spikes sticking out in a formidable manner. The memory of it makes my feet ache; the nails tortured me so I walked barefoot one hundred miles. We met some Indians and I traded my shoes for several pairs of moccasins. Believe me, I was the happiest tenderfoot in existence.

Wolfe Londoner

"There were no flies here when I reached Denver— no, that is no joke; flies came with the increase in population. The pioneers did not have to worry about flies, and the only bathtubs were Cherry creek and the Platte river.

"I ran a store in California Gulch for awhile, and, in 1863, I opened a store in Denver, at Fifteenth and Blake I had a neighbor, Alvin McCune, who was a practical joker, and we used to go at each other hot and heavy. I once had him paint a lot of wagons for me. The town began to grow, and, instead of carrying home their own goods, customers insisted upon having them delivered, so I had to get some wagons. There was one wagon that did not need repainting. It had on the back the words, 'Come and See Us.'

"One day Alvin saw it standing in front of the store; he ran it into his store and changed the words to 'Come to Jesus,' and put it back without my knowing it. That wagon was driven all over town before I found it out, and then I had a hard time to pacify the people, who thought I did it purposely. I tried to talk to McCune about it, and I really was angry, but the angrier I got the more he laughed.

"I am one of the few men who ever got even with Gene Field. It was near an election, and I had taken quite a prominent part in politics, in one instance, trying to influence the colored vote.

"Gene Field wrote an article, saying that I would present every colored voter who called at my store with a watermelon. They came in droves, all clamoring for melons. Fortunately, I found a wagon of Georgia melons on Market street and I passed them out.

"The next day I put an 'ad' in the News that Gene Field wanted a watchdog, and set a time for owners to bring dogs to his office. At the appointed time there was yelping and fighting and scrambling of dogs in Gene's office. He climbed on the table and screamed for help, while the owners of the dogs fought lustily with each other.

The Provisional Government

"To return to that watermelon incident"—the memory of it caused Mr. Londoner to smile. "It placed me in high esteem with the colored people. At a big colored meeting, at which prominent Denverites spoke, I was introduced by the negro chairman in this way: 'We now come to a man who is the friend of colored people—speaks to us on the street, treats us to watermelons. Though he has a white face, he has a heart as black as any of us.'"

The first Press Club in Denver was started over Mr. Londoner's store on Blake street, and he prizes among his possessions a cup which was presented to him by the Press Club.

His famous "cyclone cellar" was known to every newspaper man and every good fellow who visited this town. "It was no misnomer," said Mr. Londoner. Many met with a cyclone at home because of a visit to that cellar.

Mr. Londoner was widely known and counted his friends by the hundreds. He was interested in everything that made for the upbuilding of Denver. He was elected county commissioner; made chairman of the building committee for the erection of the court house, and gave up his business to do faithful and conscientious work in this building committee. He was proud of the fact that not a penny's worth of graft occurred in the construction of the court house. He was elected mayor of Denver, was a Shriner, and active in Masonic circles; a member of the National Editorial Association, and, in every way, a good citizen.*

Joseph B. Donavan

Joseph B. Donavan had a high standing with the Indians because he always gave them a square deal.

---
*Since this writing Mr. Londoner has passed away.

Among his frontier relics is a necklace of beads and claws, and it tells a history. With the settlement of the prairies the Indians found horse and cattle-stealing profitable. They were shrewd enough to shield their wrongdoers, and their attacks upon the quiet herds without any redress fired the blood of the white settlers. One day they seized the chief of a Cheyenne tribe and put him through the rigors of a frontier third degree, but he failed to disgorge. The white council deliberated, and resolved to give the chief the benefit of an Indian execution as practiced upon themselves by the savages.

Slo-a-necka was the chief's name, and slow strangulation was the method resolved upon. The execution was set for sunrise the following morning. The chief was roped to a wagon for the night.

Joe Donavan was a member of the white council and he strongly urged the chief's innocence. Towards midnight, Donavan stepped from his blankets, cut the thongs, and ordered Slo-a-necka to mount his horse and ride away. The next morning, Donavan was threatened with the chief's punishment. He told them that he knew the chief was innocent and felt sure that he would bring the real offenders to justice within forty-eight hours.

A day or two after, Slo-a-necka, with a squad of his braves surrounding five Indians bound to their ponies, rode into camp and delivered the prisoners to Donavan. They were of another tribe—Arapahoes, and had full justice meted out to them.

Donavan later negotiated a treaty with Slo-a-necka, who became the deadly foe of cattle and horse thieves on the frontier.

Three years later, Joe Donavan lost his way in the mountains and entered an Indian camp by chance. A squaw, the daughter of Slo-a-necka, came forward to greet him. She knew Donavan from her father's description of him, and, removing the necklace of beads and claws from her own neck, she tied them around Donavan's with great ceremony.

Mr. Donavan had many close calls in his perilous career as scout, and he was loved, as well as feared, by the Indians.

Dr. O. D. Cass

Dr. O. D. Cass came to Denver in 1860. He practiced medicine for seven months. The following story will show that the early day life of physicians was not enviable. He said:

"One evening in 1860, while sitting in my office, the door opened and in stalked a man about five feet nine inches in height, bearded like a pard, trousers in bootlegs, his dark hair covered by a black slouch hat, beneath which I saw a pair of glittering black eyes.

" 'Are you the doctor?'

" 'Yes, sir.'

" 'Well, I want you to go and attend my woman, who's sick.'

" 'What's the matter with her?'

" 'I don't know, but I want you to go and see her.'

" 'Well, my fee is $25, which must be paid before I go.'

"The words had scarcely passed my lips before the stranger whipped out an ugly looking six-shooter, and, thrusting it in my face, said: 'Damn your fee; follow me, sir, and be quick about it.'

"Thus positively adjured, I stood not upon the order of my going, but went at once. He led me to the door of his cabin, opened it, pointed to the patient, and immediately disappeared in the darkness. I attended her for a week and cured her. I did not in the meantime see or hear of my conductor. The woman having recovered, he came again. Striding up to my desk with the air of a cavalry brigadier, he said:

"'You cured her, did you?'

"'Yes, I think she's all right now.'

"Laying five twenty-dollar gold pieces of Clark and Gruber's mintage on the desk, he added in a milder tone:

"'Will that pay you for your services?'

"'Yes, sir, abundantly, and I'm very much obliged.'

O. D. Cass

"'See here, doctor, I've taken a notion to you. There's a good many rough fellows about town, who drink and fight and make trouble for honest people. If any of 'em ever interfere with you, you send for me. My name's Charlie Harrison.'"

Harrison was the chief of desperadoes, who shot at a word, and who had killed nearly a score of men.

Dr. Cass had been in California in the golden era in that State, and his experience there taught him that handling Rocky Mountain gold dust would be more profitable than practicing medicine, so he decided to engage in banking and gold brokerage. In the spring of 1861 he was joined by G. W. Wilcox and Joseph B. Cass, his brother. Together they established the Exchange Bank. It did a large and profitable business, which soon included deposits, loans and discounts.

During the Civil war, gold went to higher and higher premiums, and their profits on gold purchases added to those derived from interest rates of twenty per cent a month became very great, running as high, at times, as a thousand dollars a day.

The firm opened a branch office in Central and became the agents there for Holladay's Overland Mail

Stage Company. In 1865 the business was sold to Holladay. Dr. Cass remained a prominent citizen of Denver until his death in 1894.

His son, O. D. Cass, is prominently identified with many enterprises that are strong factors in the development of Colorado today. He is always ready and willing to contribute to religious and philanthropic movements, and possesses the esteem and respect of all who know him.

CYRUS H. McLAUGHLIN

No Colorado pioneer is more widely known than Cyrus H. McLaughlin, whose name is now enrolled upon the list of the dead. In 1859, while at Leavenworth, the Colorado gold excitement broke out, and Jones and Cartright of that town, who were doing an express business, believed that the gold that had been sent out had really come from California. McLaughlin was sent to investigate. He reached Golden without difficulty and then climbed over the mountains to Gregory diggings. When the miners learned that he represented an express company, he was loaded down with gold dust and he came back to Denver with thirty thousand dollars in dust in an old carpet sack. This he kept by him day and night, sometimes sleeping in the coach with it for a pillow,

Cyrus H. McLaughlin

and, on one occasion, drove the stage himself, with no passengers, for fifty miles. He arrived safely in Leavenworth, the bearer of the first trustworthy reports from the new camp.

In 1860, he came back to Auraria and started in as a compositor on the News, his occupation being that of a journeyman printer. In 1861 he took up some land on the Platte below Denver and opened a dairy and farm. The Indian scare in 1864 caused him to leave his farm and seek Denver for protection. He secured a position in the army department, which he held until 1866, when he again went back to his ranch. That same year he was elected a representative to the Territorial Legislature, and in 1867 he was re-elected and made speaker of the House.

Mrs. C. H. McLaughlin

His wife, a beautiful woman, with many fine traits of character, died recently.

O. P. BAUR

It may be of interest to the people of this day and age to know that the Baur confectionery store was founded in pioneer days.

Adolph Schinner owned a bakery and grocery store in the early times, and opened the first confectionery and ice cream house in Denver. O. P. Baur was one of his clerks. The latter bought out the business, established the Baur Confectionery Company, and, from that day to this, that company has catered for all the swell functions of the city, with unvarying excellence.

CAPTAIN RICHARD SOPRIS

Captain Richard Sopris was a pioneer of 1859, and in the fall of that year was elected to represent Arapahoe

County in the Kansas Legislature. In 1860 he headed a party of thirty or forty men, exploring the wilderness west of the snowy range, in a search for gold mines. The captain traveled on the back of a large mule, an animal which had a certain gait up hill and down hill. The "engineer" of the party, Charles P. Marion, who also acted as historian of the expedition, conceived the idea of measuring the distance the captain's mule could walk in a given time, and, by keeping a record of the number

SOPRIS GATEWAY, CITY PARK DENVER

of hours they traveled each day, he arrived at the number of miles covered by the party in the trip.

A rough sketch of the country passed over, distances between streams and mountain ranges, based on "mule measurement," was given to Governor Gilpin, who included it in his map of Colorado, and surveys of later years proved the figures given by Marion to be about right.

After serving a year or two in the Civil war as captain in the First Colorado Volunteers, he was elected sheriff of Arapahoe County. Later, he was made mayor of Denver and re-elected. He discovered Glenwood Springs, and Mt. Sopris was named for him.

Mr. Sopris was an active and useful citizen in Denver, and, in 1881, he was appointed park commissioner. He immediately began the difficult task of making a park out of the three hundred and twenty acres which the city had purchased from the State. He raised a fund of five hundred dollars from the owners of land in the vicinity and set out cottonwood trees, which formed the first shaded drives and walks in the City park.

He died at the age of eighty, and his son, S. T. Sopris, erected a four thousand dollar gate at the Seventeenth avenue entrance to the City park, which is a lasting testimonial to the public-spirited pioneer, Captain Richard Sopris.

Elizabeth Allen Sopris, his wife, was prominent in the work of establishing religious organizations in Denver. Her home was often the meeting place of pioneers interested in church and Sunday school work. She and her two daughters, Indiana and Irene, aided greatly in giving Denver its first Protestant churches. Mrs. Sopris was one of the founders of the First Congregational Church, and, until old age prevented, a constant attendant and an earnest worker in its upbuilding. She lived to see the "settlement at the mouth of Cherry creek" grow into a metropolitan city and its log cabin churches changed into the stately edifices of today. Her death occurred on December 18, 1911, at the age of ninety-seven.

PART IV
THE DEVELOPMENT OF PIONEER ENTERPRISES

CHAPTER X

ESTABLISHING FORCES OF CIVILIZATION

CHURCHES

In relating the stories of how the pioneers built the city and the state, it will be impossible to take in the long list of pioneers. Each one has left the impress of his individuality upon the land which he adopted as his home, and my effort is to show how the influences, created and set in motion by the early settlers, have been woven into the social, industrial and political fabric of our State.

The influence of the Christian religion was present in Denver from the beginning. In the fall of 1858, the Rev. G. W. Fisher preached in the open, under cottonwood trees, and in the homes of the pioneers.

The directors of the two town companies encouraged church building by donating lots. The Auraria Town Company, January 17, 1859, unanimously adopted the following resolution:

"Resolved, That there be and there is hereby donated to the first four religious societies that will build a church or house of worship in the city of Auraria, one lot to each, to be selected by anyone appointed by the societies for that purpose."

The Rev. Mr. Fisher preached faithfully to the isolated community during the winter of '58-'59, but there were no churches built.

Albert D. Richardson, in June, 1859, wrote: "When I asked a miner if there was any church, he replied, 'No, but we are going to build one before next Sunday.'" This clearly illustrates the pioneer spirit.

Richardson vividly describes a "Sunday morning."

"One Sunday morning, while walking through the diggings, revealed nearly all the miners disguised in clean clothing. Some were reading and writing, some ministering to the sick, and some enacting the part of every-man-his-own-washer-woman, rubbing valiantly away at the tub. Several hundred men in the open air were attending public religious worship, perhaps the first ever held in the Rocky Mountains. They were roughly clad, displaying weapons at their belts, and represented every section of the Union and almost every nation of the earth. They sat upon logs and stumps, a most attentive congregation, while the clergyman, upon a rude log platform, preached from the text: 'Behold, I bring you good tidings of great joy.' It was an impressive spectacle—that motley gathering of goldseekers among the mountains, a thousand miles from home and civilization, to hear the good tidings forever old and yet forever new."

When spring opened, the prospects were dismal; it was doubtful whether the infant city would live to see another winter. And, when the gold excitement broke out in May, there was no time for church building. However, the Rev. Mr. Fisher kept on talking of the "gold that was sure and pure."

Mr. Goode, a Methodist minister, organized the first church in Denver, August, 1859, with Jacob Adriance as secretary, which was the beginning of the Trinity Methodist Episcopal Church.

The first Methodist Episcopal Church Society was incorporated July 22, 1863. The Lawrence street church was the first building owned by the society.

On the first day of April, 1888, the first services were held in the basement of the present Trinity church, and $60,000 was raised in less than one hour towards the cost of completing the church building.

Mr. Peter Winne, who is a man of splendid character and sterling worth, has been a member of this church for fifty-two years. He was a potential factor in the building of the church, and, at the age of seventy-five years, he is still an active member.

From the choir in this church, Mrs. Wilberforce Whiteman has lifted her rich contralto voice in God's praise for nineteen years.

Rev. J. H. Kehler, an Episcopalian, who was familiarly called Father Kehler, came to Denver, January, 1860, with his four daughters. Immediately upon Mr. Kehler's arrival, he inaugurated regular services at Goldrick's school house. One stormy Sunday morning there were only two persons in the church, Mr. Amos Steck and Colonel J. H. Dudley. They thought, of course, they would be dismissed without a sermon, but Father Kehler, equal to the situation, selected the text: "Where two or three are gathered together in My name, there will I be, in the midst of them," and thereupon preached an excellent sermon.

John M. Chivington of the Methodist Episcopal church came in May, 1860. In that same year, W. M. Bradford of the Methodist Episcopal Church South put up the first building that was erected for church purposes in Denver, but the Civil war scattered many of the members, including Preacher Bradford, who hastened away to the South. The church was closed for awhile, and it was sold later to the Episcopalians, when it became St. John's Church in the Wilderness.

The Development of Pioneer Enterprises 135

Following Father Kehler came Rev. H. B. Hitchings, who preached six years and was succeeded by Rev. George

M. Randall, a learned, eloquent man, greatly beloved by his congregation. Later, he became bishop.

Rev. Walter Moore followed, and was in turn succeeded by E. V. Finch.

While on a trip around the world Rev. H. Martyn Hart of England stopped in Denver and preached a sermon in that little church, which was followed by a call to the parish. A man of honest purpose, untiring energy and unlimited faith is this dean of St. John's Cathedral. His daughter, Miss Hart, is an earnest worker in the church.

Bishop Joseph P. Machebeuf was the founder of Catholicism in Colorado. He was sent by the bishop of Santa Fe, with Rev. J. B. Raverdy, to take charge of the Catholic mission in the Pike's Peak region. They reached here October 22, 1860. The directors of the Denver Town Company had donated the whole block bounded by Fifteenth and Stout and Sixteenth and California to Rev. J. B. Miege, who had come to Denver to establish a church. But funds ran out and the building stopped half finished. Bishop Machebeuf bent his energies to the fund problem, and by the end of the year the building

Bishop J. P. Machebeuf

was ready for service. It was through his influence that the first organ came from St. Louis in 1862, and with it came an eight hundred-pound bell. It was the first church bell, and it was hung in a tower in front of the church.

Said a pioneer: "The first sound of a church bell that broke the stillness of these valleys and echoed among the pine-clad hills stirred emotion in the heart of many a strong man and brought tears to the eyes of many a pioneer woman who had been wooed and wedded and had worshipped to the sound of church chimes."

Christmas night, in 1864, the storm blew down the tower and the bell was broken in several pieces. But the bishop was tireless in the service and advancement of his church. A new bell was brought from St. Louis, which was hung in the church tower. This building remained the cathedral until the new cathedral was built, which is the most magnificent church edifice in Colorado.

In 1860 Isadore Deitsch, A. Jacobs, A. Goldsmith, Julius Mitchell and Fred Z. Salomon organized a small society,

Immaculate Conception Cathedral

The Development of Pioneer Enterprises

which became the nucleus of the present Jewish Temple Emanuel congregation. In 1878 the society was reorganized as the Congregation Emanuel. The first Temple Emanuel was built at Nineteenth and Curtis, and Rabbi Fleisher conducted the first services held in it. The present Temple Emanuel was erected in 1898, and dedicated January 29, 1899. Rabbi William S. Friedman, a learned man and eloquent speaker, conducts the services in it.

Following out the purpose of this book, I have written only of the churches that were established in the early pioneer days. The pioneers brought no prejudices, political, social or religious. I remember hearing the good Bishop Machebeuf tell of asking Colonel Chivington for money to help build his church. "But," said Colonel Chivington, "I am just about building a church of my own." "Very well," said the bishop, "you are about to begin, but I have already begun; my case is the most urgent." The colonel regarded the argument as good and handed him a liberal donation.

Father Dyer, so called because he was one of the first ministers of the Gospel who settled in the Rocky Mountain region, preached in the streets, in the saloons, in the gambling houses, and wherever he could gather a crowd. He would fearlessly proclaim the truth, and, at the close of the service, some self-appointed steward would pass the "hat" among the "boys" and Father Dyer's exchequer would be greatly enlarged with the "gold dust from the diggings," as that was the "circulating medium" of those days.

Though he would terrifically portray the awful calamity that would surely come upon his hearers if they did not repent of their sins, his genial manner, quaint humor and ready wit insured him a welcome in every miner's cabin.

A man who had become dissatisfied with the church because of some difficulty, and had withdrawn from it, said to Father Dyer: "I have been out of the church three years and have been watching church members all that time, and I have come to the conclusion that they do not live up to their professions."

"My dear brother," replied Father Dyer, "I think you have been out on picket duty long enough; you had better come into headquarters and be relieved."

It is the earnest man with earnest work to do who, in unexpected moments, flashes wit like that. Often there is as much religion in laughing as in crying. The melancholy frog always croaks; he never gets very high above the earth, but the lark, all life and song and joy, brushes with its wings the gates of heaven.

The following incident was told to me by Father Dyer: "In the spring of 1864 I received my mail at Laurette, better known as 'Buckskin Joe,' in Park County, Colorado. I was sent there by the Conference to take charge of a church. Falling short of funds, I took the contract of carrying the mail every week on snow-shoes from the above place to Cache Creek, via California Gulch, seventy-five miles and back. Somebody got a corner on flour, and it went up to $40 per sack, and, for once, I had a sack to spare. Some of my friends urged me to take it over there, as they were nearly out. I could not find a pony for sale, but I found a man who said he had a cow that would pack, and I bought her. I procured a pack-saddle, sewed a gunny-sack over the bag of flour, and girted it on as tight as I could. Then I tied my cow to a post and went in the hotel to eat my breakfast. An old friend, Mr. Moody, offered to help me start, but by this time my cow got mad. We each had a rope; Mr. Moody led and I was to drive her. He started and the cow trod after him on a down grade. He ran his best; the cow jumped just as high and far as she could and struck just behind him. I held on as tight as possible, and at the length of two blocks he took around the corner and she after him. Just then the girth broke, and away went pack-saddle and flour. After this novel scene I gave up the idea of trying to feed the hungry with temporal bread, but continued in my effort to dispense the bread of life. Some minister might think the above was unbecoming, but I had either to leave the work and Conference, or earn a living, and I was not educated up to the point that a man was justified in leaving because the people did not pay a good salary."

Stories of the pioneer preachers would fill a volume. I rejoice that it was my privilege to know Father Dyer, Bishop Machebeuf and Bishop Randall. There are men in Colorado today who hold them in sacred remembrance. The goldseekers, dreadfully in earnest after earthly riches, saw that these men were just as much in earnest after the better riches of the world to come—men all aflame with celestial fire—and they yielded them what Christian earnestness always compels from men—respect, admiration, confidence and a following.

Schools

The arrival of O. J. Goldrick, the pioneer school teacher, in August, 1859, was spectacular. He was clothed in a faultless suit of black broadcloth, immaculate linen, wore a glossy silk hat of the style then called "plug," and was teaching an ox-team the meaning of "Get up" by the heavy lash of a whip. He was born in Ireland and was a Dublin University graduate. Following his natural inclinations, he became the first school teacher in Denver, and the Beau Brummel of pioneer days. He seldom appeared except in black broadcloth, which made him a conspicuous figure on the streets of Denver. Soon after his arrival he circulated a subscription paper in Denver and Auraria and secured pledges amounting to $250 in support of a school. On the third of October he opened his school, in a log cabin in Auraria, with thirteen children in attendance. In a week or two the number increased to twenty.

Lewis N. Tappan, who came from Boston to Cherry Creek in the fall of '59, was walking through the streets

O. J. GOLDRICK   LEWIS N. TAPPAN   ABNER R. BROWN

MISS LYDIA MARIA RING   MISS INDIANA SOPRIS

of Auraria when his attention was attracted by a crowd of children engaged in the ordinary games of childhood. He stepped into the little log cabin nearby and was met by an affable, polite gentleman who informed him that his name was O. J. Goldrick. During the conversation Tappan suggested forming a Sunday school, which should be non-sectarian. The proposition was cheerfully indorsed by Goldrick. Mr. Tappan then found the Rev. Mr. Fisher, the pioneer Methodist minister, and, together, they commenced the canvass of the towns for pupils.

November 3, 1859, the following notice appeared in the "News:"

Union Sunday School

A Union Sunday School for the children of Auraria and Denver will be held every Sunday at 3 o'clock p. m. at the house of preachers Fisher and Adriance. The school will be not only a union school, but a union of all denominations.

At the appointed time came twelve pupils. Mr. Tappan wrote to the Baptist Sunday school of Lawrence, Kansas, soliciting a supply of books. They were freighted across the plains by Jones & Cartwright, free of charge. Upon examination, Mr. Tappan discovered, to his surprise, that they were the same books which he had solicited from his old Bible class in the Rev. Dr. Stowe's church in Boston for the Kansas Sunday school. This box of books had an eventful history. After serving its time in Denver, it was sent to the first anti-Mormon Sunday school in Salt Lake City.

D. C. Collier was elected superintendent of the Union Sunday school, and Goldrick became a teacher. The second Sunday fifteen children took their seats on the rough wooden benches, and the school, keeping pace with the wonderful advance of the country, continued to grow, until it taxed the capacity of the two rooms. By that time denominational schools were formed, and, having passed the period of usefulness, it was discontinued, leaving only pleasant memories of the men who founded and guided it.

Goldrick took part in every movement for improving the environment of the pioneer. He was an educated man, with a sincere love for his fellow man, and his name was a household word from the day of his arrival to the day of his death.

In December, 1860, a mass meeting was held in front of the old Lindell hotel to take action toward organizing a school district. Goldrick was the leader and he used a goods box for his rostrum.

The "school act," passed by the Territorial Legislature convened in Denver September, 1861, marks the actual beginning of a duly organized public school system for Colorado. However, no provision was made for school funds until the second session of the Legislature, July, 1862. Under the new school law, Goldrick was chosen the first county superintendent.

In 1864, he discontinued school work and became traveling correspondent in the mining districts for the News. On one occasion, while in the mountains in Clear Creek County, he figured prominently in a lynching. A Mexican had been caught robbing a sluice box. This was his second offense and it was promptly decided that he should be hanged. Professor Goldrick had always declared himself as opposed to lynch law, but in this case, he said, "circumstances must occasionally induce a patriotic citizen to revise his opinion." However, he urged that the doomed man should be given "the consolations of religion." "Pray!" he thundered at the Mexican, "I tell you, pray!" But the miserable man had no words at his command. Whereat the professor solemnly bowed his head, told, at some length, the black record of the man, which he assumed Divine Providence would accept as sufficient excuse for the hanging, and, in conclusion, said:

"This man is unfit to live. He is an outcast, and unworthy of associating with decent people, and so, O Lord, take him to Thyself!"

Denver pioneers enjoyed the peculiarities of Pro-

The Development of Pioneer Enterprises 143

fessor Goldrick and told many stories about him, which the professor listened to with calm indifference.

He wrote spicy "locals" for the Rocky Mountain News while teaching school, and, on account of one of them, he received a challenge. He was not a coward, but he had a nervous dread of firearms. However, he bravely accepted the challenge and braced himself for the trying ordeal by long swigs of whisky. He appeared on the "field of honor" thoroughly intoxicated. His opponent was in a similar condition. The seconds, who had prepared the affair as a practical joke, took the cartridges out of both revolvers. At the word "fire," the two weapons snapped, and Goldrick fell to the ground, his nervous system broke completely down and he believed that he was shot. His second, to carry on the joke, emptied a bottle of red ink on the fallen man's snowy shirt-front, and when the professor opened his eyes he caught a glimpse of the spreading red stain and moaned, "My God, I am dead." It took quite awhile for his second to persuade him to the contrary.

Next in importance to the name of Goldrick in the early school annals of Denver stands that of Lydia Maria Ring. Professor Goldrick's log school house was in Auraria. Miss Ring opened her school, May, 1860, in a little log cabin on the corner of Market and Fourteenth—the very first school in Denver before that settlement was united with Auraria.

Miss Ring was from Massachusetts, and came to the Cherry creek settlement by caravan. She was not easily daunted by the hardships and perils of those days, and lived alone in a tent for weeks before she could find comfortable quarters. She had an attractive personality, was always well dressed, and became a social, as well as an educational, leader. In the early files of the News it tells of a living patriotic panorama, given at the old People's theater, during war times, and Miss Ring played the part of Columbia, with the belles of Denver grouped around her as States.

Miss Sopris, now Mrs. S. H. Cushman, taught in Auraria May 7, 1860, a few days before Miss Ring taught in Denver City.

So much for the picturesque private schools.

The first free school was opened in District No. 2 December, 1862, with Abner R. Brown as principal and Miss Ada Simonton as his assistant. A few days later, School District No. 1 opened its first public school, with

H. H. Lamb as principal and Miss Sopris as assistant. The schoolrooms were usually in the upper stories of buildings, and were furnished with long homemade benches, rough desks and a long rod, which was considered a necessary piece of furniture.

Comparatively little progress was made by the public schools of Denver until the coming of the railroads, in 1870. The population consisted mostly of men without families, who were not interested in educating other people's children. About that time, big-hearted, open-handed Amos Steck, one of Denver's pioneer builders, gave two lots on Arapahoe street, between Seventeenth and Eighteenth, for the erection of a school building. The pioneer period of Denver's schools closed with the completion of the Arapahoe school building. It was proudly spoken of by the orators of that time as our magnificent temple of learning.

Mary C. C. Bradford, State superintendent of public instruction, is keenly alive to the demands of her position. When asked for information in regard to the present educational situation in Colorado, she said:

"From the humble, but inspiring, beginnings of pioneer days, the school system of Colorado has progressed until it numbers about seven thousand persons actively engaged in educational work, and the professional spirit evidenced by the entire teaching force of Colorado is greater than ever before in the history of the State.

"The University of Colorado, State Teachers' College, State Normal School, State School of Mines, State Agricultural College, Colorado School for Deaf and Blind, State Industrial School for Boys, State Industrial School for Girls, State Home for Dependent and Neglected Children, State Home and Training School for Mental Defectives—all institutions either purely educational or such in some phases of their activity—show cultural development, practical efficiency, and skill in administration.

"In both city and country schools there exists a clear consciousness of the chief functions of public education —that of making citizens worthy to be entrusted with the welfare of the State. The two hundred and seventy-five thousand children of school age in Colorado are receiving increasingly practical education, an education that means the interpretation of life in terms of truth, beauty, efficiency and service."

Under the leadership of Governor John Evans, in 1863, the Denver Methodists laid the foundations of the Colorado Seminary. This was the first school for advanced learning in the Territory of Colorado. The school was opened November, 1864, and maintained until 1867, when, in consequence of accumulated indebtedness, it was closed. The property was sold, and bought by Governor Evans. In 1879, the Colorado Seminary was reorganized under the original charter. A new board was appointed, and Governor Evans returned, as a gift, the seminary property he had bought twelve years before to save it. To this he added $3,000 for laboratory apparatus. Vice-President Bailey gave $13,000, and the business men generally contributed liberally to reinstate the seminary. In 1880, a second and co-ordinate corporation was formed, under the name, "University of Denver." All the property is owned and the material affairs managed by the seminary corporation, while the university corporation controls and directs the higher departments of university training.

Rev. David H. Moore was elected chancellor of the new university and president of Colorado Seminary. Dr. William F. McDowell was the next chancellor, and, in January, 1900, Dr. Henry A. Buchtel entered upon the duties of chancellor. A large tract of land was donated by real estate men in South Denver, and the permanent home of the university was established there.

Newspapers

In the pioneer history of Denver, nothing of any importance was consummated without the personal participation of William N. Byers.

From that April day in 1859, when the News was established, to the day of its sale to W. A. H. Loveland, he used its columns to point out the great natural resources of the country, and to urge their development. He gave to the outside world, through his reports, the earliest and best intelligence of the growth of Denver. No man has done nobler and more unselfish work for the upbuilding of Colorado.

The Development of Pioneer Enterprises 147

"The pioneer newspapers of Denver," said Mr. Byers, a short time before his death, "were the Rocky Mountain News and the Cherry Creek Pioneer. The question as to which came from the press first has been often discussed and disputed, but our information at the time was that the News had priority by about twenty minutes.

"My printing outfit was located in an attic over Uncle Dick Wooton's saloon. Naturally, this saloon saw

a good deal of roughness, and many of its frequenters were 'mighty handy with their pistols.' Stray shots were frequent, and we, of the printing office overhead, soon learned that an inch pine board wouldn't stop a Colt's navy bullet, so we got more boards and doubled the floor under our beds. None were killed in that campaign.

"The Pioneer outfit was brought from St. Joseph, Missouri, by Jack Merrick. He was a 'jolly, good fellow,' and he wanted to get acquainted before he settled down to work. He was mighty busy at that before we came, and then he set to and gave us a very close race. The extraordinary event of a newspaper in the Rocky Mountain region, and the race, enlisted the interest of the people, and all afternoon there was a continuous procession of people over the 'log walk' across Cherry creek to see the process of making the first newspaper, and, more particularly, to determine which one was first to appear.

"Merrick got out the first number of the Pioneer, and then he took a rest. Two or three days later, my partner, Mr. Gibson, went around and traded an armful of 'grub' for the outfit, and carried it back with him to the News office. That ended the Pioneer, and marked the first newspaper death in Colorado. Jack took his 'grub' and went prospecting. Early in the spring of 1860, a third printing press reached Denver. It was brought out by H. E. Rounds and Edward Bliss of Chicago, but, without starting into business, it was consolidated with the News, and the four proprietors became jointly and equally the News Printing Company. In 1863, Rounds and Bliss were bought out by Byers and Dailey.

"In the spring of 1860, Thomas Gibson, who had sold his interest in the News to John L. Dailey, returned to Denver with another printing office, and, May 1st, issued the first number of the Daily Rocky Mountain Herald, which was the first daily paper published. A few weeks later, the News issued a daily, and, soon after, published another edition called The Bulletin. Late in that year, another paper was established in Denver, by Moore and Coleman, called The Mountaineer. Early in 1861, it was bought out by Byers & Dailey. I believe there were no other newspaper changes in Denver until 1864, when the News office was destroyed by the Cherry creek flood, and the Herald was purchased by Byers & Dailey. For several years following, the News had the field entirely to itself.

"I think this covers briefly the pioneer press history of Denver. In common with the fortune of all other pioneer enterprises," he continued, "the press met with great trials, difficulties and misfortunes. Our paper sold at twenty-five cents a copy. I sent to Fort Leavenworth for paper and had to pay a dollar a pound for freight. We got along as best we could, printing on wrapping paper, druggists' paper, tissue paper—in fact, any kind of paper that we could get, and we missed several issues in the summer of 1859 because there was nothing to print on.

"My memories in connection with the business are varied, generally pleasant, and always interesting. There were trials and many disappointments. There were times when I found it prudent to disguise myself or to vary my route homeward when I left the office after night, because of threats against my life. The office was often threatened. Once only was it attacked. For years it was the rule to keep arms always in reach; the compositor stood at his case with a gun leaning against his stand. The cause for such precaution was the outspoken tone of the paper against lawlessness and disorder."

John L. Dailey came to Colorado with W. N. Byers, in 1859. In July of the same year he became one of the owners of the News. He took charge of the business department, contributed to its columns, and became a factor in the success of the paper.

The big flood in 1864 swept the News building, with all its material and fixtures, away.

Parts of the press were recovered from the sands at bedrock, in 1872, and are among the curiosities of the State Historical Society at the capitol. Another building was erected for the News on Market street. This building Mr. Dailey took down piece by piece in 1900, and presented it to the city for restoration at the City park, there to stand, one of the most interesting relics of pioneer days.

Mr. Dailey was connected, in many ways, with the building of Denver. He was straightforward and upright in all his dealings with his fellow man, widely known and highly respected. His daughter, Miss Annie Dailey, is one of Denver's most gifted artists.

In 1870 the Rocky Mountain Herald passed into the hands of O. J. Goldrick, who became its editor, with Halsey M. Rhoads as business manager. Mr. William Ferrill is the present publisher of the paper.

The following is the list of Denver newspapers in the order of their establishment: The Rocky Mountain News, the Denver Times, the Denver Tribune, the Denver Republican, the Denver Herald (German), the Denver World, the Denver Sun, the Denver Post.

The newspapers of Denver today have the mechanical equipment and the talented working force that place them on a level with any city in this country or Europe.

Pioneer Printers

In response to a call issued by Angelo Noce, twenty-one old-time printers assembled and effected a temporary organization of what is now known as the Colorado Pioneer Printers. A permanent organization was effected July 22, 1912, with Clarence E. Hagar, president; Angelo Noce, first vice-president; Sam S. Landon, treasurer, and Joseph G. Brown, secretary.

Chas. S. Semper

The charter members were as follows: Angelo Noce, Clarence E. Hagar, Joseph G. Brown, August Koester, Sigmond Friedenthal, Charles F. Hynes, Halsey M. Rhoads, Samuel S. Landon, T. B. Caswell, Azel R. Logan, John B. O'Connell, Al G. Dobbins, Byrd L. Wilson, John Frederic, John Henderson, Frank Zern, John J. Bucher,

The Development of Pioneer Enterprises

Frank Kratzer, T. J. Kendrick, Frank C. Birdsall, Charles S. Semper.

Today, the society has an active membership of one hundred and forty. The nature of this association is fraternal and social. All printers, editors, writers or others who were practically connected with the printing or publishing business in Colorado twenty-five years ago, or prior thereto, are eligible to membership. The officers are elected annually. Mr. O. L. Smith is now president.

Charles S. Semper is, at this writing, the sole survivor of those who issued the first copy of the Rocky Mountain News, in 1859. The aged printer is a Confederate veteran. He came to Denver in 1858, joined the South in the Civil war, and took part in most of the great battles.

Edward Keating

Mr. Semper and his wife are living on a farm near the town of Semper. The aged couple say that they ask nothing more than to be allowed to end their lives on the homestead taken up many years ago.

The Denver Press Club

The Denver Press Club bears a double distinction. It is the only organization of its kind in the country that is composed entirely of bona fide newspaper men—writers. It has been in existence almost eleven years. The Gridiron Club, made up of Washington, D. C., correspondents and writers, is the only similar organization that approaches the Denver newspaper men's club.

Geo. E. Lewis

The Denver Press Club was organized in March, 1905. Its vicissitudes since that time have been numerous, but it surmounted all obstacles, and today stands as a model, the country over, of the ideal newspaper man's organization.

The membership of the club is about one hundred and fifty. Its associate membership list includes some of the most prominent men of the country — senators, financiers and others of large affairs. The honorary list is confined to President Wilson and ex-Presidents Roosevelt and Taft.

Edward J. Keating, now United States Congressman from the First District, Colorado, was the first president of the Denver Press Club. He served two terms. George E. Lewis is the present head of the organization.

An organization formed by Gene Field, "Bill" Nye. Wolfe Londoner—one of Denver's first mayors—and others of the old-time "scribes" furnished the inspiration for the present club.

The club quarters are in the Denham building, and the place is the mecca for most of the writers who visit Denver.

CHAPTER XI

SOCIAL AND ECONOMIC CONDITIONS

Denver a Culture Center

A. E. Pierce

Mr. A. E. Pierce, a fifty-eighter, has linked his name with history by being the first to make Denver a culture center.

Mr. Pierce said to me recently: "When we walk down Sixteenth street today and see the new skyscrapers rising up around us, it is hard for us to appreciate what Denver was in 1858. I have witnessed this transformation from 'grass roots.' It was my fortune to have been one of that little band of argonauts who crossed the 'Great American Desert,' as it was called in our old school atlas, to the new Eldorado, in 1858. I was in Omaha when a prospector returned and showed a few flakes of precious metal in a goose quill. This was enough. A caravan to cross the plains was at once formed. With it I cast my lot. We took the North Platte route. It was midwinter when, one day, we crossed Clear creek, drove over the hills of what is now North Denver, and came in sight of the little settlement on Cherry creek and South Platte. Small as the camp was, it was a welcome sight to us. We had tramped beside our patient

A. E. Pierce

oxen over eight hundred miles. We never rode; the load was sufficient without.

"When Gregory discovered gold in the gulches and lodes at Black Hawk, there was a stampede for the new camp. My partner and I were among the first. In a brief time the hills and gulches swarmed with prospectors.

"At this time there were no mail facilities, except via Fort Laramie, a government post two hundred miles to the north. The Auraria-Denver camp appointed one Henry Allen postmaster, and employed a man to carry the mail to and from the fort. He was paid twenty-five cents for each letter. Letters forwarded to camps in the mountains were taxed an additional twenty-five cents. I well remember receiving one in Russell Gulch for which I paid fifty cents in gold dust. It contained about two lines from an old chum, saying: 'Let me know where you are so I can write to you.'

The Circulating Library

"On my return from Russell Gulch in the fall of '59, I found the two towns had grown apace, but there was a great dearth of reading matter. Not a book, magazine or eastern paper could be bought. Although I was down and out financially, I managed to scrape together enough gold dust to send to St. Joe for a supply of pictorial and other papers and paper-bound novels. In course of time the stock arrived, in two large packages, by the Pike's Peak Express, with $10 express charges. I had enough money to get one of these packages out of the office and opened it up on a work bench under a big cottonwood tree. I soon sold the stock out to the mentally hungry pilgrims. Then I had money to take out the other package. This stock vanished with equal rapidity, but I now had money to do business and ordered

The Development of Pioneer Enterprises

a larger stock, and also got together a number of bound books. From the work bench I moved into the little room where mails were received and given out. I then ordered a supply of bound books and started a circulating library, which became a popular and well-patronized institution. I had labels printed and pasted on the cover, 'A. E. Pierce Circulating Library.'

"I very soon found that in providing the new town with reading matter I had struck a 'pay streak.'

"Of course, Denver was envious that Auraria should have the only literary depot, so I opened a branch on the east side in William Graham's drug store. A little later on I consolidated the two news depots and moved into a new store. I built up a large trade, supplying not only the local demand, but all the mining camps, with the latest papers from the East. I had papers on my counter from all over the United States and was able to give every newcomer the latest news from his own State, for which he was always glad to pay a quarter. The standard price for a newspaper, regardless of age, was twenty-five cents. In 1860 I sold out to Woolworth & Moffat, as I desired to take a trip back East.

First Reading Room and Library

"February 10, 1860, I organized a reading room association. The rooms of the library were in a building near the bed of Cherry creek, below the site of the present city hall. The original officers were: President, Major R. B. Bradford; vice-president, Captain C. P. Marion; secretary, O. J. Goldrick; treasurer, A. E. Pierce; librarian, James Kime; directors, R. B. Bradford, O. J. Goldrick, C. H. Blake, G. W. Bark, T. H. Warren, W. M. Slaughter, William Graham.

"The association was known as the Denver City and Auraria Reading Room and Library Association. Each member paid into the treasury fifty cents at the beginning of every month. We had one hundred members. Their names were in a book, together with the constitution and by-laws and a list of officers, which book I presented to the present city library when the late R. W. Woodbury was its president. It is an interesting relic.

"I thank God," continued Mr. Pierce, "that I have been permitted to live and have some part in so important an era of western life and history. There was a joy in pioneering. The pioneer lived 'the simple life,' close to nature. He was care free; he rolled himself up in his blankets and slept on the ground; his menu was limited—bread and meat and coffee for breakfast, the same for dinner, and likewise for supper. There was usually a pot of boiled beans, and, as a dessert, stewed dried apples, or pie from the same filling. The first ripe apples that appeared on the streets of Denver in 1860 sold readily for twenty-five cents apiece."

The Society of Colorado Pioneers

Mr. Pierce said: "To be entitled to membership in the Society of Colorado Pioneers, one must have arrived in Colorado and resided here prior to January, 1861. Efforts have frequently been made to extend this time to a later date, but the old pioneers have resolutely stood against it.

"There is a reason for this. The years 1858, '59 and '60 were, in a peculiar sense, pioneer years. Especial recognition has always been accorded those who came as early as '58. It was the 'picket line,' or advance guard. The number coming that early was quite limited. But during the years '59 and '60 thousands came. These were the pioneers who scattered all through the mountains, opened the mines, built towns and located ranches in the valleys. They laid foundations upon which those coming later built.

"The early pioneer came to a silent wilderness. He took hold of the territory 'in the raw.' He had nothing but his hands, his energy and his courage to start a new civilization in the wilderness. Within two years he had so far advanced that he was ready to ask his 'Uncle Samuel' to take him right into his family circle. Those coming to the Territory later found a well-organized community, all the comforts of home, as it were, a place to sleep and a place to eat. Doubt had given way to certainty. Instead of prospectors washing out a few flakes of gold from the sands of Cherry creek, or some other still less auriferous stream, stamp mills were pounding out the real stuff in Clear creek and other canyons, and a private mint coining genuine golden eagles, while the poorest man had some of the 'stuff' in his buckskin sack.

"Yes, it was different after 1860, and, no matter what may happen to the Society of Colorado Pioneers in after years, the fact must ever remain the same—the real pioneer was the one who first turned the sod. I accord all credit to those who came a little later, or even some years later. Some of these have been empire builders, but, even so, they found the trenches dug, the trail blazed, the foundation laid, and all the evidences of civilization—the press, the school, the church and society, as well as the dance hall, gambling hall and brothel—yes, all these adjuncts to modern civilization, while the real pioneer had—all these things to get.

"Probably, some day, the doors of the pioneer society will be opened, and those who came at a later date will be enrolled; but not until most of the 'real stock' have passed over the range and become extinct, as the buffalo of the plains."

The society numbers several hundred members at the present time, and Mr. William R. Beatty is the president.

PIONEER LADIES' AID SOCIETY

This society has for its special object the care of the unfortunate pioneers. It was organized as an auxiliary to the Society of Colorado Pioneers in September, 1889, by the following women: Mrs. William N. Byers, Mrs. Birks Cornforth, Mrs. L. W. Cutler, Mrs. J. F. Henderson, Mrs. Alvin McCune, Mrs. C. H. McLaughlin, Mrs. H. W. Michael, Mrs. D. Mitchell, Mrs. R. Moseley, Mrs. A. G. Rhoads, Mrs. Andrew Sagendorf, Mrs. Richard Sopris, Mrs. Augusta Tabor and Mrs. Justina Trankle. In 1894, when it was incorporated, the society had a membership of one hundred and fifty. From the time of its organization this society has held the regard, sympathy and good will of the people.

THE PIONEERS' PICNIC

The far-famed Elitch's Gardens became a beauty spot in pioneer days. Mrs. Martha Hagar, with her husband and sons, came to Colorado in the early times and settled at Empire, where they were constantly in dread of Indians. The town was then a distributing point of rations for the Utes. They passed through a period of merciless Indian savageries and butcheries, and finally, after the death of her husband, Mrs. Hagar moved to Denver.

Here she married William Chilcott, and for many years the couple made their home on the property now known as Elitch's Gardens.

Mrs. Chilcott, with her own hands, planted many of the shade trees that adorn the gardens today. Through her continued labor and care the dreary desert place was changed into a pleasant ranch, which soon became famed for its beauty. The many fine reports of it caught the attention of John Elitch, who bought the property and made it one of the beauty spots of Denver.

To the pioneers, the resort, even in its modern altered condition, is always a reminder of the gentle lady who planted the first trees.

On the twentieth day of every June the men and women of the Colorado Pioneer Society, with ribbons and badges on their coats and dresses, enjoy a reunion at Elitch's Gardens.

Early in the afternoon they begin to crowd through the gate with great bulging baskets of "goodies."

Pioneer Day at Elitch's is an important event, and several hundred from far and near usually gather amid the flowers and trees and song birds of the beautiful spot to live over again, in memory and reminiscences, the days when Colorado was new.

It is with feelings of admiration and gratitude that I mingle with the men and women who helped to blaze the path of civilization westward. I have seen faces whose seams began when danger and privations were daily companions beam in recognition of an old-time friend, and hands which helped to hew out the foundations of an empire clasp in warm remembrance.

I have listened to men who were among the first to find gold in the mountains talk of the days when, to be a prospector, with all a prospector's hopes, was greater than to be the crowned head of a kingdom.

The gathering always presents to me a scene of mixed festivity and sadness. I remember the picnic last year. The day was superb with the radiance and charm of early spring; the gardens never looked prettier, with every flower bed a riotous mass of color; all the amusements were going in full blast, to the delight of hundreds of children, who were boastful of their pioneer lineage.

I heard one lady say in plaintive tones: "I have been coming to these reunions year after year, and my sister and her husband have been with me, but this year

The Development of Pioneer Enterprises

I am alone—both have gone over the Great Divide since last June."

I turned to converse with Mrs. D. C. Oakes, the widow of D. C. Oakes, a sweet faced lady, who sat at one side and wore a badge labeled Honorary President of the Pioneer Ladies' Aid Society.

"In the days of Indian raids," said Mrs. Oakes, "my husband built a fort for the refuge of people. It was formed of square hewed logs, with a well in the center, and was termed 'Major Oakes' Folly' by those who did not realize the danger. We lived there six months. The Indians kept close watch, and it was only under the cover of darkness that the men got out to buy provisions. Our cooking utensils and furniture were limited, but it was a comfort to feel that we were safe from the tomahawk of the red man. After the Indians left, the people went to look for their former homes, and they found only heaps of ashes."

Mrs. Oakes came to Denver in 1859, and has seen it grow from a village of log cabins, with its stirring scenes of ox teams, scouts, trappers, Indians and prospectors, to skyscrapers, automobiles and flying machines—truly a wonderful period of history-making.

She has given a building site to the Territorial Daughters for the construction of a home for Colorado pioneers.

I was introduced to two of the "boys"—Eugene La Velle, ninety-seven years old, and A. J. Randall, ninety-two, who seemed to be entering into the pleasures of the day with all the enthusiasm of boys.

"I remember the first hanging," said W. T. Eubank, another pioneer. "He was an old Dutchman, and when the rope was placed around his neck he took off his shoes and handed them over to the man who had defended him, saying: 'It's all I got to give yer; take 'em.'"

Mr. James H. Pierce of Morrison remarked proudly:

"I am the only survivor in Colorado of the Green Russell expedition. I often live over in memory the day we pitched our tents under the cottonwood trees on the Platte."

And there was handsome Major Boutwell, who has watched Colorado grow from "infancy to manhood." The distinction of which he is proudest is that he is a pioneer.

Harry Ruffner, with his smile that never comes off, was posing for a picture. He was born at Fourteenth and Blake in the old Colorado house, which his father owned, and is now secretary of the Sons of Colorado, a society of native sons. He talked of the playgrounds of the town in the early days along the banks of the Platte river, and the old swimming hole at a spot just north of the present Union depot, where all the kids in town gathered and swam in the water on summer afternoons, protected from public gaze by the willows on the banks.

"Many a time," said Mr. Ruffner, "have I watched the cowboys, surrounded now by a golden and romantic haze, driving the great herds over the plains. I could tell them miles distant, because of the cloud of dust that preceded them and rose to the high heavens.

"I have seen the patch of ground in Henry C. Brown's ranch transformed from a pasture lot to a million dollar hotel site in thirty-five years, and I am ever ready to honor the brave men and women who have made Colorado a great and glorious commonwealth."

The tones of a violin drew me to where the dancers moved through the quadrille, the Varsouviana and the Virginia reel, a little more stately, but with just as much enjoyment as in the early days. It is surprising how the sturdy old pillars of the State retain their nimbleness.

*Hugh Steele kept time to the music with graceful step, and *Major Boutwell bowed with dignity to his

---
*Both have since passed away.

white-haired partner—the partner who has stood at his side for fifty years, and both entered into the dance. George Twombly and his handsome wife led the Virginia reel.

Mrs. Elitch Long, "the lady of the gardens," moved among the throng, her face beaming with smiles, and giving a pleasant word to both young and old. Through her untiring energy the gardens have been run on a very high plane, and have always attracted the cultured people of Denver.

For this beautiful work, she is appreciated and recognized as one of our state builders.

Fannie D. Hardin, the moving spirit in the Pioneer Aid Society, was there. She mingled with lads and lassies of seventy and eighty, and danced the old steps with rhythm and grace that attracted attention. Mrs. Hardin's father, Samuel W. Walthall, fought in the war of 1812. Her parents were Virginians and died before she was twelve years old. While she had ancestors and relatives of historic connections, she deserves attention on her own account.

"I came to Colorado in a 'prairie schooner,'" said Mrs. Hardin, "in company with my sister and brother-in-law, Mr. and Mrs. A. R. Malone. We camped one night on the Platte, and the next morning we received a call from some friendly Indians. I wore a bright turkey red calico dress, and I made a great impression on one of them. He asked my brother if he would exchange me for five ponies, and, thinking it a joke, my brother nodded yes. He did not know the Indian method of courtship. A few hours later, to his surprise, he saw the Indians returning with five ponies. He turned to me and said, 'Hide!' I jumped into the wagon and he covered me over with a feather bed. In order to get rid of them he had to tell them that I had gone, and, after talking, they went away, showing great disappointment. It is rather interesting to know how much they thought I was worth—five ponies," said Mrs. Hardin, with a laugh. "And, being an Indian proposal, it was an unusual experience."

A few years later this bright young girl was married at Fort Weld, on Christmas eve, to Lieutenant G. H. Hardin. The wedding was one of military pomp. Father Kehler, founder of St. John's church of Denver, performed the ceremony.

When Lieutenant Hardin finished his time of service, he went to his big ranch on the Julesburg Short Line, at Hardin, Colorado, a station named for him. He died in 1885. After his death, Mrs. Hardin, with her son, Arthur B. Hardin, ran the ranch successfully for four years, and for twenty-five years Mrs. Hardin has been in the hotel business in Denver, proving by her energy that she is a woman worth while.

At six o'clock, the lunch baskets were opened and the empire builders of '59 and '60 lived the glory of it over again while they sat and ate in the long afternoon shadows, exchanging reminiscences that thrilled the blood and quickened the imagination.

The Old Dugout

The story of the "old dugout" will illustrate the increase of values in real estate.

Richard E. Whitsitt, in 1860, bought four lots at the corner of Sixteenth and Curtis for $700. In 1865, Whitsitt sold them to John Fetter for $950. One year later the First Baptist church bought them for $1,150. The church first made the corner famous, and many old-timers can recall the site of that day. The congregation commenced the erection of a church building and the basement walls were completed to the height of about four

The Development of Pioneer Enterprises 165

feet above the sidewalk; owing to lack of funds a rough board roof was built over them, and this was called the "Baptist dugout." The hall that was used as a church had originally been intended as a basement of a sumptuous structure. In 1872, there were unmistakable evidences that the transplanted population of Colorado was beginning to grow up with the country and must needs have opportunity to grow up in the way it should go. The board was perplexed to know how to provide desk room for Colorado babies, that seemed to come into the state at an unprecedented rate, all six years old and with

"THE BAPTIST DUG-OUT."
E. L. SCHOLTZ

an insatiable thirst for knowledge. This perplexity has been handed down as a legacy from board to board to the present day. The school houses were crowded and vacant buildings were few in those days. The old dugout was rented and fitted up as a schoolroom. It was used on week days as a public school and Sundays as a church. Later on, a large brick room was built on it by Charley Leitsenour for a beer hall, named "The Walhalla," which eventually became a public hall for meetings, balls, conventions, shows, lectures, theatricals, social parties, political speeches and occasional church purposes.

The second session of the State Legislature was held

there, Governor Pitkin was inaugurated there, Professor N. P. Hill was elected senator within its walls, and both Henry R. and E. O. Wolcott served as legislators in the old building.

In 1875, the First Baptist church sold the corner to Lewis C. Ellsworth for $7,500. Ellsworth sold the four lots in 1884 to Jerome S. Riche for $90,000. Mr. Riche is one of Denver's successful pioneers, whose genius and working energy have been directed towards the upbuilding of Denver. He is always ready to act on his own initiative and has long been regarded as an investor of fine judgment. This purchase instilled in others confidence in Denver real estate.

The increase in value was now on in earnest and the lots which originally cost $700 Mr. Riche sold, in 1897, for $300,000 to William Church. It is now the site of the leading drug store of the city. Mr. Ed. B. Scholtz pays as much rent for the corner store a month as the original cost of the four lots. He came to Denver in the early days and was a clerk in a drug store before he went into business for himself. He worked his way without any help, and now owns and controls a chain of drug stores in Denver. He was the first president of the Sons of Colorado, and, owing to his real western enterprise and enthusiasm, was made president of the Chamber of Commerce. Today he holds an enviable position in the hearts of the people of Denver as one of its most popular citizens.

Wheat

About the last of October, 1859, two heads of wheat were accidentally discovered in a garden in Denver. The grain was large and fine, which convinced the pioneers that a very superior quality of wheat could be grown in this country. The gateway of opportunity swung wide, and John W. Smith was the first to drive into it. He arrived in Denver June 3, 1860, with a wagon-train loaded with merchandise for a general store and machinery for a planing mill, a flour mill and a quartz mill. From the day of his arrival, he was one of the most substantial men in the community, for he brought with him twenty thousand dollars in cash.

He set up the quartz mill in Mosquito Gulch, Park County, and the planing mill was established in Denver. Both of these

John Smith

he sold at a large profit. The flour mill was a small, portable buhr gristmill, and, with it, he ground the first wheat and made the first flour ever made in what is now Colorado. He charged $1.50 a hundred for grinding and ten cents for sewing every sack. He also had a general store on Blake street. In the period of fifteen years between 1860 and 1875, John W. Smith erected five flour mills in this city; the one best known was the Excelsior Flour Mills, which he sold to J. K. Mullen. For many years he derived a large income from his milling interests alone.

He was one of the first to attempt to irrigate the dry plains. In 1863, he invested $40,000 in the construction of the Platte water canal, familiarly known as the Smith ditch, which is now owned by the city.

He erected, in 1868, the hotel named the American house; it was the first large building to have steam heat, and the first to have an electric elevator installed.

The opening of the American marked the beginning of smart functions, some of which have never been surpassed. All the distinguished people who came to Denver in the '70's were guests at the American.

John W. Smith was one of Colorado's most enterprising pioneers. Richard E. Leach, in his sketches of departed pioneers, says: "Not content with but one line of activity, he was, at different times in his career, merchant, miller, manufacturer, miner, irrigationist, hotel proprietor, banker and railroad builder, enjoying equal success in whatsoever pursuit he followed. Few men have scattered their energies over so large a field of endeavor without meeting with disaster in the end. Few men who gave their attention to such a variety of interests ever accomplished better results for themselves and for posterity."

Mr. J. K. Mullen

Another man shrewd enough to grasp the opportunities in the milling business was J. K. Mullen. He came in the early '70's, and, securing a position in a mill, studied the details of the business both from the mechanical and financial standpoint. His employers showed their appreciation of his industry by soon placing him at the head of the mill. In the course of a few years he bought the Excelsior Flouring Mills from John W. Smith. Later on, he began the construction of the Hungarian Flour Mills and installed the roller system of making flour in Colorado. Today

J. K. Mullen

he is operating ninety-one mills, elevators and warehouses in Colorado, Nebraska, Kansas, Utah and Oregon.

He has more acres of ground under cultivation than any other man in the State, except Governor Benjamin H. Eaton, and is president of the following companies: J. K. Mullen Land and Cattle Company of Lamar; Tamarack Land and Cattle Company of Logan County; The Harmony Land and Cattle Company of Logan County; Platte Land and Cattle Company of Platte County. The invested capital amounts to $5,000,000, and the business aggregates $18,000,000 annually.

Mr. Mullen is at the head of this vast business today, and is a splendid example to all young men as to what industry and energy can accomplish. He has built near his own home, beautiful homes for his four daughters. He and his estimable wife are spending the closing years of their lives surrounded by their children and grandchildren.

BANKS

The development of the banking business is another instance of the keen business sagacity of the early pioneers.

In September, 1859, Charles A. Cook and Jasper P. Sears formed the firm of C. A. Cook & Co., and came to Denver from Leavenworth, Kansas, with a stock of general merchandise. They were soon doing a flourishing business, mostly wholesale. The medium of ex-

Jasper P. Sears

change was gold dust at this time, and they gradually drifted into the purchase of it as a subordinate part of their business, with the ultimate result that they became full-fledged bankers. There arose a demand for small currency in trade, and, to meet this, Cook & Company issued script "shin-plasters," engraved on steel, of ten, twenty-five, fifty cents and one dollar denominations, redeemable in gold or other legal currency at their store bank.

The circulation of these "shin-plasters" proved a great convenience in the mining camps, and the face value of them was never discounted. When gold was at a premium during the Civil war, the private notes of the above named firm went to a premium also over the government notes.

All the old-timers remember "Jep" Sears, as he was familiarly called. He saw the city grow from a few log cabins and tents to be the metropolis of the West, and he took an honest pride in being one of its founders. He was a capital story-teller; his imagination could always supply all that was needed to embellish a story, and a slight impediment in his speech made his manner of telling it inimitable. He loved to tell about the time that he and his friend rode out toward the foothills to secure a deer for Christmas. He was mounted on a really good horse from the States, and his friend was on a broncho. A straggling band of Indians on the warpath discovered him and his friend and immediately gave the warwhoop. The race toward Denver was on. He quickly realized that his mount could easily run ahead of the ponies ridden by the Indians, but the broncho bearing his friend was a laggard. He was in the lead, but he was too chivalrous to abandon his friend, who was bending low and plying the whip with all his might. "Jep" kept looking back; he saw that the Indians were steadily gaining, and, growing uneasy, he shouted: "Come on,

The Development of Pioneer Enterprises

Bob; they are gaining on you," which brought from Bob the response: "Damn it, do I look like I was trying to throw this race?"

I heard him tell this story, and when he finished he laughed a long, loose laugh that rolled away into a thousand indescribable chuckles. Then he elevated his chin, which was a habit when about to draw a conclusion of some kind, and said: "Really, my friends, there is not much needed to make a merry Christmas; it is all a question of circumstances and how you look at it."

George W. Brown was the first banker and broker of the Territory. He opened his office in 1859. A few months later, Turner & Hobbs of Independence, Missouri, opened an office under the management of George W. Kassler. Both of these offices closed in the early '60's.

George W. Kassler was for thirty years actively and honorably identified with the business life of the city of Denver. He was always respected and esteemed by his associates.

George Kassler

Warren Hussey was one of the first private bankers and dealers in gold dust of prominence in Denver. In 1864, Hussey, in partnership with Mr. Nolan of Denver, established a like bank in Virginia City, Montana, at the rich gulch mines of Alden Gulch, and, about 1866, Hussey established a leading bank at Salt Lake City. He was one of the active and widely known business men of early Denver.

Austin M. Clark, Milton E. Clark and C. H. Gruber came to the new town on Cherry creek in 1859. They noticed that miners coming down from the hills with gold dust and bright yellow nuggets had no place in which to store it. So they built the two-story red brick structure on the corner of Market and Sixteenth. Over the door was the sign, "Bank and Mint." It was a square two-story brick building with a square flat turreted tower. The interior was finished quite sumptuously and was the show place of the town. The windows were heavily

barred and were made doubly secure by iron shutters. Denver was a wild town then and there was no telling when the "bank and mint" might be attacked by desperadoes bent on securing booty. The bank opened July 20, 1860, and George W. McClure was placed in charge of the minting department.

At first, only $20 pieces were coined, and they were of pure gold, thus exceeding in value the government

The Development of Pioneer Enterprises 173

coins with their alloy. The first smaller coin issued was a $10 piece, which was presented to William N. Byers, proprietor of the Rocky Mountain News.

In 1861, additional dies were secured to coin the $2.50 and $5 denominations, and these were coined with alloy, according to the United States standard, the pure metal being too soft for practical purposes. This money found a ready circulation, and, in a little less than two years, they coined and circulated over $3,000,000. They also issued handsome steel engraved $5 notes, payable in gold at the Clark & Gruber bank. These notes were quite elaborate affairs and bore engravings of Mr. Gruber and of Indians chasing a herd of buffalo.

In 1862, when the stringency of the money market, due to the Civil war, became so marked that the United States currency was at a discount for gold, the Clark & Gruber bank notes were in great demand. They were worth $5 in gold and the bankers were good for demand.

It might be a singular fact that paper money issued by a private firm in a little western town was worth considerably more than money issued by the United States government, but these Denver bankers had the gold back of their paper issue, while the United States then had not the like security.

It was not until 1862 that the legality of the Clark & Gruber money was brought into question. At that time it was decided that the best solution of the problem would be to have the government purchase the plant and establish a mint in Denver.

In 1862 the government purchased Clark, Gruber & Company's mint—the transfer was made March 3, 1863, and a brand new sign was placed over the door: "The Mint of the United States," but it did no coining, and was only for assaying and casting bullion.

In 1895, Congress appropriated $500,000 toward building a new mint in Denver. A site at West Colfax,

Evans and South Thirteenth streets was purchased, and the erection of the present magnificent building commenced. The passing of the old mint building removed almost the last of the landmarks in Denver of the '60's.

Charles B. Kountze

Mr. Luther Kountze came to Denver in 1862, and opened the second banking house of the series of private banks organized by the four Kountze brothers—Augustus, Herman, Luther and Charles B. Kountze. The first bank of this system was opened in Omaha by Augustus Kountze in 1856. The bank in Denver was in a corner of Walter S. Cheesman's drug store on Blake street. After the fire in 1863, the firm built a two-story brick building on the corner of Holladay and Fifteenth streets, and moved into it in 1865. The following year (1866) the bank became a national bank.

Charles B. Kountze came to Denver to enter the bank

in 1864, when nineteen years of age, and in 1866, at twenty-one, he became its first cashier. At the age of forty-six he was supreme controller of the Colorado

The Development of Pioneer Enterprises

National, an equal sharer in the First National of Omaha, and that of Kountze Brothers in New York. There is scarcely a western state in which he and his immediate family have not possessions.

Denver became the home of Mr. Charles B. Kountze, and banking was his permanent vocation. His fortune was not the result of greed, but the reward of honest industry, energy and the legitimate exercise of ability. He never sought his own advantage in the ruin of his fellows, but made profits in the general advancement of the community. He showed his faith in Denver by investing largely in real estate and helped to build up a greater Colorado.

Mr. Kountze was a man of irreproachable life, always generous and true, with a marvelous grasp of affairs and the courage of his opinions. He possessed the confidence and esteem of all who knew him. He married Miss Mary Estabrook, a woman of rare beauty and many fine personal traits. Her deeds of charity have helped many an unfortunate one over the rough path of poverty.

Their son, Mr. Harold Kountze, has the business instincts of his father, and has taken his place in the Colorado National Bank.

BOULDER

How Boulder Was Settled

While precedence is accorded to Denver as to date of location, the settlement at Boulder was almost simultaneous with that of the first goldseekers at the mouth of Cherry creek.

On the seventeenth of October, 1858, a party of emigrants pitched their tents near the site of Boulder. They built a number of log cabins and there laid the foundation of the town.

In the following January, Colonel J. S. Bull, Charles

Clouser, William Huey, W. W. Jones, James Aikens and David Wooley explored the adjacent canyon a distance of twelve miles, where they found gold. The canyon was named Gold Run, and the place of discovery Gold Hill. One hundred thousand dollars was taken from Gold Hill during the following summer.

Boulder has been, from its earliest days, a place of learning. The first school house built in Colorado was in Boulder, and it was built by everybody giving what they could. Mr. Nichols found a big tree, which he cut down, intending to donate it to the school. He went for a team to haul it to town, and when he returned a man had it on a wagon and was moving it off. Mr. Nichols demanded his property. The man refused, saying: "You will have to fight for it," which Mr. Nichols proceeded to do, and, after a hard fist combat, the rogue agreed not only to surrender the property, but to assist Mr. Nichols in getting it to town.

Some Pioneers

Mrs. Mary A. Ellis, a gentle, blue-eyed woman exquisitely fine in manner and taste, is proud of being the fourth school teacher in Boulder. There is no pride like

MRS. MARY A. ELLIS AND MRS. L. R. WIDNER

FIRST SCHOOL HOUSE IN BOULDER 1860

that of being able to impart knowledge. She taught seventeen classes in a half day, because every family brought school books across the plains and they were all different. Mrs. Ellis is full of the spirit of Colorado, and, at the age of eighty, writes verses expressing her love for the State. Mrs. L. R. Widner, who is over eighty, lives with her. They have been friends for fifty years, and it is beautiful to see those cultured and refined old ladies spending the evening of life together.

Mrs. Widner often comes to Denver to visit her daughter, Mrs. Platt Rogers, and when she gets tired of the style and fashion of the city, returns to the cottage in Boulder, where, with her old-time friend, she reaches the summit of contentment.

The pioneers of Boulder talk simply and without ostentation concerning the things which we of today call great—the hardships and inconveniences endured while building up the State.

The town was named because there were so many smooth, round boulders everywhere.

*Mrs. Annie A. Brookfield is the only woman survivor of the fifty-niners who founded Boulder. She was made queen of the carnival when she was eighty-eight years old. She is still a handsome woman, with silvery hair and a mild, humorous way of talking. She said: "Mrs. Safely brought the first set of chairs to Boulder. I have one of them in my house now. It's a rocker, and if you sit down in it you'll go right over on your face—it kicks like a broncho."

The first coal oil lamp in Colorado was owned by Mrs. Andrews of this city. Her house was partitioned with white cotton sheets, as was the custom in those days. The first night the lamp was lit the door was thrown open and the white walls added considerably to the bril-

---

*Mrs. Brookfield recently passed away.

liancy of that nocturnal luminary. The neighbors, who had been so long accustomed to the flickering rays of a "taller dip," thought the Indians had come and were burning the house.

Mr. Andrews was calling his cows, which they thought was a cry for help, and a neighbor rushed to his assistance, calling: "I'm coming, I'm coming." The alarm spread, and all the people in the town fled to a place of safety.

Colorado State University

The Colorado State University was incorporated by an act of the Territorial Legislature, but was not put well under way until Colorado became a State. Nothing concerning Boulder would be complete without special attention to this great educational institution. Its present state of excellence is due to the loyalty of the citizens of Boulder, and to the wise and energetic university presidents. The university was founded in 1875 through the influence of David H. Nichols. He was a representative from Boulder County in the Territorial Legislature.

The Legislature expressed its willingness to appropriate $15,000 for the building of a university, provided the citizens of Boulder would contribute the same amount. Mr. Nichols mounted a horse and rode to Boulder. He went among the citizens of the little town, and, in a few hours, raised the $15,000. The next day he rode back to Denver and secured the appropriation. The university opened its doors September 5, 1877, with two instructors and forty-four students. Dr. Joseph A. Sewell was the first president.

The ground, covering sixty-three acres, was donated by the citizens of Boulder, and with the buildings, was considered worth $35,000, and now the buildings and equipment are valued at $1,345,000.

The Development of Pioneer Enterprises

The second president, Mr. Horace M. Hale, was a careful economist. On one occasion, a caller found the president riding a sulky plow, with which he was shaping up the campus. "It saves $1.50 a day of the university funds," said President Hale.

James H. Baker, who assumed the presidency in 1892, tells that he once called on President Hale and found him puttying up the cracks in the window.

Dr. Baker was successful in building up this institution. Through his efforts it was carried over a very trying time. When the State University appropriation of $110,000 was not available, and there was doubt that the sum would ever be paid, Governor Thomas, after consultation with Dr. Baker, authorized a loan to cover the State's deficiency. Dr. Baker organized a committee, and the loan was secured, mostly from the people of Boulder, Denver and Pueblo. The State afterwards made good the loan.

Dr. James H. Baker

The State of Colorado owes Dr. Baker a debt of gratitude for the advancement and splendid educational standing of this institution.

The University of Colorado is the culmination of the public school system of the State, and is maintained by the State, to provide, at a minimum cost, higher and professional education for those graduated in the high schools. It enables them to pursue their studies at any extent and in any direction they may choose.

The university ranks in high standards and in all that pertains to true university work with such state universities as those of Michigan, Wisconsin and California.

The Chautauqua at Boulder is a magnet throughout the session for educators, clergymen and cultured people.

Boulder and Colorado Springs claimed the right to the anniversary of the quarto-centennial of Colorado as a State, and both towns celebrated. At Boulder, the pioneer days, the industrial and educational development of Territory and State, were reviewed by Governor James B. Orman, Senator H. M. Teller, Congressman James C. Bell, State Senator Barela, Mrs. Helen M. Grenfell, then State superintendent of public instruction, and the newly elected United States Senator, T. M. Patterson.

The city of Boulder is, at this writing, one of the most beautiful and bustling little cities in the State. The far-famed "Switzerland Trail," a railroad trip that is taken by thousands of tourists annually, is located in Boulder County.

South Boulder canyon, through which the Denver and Salt Lake Railroad runs to the top of the Continental Divide, is also located in this county.

Boulder County produces heavily in all avenues of agricultural development. The lignite fields of northern Colorado are in Boulder County, at Louisville and Lafayette. These supply most of the steam coal used in Denver.

Switzerland Trail

PART V
THE TERRITORY OF COLORADO

CHAPTER XII

ESTABLISHING LAW AND ORDER

The Migratory Legislature

The creation of the Territory by Congress gave the country a government of unquestioned authority, and the effect was in every way beneficial.

William Gilpin, upon assuming the duties of office in 1861, ordered a census taken, which showed a population of 25,331 in the Territory and 3,000 in Denver.

For a time the location of the capital was uncertain. The governor called the First Territorial Legislature, which was composed of thirteen representatives and nine councilmen from designated districts, to meet in Denver September 9, 1861. A small frame building where the McClintock block now stands was rented for the House of Representatives, and the Council was located in a building on Larimer

William Gilpin

street. At that session of the Legislature, by an act approved November 5, Colorado City was made the capital, and the time fixed for the meeting of the next session there in June, 1862.

Judge Wilbur F. Stone, who was a member of that Legislature, says:

"In the meantime, Congress, at that December session, had amended the organic act by increasing the number of the Territorial Council to thirteen members and the House to twenty-six, and these additional members were elected in December, 1861. Near the first of June, 1862, Delegate Bennet, at Washington, discovered that if the Legislature met in June there was no appropriation to pay for it, as June was in the same fiscal year as the preceding session, so he had Congress pass a joint resolution to change the date of the Legislative session from June to July. The members of the southern districts not having heard of this change met at Colorado City at the June date, where they learned the news and had to journey back home horseback, some of them one hundred and fifty miles.

"The Legislature assembled at Colorado City July 7th, the postponed date fixed by Congress, and organized by electing the speaker of the House, the president of the Council and the other requisite officers, but there were no conveniences for transacting business, or even living, in the little almost unoccupied village. The House met in the one room of a rough board building, unfinished and unfurnished, while the Council convened in a room used as the dining room and kitchen of the only boarding house in the place—a log structure kept by 'Mother Maggard.'

"Most of the members camped out, slept in their blankets in tents or on the open ground, cooked their own 'grub' and 'bached,' as in the mining camps. After spending four or five days in a grotesque sort of 'horse play,' the Assembly, by joint resolution, adjourned to hold the session in Denver. It was near sundown when, after much wrangling and many comic motions, resolutions and 'bills' were offered and ruled 'out of order,' that the joint resolution to adjourn—for a 'change of venue'—was adopted, and in fifteen minutes afterwards the Assembly broke camp, hitched up teams, saddled horses and mules, and a long caravan started up Monument creek toward the 'Divide' for Denver.

"The outfit traveled all night, singing songs and making speeches. At sunrise a stop was made for breakfast —such as could be had for man and beast—at Coberty's ranch, near Castle Rock, and about two o'clock of that day the dusty and very thirsty caravan trooped into Ferry street, West Denver, every man singing 'Old John Brown's Body' at the top of his voice.

"A detailed description of that nocturnal exodus of the pioneer Legislature from the first capital at the foot of Pike's Peak to the mouth of Cherry creek would present the most amusing historic episode in the annals of Colorado's genesis and evolution.

"That Legislature, which was held in Denver in commodious and well-furnished rooms on the west side of Cherry creek, contained as members a large proportion of men of distinguished ability and legislative experience. They passed a code of laws, civil and criminal, of an excellent character, and so well adapted to the needs and exigencies of the people, their pursuits, and the conditions of this country, that many of them, in substance, remain the laws of the State to this day."

At this session the capital was located at Golden City, where it remained until December 9, 1867, when an act was passed making Denver the capital, but this location was not made permanent until after statehood, when it was fixed by a popular vote of the State, under a provision of the State constitution, authorizing a general election for such purpose.

H. C. BROWN'S GIFT

Way out on the brow of what is now Capitol Hill, Henry C. Brown built a little frame house, in the spring of 1864, as evidence of his homestead right to one hundred and sixty acres—a quarter section—for which he had

filed a claim. When Mr. Brown began building his claim cabin, R. E. Whitsitt of the Denver Town Company appeared on the scene and wanted to know what he was doing there.

"I seem to be building a little house," replied Mr. Brown.

"You have no business to be building houses here," said Whitsitt. "This is included in the original plat of Denver City. You get right out."

"Dick, this is my land," said Mr. Brown, stepping

forward and emphasizing his words with his hammer. "I am not going to get out, and you can't make me."

Mr. Whitsitt uttered a sulphurous remark about "land jumper" and dashed down the hill. The town company entered no further protest against Brown's right to his one hundred and sixty acre tract. It is now known as H. C. Brown's Addition and Second Addition to Denver.

December 9, 1867, the Territorial Legislature moved the capital of Colorado from Golden City to Denver.

January 11, 1868, H. C. Brown donated to the Territory out of the heart of said tract, the ten acres bounded by Colfax, Grant, Thirteenth and Lincoln avenues, under the above act, as a site whereon to erect the capitol and other buildings. He did this upon the assurance and expectation that lands contemporaneously donated by John W. Smith, Henry M. Porter and Judge Clements would be at once sold and the moneys devoted to the erection of the capitol buildings thereon.

The Territory did nothing. August 1, 1876, Colorado was admitted into the Union as a State, and the location of its capital left to be determined by a subsequent vote of the people.

May 9, 1879, nothing having been done, Mr. Brown determined to force either the erection of the building, or else an abandonment of all claim to the land.

He therefore, on May 9, 1879, filed a deed of revocation and commenced to build a board fence around the land. As he anticipated, the State brought suit to recover the land, and, in 1881, passed an act levying a half-mill tax to erect a capitol building, and in 1883 voted $300,000 in bonds for the same purpose. The litigation was protracted. It went to the Supreme Court of the State, and twice to the Supreme Court of the United States. James H. Brown, the son of Henry C.

Brown, barely twenty-one at the time, represented his father therein.

January 4, 1886, the decision of the United States Supreme Court ended the litigation in favor of the State. The State then purchased the adjoining block between Lincoln avenue and Broadway from W. S. Cheesman and George W. Kassler for $100,000, and immediately commenced the construction of the present capitol building.

The Tenth General Assembly was the first to occupy it, in 1895.

The building received its finishing touches in 1900, and its total cost was $3,000,000. It was constructed entirely of granite and marble from our Colorado quarries.

In the governor's private office of the capitol building stands a life-size oil portrait of H. C. Brown, the gift of his son to the State.

Loyal to the Government

Gilpin's appointment was at the beginning of the Civil war. There was a strong southern element in Colorado, and many went to join the southern army. A majority of the people, however, were loyal to the government. A better illustration cannot be cited than that related by Judge Wilbur F. Stone:

"Soon after the Territorial organization, two young men who had been working for a miner at Gold Run, in Summit County, stole a large quantity of gold dust from their employer. They were pursued, captured, brought back to the gulch, tried by a 'miners' court' and sentenced to be hanged. In the meantime, A. C. Hunt, then United States marshal for the district of Colorado, learned of the affair while passing through Park County in charge of some prisoners, and at once dispatched to me a warrant for the arrest of the culprits, sending me, at the same time, a commission as deputy to execute the warrant. I was then at Buckskin Joe, in Park County, and, mounting my horse, rode with all speed over the range twenty miles to Gold Run, which I reached just as the crowd of nearly a thousand miners had gathered to see the execution.

"Under a pine tree two graves had been dug, and beside them was placed a wagon, upon which the two condemned criminals were standing with ropes noosed about their necks and fastened to the tree above, looking down upon their open graves and waiting the signal when the wagon should be drawn from under them. A hollow square of men with loaded rifles inclosed the wagon.

"I jumped upon a pine log and harangued the crowd, urging them to allow the prisoners a trial in the Territorial courts. The people feared an escape and were inflexible. The crisis had come. Suddenly breaking through the guard, and leaping upon the wagon, I claimed the criminals as my prisoners.

"Instantly, every rifle of the guard was leveled at me. Snatching the warrant from my pocket I held it up, showing the seal and the American eagle on the corner, and commenced in a loud voice to read the formal printed mandate of the warrant. 'The President of the United States to the Marshal of Colorado, greeting: You are hereby commanded to take the bodies of—' I got no farther with the reading than this, for those words were no sooner uttered than a voice in the crowd shouted: 'Boys, we can't resist the President of the United States. Hurrah for Abe Lincoln!' The crowd echoed the cheer, 'Hurrah for Abe Lincoln!' A serio-comic mixture of the sublime and the ludicrous. Immediately, the guns of the guard were brought to a 'present arms.' With my camp knife I cut the ropes which bound the prisoners, pushed them before me through the crowd, remounted my horse, and, accompanied by a single assistant—a stanch fellow named Bill Burdett, who was a faithful guard at the

State penitentiary at Canon City—marched back across the mountains in the night, by a lonely trail, and sent the prisoners to Denver, where they were tried, convicted and sentenced to a term of years in the penitentiary at Alton, Illinois.

"And so were the foundations of law and order laid by the pioneers."

The Civil War

News came that General Henry H. Sibley, in command of the Confederate forces of Texas and New Mexico, contemplated a campaign against New Mexico and Colorado. The little community here was in a gloomy and discouraged position, menaced by influences that were plotting to place Colorado in the Confederacy; isolated by six hundred miles of plains from the East; in the midst of tribes of savages, one couldn't tell what might happen in the interval of long waiting.

Governor Gilpin appreciated the gravity of the situation. He was a man of unwavering loyalty to the Union, and appointed his staff more on the lines of a military than a civil government. R. E. Whitsitt was adjutant general; John S. Fillmore, paymaster; Samuel Noer, quartermaster general, and Norton C. Fisher, purchasing agent. This at least proved the allegiance of his own constituents to the Union.

He issued a call for a regiment of volunteer troops with which to hold the Territory for the Union. Recruiting offices were opened in Denver, Colorado City, Golden and Boulder. Before the close of September the regiment was formed, but there was neither arms, ammunition, nor supplies for soldiers in Denver at that time, and no money in the treasury of the Territory.

The governor met the emergency in a way that he believed right and justifiable. He ordered his militia staff to go and buy all the guns they could find in Colorado, and issued drafts, directly upon the treasury at Washington, to pay for them. A mass of weapons, dissimilar in quality and structure, were soon collected— old rifles, shotguns, old muskets, and anything that resembled a firearm. In a few weeks one thousand men from the mountains and the glens rallied around him, in appearance a motley crowd, clad in all the odd fashions ever seen in a new mountain district, but never were there better soldiers than those who constituted the First Colorado regiment. John P. Slough was appointed colonel, Samuel F. Tappen, lieutenant colonel, and John M. Chivington, major. Chivington was asked to be the chaplain of the regiment, but he refused and asked that he be appointed to a fighting position.

This regiment received orders to proceed with all possible haste to Fort Union, New Mexico, and report to General Canby, who was in charge of the Federal troops, for service. At Fort Union they were given uniforms and arms. Pressing southward, they met Sibley's force at Glorieta Pass. Chivington, with about one-third of the command, was ordered to march to the west end of the pass, and his attack in the rear saved the day. Sibley's force was driven back into Texas. The heroic men of the First regiment, raised through the powerful efforts of Governor Gilpin, saved New Mexico to the Union and made the attempt to conquer Colorado a failure.

The Removal of Gilpin

When the drafts, amounting to $375,000, which Governor Gilpin had issued, on payment of military supplies and expenses, reached Washington, they were repudiated by the Treasury Department, and went to protest. The governor had no authority to use funds for military purposes. He was attacked by the infuriated holders of the drafts, and there was an uproar over them at Washington. He endeavored to obtain payment of the drafts by a personal visit, but was unsuccessful, and the matter finally became one for Cabinet consideration, which resulted in the removal of Governor Gilpin.

I knew him, and often talked with him. He was a man of vast historical, political and scientific information. He made a study of the onward march of civilization. I heard him talk in the early days of the possibilities of agriculture in Colorado by means of irrigation, and the development of the resources of the region by building railroads. He was the first to predict the connection of America with Northern Asia by a railroad through Alaska. It was called chimerical at that time, but would we call it so today? When Denver was just a village he made an effort to organize a company to build a railroad from Denver to the City of Mexico. He was laughed at as "visionary," but the enterprise has since been consummated. His aphorisms and quaint expressions were in the mouths of everyone. He spoke of Denver as the "mining laboratory of the world; the paragon of all geographical positions," and the mountains as the "cloud compelling peaks of the Rockies," and "the vertebrate Sierra of the continent." His constant dream was "the resplendent future of the Pacific Northwest." Above all, he was patriotic, and the saving of Colorado to the Union at the commencement of the Civil war was his greatest historic act. Colorado should never forget her debt of gratitude to Governor Gilpin.

He was an honest, brilliant man, and his personal character was beyond reproach.

Later, a second Colorado regiment was formed, and this force won great praise at the time of Price's invasion of Missouri in 1864.

The glorious fight made by the Colorado boys for the preservation of the Union should be kept fresh in the minds of the people.

The State has erected a monument to the memory of the

*Colorado Soldiers
of the Federal Army
Who Fell
During the Civil War*

From Milo H. Slater's dedicatory address, I quote the following: "During the Civil war, no other State or Territory in the American Union supplied to the Federal army so many soldiers in proportion to its population as did the Territory of Colorado. In making this statement, I am uttering no idle boast, but merely speaking a significant truth, a truth which is of historical value. It is a truth which reveals a distinct feature in the composite character of Colorado pioneers."

Captain J. D. Howland

In closing this chapter, I must speak of Captain John D. Howland, Colorado's famous artist, who came to Denver in 1858, when he was about sixteen years old. His precocity in art was then attracting attention. He had numerous adventures, and, in 1861, enlisted in Company B, First Colorado Infantry. He went to New Mexico with his regiment and took part in all its campaigns. After an exciting career as a soldier, he went to Europe to study art. As a soldier, he never gave up his drawing, and the sketches he made then furnished valuable material in later years. He returned to Colorado after five years of study and travel, and became a prominent figure in the life of the State.

He served as a member of the Indian peace commission, appointed by President Andrew Jackson after the massacre at Fort Kearney, and helped to bring about peace with the Sioux and other tribes. In later years, he devoted himself entirely to his art.

He made a strong fight for a place in the world of artistic endeavor, and he won. For years he has enjoyed wide fame, because of his studies of the native wild animals of the West, and his pictures are scattered over the earth, in salons and private collections. No one has painted the buffalo, Indian and coyote with the inspirational touch of "Jack" Howland. Apart from being a great artist, he possessed a strong personality, and, as Captain Howland, was delightfully interesting.

Always neatly dressed, his hat careened at a slight angle, his hair touched with gray, lending additional distinction to his expressive features, Captain Howland was for many years a striking figure on the streets of Denver. The Grand Army button always gleamed from his lapel, and he walked with a vigorous military step.*

*J. D. Howland passed away recently.

CHAPTER XIII

UNDER EVANS' ADMINISTRATION

FIRE

In May, 1862, President Lincoln appointed John Evans to succeed Governor Gilpin. He was a very different type of man from his predecessor—a captain in civil life. His administration extended to 1865 —a trying period in the pioneer life of Colorado.

John Evans

On the nineteenth of April, 1863, one-half of the business part of Denver was destroyed by fire. The alarm was given between the hours of two and three in the morning, and, before the town was fairly aroused, the flames had made such headway that all effort to extinguish them seemed unavailing. The most that could be done was to save the contents of the burning buildings.

The loss of property by this fire exceeded two hundred and fifty thousand dollars and embraced the principal business portion of the town. Before the wreck of the burnt district was cleared away, while the ashes were still hot and smoking, the work of rebuilding began. The new structures were principally of brick, and the indomitable energy that characterized the pioneer caused a fine city to spring up, and commercial transactions soon resumed their former bustling activity.

Denver's Volunteer Fire Department

There was a volunteer fire department in the pioneer days, and the first fire extinguished by this volunteer department was in August, 1860. The first chief was Phil Trounstine.

Although the business section of the town was burned in 1863, all efforts to establish a regular fire organization were unsuccessful until the city was found to be at the mercy of a band of incendiaries.

A meeting was held at the grocery store of C. C. Davis and Rodney Curtis, and the Denver Hook and Ladder Company No. 1 was formed.

March 25, 1866, the company ordered a truck, left to the selection of A. Jacobs, who was in Cincinnati on business at the time. Colonel Howard had a rude truck built at the government shops in West Denver, which he offered to the company for use in drills until their truck arrived, and it was gratefully accepted. A committee was appointed to select a uniform. which was as follows: Black eight-cone leather hat with white shield, tipped with a gilt eagle head; across the top of the shield the word "Denver," and below it a figure "1" crossed by a hook and ladder; red shirt with black necktie; black leather belt with the word "Denver" in white letters between a hook and ladder at the back, and black doe-skin trousers.

Boys in Fire Uniforms

The uniforms arrived about the first of July, and on the seventh of the month the company made its first appearance in full uniform. They took out the truck, paraded the streets, and made a run down Sixteenth street, and then down Larimer over the bridge. It must be remembered that the leading men of the town formed this fire company. The first ball of the company took place Christmas night, 1866, in Cole's hall on Larimer

street. The ladies of the city lent their assistance in decorating the hall. Loads of evergreen came from the mountains, while furniture, paintings and hangings were loaned by leading citizens.

These balls were held annually and were the chief social events of the city. Tickets to the balls were $10 each, which made them a source of revenue to the company. In 1867, the city purchased a fire bell for $1,200, and this was hoisted on a skeleton tower behind the fire house. A windstorm took the tower and bell down on Thanksgiving eve, but no damage was done. This bell was used until 1873, when a new one, weighing 3,600 pounds, cast from a piece of Spanish artillery of the date of 1697, which was captured by the United States troops at Vera Cruz, replaced it. The James Archer Hose No. 2 was organized January 31, 1872. This company had very fancy uniforms. After the ball, on one occasion, a large number went to the home of Mr. and Mrs. Samuel H. Fisher, where an elegant supper was in readiness. It was morning when the joyous party broke up, and the Archer hose boys, in their uniforms of white duck trousers, blue blouses with white satin collars and cuffs, had to walk home through a blinding snowstorm.

It was only a short time after the organization of the Archer Hose that the famous J. E. Bates Hose No. 3, and the Woodie Fisher Hose No. 1 were organized. Denver could now boast of a fire department consisting of one hook and ladder and three hose companies. The Holly system of waterworks was in operation, and about fifteen miles of water mains extended through the thickly populated part of the city.

The old bell was moved to the Archer hose house. Quite a contrast to our up-to-date fire department was the method of alarm. Upon the resignation of Mr. Trounstine, July 31, 1873, Joseph L. Bailey was appointed chief. He led the volunteer companies until April, 1875.

About this time the Broadway Hose No. 6 came into life. Looking over the list of charter members of this company, it would appear to be one of a directorate of some gigantic corporation or syndicate. Among the names are T. M. Patterson, Clarence J. Clark, R. F. Burrill, J. B. Vroom, T. N. Haskell, G. G. Symes, Charles A.

Treat, Bela M. Hughes, C. H. McLaughlin, John W. Horner, W. J. Berger and J. F. Brown.

In 1876, a huge fire tower was erected, and shortly afterwards a fire alarm system was introduced. Thomas S. Clayton was chief of the fire department at this time.

The crude but ever willing and enthusiastic Denver volunteer department saved millions to the city, and proved at many big fires that they were firemen of no mean caliber. The question of reorganizing the fire department on a paid basis was agitated for some time, but it was not until June, 1881, that any definite action was taken in the matter. Julius Pearse was appointed assistant chief of the paid fire department, and, shortly after, was made chief of the paid department. He served in that capacity until 1897, when he resigned to organize the Julius Pearse Fire Department Supply Company, which company he still heads in the capacity of president. Mr. Pearse has patented and manufactured numerous appliances used throughout the United States in fire fighting, and his company has the distinction of having installed and equipped ninety-five per cent of the fire departments in the West.

Cherry Creek Flood

Cherry creek, with its broad, sandy bed, was considered a very inoffensive stream. But, on the night of May 13, 1864, it swept through the town, carrying away in its mad course dwellings, saloons and business buildings. The old city hall that stood at the Blake street crossing was swept away, and, with it, the iron safe, which was never found afterwards, in which were the town records and various municipal documents, papers conveying real estate titles, and their disappearance caused the historic controversy called the "city lot question." The Rocky Mountain News building was on a foundation of large rough stones laid in the middle of the creek, connected with the banks by a board bridge on piles and which had been so constructed to establish itself on both sides during the rivalry between the two cities. Those huge stones were picked up and whirled away with the iron safe like chips of wood. The entire property, worth between ten and twelve thousand dollars, was carried away. John L. Dailey, one of the proprietors, and four of the employes were sleeping in the building and made a hasty escape in scant clothing. Many people were rescued from their falling houses in boats. August Mortz, on some wreckage, floated eighteen miles down the Platte before he could get ashore.

Said Mrs. Samuel Monk: "I heard a terrible sound rolling through the air, like the discharge of a cannon.

MRS. SAMUEL MONK

CHERRY CREEK FLOOD

I threw open the door and beheld a gigantic wave, like an approaching Niagara, reflecting on its crest the light of the moon. At first it was slow and majestic in its movements, then it came faster and faster, mounted higher and higher, tearing up solid soil until it held in suspension nearly half its volume in sand. Trees were toppled down, houses fell, and everybody rushed in fright away from the mad torrent.

"After the sorrowful tales were told and the gloom wore away, we found much to laugh at. One lady awoke her husband and asked him to get up and see what was the matter; 'she heard a noise like the screaming of people.' He said it was the wind, and gave himself up to sleep, but she 'refused to be comforted,' and aroused him again. He said, 'If I go to the door and look out, I suppose you will be satisfied.' Stepping on the floor, he plunged knee-deep in water. Then, muttering a few crusty words about leaving the children's bathtub in the middle of the floor, he took another step, only to discover that something was radically wrong. They were saved from a watery grave by the gallant men on horses, who were dashing through the surging waves, rescuing families from their flooded homes."

Cherry creek left the old bed and broke another for itself farther north, undermining the bluffs, and, by the various magic of created things, formed new knolls and mounds, which stood fixed and permanent in their sudden heights as if the Divine Architect was remodeling the earth.

Many slept peacefully through it all, awaking long after the sun's bright beams had dispelled the darkness and revealed their narrow escape from death. West Denver was overflowed, stretching as a lake half a mile west to the Platte river, and people were rescued from houses surrounded by water for two or three days after the flood came.

One man's house was torn from its foundations and carried by the flood wave to a hill, where it was stranded like the ark on Mt. Ararat. The next morning, when viewing the topography, he exclaimed: "Has the earth been turned upside down, wrong side out, or have I lost my wits?"

A gentleman living on the North Side advertised:

"Lost—On the night of the nineteenth, four first-class building lots. They are probably stateward bound. Anyone who will overtake and return them will be liberally rewarded by the owner."

Another requested the removal of other people's lots from his real estate.

A negro woman and five children took a deck passage on their cabin roof for a couple of miles, and were safely anchored on the limbs of a cottonwood tree.

The loss was heavy, and fifteen or twenty people were drowned.

Within a month, Byers & Dailey built the Commonwealth printing establishment and resumed publication of the News.

Robt. W. Speer

Of course, there were many theories and speculations about water spouts, cloudbursts and so on. When the facts were developed, it was found to be the result of a storm on the Divide, of rain and hail alternately, which raged almost continuously for several days. One good effect of the flood was the washing away of all hostile or sectional feelings between the east and west divisions of the city.

The turning of the bed of Cherry creek was

then energetically discussed, and became an intermittent disease with which Denver was afflicted until Robert W. Speer became mayor in 1904. He solved the problem by confining the stream in a narrow channel with stone and cement walls. The space back of each wall was filled in and edged with trees, paved roadways and lights. The Speer boulevard is today an attractive driveway.

CHAPTER XIV

THE INDIAN WAR

The Reign of Terror

To call it the "reign of terror" but feebly expresses the state of affairs existing in Colorado in 1864.

Occasionally a straggling Indian, mounted on the inevitable pony, would ride straight up to the windows (for fences were few and far between in those days), flatten his face against the window pane and scream, "How," which, although a polite greeting enough, served to frighten timid women and children well nigh out of their wits. A lady, in replying to such a salute, opened her mouth wide and lifted her false teeth out on her tongue. The Indian, who had never seen the like before, regarded her as a spirit, and beat a tumultuous retreat.

One day as Mrs. Steck was arranging her bonnet before a glass, by the side of her serene face was reflected the squalid features of a squaw, who had stolen into the room unawares, and seeing her own image in the glass, was thrown into a paroxysm of delight by contemplating her beauty, perhaps her toilet, which was nothing more than a string of beads around her neck and a blanket about her waist. Beyond the advantage of protection from the weather, they were in the most unsophisticated ignorance as to the ordinary uses of clothing. But so great was their vanity they would give anything they possessed for a mirror.

The Hungate family, father, mother and children, had been murdered at a short distance from Denver, and threats had been made to sack and burn the city. The nerves of the people were strung to the highest tension, and they were ready for a panic at the least intimation of danger.

Late one evening a man dashed into town, frightened almost out of his senses, and reported that a large company of hostile Indians were driving off stock and murdering the ranchmen. The scene that followed was indescribable. Every bell in the city sounded the alarm. Men, women and children pushed through the streets *en deshabille*, and literally crazed with fear. The United States branch mint was prominent among the places of refuge. In the general alarm, wells, cisterns, dark alleys and dry goods boxes became hiding places for the terror-stricken inhabitants. One man said to another, "My gun has been idle for so long, I wonder if it will go off; I believe I will shoot at that dry goods box and see." Immediately the box rose up on two legs, and a voice from within shouted, "Don't shoot."

Mrs. Sears stopped to leave things in order, and pack her new silk dress in a valise which she intended to carry on her arm; her delay excited the alarm of her son, "Jep" Sears, who went in search of her. She saw him coming, and supposing him to be an Indian, she made a rapid exit from the back door. He followed, calling her to stop. The old lady, being a little deaf, failed to catch the words, but the voice excited her all the more, and impelled to her highest speed, she never stopped until she reached a place of safety, where, trembling and exhausted, she discovered she had been running away from her own son.

So great was the confusion incident to the fright, it is believed that one hundred Indians could have taken the city.

The armory was opened and the arms distributed to the distracted men, who rushed around like peripatetic arsenals.

Mr. Rodney Curtis, then a dapper young man of Denver, heard that it was a false alarm, and made all possible haste to the mint, to relieve the fears of the panic-stricken people. Said Mr. Curtis: "Just as I stepped inside the door, a woman rushed up to me and said, 'Hold my baby while I go and find my other children.' With that she placed the child in my arms and dashed wildly away through the crowd. I experienced an overflowing sensation of goneness. It was done so suddenly that I could not state to a certainty who the mother was.

"The little fellow fixed his big eyes on me and commenced to screech. I couldn't walk with him, the crowd was too dense. I bounced him up and down, sang all the Mother Goose melodies that I knew, whistled and smiled at him, while I felt as savage as a Sandwich Islander. There is no romance in taking care of other people's children.

"He yelled incessantly. I looked at my watch; an hour had gone. Saints and angels; why had she perpetrated this joke upon me? I gave the baby another bounce. He knocked my hat off, caught at the end of my cravat and tore that off. And I was in a very dilapidated condition when the mother finally appeared. She commenced to apologize, but I stopped her, by saying: 'Don't speak of it.' I meant it, too, for it was too dreadful to talk about. After pulling myself together, I mounted a goods box and exclaimed: 'It is a false alarm.'"

A train of Mexican freighters camping for the night, about fifteen miles east of Denver, were throwing their arms high in the air and shouting at their unruly cattle, which caused the headlong arrival of the ranchman into the city, who so admirably succeeded in imparting his fears to the citizens.

The city soon resumed its businesslike tranquillity, but the great scare furnished a topic for conversation long after.

These panics were not confined to Denver alone. A

Mrs. C——, who owned a ranch way up the country, had sent her men out to gather in the stock. While sitting alone in the house, cogitating on the various Indian rumors, she began to feel afraid, and looking out the back door she saw an Indian in the willows. She remembered hearing the boys say something about having seen fresh tracks in that gulch, and now she was satisfied that they were Indian tracks. There were sixty guns in the chamber above, that had been left there by the government, and quick as thought she rushed upstairs, seized a gun, rested the muzzle on the floor and while examining it to see if it were loaded, it went off, sending the bullet with such force that it tore up the floor, went through and through her new patent churn in the kitchen and battered up the milk pans in the cellar most shamefully. Without stopping to meditate on the danger and power of that weapon, she took another, tore out a port-hole, and seeing the black head just above the willows, she took aim and fired. The bark flew in every direction, and lo and behold, in the heat of her imagination, she had shot an old stump.

The ranchmen clubbed together, built forts and block houses, and moved their families to them for safety.

Capturing Spotted Horse

Spotted Horse was the chief of a band of Indians who, by their savage atrocities, caused a reign of terror along the Platte in the spring of '64. Houses and barns were burned for a distance of two hundred miles; men, women and children were massacred in a most terrible manner.

Spotted Horse, with his small band of warriors, hideous with paint, feathers and shot-gun, had Denver effectually besieged. There were troops at Fort Kearney, four hundred miles east, but they made no effort to pun-

Indians Attacking Stage Coach

ish the murderers. Occasionally, with colors flying, they escorted an immigrant wagon or freight train and gently pushed the playful Indians back.

Their kindness was carried a little too far; it was about to step into eccentricity. Matters began to assume a solemn form. It was death to the pioneers from starvation and the tomahawk, or death to Spotted Horse and his band.

At this critical moment the "Colorado First," a regiment of brave men who volunteered to fight the rebellion, returned from New Mexico.

Major Downing, with a fraction of his regiment, consisting of about sixty-five men, was ordered to proceed down the Platte and clear the road.

The major had won a reputation for undaunted bravery. "Sure," said Mike, "he is a very Daniel; he has a charmed life. I have seen him sit on a high rock, in the thickest of the fight, and repair his revolver when the bullets were falling thick around him, and never a wound did he get. I have seen his coat perforated with holes like a sifter, and a twenty dollar gold piece mashed to a cup in his vest pocket, yet there is not a scar on his body, and I'll venture to say he will never be found dead walking around."

Jacob Downing

Spotted Horse, a bloodthirsty and cunning Indian, was a formidable foe.

But the major, cool, deliberate and calculating, was equal to the occasion. He reached the American ranch one hundred and forty-five miles below Denver, where Spotted Horse and his warriors made their rendezvous, and pitched his tent.

As he sat in his camp one morning viewing the country through a field glass, he saw a man dressed in citizen's clothes on the opposite side of the river. He immediately detached ten or twelve men to capture him, and if possible to bring him to the camp alive, for he knew from his walk that he was an Indian, probably one of their scouts on a tour of observation.

When brought into camp he proved to be none other than the famous Spotted Horse.

The major surveyed him for a while in meditative serenity; then offered the Indian, who sat in sullen silence, his life, if he would surrender his band. This he refused to do.

He then ordered his men to drive a stake and prepare to roast the Indian alive.

The chief gathered his coat around him and sat contemplating his funeral pyre with stoical indifference.

When the fire was kindled the major gave orders to bind him to the stake, saying, "You have seen many a white man die this horrible death, and now we propose to let you know how it is yourself."

This unnerved him; he pleaded for his life, and promised to lead the soldiers to his camp. The terms were agreed upon, and in the shortest possible time the command was moving, with Spotted Horse strapped on a horse in advance.

They camped that night in a little ravine, and the chief informed them that his warriors were only a few miles ahead, up the canyon that they were approaching.

About eleven o'clock at night the major and his command stole away, leaving the camp fires burning to make the Indian scouts believe that they were still there. Reaching the spot designated by Spotted Horse, early in the morning, the order was given to halt and form in line of battle.

At a given signal he opened fire. The Indians made a bold resistance, but finally surrendered.

This was the first Indian battle in Colorado, and the result was, forty killed and one hundred wounded, their village destroyed and their chief a prisoner.

Spotted Horse was sent to Washington, and afterwards went to Europe with a showman, where he was gazed upon by thousands as a fine specimen of the North American Indian.

Peace was restored along the Platte, and Major Downing sustained the loss of only one man.

Taking the Baby to His Father

In the spring of 1864 the Indians started on the warpath. Stages and wagon trains were waylaid and passengers massacred. For a time communication between Colorado and civilization was almost stopped; the road was dotted with the bones of the dead and sprinkled with the blood of the wounded and slain.

An incident more vivid and thrilling than any of fancy's written tales, and highly illustrative of the anguish of mind and body endured by the traveler during those perilous times, was told to me by Mrs. Bowman, a very interesting and intelligent woman.

"I was full of youth and vivacity and my constant buoyancy of spirit made me a joy to my friends. My husband had left me and my beautiful baby boy in Atchison, where I waited impatiently his summons to join him in Denver. After a few months he wrote of being lonesome, and of his great desire to see the baby. I decided

The Territory of Colorado

to go to Denver and take the baby to his father. I knew that Ben Holladay had withdrawn his coaches, and the United States mail had been discontinued, because of Indian depredations, but I feared no evil. I never borrowed trouble, and had one risen from the dead and prophesied the danger before me, I would not have believed. My husband telegraphed a friend to see that everything was provided to make my journey as pleasant as possible. Accordingly, I was fitted out with a light wagon, nicely covered, and drawn by two spirited, fleet-footed mares. I hired a negro driver, by the name of Lee Ayres, a large, strong man and known to be perfectly trustworthy. I also engaged a white man to assist in attending the team and help about the camp. My companion was a woman, somewhat older than myself. I had known her from childhood and called her 'Muzzey.' She was a very devout Christian, and exacted of me a promise that I would not travel on Sunday. I said, 'All right, "Muzzey," you can pray and I will watch.' The fact of our husbands both being in Denver formed a strong sympathetic link between us, and the hope of meeting them inspired us with courage to undertake the hazardous journey.

"For the first four days out, we lingered with a train of ox teams. Picturesque Indians with feathers in their hair, crowded about us, begging for whisky and swearing in pure English. They had acquired a Billingsgate vocabulary of unrivaled opulence.

"A kind friend, thoughtful of protecting my complexion, made me a lavender berage sun-bonnet, lined with pink, and finished with a long skirt; they were greatly in vogue in those days. An Indian, regarding it as a curiosity, snatched it from my head, placed it on his own, and went galloping over the plains, performing wild and dexterous evolutions, with the long gauzy skirt of the bonnet floating around his head like a cloud.

"True to my promise, when Sunday came, we camped. I can never forget that Sunday's camping on the plains. It added ten years to my life. The sun seemed to stand still, and I thought, if this is time, what is eternity?

"Ten days after we left Atchison, the telegraph wires were cut and the operators deserted their stations. We met men on horseback, who rode wildly from ranch to ranch, heralding the news of savage warfare. They told us the Indians were on the outbreak back of us. We could not retrace our steps, so we left the ox teams and pushed forward. I stopped at Fort Kearney and asked for an escort, but was gruffly refused. All that was left to us was to go on. When evening came, we were out on the rough green plains that 'no man reaps,' in the midst of an eternal and infinite solitude, with the horrible death at the hands of the 'red man' staring us in the face. My heart seemed beating a funeral march, my watch served only to arouse the old superstition of 'death ticks.' Oh, what a procession of phantoms went moving through my highly excited brain.

"Between four and five in the morning, when it was beginning to look rosy in the east, we stopped in a little ravine to feed our horses and eat our breakfast. Lee Ayres, in a feeble effort to dispel the gloom, said, 'We are just like morning glories, out the first thing in the morning.'

"Suddenly our attention was arrested by a smoke that rose higher and higher, and grew blacker and blacker, until the whole heavens seemed to be draped in mourning. Lee Ayres climbed to the top of the wagon and gazed, as if looking into some destruction; his countenance betokened a soul stricken dumb. At last, in smothered tones, he said, 'Oh, my God! We are gone.' The ox trains in front of us were all on fire. The black smoke from the burning bacon drifted towards us and prevented the savages from seeing our little wagon in the ravine. The agony that we suffered made that half hour a living age. We felt that death was overshadowing us and we knelt in prayer. The good woman at my side seemed to be whispering her dearest secrets into the ears of God. Her face shone with a heavenly light, that fell upon me like a benediction, and I felt resigned to say, 'Father, not my will, but Thine, be done.' Lee Ayres said, 'I will crawl on my hands and knees up the ravine, until I can command a better view, and if I find that death is inevitable, you must kill your baby, I will kill you and then kill myself; they cannot have us alive.' 'Kill my child!' I cried. 'My dear little innocent babe. Oh, no! I can never do that.'

"When Lee returned his face was lit up with renewed hope. He said, 'The Indians are gone and we will make the drive for life.' As we neared the conflagration, the horses became unmanageable, and the one on the right jumped out of the traces. The Indians had gotten some distance up the ravine when they caught a glimpse of our moving wagon. They turned with a fiendish whoop and commenced firing upon us.

"The white man sprang to the tongue of the wagon, and, drawing a knife commenced to cut the harness from the horses, saying that he intended to make his escape.

" 'Stop,' commanded the negro, leveling his revolver at him; 'if you cut another strap you die.' The miserable wretch crouched on the tongue and watched him with glittering eyes. The Indians were rapidly gaining upon us.

"The negro driver said to me, 'Give your baby to Muzzey and drive, while I shoot at the Indians.'

"Superhuman strength seemed to be given me. I clasped my child to my breast with one hand and seized the reins with the other. The horses went dashing, rearing, plunging around burning wagons. On either side were horses and oxen struggling in the agonies of death, and men dead or dying, wrapped in winding sheets of flame.

"All passed before me like a horrible panorama and left an indelible picture on my mind. On we went, our ears ringing with the whoops of the Indians and our wagon top stuck full of arrows. When we reached the top of the hill, we could see Thompson's ranch, the point for which we were striving, for there they had arms and ammunition.

"Presently we heard a bugle sound, and the clear, liquid tones were sweeter than any music I ever heard before or since. It seemed to my troubled soul that heaven had opened and the strain floated from the angel choir. We bent our heads in thanks.

"My husband had gone to Fort Cottonwood, secured a guard of sixty soldiers and set out to meet us. He lifted me from the wagon. I laid the baby in his arms, saying, 'I have brought him to his father.'

"With eager joy he drew the veil from the baby's face. Like a piece of rare sculpture he lay, the long lashes rested upon his marble cheeks, and the golden locks clustered around his chiseled features that bore no trace of pain—dead, dead, my baby was dead.

"All grew dark around me and I fell senseless at my husband's feet. Heart and brain were both shattered. It seemed that my faculties would never recover their former intelligence; for weeks and weeks the savage war whoop rang in my ears, and my feverish lips murmured, 'Taking the baby to his father.'"

Battle of Sand Creek

The scope of this work does not admit of a detailed account of the part our pioneers took in the Civil War or of the Indian wars. I shall tell only enough to show

The Territory of Colorado

what the pioneers encountered in the upbuilding of the State.

In the autumn of 1860, the Arapahoes and Cheyennes, under a treaty, ceded their lands here to the general government and left this part of the country for their reservations. Their hearts were filled with hatred for the white man.

The war between the States took so many men from Colorado, that the Indians believed it to be their opportunity to unite in a general uprising, to drive out and exterminate the whites and place themselves in possession again of the entire country.

Colorado was made a separate military district and Colonel Chivington was placed in command. He came to Denver in 1860 as the first presiding elder of the Methodist Episcopal Church in the Rocky Mountain district. When the Civil War broke out, he stepped from the pulpit to the battle field, without any military training whatever. There was in him the peculiar quality of the great warrior, that made men willing to follow wherever he led.

The Indian uprising through 1864 had grown to be somewhat terrible. Governor Evans held peace councils with them, to no effect.

General Curtis notified the governor that peace was not to be made with the Indians without his instruction.

Denver was threatened with famine; all provisions had to be hauled here from the Missouri River in wagon trains; freighters could not venture out; the glare of burning houses could be seen from the city at night; stage stations were burned; men, women and children were horribly butchered.

During the excitement, the Third Regiment was enlisted to serve for one hundred days in a campaign against the Indians. "I saw the mounting of that regiment," said a pioneer, "and it was funny. You see, to fight the Indians it was necessary to be mounted, but how to do it was a perplexing question, for horses were scarce in the country. The Ford brothers had brought in one thousand California bronchos. They made a proposition to the quartermaster to furnish horses, which was accepted. Ford employed professional horse trainers, and after a few days of choking and throwing, the horses, tired and exhausted, but not tamed, were reported ready for use.

"The soldiers went out on the prairie for their evening drill, and the prancing steeds were led, four abreast, and placed in position. The commanding officer rode up and down the line, and viewed his soldiers.

"He thought he had never looked upon a fairer sight, and straightening himself with stately grace, he gave the command to mount. The attempt to execute this maneuver startled the horses out of their senses; some of them stood straight up in the air on their heels, and quickly reversed the position; some stuck their heads down, clumped their feet together, and elevated their backs with such force that the men were sent skyward, and the horses passed all the jack-rabbits on the way, in their efforts to get out of the country. But the Third Regiment was afterwards mounted, and the exploits of that fine body of men deserve the gratitude of every citizen in Colorado.

"On the 29th of November Governor Evans issued a proclamation of war against the Arapahoes, Cheyennes, Sioux and all who were on the warpath. Shortly after, the hundred days men, under the command of Colonel Chivington, fought the battle of Sand Creek, which was considered by the philanthropists of the East one of the greatest Indian massacres of modern times. But it brought peace and quiet to the terror-stricken people of Colorado, by crippling the power of the most numerous and hostile tribe of the plains, and men resumed their struggle for daily bread without fear of the savage."

Congress took notice of the public indignation, and the result of the Congressional investigation was that Colonel Chivington was removed and Colonel Thomas Moonlight was placed in command of the Colorado military district. But Colonel Chivington was sustained by almost every frontiersman, and all who were familiar with Indian character. Jim Baker was heard to say that the Sand Creek affair did more to command the fear and respect of the Indians than all the other fights put together. It broke their power and they were compelled to accept the reservation system, which practically ended the savage war in Colorado.

Colonel Moonlight had a laughable experience some time later. He was in command of a company of mounted troops and was close upon a band of Indians, far down the Platte. One night while the colonel and his men were in camp, the savages adroitly managed to steal and run off every one of the horses, leaving him and his men to foot it out of the Indian country. The Indians were so pleased with their brilliant achievement in horse stealing that they let the colonel and his troops go unmolested.

Treaty With the Indians

A treaty was made with the Indians in 1867 whereby the Arapahoes, Cheyennes, Kiowas and Comanches gave up their lands east of the Rocky Mountain range and settled upon the reservations provided for them in the Indian Territory. In 1868 they repudiated the act and began a general assault upon the borders of Colorado, which was followed by many bloody scenes similar to those of the outbreak in 1864-65.

General Sherman, who took command of the department in March, 1868, received orders to drive the Indians out of the country, but his forces were scattered and not sufficient in numbers for speedy effect. August 28, the mutilated remains of Mrs. Henrietta Dieterman and her boy, about five years of age, were brought into Denver. The exhibition of the dead bodies excited fierce indignation.

It was impossible to get either troops or ammunition from Fort Hays, Reynolds or Wallace, and Secretary Hall, who was then acting governor, called for volunteers to carry a message to the officer in command at Fort Wallace. Theron W. Johnson and a man whom he selected were chosen for this perilous undertaking. They ran the gauntlet and delivered the message. The result was that Colonel George A. Forsythe, with a body of fifty scouts, moved toward the Republican River. He reached the Arickaree branch of the Republican, and while encamped, he was attacked by a force of seven hundred Indians. Finding himself overpowered, he retreated to a small island in the Arickaree, where he was immediately surrounded. The little band dug rifle pits from which they repelled a number of furious charges. The fight was continuous; their courage and daring are without a parallel in the annals of border warfare.

Twenty-one of the fifty scouts were killed and the survivors resolved to perish to the last man rather than surrender.

They fought off their assailants for three days, when the Indians began to withdraw.

Meanwhile two brave men crawled through the lines of the beseigers by night, made their way to Fort Wallace, and upon their report, Colonel Bankhead proceeded with a small force to Forsythe's relief. By this time, under orders from Sheridan, fifteen companies were then marching to the borders of Colorado. Soon the Federal troops had control of the situation and in due time peace was restored by driving the Indians out of the country and keeping up the pursuit until they could fight no longer, ending with Custer's terrible slaughter of the Cheyennes,

Arapahoes and Kiowas under Black Kettle on the Washita, where one hundred and two warriors were left dead upon the field, the old Black Kettle being numbered among the slain.

The dispersion of the Indians from Colorado was owing chiefly to the industrial acquisition of the white man, and would make a history in itself. The Southern Utes have been allotted a reservation in the southwestern corner of the State, and there is found the only remaining relic of savage life in Colorado.

CHAPTER XV

THE GROWTH OF DENVER

The Lot Question

The early pioneers of Denver were merely "squatters." They could acquire no valid title to lots, for the Indian right, as first in possession, extended over the land. An effort was soon made to provide a remedy by law for this peculiar condition. In 1860, by a treaty with the Arapahoes and Cheyennes at Bent's Fort, the title passed to the United States. It was difficult to get Congressional attention, owing to the important demands of the Civil War, and it was not until 1864 that Congress passed the "Grant bill," a law which was called, "The Relief of the People of Denver, Colorado Territory." It was intended to correct all defects of title growing out of the conditions under which Denver was founded. Out of it grew the "lot question," which caused bitterness of feeling, personal animosities and great public excitement. Even the Cherry Creek flood was drawn into it, to account for the loss of records that were in the "old safe," which was washed away and never found. But the victims of the loss strongly asserted that the titles were destroyed in some other way. It was long before the bitter feeling aroused by the "lot question" passed away.

How Broadway Was Laid Out

In 1859, Thomas Skerritt, with his sixteen-year-old bride, traveled over the plains in an ox team, from Chicago to Denver. Where Englewood is now located he took up six hundred acres of land, in 1864, and lived there continuously to the day of his death.

For the public guidance as well as for his own convenience he secured the service of surveyors to mark off with stakes the section lines bordering his ranch lands and extending towards Denver. He then locked the back wheels of his heavy wagon, and made a straight track, by the aid of the section line stakes, all the way from his house to Cherry creek.

Three times back and forth went the wagon, and when the work was done there stretched away in unswerving line across the prairie what is now the busy thoroughfare of South Broadway—that portion of Broadway south of Cherry creek.

David J. Cook was widely known in territorial days as a pathfinder, officer of the law and private detective. He was a terror to evildoers in the times when border outlaws and thieves needed to be ruled with an iron hand. No desperado ever escaped him. If he took the trail after a band of marauding Indians, horse thieves or highway robbers, he never returned empty-handed. He knew that his errand meant death to him if he failed; the criminals of the border neither gave nor asked quarter. If they got a drop on an officer of the

David J. Cook

law, they ended his career with a bullet through the heart. General Cook wrote a book entitled "Hands Up," in which he related numerous experiences with bandits and criminals in the mountains and on the plains.

He served as a peace officer continuously from 1866, and died a member of the police force, at seventy-one years of age. He bore a reputation for personal bravery unsurpassed by any western official. He was polite, modest and retiring and seldom took credit for his deeds of daring.

Sam Howe, the veteran detective of the Denver police department, is the oldest officer in term of service

Sam Howe

in the State. He was appointed a member of the Denver police force in 1873. When he went to Marshal Hopkins, after receiving the appointment, Hopkins said, "He won't last long." But the frail looking young man was soon a terror to evildoers, and to quote Mr. Howe, "has lasted 'bout as long as the rest of that bunch." His famous "scrap-books" contain many of his thrilling adventures. The wildest tale of the dime novel manufacturer is an idle prattle when compared to the real story of Sam Howe's career.

Old Lige

Among the prominent personages in Denver from 1864 to 1886, was old "Lige." He was colored, but he wasn't a plain, ordinary black man; he was an individual, and his name was high-sounding, Mr. Elijah Wentworth; but no one knew him by that name, for every man, woman and child in Denver called him "Lige;" even tourists knew him by the name "Lige" and laughed over the comical darky. He was an essential figure at that time and as often quoted as the "all kinds of shoe laces" man of today.

"Lige" was bow-legged and gray-haired and his age was an unsolved mystery. He had no particular calling, but he often said, "I'm handy at most anything," which he proved by always having plenty of money. He was "barker" for hotels and rang an old bell while he told in his own peculiar way the attractions of that particular hotel. Many a one was induced to remain and see Denver grow by the eloquence of old "Lige." He was a great booster for Denver.

But his real fame was in restoring straying and lost children to anxious and weeping parents. This was "Lige's" specialty. He would sing rhymes of his own making and ring his bell from one end of the city to the other until the child was found. His voice was loud and far-reaching; but one day a voice called him, and "Lige" went willingly to his home beyond.

Old "Lige"

THE FIRST GROCERY BUSINESS

"The foundation for Denver's grocery business," said Mr. S. T. Sopris, "was laid in 1860, by Captain Scudder and Freeman B. Crocker. A small tent was used for sleeping quarters and for storage of goods at night, but business was transacted out in the street under the shadow of cottonwood trees. A wheelbarrow answered as delivery wagon for articles that customers could not carry home. Captain Scudder pushed the wheelbarrow and was usually whistling or singing as he went. He had been captain of a fishing boat, sailing from Gloucester, Mass.; he was a jolly soul, a typical New England coast skipper.

They were good men, those pioneer merchants, and they became prominent in mercantile and political affairs. Scudder was a county commissioner for two or three terms and a member of the first Territorial Legislature for two or more terms. Crocker was active in the organization of our public schools, a member of the city council, county commissioner for many years and at the time of his death was president of the board of public works. He was always spoken of as a worthy public official.

Captain Scudder

Early Day Amusements

Denver has been from its earliest history, a great theatrical center. The first theater was opened October 24, 1859, in a building known as the Apollo, which was built by the Barney brothers. The company that opened it was run by C. R. Thorne, who produced a line of legitimate performances. In the opening play, "Richard III." he played the title role himself.

Apollo Hall in the Early '60s

The company soon went to pieces. Then Madame Wakely came, and her players became prime favorites.

The Territory of Colorado

Other companies appeared from time to time at the Apollo. Jack Langrishe was the first of importance. Mike Doherty was with him; he was one of the best Irish comedians that had been seen in the West.

Then a large theater of wood was built on the corner of Sixteenth and Lawrence. It was opened November 30, 1861, and shortly after came into the possession of Langrishe, who maintained a stock company here.

This theater was destroyed by fire. Soon after the fire the Governor's Guards building was erected. A stage was built at one end of the large hall and concerts were frequently given there, with an occasional theatrical performance.

In 1876 N. C. Forroster came to Denver at the head of a good company and played at Guards' hall. Theatrical performances were continued here until the Tabor Grand opera house was opened in 1882.

Society

The Goss girls, Hattie, Kate and Dell, were favorites in society in the early days. Their home was in Boulder,

HATTIE GOSS   MRS. GEO. CLARK   DEL GOSS

but they attended the social affairs in Denver. Dell married Rodney Curtis; Hattie, Fred Zell; and Kate married

George T. Clark, one of the early mayors of Denver, who was called the "boy" mayor because of his youth at the time of holding office. The George Clarks had the first piano ever brought to Denver. It was a small square piano of rosewood, inlaid with pearl.

Mrs. Clark is still a handsome woman and lives in Denver. While taking a cup of tea with her at the home of her daughter, Mrs. W. G. Wigginton, we talked of society in the pioneer days.

"The Rocky Mountain News did not run a society page," said Mrs. Clark, "but there were many social gatherings of bright and congenial people.

"There were no bridge parties, no afternoon teas or receptions, for the pioneer women were too busy with their domestic duties to frivol away afternoons; besides, we scorned amusements that were not shared with our husbands.

"Our dances were usually given at one of the hotels. They began promptly at eight o'clock; we tripped the light fantastic, to the music of a 'fiddle' and a flute, and John Lewis, who recently passed away, was the professional caller. Supper was served about midnight, and the dance went on till the break of day.

"The theaters were unusually good, though the buildings were crude. The troupes, as they were called at that time, came in a stage and played a week's engagement at the little theater on Larimer street, and later at the Denver, which stood where Spengel's store now stands.

"Driving in the evening was one of the great pleasures. Everybody owned a horse and buggy, and from Denver to Ford's park, out northeast, was simply a race track. The greatest sport was in trying to pass one another on the way. George Estabrook, big-hearted, open-handed George, had the finest stable in town, and is still noted for his string of thoroughbreds.

The Territory of Colorado 225

"His sister, beautiful Mary Estabrook, now Mrs. C. B. Kountze, was considered the best horsewoman in the country."

The photographs are from Mrs. Clark's old album, with her remarks as she handed them to me.

"Anne George, a beautiful Southern girl, who married Jasper Sears. She is still a resident of Colorado and is the mother of Mrs. Eugene W. Taylor, a well-known newspaper woman.

Mrs. Anne Sears Stevenson

"The charming and popular Jennie Rollins, now Mrs. L. C. Greenleaf.

"Mrs. George Kassler came here as a bride; a woman of refinement and culture, who impressed all who knew her.

"Mrs. Avery Gallup was handsome, and a great favorite.

"Mollie Voorhies was always bubbling over with vivacity. She is now the widow of O. H. Harker.

"Miss Diadema Adams, who married A. W. Bailey, was a very pretty girl and developed into an artist of some distinction.

"Mrs. Fred Clark, the mother of Mrs. A. G. Reynolds and Mrs. Everett Steele. Mrs. Clark was always one of the most elegantly dressed women in the town.

"Mr. and Mrs. Henry M. Porter. Mrs. Porter had pretty golden hair in those days.

"Mrs. Moffat enjoyed social life at that time, and while Mr. Moffat shunned dances and parties, he insisted upon his wife taking part in these pleasures. She often went with a married couple and promptly at the appointed time Mr. Moffat called to take her home.

"In the early days the prominent visitor received

marked attention, which formed a splendid side to social life. In 1865, Speaker Schuyler Colfax, later Vice-President, came to visit his sister, Mrs. Daniel Witter, who was a prominent woman socially. A ball was given for him and tickets sold rapidly at sixteen dollars each. Colfax avenue was named for him.

"On one visit, he brought his cousins, Sue and Carrie Mathers, to visit Mrs. Witter. Sue later married Frank Hall and Carrie became the bride of O. J. Hollister, a well-known newspaper man of Central.

"In 1866, Bayard Taylor came to Denver in company with the noted American artist, William H. Beard. General Sherman came in 1868, and with him were Generals W. R. Hazen and W. J. Palmer. Professor Louis Agassiz came and was a guest at the Planter's house, where a banquet and other festivities were given in his honor. Albert Bierstadt, the famous landscape painter, was royally entertained.

"General Hancock, with an escort of soldiers, came in 1867, but remained only a day or two. Professor Hayden of the United States Geological Society, with several associates in scientific work, arrived in 1868. General Grant was received that year and given the freedom of the city. Cyrus W. Field of Atlantic cable fame, came in 1869 and was given a warm welcome. The Grand Duke Alexis reached Denver in January, 1872. He engaged in a great buffalo hunt on the plains, under the direction of W. F. Cody, known better as 'Buffalo Bill.' A conspicuous event of the Grand Duke's visit was a ball at the American house.

"But the coming of the railroads made distinguished visitors so numerous that public festivities could not be provided in honor of them.

"Those were happy days," said Mrs. Clark, in conclusion, "and the few of us who have weathered the hardships of many years find that feeling of frendship, love and loyalty which bound us together then, still enduring."

The Foundation of Daniels' and Fisher's Stores

An ox-team and wagon-load of general merchandise jolted into the pioneer town of Denver, October 6, 1864. This was an important event, for it was the beginning of the Daniels and Fisher Stores Company of today.

The man at the head of the firm was W. B. Daniels, who remained in New York, engaged in the wholesale clothing business. Mr. W. R. Kenyon was placed in charge of the store here, and it was one of the cornerstones on which Denver built her reputation as the future metropolis of Colorado.

The business prospered from the very first. It became necessary to increase the accommodations, and the new company was Daniels & Eckhart.

Trade poured in steadily, and it became necessary to move into a still larger building. In the fall of 1869, a new store was opened on Larimer street. Quite a pretentious building for brave, strenuous little Denver, and in consequence the whole undertaking was condemned by the pessimistic element as too foolhardy to succeed. But the little dry goods house continued to grow.

An anecdote which well illustrates the resourcefulness necessary to successful trading in the early days may not be amiss here. An enthusiastic buyer for the firm had placed an order for trouser buttons, the ordinary, four-hole kind, not wisely, but too well! When the consignment arrived, containing hundreds of great gross. Mr. Daniels wrathfully remarked that there were more trouser buttons in the shipment than there was population in the State. The discomfited buyer, however, was by no means checkmated, but straightway hied him to a "keno" parlor and bargained with the proprietor with

FIRST STORE

WM. B. DANIELS

MAJOR WM COOKE DANIELS

THE TOWER

such good results, that the trouser buttons, transformed by the simple process of renaming, into keno counters, changed hands there and then, at a handsome profit to Daniels, Eckhart & Co. As these keno rooms were never closed, night or day (a bean lunch being served to the patrons shortly after midnight, that the pangs of hunger might not interrupt the game and, incidently, the profits), a constant demand for the new style of counter was thus assured, the so-called "counters" which had dropped on the floor during the progress of the game being swept away next morning as a matter of course.

In the spring of 1872 it was decided to make another change in the firm. A promising young man, Mr. W. G. Fisher, had been admitted into the business some time previously, and he formed the company of the reorganized firm. Mr. Daniels and Mr. Eckhart finally decided that they could not agree on some vital points connected

MR. W. G. FISHER   MRS W. G. FISHER

with the business and this disagreement led to Mr. Eckhart's complete retirement from the firm.

In October, 1875, the new firm, Daniels & Fisher, bought the corner of Sixteenth and Lawrence streets, and there they laid the foundation of the present store. People then said, "You may be able to build away out there, on the very borders of the city, but you won't be able to carry the trade with you."

The growth of the Lawrence street business was phenomenal, which was in a large measure due to W. G. Fisher, junior partner, who was a man of business ability, wide sympathies and practical philanthropy.

On Christmas day, 1891, the store suffered a heavy loss through the death of its senior partner, Mr. W. B. Daniels. A most remarkable man, Mr. Daniels was often spoken of in financial circles as "the A. T. Stewart of the West." Not only had Mr. Daniels unerring instinct in regard to merchandise, but his powers as an organizer and financier were altogether exceptional. It is owing to his liberal and progressive policy that the Daniels & Fisher Stores Company stands where it does today, in the front rank of America's department stores.

Colonel L. C. Ellsworth was then appointed administator of the Daniels estate, and with Mr. W. G. Fisher, surviving partner, carried on the business.

Mr. Fisher's death in 1897 was a loss not only to the store but to the entire community.

He came to Denver in 1870 and was identified with the firm of Daniels & Fisher for more than a quarter of a century. No man in the great establishment was better known to customers or clerks than Mr. Fisher himself. He was as easily approached by the small customer as the large one. His simplicity of character flowed out into great kindness; every public movement received from him cordial and generous support; every charity based its first foundation on his generous purse.

The unwavering principles of honor and right were behind all his transactions. He worked his way from the smallest beginning until he stood, modest and unassuming, a leading figure in the business interests of Colorado.

In social life he drew many friends to him and his generous nature made him a true companion.

When the news came of his sudden death in New York, where he had gone on business, the whole city mourned.

His widow, generous and open-hearted, still lives in her elegant home on Logan street, admired and respected by the whole community. Her fine intellect has been broadened by extensive reading and travel. She is at all times courteous and kind to her associates and those with whom she comes in contact; conscientious in the discharge of her duties as a friend and as a citizen, and ever ready to aid, with her influence and means, whatever she considers a benefit to the city of Denver. Her large ballroom is often thrown open for public-spirited and charitable purposes. She is a member of the west-central committee of the national board of the Young Woman's Christian Association.

At Mr. Fisher's death the business management passed into the hands of Mr. W. C. Daniels, son of the late senior partner, who from the very first displayed remarkable business instincts. Under his able direction, the store assumed many new features, not only new to Denver, but new to the entire department store system.

In July, 1897, Mr. Daniels bought Mrs. Fisher's interest in the business, becoming practically the sole owner, and May 1, 1900, the Daniels & Fisher Stores Company was incorporated.

Mr. W. C. Daniels resides abroad. and Mr. Charles MacAllister Willcox is general manager of the business.

Equal Suffrage

At a session of the Territorial Legislature in 1869, ex-Governor John Evans and D. M. Richards of Denver endeavored to secure consideration of a measure introducing the question of woman suffrage in Colorado, but they were not successful. In 1870, Territorial Governor Edward McCook recommended an extension of the franchise to women. This was rejected. It was not brought up again until 1876. In that year a convention anticipating

The Territory of Colorado

the admission of Colorado as a State was held in Denver, January 10, which resulted in revival of interest in the women's movement.

A committee from this convention appeared before the constitutional committee, which was held in Denver in the winter of 1875 and 1876, and asked recognition of equal suffrage in the constitution to be framed for the new State. The proposed amendment for equal suffrage was lost by a vote of twenty-four to eight, but the following section of the report of the committee in charge of the matter was inserted by Judge H. P. H. Bromwell, and adopted: "Section 2, Article 7. The General Assembly may, at any time, extend by law, the right of suffrage to persons not hereinafter enumerated, but no such law shall take effect or be in force until the same shall have been submitted to a vote of the people at a general election and approved by a majority of the votes cast for or against such law."

Following the adoption of this section, the convention adopted a resolution instructing the First General Assembly of the State of Colorado (1877) to provide a law whereby the question of woman's suffrage should be submitted to a vote of the electors. Accordingly, an act was passed at the next session of the Legislature submitting the question to a vote of the people. A campaign led by the Woman's Suffrage Association was made in that year, but the proposition was defeated at the general election October 1, 1878, by a vote of ten thousand for and twenty thousand against.

In 1891 another effort was made to have the word "male" expunged from the constitution, so that woman's suffrage would have a constitutional right. Under act of the Legislature of 1893, the question was again submitted to a vote of the people at the general election of that year, and at this time the victory was won for woman's suffrage. The vote was as follows: For, 35,689;

Helen Ring Robinson

against, 29,461, showing a majority of 6,347 for equal suffrage.

As members of the Legislature and as officers in positions of public trust, the women have been valuable acquisitions to the body politic. Mrs. Helen Ring Robinson, a woman of fine ability, was the first Colorado State Senator.

Women's Clubs

In connection with equal suffrage, it seems appropriate to speak of women's clubs. The great development of the club movement in Denver and the State has been since 1880.

The Denver Fortnightly was organized April 13, 1881. The object of the club is, "The union of congenial friends for study and discussion." It has a membership of thirty, and while it has no philanthropic committee, many of its members are actively identified with charitable and benevolent work in other organizations. The Fortnightly was instrumental in forming the Woman's club of Denver and the State Federation. Its motto is, "To the truth add other truth." Its flower, the Marechal Niel rose.

The Monday club was founded in 1881, almost simultaneously with the Fortnightly club. It was organized "to bring together women interested in intellectual culture."

Among the pioneer organizations is Der Deutsche Damen club. It was formed in 1884 for the study of German literature, history and music and also for social purposes.

The Round Table was organized in 1888 for the purpose of studying history and literature. The membership is limited to thirty. The Rocky Mountain columbine is the club flower, and the club motto is, "Step by step we gain the heights." Mrs. Alice Polk Hill founded the Round Table and has been its president for twenty-five years.

The Tuesday Musical club was organized in 1892 for musical advancement and for the study of the literature of music. Candidates for membership are required to pass a rigid examination in musical theory and practice.

The original Clio club was organized in 1892. In 1895 was formed The Monday Evening Clio for both men and women. In the same year a Junior Clio was organized, and in 1896 the Young Ladies' Clio was formed for historical and literary study.

The Sevigne club was organized in the month of December, 1892, for the purpose of studying and speaking the French language. No English word is spoken at its meetings.

The first meeting to consider the organization of the Woman's Club of Denver was held at the home of Mrs. Charles Denison in the spring of 1894, and soon after a meeting was held in the basement of the Unity church, when an organization was formed with about two hundred members. It is impossible in my limited space to tell of the methods and the influence of the Woman's club. It has prompted the organization of many small but helpful literary associations, and the result is that the women of Denver have been lifted to a broad, intellectual view of life.

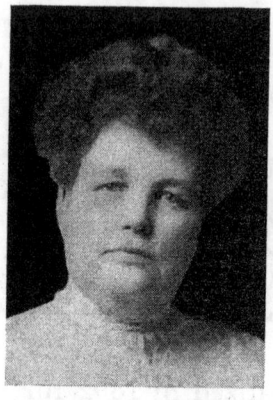

Mrs. Sarah Platt Decker   Mrs. J. D. Whitmore   Mrs. Luther M. Goddard

Mrs. Chas. H. Jacobson   Mrs. Dewey C. Bailey   Mrs. E. P. Costigan

PRESIDENTS OF THE WOMAN'S CLUB IN ORDER OF SUCCESSION

Miss Minnie J. Reynolds organized the Woman's Press club in 1898. She was its first president. The object of the club is, "To advance and encourage women in literary work, to cultivate acquaintance and friendship among women of literary tastes, to secure the benefits arising from organized effort, and to drive dull care away."

There are many philanthropic and patriotic associations, but in a book with the limitations of this one I can mention only the clubs that were pioneers in the club movement.

J. C. Smiley says: "The statistics of 'the club movement' reveal the interesting facts that in number of women's organizations and in aggregate membership therein, Colorado, in proportion to population, surpasses every other State in the Union; and that Denver in proportion to population, not only leads in Colorado, but is in advance of every other city in the Union."

THE COLORADO FEDERATION OF WOMEN'S CLUBS

The Colorado Federation of Women's Clubs was organized in Denver on April 5, 1895, with a membership of thirty-five clubs. The first annual meeting was held in Colorado Springs October 25, 1895.

For the first few years the programs consisted of papers and discussions suggested by the different clubs, but in 1903 the reports of the standing committees were made a part of the regular program.

The Federation has grown from thirty-five clubs to one hundred and fifty clubs and has been a vital force in the advancement of the State along legislative, educational and humanitarian lines. The work is divided among twenty-two committees, some of the most important being: The traveling library committee, which established the traveling libraries, that have now become a State institution, and have been of incalculable value to remote and isolated districts.

The art committee, which collected and arranged a traveling art gallery to bring the masterpieces of the world within the reach of all who are interested in art.

The scholarship committee, which has helped one

hundred and seventy-eight girls to complete their education and become self-supporting.

The education committee, which has been of great assistance in bettering school conditions, especially those relating to rural schools.

Mrs. E. M. Ashley

The legislative committee, which has taken an active part in securing the passage of laws for the help and protection of women and children.

The conservation committee, which has been a factor in the preservation of the natural resources of Colorado and the protection of its birds and plants.

The bureau of information, which is of special service to club women in the arrangement of programs and the preparation of club papers.

The industrial, State institutions, health, household economics, civics and civil service committees are all of very great value, along their various lines, to the entire State.

The greatest value of the Federation, however, has been that it has shown women the opportunities that were waiting for them on every hand and given them the power of achievement that comes only from the organized efforts of a large number of enthusiastic women working together for a definite purpose.

The Territory of Colorado

The presidents of the Federation have been: Mrs. E. M. Ashley, Denver; Mrs. M. D. Thatcher, Pueblo; Mrs. J. H. Baker, Boulder; Mrs. T. M Harding, Canon City; Mrs. Mary C. C. Bradford, Denver; Mrs. Isabella Churchill, Greeley; Mrs. J. D. Whitmore, Denver; Mrs. H. L. Hollister, Pueblo; Mrs A. H. McLain, Canon City; Mrs. P. J. McHugh, Fort Collins; Mrs. W. R. Garretson, Denver.

Mrs. E. M. Ashley, the first president of the Colorado Federation of Women's Clubs, came to Denver in 1861, and since that time she has participated in all measures designed for the advancement of women.

She was an active worker in the campaign for equal suffrage in 1893, and was vice-president of the board of lady managers of the World's Columbian Exposition. She is a woman of fine education, great kindness of heart and an easy grace of manner.

The Territorial Governors

William Gilpin, the first territorial governor, was appointed by President Lincoln July 8, 1861, and was removed from office April, 1862. John Evans was appointed by President Lincoln April 19, 1862.

I have told of the fire, flood, Civil War and Indian outbreak during his administration. The measures taken by him in the trying period of his administration were wise, patriotic, and above all, successfully carried out. He filled the executive chair to his honor and credit for over three years and resigned the office in 1865.

The accompanying picture shows, in the order of their services, the territorial governors appointed after Governor Evans.

John L. Routt was the eighth and last territorial governor. He was appointed by President Grant in 1875.

240   *Colorado Pioneers in Picture and Story*

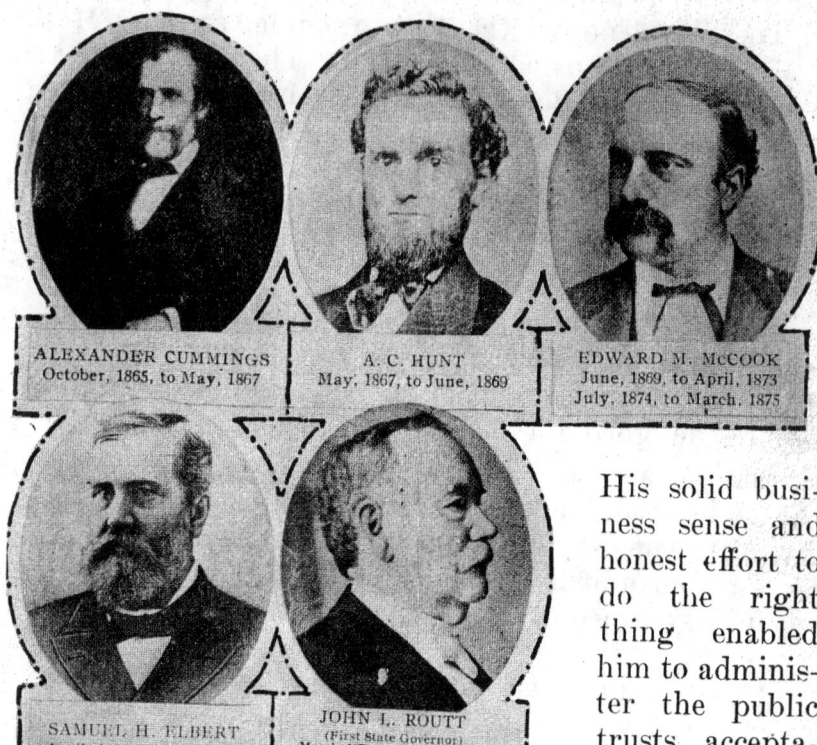

ALEXANDER CUMMINGS
October, 1865, to May, 1867

A. C. HUNT
May, 1867, to June, 1869

EDWARD M. McCOOK
June, 1869, to April, 1873
July, 1874, to March, 1875

SAMUEL H. ELBERT
April, 1873, to July, 1874

JOHN L. ROUTT
(First State Governor)
March, 1875, to November, 1876
November, 1876, to January, 1879
January, 1891, to January, 1893

His solid business sense and honest effort to do the right thing enabled him to administer the public trusts acceptably to the people. Statehood was consummated during his term of office, and he was elected the first governor of the State upon its admission into the Union.

He was a man of honesty and great virtues.

A story will illustrate Governor Routt's fine sense of humor:

A party of friends were in his office one day, telling of their skill as fishermen. The governor was busy at his desk. Suddenly he looked up from his work and said: "You fellows with your little ten-pound trout and twenty-pound catfish will have to take a back seat, for I caught a pickerel that weighs one hundred and sixty-five pounds."

His wife was Miss Eliza Pickerell, weighing one

hundred and sixty-five pounds, a member of a prominent Indiana family of that name.

CONGRESSMEN

The territorial representatives in Congress are merely the agents of their constituents and have no vote in legislation. During its territorial period Colorado had five representatives in Congress. All of them were elected twice: Hiram P. Bennet, elected in 1861, re-elected in 1862; Allan A. Bradford, elected 1864; George M. Chilcott, 1864, re-elected 1866; Allan A. Bradford, re-elected 1868; Jerome B. Chaffee, 1870, re-elected 1872; Thomas M. Patterson, elected 1874. The second election of T. M. Patterson was for the regular term as a member of Congress after the State was admitted.

MAYORS

The first mayor of Denver was J. C. Moore; the second, Amos Steck, elected April 1, 1863. H. J. Bredlinger was next and served from April 1, 1865, for one year; George T. Clark came next, and then Milton M. De Lano served two years. Edward Chase was in the council during De Lano's first term, resigned, and was elected several times thereafter. It was the universal opinion that no straighter or more honest man ever served the city than was this same Edward Chase.

George T. Clark

William M. Clayton was mayor from April 1, 1868, to April, 1869. He believed in economy. That was his watchword. He often shouldered a shovel and opened clogged-up ditches to save the city money.

He was so careful of the city's funds that he saved enough during his administration to pay the municipal expenses for the following year without a tax levy being necessary. But he was not mean or stingy. He conducted a general store, and when the Indian raids and fighting caused hard times he gave credit to everybody until times got good again.

PART VI
THE PIONEER STATE BUILDERS

CHAPTER XVI
CHANGES IN MEANS OF COMMUNICATION

Freighters

The splendid State of Colorado is the gift of the pioneers to civilization. Toilers they were in the days of 1858-59 and '60. Men gifted with both brain and brawn, who fought their way through countless obstacles, and while they were carving a State out of the wilderness Denver was the scene of magnificent human progress.

I will now trace the development of pioneer enterprises to the time that Colorado became a State, and to show that the pioneer spirit of hope and courage is not dead in Colorado, I will draw a line from 1876 to the present and end each story with a brief mention of the men and women of today who are pushing forward the work of State building. In the onward march of civilization, the enterprises of the hour require the work of the pioneer. The problems are different from those in 1858, and in the present phases of government, economic reform and social betterment, the leaders in State building are not less intrepid than those who led the way in 1859.

There was not a railroad west of the Missouri river in 1859. Every pound of freight, every emigrant and every letter had to be carried by wagon or on horseback in the face of hardships untold and at the risk of life. Many were engaged in freighting, but the first organized system of wagon trains to cross the plains to Denver was that of the trading and shipping firm of Russell, Majors & Waddell.

In the spring of 1859, when the rush for Pike's Peak commenced, this firm organized the Pike's Peak Express Company. They bought the Hockaday line of coaches, running from the Missouri river to Salt Lake, and turned the line, so that the main road branched off at Kearney and headed for Denver.

So extensive was the business of this firm that as early as 1859, Russell, Majors & Waddell had upon the

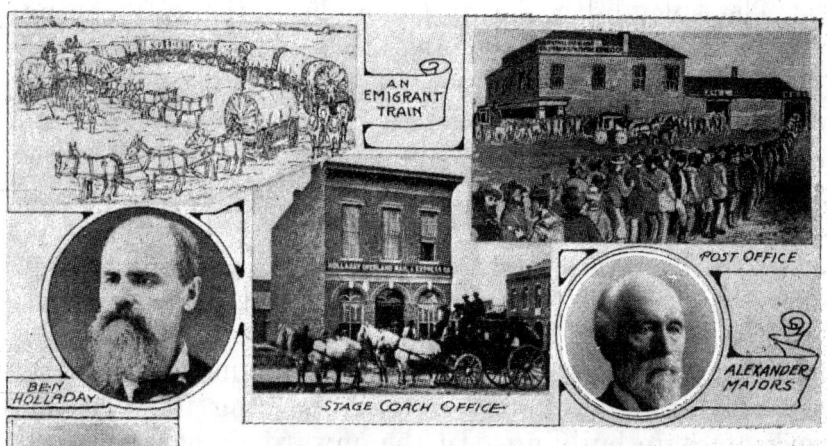

plains 5,000 wagons, 20,000 oxen and 10,000 mules and horses. They were the greatest inland freighters in the world.

At one time their influence was greater in the affairs of the government than are the railroads of today.

The Central Overland California and Pike's Peak Express Company succeeded the Leavenworth and Pike's Peak Company, and their arrival and departure in Denver were events of importance. With the arrival of the "mail-coaches" there was a great rush to the "postoffice" —a pretentious frame building erected by Major R. R.

Bradford at Sixteenth and Holladay. Amos Steck was behind the "pigeon hole." There was always a string of men a block or two long waiting to get mail. Letters cost twenty-five cents each. Gold dust was the principal circulating medium at this time. Every person carried a buckskin bag in his pocket and every merchant was obliged to provide himself with Troy scales to weigh the "currency of the realm." The weighing of the gold in payment for letters consumed time in delivering the mail. Young Steck had a remarkable memory for faces and names, and by calling out far down the hitching, halting line, would relieve them of tedious waiting. Letters often failed to reach those for whom they were intended, from the fact that men frequently dropped their real names and took common ones, like Sam Smith or Jack Jones.

A story is told of one Noah Davis, who was mining in Park county in 1860, under the name of Jack Jones. A friend from Gregory Gulch informed him that four letters were waiting for him at the postoffice. Jack Jones, as he was called, had not heard from his wife for a long time, so he tramped ninety-four miles over the mountains, only to find that another Jack Jones had taken the letters from the postoffice.

The first mail delivered by the government in Denver arrived August 10, 1860, and the first postmaster appointed at that time was Park McClure. Previous to that, letters were delivered by the express company.

In 1862, Ben Holladay became the owner of this line of coaches. He was the great transportation king of the plains. No other one man owned and managed a transportation system at once so vast and so difficult.

The Indian depredations of 1864-66 almost broke up his stage line. The red men burned the stations, stole the stock and killed the white men. The financial loss was about a half million. In 1866 Holladay sold the Overland stages to Wells Fargo & Company. This company continued the romantic enterprises until the coming of the railroads.

The first transfer company was started by the Ben Holladay stage line. Jack Hughes succeeded Holladay, Wall & Witter following him; then William H. Pierce & Company, known as "Tip" Pierce. His successor was Mr. Simonton. The Denver Transfer Company succeeded Simonton; Marrs & Middleton succeeded the Denver Transfer Company. Then came Austin & Reynolds; Kuykendall, Cobb & Martinez were their successors. Then followed Kuykendall, Cobb & Kuykendall. The Denver Omnibus and Carriage Company was next, which was organized by John M. Kuykendall. Later he organized the Denver Omnibus and Cab Company. He is president and general manager of both these companies.

In spite of the ever-increasing responsibility of his personal business, Mr. Kuykendall gives a great deal of time to public-spirited works for the upbuilding of Denver.

Mr. Kuykendall said: "I have lived in Denver forty-five years, and believe it has a great future. I am very much attached to Denver. There is no other place on the globe

John M. Kuykendall

that would feel quite like home to me, and I hope I may be able to spend the rest of my days in this city."

Mr. Kuykendall has an affable southern manner; he is genial in disposition, generous of heart and has a level business head.

He married Miss Thomason of Cheyenne, the daughter of Mr. Zachariah Thomason, a wealthy cattleman of Colorado and Wyoming. She is noted for a sweet benevolence of character and rare social graces. The Kuykendall home on Seventh avenue is one of the most elegant in Denver.

THE PONY EXPRESS

The distance, the perilous and time consuming means of communication between the new country and the old States, caused leading men to constantly calculate ways and means for the bettering of conditions. The conflict between the North and the South increased the clamor for faster mail service. The people were eager to hear the news and the war talk added to the demand for swifter information.

In the winter of 1859-60 Senator Gwinn of California, several money magnates of New York and Alexander Majors of Russell, Majors and Waddell, the transportation kings on the plains west of the Missouri river, met in Washington, D. C.

The result of that meeting was the inception of one of the most daring and romantic business ventures the world has ever known; the pony express, by which the time of transmitting news across the continent was reduced from twenty-one to ten days.

The telegraph then extended only to St. Joseph, and, between that point and San Francisco, there was nothing to break the monotony of mountain and plain but two settlements, the Mormons in Utah and the Pike's Peak settlement. The project was deemed absurd and absolutely impossible.

At first Russell was the moving spirit of the enterprise; Majors and Waddell thought the expense would be too great. Russell was laughed at by everyone, including his partners; Majors wrote to Russell's family that he had long doubted Bill's sanity, and this time he had gone crazy sure, and they had better come and take him home before he did anything dangerous. However, the plans for the pony express were perfected, and on the morning of April 9, 1860, 10,000 people gathered at St. Joseph to witness the start. A grand celebration was given in honor of the affair; speeches were made, cannons were fired and a special train arrived, with a messenger from New York and a "pony express extra" describing the enterprise. A beautiful black pony was brought out, saddled, a rider mounted him and stood in readiness. The mail bag was left open until the last moment, for dispatches; then, at a signal, he started, riding like a jockey at a race.

Five hundred fleet footed horses, of the tough and tireless kind, were secured for the pony express service; two hundred men were engaged, and eighty of them were selected as riders. The riders were chosen because of their expertness in the saddle, their hardihood to withstand the fatigue of the run, their bravery to face the dangers of their lonely routes and their judgment to get all the speed out of their horses and not overtax them. They were paid $125.00 a month and must weight one hundred pounds or less.

In order to keep the weight at a minimum, the arms of the pony express riders were limited to revolver and knife. Each rider had six to ten relays of ponies, making his ride sixty to one hundred miles. Day and night the mad race went on, until, at the end of ten days, a foam flecked pony dashed up to the telegraph office in far off Sacramento, where the news was again put on the wires and flashed to San Francisco. Messages carried by the pony express were required to be written on tissue paper. The rate charged was $5.00 an ounce, and the weight carried each trip was limited to ten pounds.

In 1860, Russell, Majors and Waddell were running their ponies into Denver.

President Lincoln's inaugural address, March 4, 1861, was whisked across 2,000 miles in seven days and seventeen hours, which was the world's record for dispatch by means of men and horses.

Five of the original pony express riders lived in Denver for a number of years. J. G. Kelly, who recently died, gave the following adventure: "We were in the midst of the Piute War, and our instructions were, 'when you see an Indian close enough, shoot him.' One of our riders came into the station with a hole clear through him. He lived just long enough to tell us an Indian shot him, as he came through a quaking-asp thicket, about three miles back on the trail. Two days later I had to pass through this same thicket. The trail was crooked and narrow; the brush was higher than the head of a man on horse back, and it cut off all view. It was a decidedly uncomfortable place in which to anticipate an attack from a lurking foe. With my heart pounding against the roof of my mouth, I put my revolver at full cock, dropped the reins on the neck of my pony, put both spurs into his flanks and went through the thicket like a streak of greased lightning. At the top of the hill I stopped, and while the pony got his breath I watched the thicket. I noticed a shaking of the bushes in several places, and, as there were neither horses, cattle or large game in the neighborhood that might account for the moving of the bushes, I concluded that there were Piutes in the thicket, but I had come through with such a rush that they had failed to get a shot at me. I opened fire on the spot where the bushes moved; they ceased to shake, and I was convinced that I had run an ambuscade. A few days afterwards two men were killed by skulking warriors in this thicket."

Of all the pony express riders, Cody has become the best known. He obtained the name of "Buffalo Bill" while furnishing buffalo meat to the builders of the Union Pacific railroad, and by this name he is known throughout the world. When a mere lad he made the longest pony express ride on record.

Colonel Alex. Majors had great affection for him, and told much about his famous career on the plains as guide, hunter, Indian fighter and pony express rider. Among the stories, he told one of how Bill Cody, when he received his first month's pay, which was a considerable sum for a boy in his teens to earn, took the money, spread it out on the table before his widowed mother, and joyously said: "Isn't it splendid, mother, that I can get all this money for you and my sister?"

Next to Colonel W. F. Cody, the most famous of the pony express riders was Robert Haslam, known throughout the West as "Pony Bob." He had many fights with Indians and "road agents" and had numerous hairbreadth escapes.

He carried the news of Lincoln's election as President, riding one hundred and twenty miles in eight hours and ten minutes, using thirteen relays of horses. He was ambushed by Indians, shot with flint head arrows through the lower jaw, fracturing it on both sides and knocking out five teeth.

The pony express was operated for over two years. It was the most unique and romantic mail service ever organized. While it was a losing business venture, it opened a way for the telegraph and railway. Alex. Majors was one of the organizers of it. He was called the "Kentucky Christian"; he never drank, never swore, and made his employes sign a contract not to drink, gamble or swear, under penalty of being "fired" without the pay that was coming, and gave every one of his employes a pocket Bible.

TELEGRAPH

A citizen of Omaha, Nebraska, Edward Creighton, completed a telegraph line across the continent, and the swift pony express was superseded by the swifter lightning.

The wire reached Julesburg, May, 1861. The new company opened an office in Denver, using the pony express or stages to carry the messages to Denver. David H. Moffat was appointed the first agent.

An enterprising Denver man, B. F. Wood-

B. F. Woodward

ward, built a line from Julesburg to Denver. The wire was strung into the office of Warren, Hussey & Company's bank in the autumn of 1863, and Judge Amos Steck, who was then mayor, exchanged congratulatory messages with the mayor of Omaha. From the time of the earliest settlement in Denver the pioneers suffered intensely from the feeling of isolation; they pined for telegraphic communication with the outside world; and the branch line from Julesburg completed October, 1863, brought great relief. The rates were very high. A message to New York of ten words cost $9.10.

The Indians called the telegraph the "white man's talking string," and when they went on the war path would often interrupt communication by carrying off great lengths of wire. The buffalo also made work for the telegraph company. They used the poles for back scratching, and a few rubs against the poles by the big animals would bring them to the ground.

The wind and lightning caused frequent damage, and it was thought at one time that the telegraph could never be successfully used in this country.

Benjamin F. Woodward, the builder and manager of Colorado's pioneer telegraph line, became identified with many other business enterprises that contributed to the development of Denver.

Telephone

The telegraph was followed by the telephone, the other great public electrical utility in Denver.

F. O. Vaille opened the first telephone exchange in Denver. Henry R. Wolcott became interested in the enterprise with him. This line was controlled by the American Bell Telephone Company, but in 1881 the Colorado Telephone Company came into existence, with H. R. Wolcott as president and F. O. Vaille as general manager.

The Pioneer State Builders 253

In 1884 E. B. Field succeeded Mr. Vaille as general manager.

Mr. E. B. Field came to Colorado in the late '70's for pulmonary trouble; a stranger in a strange land, he sat under the trees in the yard of his little home on South Broadway, sick but hopeful. He was a poor man then; it was necessary for him to work to support his family.

He knew nothing of telephone or electrical apparatus at that time, but from the moment he entered the service of the telephone company he gave energy, industry, experiment and ceaseless seeking to theoretical and practical telephone work. He forged rapidly to the front, and his present position is a brilliant example of the results that can be obtained by push and perseverance.

E. B. Field

Mr. Field wrestled incessantly with rival companies, for he believes that the Telephone Company must be conducted as a unity to insure satisfactory results for the people. Under his management the Telephone company became a factor in the commercial growth and prosperity of Colorado.

Then came an era of expansion, reorganization and the fitting of the telephone for all demands that could be made upon it. Mr. Field was omnipresent at every stage, overlooking and controlling every movement, until the telephone system expanded to the "Mountain States Telephone and Telegraph Company." He is now the executive head of a corporation that controls the entire telephone systems of Colorado, New Mexico, Arizona, Utah, Idaho, Montana and Wyoming, a territory representing one-fifth of the total area of the United States, in which lives two per cent of our entire population.

Thousands of miles of wire connect cities, villages, mines, mills and ranches from El Paso, Texas, north to Santa Fe, New Mexico, then up to Trinidad, Pueblo and Denver in Colorado, and still northward to Cheyenne, Billings, Helena and Boise, then down again to Salt Lake City—all controlled by the one company. Some idea of the stretches of barren territory covered by Mr. Field's system may be gained when it is stated that the lines that have been constructed over mountains and plains were built to last, and, when once erected, are never removed, so that hundreds of once prosperous mining camps that are now deserted still get the highest grade of communication. The business men of the West appreciate his ability to organize, and his persistence in overcoming reverses.

E. B. Field is a man with a big brain and a big heart. The employes of the Telephone company are all attached to him because of his kindness and consideration for them. With intuitive insight he has worked his way over the hard trail to prosperity, holding out always a willing hand to help the weak in the race. He is public spirited, and, when called on to further any public movement, is never hesitating or slow to respond.

Mrs. Field is a woman of fine culture and great kindness of heart; she is active in philanthropic and club work. Her deep interest in human beings makes her benevolent, and no one will ever know the vast number of people who have experienced the result of her generosity. On that subject she is silent. Mr. and Mrs. Field have one son and three daughters, Mrs. Mary A. Fairchild, Miss Martha L. Field, Mrs. Grace W. Marvin and Mr. Edward B. Field, Jr., who is vice-president and treasurer of the Telephone company.

Mrs. E. B. Field

Mr. Field has been treasurer and director of the Denver Chamber of Commerce. He is a member of the Denver Club, Denver Athletic Club and Denver Country Club, a Royal Arch Mason, a Knight Templar and a Mystic Shriner.

CHAPTER XVII

THE PIONEERS FACED THE QUESTION OF SUPPLY

Water

An Auraria City Water Company was formed in February, 1859. The plan was to bring the water by a ditch from a high point up Cherry creek to a reservoir, which they intended to bank up as high as the ditch flow would permit. This project was never carried out, yet it was the beginning of the vital water question.

In 1860 the Capital Hydraulic Company was organized, with A. C. Hunt, Andrew Sagendorf, John M. Clark, Amos Steck, Turner and Hobbs, R. R. Bradford, J. B. Doyle and F. Z. Salomon as promoters. This company proposed to construct a hydraulic canal from a point up the Platte, with reservoir near the mouth of Dry creek.

Work was commenced on the ditch in 1860, but the promoters became discouraged, and the Capital Hydraulic disintegrated.

In 1861 the pioneers again put their shoulders to the wheel. Their project then became known as the Witter ditch, and later as the Mullen Mill ditch. They abandoned the reservoir plan and started the ditch directly from the river at Little's ranch. After many trials and difficulties the ditch was completed to Denver. It cost a large sum of money for those days, but nothing ever gave more relief and satisfaction as watering the town by the old ditch.

While the mountains and plains surrounding Denver

The Pioneer State Builders

were magnificent, the town itself was dreary—no trees, no grass, no flowers, no water for irrigation; all the water for domestic purposes was obtained from wells or hauled from the river. Dust laden breezes often swept through the streets. December 23, 1864, a terrific wind-storm commenced, which continued for three days without interruption. People were taken off their feet by the powerful gale, and the air was darkened with flying rubbish. Major J. H. Fillmore, a prominent citizen, was prostrated by the storm, and death soon followed.

In 1865, winding its way from far up the Platte, around the bluffs of Capitol Hill, came what is now called the "old city ditch," and its coming marked the beginning of tree planting and lawn making. Clear, sparkling water flowed at the sides of the streets, trees grew rapidly and yards were beautiful with grass and flowers. The gurgling water at the sides of the streets continued until the coming of the asphalt pavements.

WALTER SCOTT CHEESMAN

In 1861 W. S. Cheesman, a man who was destined to wield a great power in the water supply, came to Denver. He had spent the larger portion of his youth in Chicago, and had learned his first lessons in finance there. He at once decided that Denver had a future similar to Chicago, and bent his energies to be part of the growing greatness. In 1861 he opened the first drug store in Denver, near the corner of Fifteenth and Blake, and ran a successful business there until 1874, when he sold out to enter another larger field of work. He became closely associated with David H. Moffat and John Evans, and the three men formed the life of commercial enterprise in Denver at that time.

In 1868 they united in building the Denver Pacific railroad to Cheyenne. Mr. Cheesman was for several

Walter S. Cheesman

years the president of this company. He was active in the building of the Denver Boulder Valley railroad and the South Park road. This railroad boom determined the destiny of Denver, and checked Pueblo or Cheyenne from becoming the metropolis that Denver is today. The Union station was built by a company organized by Mr. Cheesman for that purpose. He also determined the location of the court house. Owing to the price then asked for the present site, the old County of Arapahoe contemplated building the court house further out. Mr. Cheesman bought the ground and resold it to the county commissioners at a price that they could pay. When others hesitated, he dared. His young enthusiasm and energy overcame all obstacles, and he made money, because he believed in Denver and always, by word or example, was ready to show his belief that nothing could keep Denver from being the great city of the West.

He had the prophetic vision and the courage that bring great things to pass. His rare judgment and firm faith are shown in the success of the large enterprises with which he was identified. He was one of the organizers of the International Trust Company, and served as a member of its executive committee continuously for more than fifteen years, a director of the Denver, Northwestern & Pacific Railway Company, a member of the Denver Real Estate Exchange. He was the most sanguine of all the young men who came in the early days, and his faith in Denver never waned. He bought real estate in hard times and good times. He founded great financial institutions as necessary links between Denver and the money centers of the East. He reached out into the mining regions of the State and helped develop mines, which in turn helped to develop Denver.

There was a strong humanitarian side to Mr. Cheesman's character. He was president of the Colorado Humane Society for many years and often exercised his power as an officer of this society to stop cruel treatment to children and animals. He was known repeatedly to leave his carriage and stop blows on overworked horses. A child or animal unable to defend itself always received his sympathy and assistance. A gentleman said: "One night when I was making my way across the street through a raging storm I saw a man coming towards me, leading a poor old lame horse. As he drew near, I saw it was Walter Cheesman. 'Where are you going?' I called out. 'I saw this old horse,' he replied, 'staked out in a vacant lot, and I am taking it where it can be under shelter tonight,' and the multi-millionaire tramped away through the slush and the rain on his mission of mercy."

It is said that Walter Cheesman hypothecated every foot of real estate he owned in the world to save a friend who was in financial difficulty.

Before Mr. Cheesman had quit active railroad work he became interested in a company formed to supply water to Denver. The company was organized October 30, 1870; the capital stock was $150,000; Colonel Archer was president; David H. Moffat, treasurer; R. R. McCormick, secretary. Forming the board of directors were: Jerome B. Chaffee, Wilson Waddingham, E. W. McCook. E. F. Hallack, F. Z. Salomon, Walter S. Cheesman and Daniel Witter.

The population of Denver at this time was about 6,000. Ultimately there was a division of interests, which resulted in a consolidation of the two plants under the name of the Denver Union Water Company. It was organized in 1894, and was controlled by a pool of stock owned by David Moffat, W. S. Cheesman and Thomas Hayden. The valuation of the company's property grew to $25,000,000. Mr. Cheesman was elected to the important position of president. He was young, alert and energetic, and entered into the business with determination and vigor, but soon found loads of trouble.

He built great reservoirs, he devised systems of filtration and distribution; under his direction the famous Cheesman dam was built. This dam created Lake Cheesman, which is the deepest artificial reservoir in the world for the storage of water for domestic supply, and forms an important element in the life of Denver. It is a feat of hydraulic engineering, and restrains 30,000,000,000

The Pioneer State Builders

Cheesman Dam

gallons of water, enough to supply Denver for three years.

The nerve-racking trials and misfortunes which attended the obtaining and maintaining of a sufficient supply of water for the city, and the struggle between rival companies, the various changes in the management, would form a book of itself. Few men have ever faced greater difficulties or fiercer oppositions than those which confronted Walter Cheesman through the long years when he was seeking with unconquerable determination to build an adequate water plant which would make it possible for Denver to become a great city.

When we compare the first part of Denver's existence—no grass, no flowers, no water for irrigation—with the beautiful city of today, we can, in a measure, realize how much we owe to the energy and courage of Walter S. Cheesman.

He was extremely reticent about personal affairs, and

no one but the beneficiaries ever knew of the money he gave away. His pleasure was in kindly acts, and he was always a willing co-worker with anyone whose object was the good of Denver and the welfare of his fellow man.

CHEESMAN MEMORIAL
Erected to the memory of Walter Scott Cheesman, by his widow and daughter, in Cheesman Park

The Pioneer Cattle Growers

The cattle grazing enterprise of Colorado was initiated by Colonel Jack Henderson. He reached Denver in December, 1858, with a load of groceries, whisky and crackers forming the largest part. He gave two barrels of whisky for a little island in the Platte, which was called "Henderson's Island," and is known by that name today. He immediately commenced grazing cattle for the pioneers, and demonstrated the fact that cattle would live and thrive on the open plains all through the winter.

The alert pioneers were quick to see the opportunity, and for many years great herds of cattle roved the range. The "cow boy" and the "cattle king" were figures around which romance and history were woven in the early days of Colorado. John W. Iliff was one of the most successful in the stock industry. In 1859 he crossed the plains to Denver and opened a grocery store, which he closed out in about a year and invested his money, two or three thousand dollars, in cattle. He made himself familiar with every detail of the business, rode the range and followed the round-up with his men, slept with them in the open, ate out of the "chuck wagon," and was as keen to detect his own brand as was any of his foremen. He secured government contracts for dressed beef, and in a short time furnished meat to the soldiers at all the military posts along the line of the Union Pacific railroad and to many Indian reservations. He established a large trade in dressed beef to butchers. Working in this way, he soon found himself in command of a thriving business, and for several years made his headquarters at the old Planter's House in Denver.*

Mr. Leach says: "The enterprise controlled by John W. Iliff rapidly assumed enormous proportions. His herds numbered from 30,000 to 40,000 head of cattle, valued at over a half million dollars. His range extended from Greeley eastward to Julesburg and from the Platte river north to Lodge Pole creek. Of this vast territory he owned personally 20,000 acres. He could travel over this area for a week at a time, and always eat and sleep at one of his own ranch houses. The chief station in this princely domain was located about forty miles from Julesburg, where there were houses, sheds, corrals, chutes and complete facilities for handling and branding stock. There were sections of fenced land on the Iliff range, some twenty or more houses, mowing machines, wagons, farming tools and nearly two hundred head of horses.

"Few men have ever grasped the cattle trade as firmly to its least detail, and fewer still have been willing to undergo equal hardships in order to acquire as much knowledge as he possessed. Too close application to business undermined his health, and Mr. Iliff succumbed

---

*I have taken the facts of this sketch from R. E. Leach's Sketches of Departed Pioneers.

to the ravages of disease at the age of forty-six. He had faith in the future of Denver, and while the larger portion of his time was spent on the range in active superintendence of his interests, he maintained his residence in this city.

"The title of 'Cattle King of the Plains' was justly his through no chance or freak of fortune, but by virtue of his steady, persistent and intelligent effort."

He took an interest in all educational matters and made many substantial gifts to institutions of learning.

Among the men who aided much to forward the growth of the stock raising industry in Colorado was W. H. H. Cranmer. He was one of the larger owners of cattle in the Byon region. His herds numbered thousands, and he amassed great wealth.

In the early '80's he came to Denver to give his children better educational advantages, and invested largely in real estate. He was interested in the movement which resulted in the founding of the Denver Stockyards by Henry A. Clough in 1880, and was one of the organizers of the Denver Packing Company. He, with Mr. Finis P. Ernest, built the Ernest and Cranmer block.

Mr. Cranmer, like all of the men who took part in the making of Colorado, lived a strenuous life. He overestimated his strength and capacity for endurance, and died at the age of forty-nine.

His widow, Mrs. Martha J. Cranmer, and six children are prominent in the Denver of today—Mrs. W. P. McPhee, Mrs. W. C. Russell, W. H. H. Cranmer, George E. Cranmer, Catherine H. Cranmer and Mrs. Grover C. Coors.

Since the time of Mr. Iliff and Mr. Cranmer great reservoirs and miles of irrigating ditches have been built; town after town has been founded; the farmers have come with their fences and have converted the range lands into small tracts of highly productive farm lands; they are growing hay and grain and sugar beets where wild grass once grew. And to these same cultivated acres is largely due to the revival of the cattle business in Colorado. Irrigation has solved the drought problem, and there is feed for the live stock all over the country.

The National Live Stock Association was organized at Denver January, 1895, when its first annual convention was held in this city.

Denver was made the permanent headquarters of the association, with John W. Springer as president, and Charles F. Martin secretary, both being retained in office by the several successive conventions.

Cattle and sheep thrive in a wonderful way on the residuum beet pulp and residuum syrup obtained from the sugar factories. Many beet growers are engaged in the profitable business of stock raising.

The Denver stock show now ranks next to the great international show at Chicago. $450,000 have been spent in the construction of a plant to house the show, and once a year the finest cattle and horses in the world can be seen in this magnificent stock pavilion.

Fred P. Johnson, secretary of the Colorado Stock Growers' Association, says: "All indications point to a profit close to $5,000,000 on the cattle feeding operations of the State for the season of 1915.

"The packing industry has been taking enormous strides for several years past. Improvements and extensions are constantly being made at the Denver Union Stockyards. Ninety per cent of the stock sold in the Denver market is slaughtered in Denver. The future in this industry is bright because of Denver's undisputed pre-eminence as the leading 'feeder' market of the country."

Agriculture

The first attempt at agriculture by irrigation north of the Arkansas river valley was made by D. K. Wall, who came to Colorado in the spring of 1859. He brought with him some garden seed, and on Clear creek, near the present site of Golden, cleared and fenced a few acres of ground. He plowed, planted and dug ditches to convey the water. His garden soon became a delight to everyone passing that way. It was on the trail to the Gregory diggings, and everyone did pass that way, for the throng from the East made directly for the famous diggings. Mr. Wall realized $2,000 on his first crop, and convinced the pioneers that vegetables and grain could be grown in this region. He became famous as Colorado's first farmer.

While many of the sturdy pioneers hearkened to the lure of the golden quest in the mountains, others felt the harvest call of the valleys, dropped the pick and shovel for the plowshare, and with the indomitable spirit of the pioneer went forth to bring the desert places into service.

They made irrigating canals from the mountain streams and turned the water down upon the dry places. In 1866 one hundred and thirty-six miles of irrigating ditches were constructed, at a cost of $1,000 per mile. Where there had been only cactus and sage brush, the pioneers grew wheat, melons and potatoes.

RUFUS CLARK

Rufus Clark came to Denver in the fall of 1859. He was convinced by the numerous failures of hundreds of those who delved after riches hidden in the mountains that mining was a precarious means of livelihood. He filed a homestead entry on land along the Platte and devoted his energies to gardening. He sold vegetables to miners who came through Denver on their way to the mountains, and in one year he made $30,000 from the sale of potatoes alone, which laid the foundation for the fortune he afterwards amassed, and made him known to fame as "Potato Clark."

He was a member of the Territorial Legislature, when the capital was located at Golden, and refused to run for re-election.

Mr. Clark always took great interest in the Salvation Army. He, with another, gave the building for the Salvation Army headquarters. He afterwards built a college in Africa, known as Rufus Clark and Wife Theological Training School. He gave the site for the University of Denver, and many thousands for charitable institutions.

GRASSHOPPERS

The Colorado crops fell short in 1865, owing to the ravages of the grasshoppers; they came in clouds and shoals and almost ruined those engaged in agriculture. The invasion of these insects made business dull and food prices very high.

They disappeared and did not return until 1875, when they came again in swarms, took possession of the country, passed from field to field, and vegetation vanished before them; even the railroad trains were stopped by their crushed bodies, which made the rails so slippery that forward movement was impossible. Farmers were reduced to bankruptcy.

Daniel Polk

Mr. Daniel Polk, one of Colorado's successful farmers, had planted a large vegetable garden on the ground now known as Overland Race Course Park, from which he expected to realize $20,000. The celery alone was worth several thousand, and the melons were the finest that had yet been grown in the Platte valley. The beautiful garden was one of the "show places"; people drove out from Denver to see the luxurious growth of vegetation.

Daniel Polk

The grasshoppers lit upon that garden of one hundred and twenty acres, and in twenty-four hours every green thing was devoured.

Mr. Polk had lost a fortune during the Civil War, and this was another great loss, but he was a captain of industry and continued to plant until success crowned his efforts. He was one of the builders of South Broadway, and was a strong type of the energetic men who made Colorado the marvel and wonder of the world.

The pioneers of South Broadway were Judge George W. Allen, Mr. Avery Gallup, E. B. Field, Mr. Wm. N. Byers, John L. Dailey, J. O. Patterson, who built the first brick house south of Cherry creek; Mr. Daniel Polk, Mrs. Alice Polk Hill and the Fleming brothers.

Judge George W. Allen still lives in his old home on Broadway; there are memories around the old place that hold him there; his children have been brought up there, and the greater number of his days have been spent there in a pleasant home life, with his cultured and interesting wife as a companion.

Geo. W. Allen

Judge Allen's many fine characteristics have endeared him to a host of friends and acquaintances. He is an able jurist, has been on the bench twenty-two years, and has won the confidence and good will of the people by his just decisions. In his home and at the bar he is an honest, scholarly and lofty figure. As a citizen he is generous, patriotic and progressive. Many local enterprises receive his active assistance.

Irrigation

Abundant flow in irrigation ditches, with glorious golden sunshine send thrills of prosperity throughout the State and make the pioneer's dream come true. Colorado products of the farm and orchard are in all the great markets of the world.

A gentleman, in speaking of Colorado, said: "In New York I saw Greeley potatoes on the menu; on the steamship, Colorado apples and peaches on the card, and in Rio de Janeiro, Colorado cantaloupes and Rocky Ford melons occupied positions of honor on the menu card of my hotel."

Agriculture took such gigantic strides in progress that a Colorado State Agricultural Association was organized in 1865, and the first agricultural fair was held. The Association offered a prize to the best lady rider. Society united in the effort to make the fair a success, and there were twenty entries in the contest. Miss Baker, who rode horseback, took the first prize, Miss Sumner the second, and Mrs. Avery Gallup the third. They refused to let Mollie Estabrook ride; she was such a famous horsewoman it was thought the rest of them would stand no chance; so Miss Estabrook, afterwards Mrs. Charles Kountze, drove Isadore Deitsch's fast horse around the track. This was considered a great social event.

The development of agriculture in Colorado carries with it the history of irrigation. The first irrigating ditch in Northern Colorado was known in pioneer days as the Yaeger ditch. It was constructed in 1859 by A. E. Lytton. He took the water out of the Cache la Poudre river in Larimer county to irrigate his garden. Later J. L. Brush took the water out of Big Thompson creek for irrigation. Mr. Hal Sayre made the survey in both instances.

In 1865 the Hon. B. H. Eaton made a large canal

and took the water from the Cache la Poudre to water 1,500 acres. After the settlement of Greeley in 1870 the Union Colony constructed four large ditches from Big Thompson and three from the Cache la Poudre, at a cost of $435,000.

*The first large ditch or canal in Colorado to furnish water for irrigating purposes was constructed by a company of Scotch and English capitalists known as the "English Company," and the example and success of this enterprising company gave the first impetus to land irrigation on a large scale that brought to agriculture in the State a wealth far surpassing that of all its gold and silver mines.

The agents of the English Company came here in the latter part of the '70's and established the Colorado Loan and Mortgage Company.

These men soon perceived the profitable character of agriculture in irrigated lands, and the need of money for proper development. They loaned broadcast from the Platte to the Arkansas valleys to enable the farmers to extend ditches, purchase agricultural implements, teams and live stock—thus farming grew apace.

The company next conceived the plan of constructing a large ditch. In the early '80's they built what came to be popularly known as the "High Line Ditch," which brought water down from the Platte canyon, conveying it across Plum creek by a high flume aquaduct, crossing in like manner Cherry creek and on over the highlands to the south and east of Denver beyond Montclair and Aurora. This was the first large irrigating ditch constructed for the purpose of conveying water for sale of the water right to land owners having no ownership title to the ditch itself.

The stimulus which this first successful enterprise gave to like undertakings has since caused the building of

---

*From Judge Stone's article on the English Company.

great canals by companies for the sale of water throughout all the great basins of the rivers of the State. The largest of these canals, in carrying capacities and length, are in the Arkansas valley, some of which are from twenty to thirty feet in width and from forty to one hundred miles in length.

The English Company also built the Windsor hotel, the Barclay block and the Mansions building, costing altogether about one million dollars.

From this condensed sketch it will be seen that the English Company was one of the first great builders of the city of Denver and the State.

The Antero irrigation system is one of the most important enterprises of the kind that has yet been undertaken.

Henry L. Doherty made the new irrigation system possible, and the completion of the Antero reservoir on the 20th of June, 1914, was the occasion of a general celebration in Denver. A half holiday was declared by both the governor and the mayor, and after a dinner in honor of Mr. Doherty, which was attended by 1,000 business men, a great number motored or took trains to the opening of the head gates, a few miles east of Denver.

Irrigation is not a new process in the growing of crops. In Egypt, India and other countries its value in agriculture was recognized many centuries before the discovery of America, and its development in Colorado shows the remarkable energy and intelligence of the men of the new West.

The success of farming by irrigation is demonstrated beyond any reasonable doubt, and agriculture is today a matter of expert practice based upon scientific knowledge, the most fascinating work of development and State building ever opened to the effort of man.

The magnificent water power electric car service, telephones, daily mail service and good roads create a de-

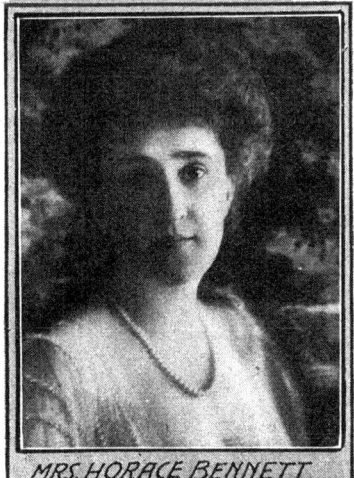

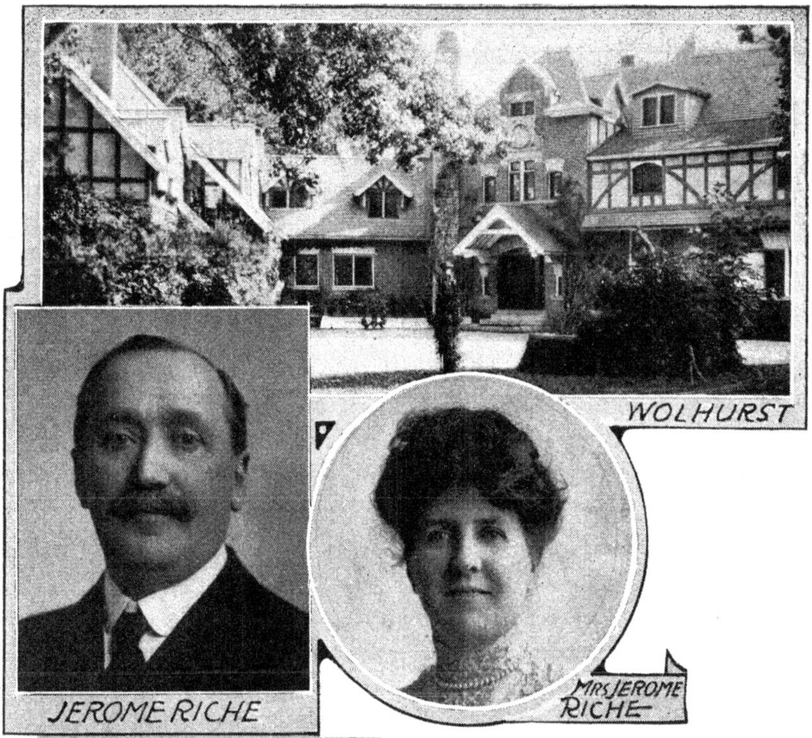

WOLHURST

JEROME RICHE

MRS JEROME RICHE

MRS. HORACE BENNETT

mand for permanent homes and summer homes in Colorado.

Wolhurst

The famous Wolhurst leads in country estates. It was once the home of the late Senator Wolcott, and was originally planned and partly built by him. After his death it became the property of the late Thomas F. Walsh, who enlarged and improved the place.

Several years ago Wolhurst was purchased by Horace W. Bennett and Jerome S. Riche, who have carried out the plans of the previous owners. The property now stands as a model for vast country estates of wealthy American gentlemen who seek the leisure and comfort of the English nobility.

Scientific farming and stock breeding are Horace Bennett's hobbies, and at this great 1,000-acre farm he gratifies these tastes to the fullest extent. The expansion of Wolhurst to a successful stock growing and crop raising farm adds greatly to its interest and attractiveness, and accentuates Colorado's wonderful development along these lines. By this work Mr. Jerome Riche and Mr. Horace Bennett have made themselves prominent as State builders.

Distinguished tourists through Colorado, presidents of the United States, titled personages from abroad, artists and authors, have been guests at this lovely country place, which is presided over by Mrs. Jerome Riche and her daughter, the beautiful and intellectual wife of Horace Bennett. In this elegant home the sweet influence of these gracious women radiate and make their names synonymous with culture, refinement and social grace.

NATHANIEL P. HILL

The miners were moving away from Black Hawk and Central because the surface ores, which yielded their gold quite freely to the stamp mill process, had been nearly all worked out.

The mills and machinery for working refractory ores had cost millions of dollars, but all had failed. At this psychological moment Nathaniel P. Hill, professor of chemistry in Brown University, Providence, R. I., appeared upon the scene. He was impressed with the waste which the methods then used for the reduction of ore involved, and devoted his scientific skill to solving the problem.

Nathaniel P. Hill

He conceived the idea of establishing works which could successfully treat these ores. To carry out his scheme he made two trips to Europe and spent several months in Swansea, Wales, and Freiburg, Germany, examining the methods employed in those places for treating ores of gold and silver.

After satisfying himself fully of the feasibility of smelting the ores of Colorado, he returned to Boston and organized the Boston and Colorado Smelting Company.

In January, 1868, the smelter started operation in Black Hawk.

Professor Hill was the first to treat successfully the refractory ores of Colorado, and by his scientific knowledge, energy and business sagacity placed mining on a sure and sound basis. The miners finding there would be a ready market for their ores, returned by the hundreds to their abandoned claims, and in less than five years the people of Central and Black Hawk, who had talked about moving away, were busy getting rich.

Professor Hill's solution of the then most grave and menacing problem of successfully dealing with our ores marked an epoch in the affairs of Colorado and made him conspicuous in the history of our City and State.

His fine judgment and probity of character suggested Mr. Hill to the people for various offices. He was elected mayor of Black Hawk in 1871, and was made a member of the Territorial Legislature in 1872.

In order to command the ore products of all parts of Colorado and also New Mexico, Arizona, Montana and Utah, it was thought necessary that the smelter should be at some railroad center. Accordingly he built a larger smelter in Denver, known as the Boston and Colorado Smelter, at Argo.

In 1879 he was elected to the United States Senate to succeed Senator Chaffee. As senator he was true to his State and true to the interest of the people he represented. He introduced and carried to a successful issue many important measures.

After he retired to private life he gave his attention exclusively to business affairs. While he determined never again to be a candidate for any public office, he took a keen interest in public affairs and found pleasure in the discussion of National or State political questions in the columns of his own paper, the Denver "Republican," which journal he became the owner of, and retained it to his death.

Senator Hill had a happy faculty of telling a story, and enjoyed relating anecdotes of his early life in the West. I heard him tell one experience when crossing the plains in 1864, the year of the Indian outbreak:

"The coach looked like an arsenal on wheels," said Mr. Hill; "there were nine men on the top and nine inside, all heavily armed. As was the custom in that time, we organized for battle, and elected as captain of the coach a man who claimed to have had numerous fights with the Indians, and in every encounter he swept them all from the face of the earth.

"This hero had a seat just opposite mine in the coach, and he talked about his Indian fights until there seemed to be enough danger floating around loose on the plains to make a volume of blood-and-thunder stories of unwieldy size.

One day as we neared the station where we were to change horses, the men on the top of the coach, just to break the monotony, fired off their guns. The brave Indian fighter ducked his head between my legs with such force that he went through the seat under me, and it was with difficulty that I extricated him. He was as white as death and trembled like a leaf—the worst scared man that I ever saw. Hardly able to articulate, he asked: 'Where are the Indians?'"

Senator Hill was a man of integrity and ability, and in his varied and successful career proved himself worthy of his long line of distinguished ancestors. He married Miss Alice Hale of Providence, R. I., who was a woman of quick perception, tact and kindness of heart. In Gilpin county, where her husband's smelter was located, her home was the center of hospitality. When they moved

Alice Hale Hill

to Denver she became a force in every charitable and social enterprise. She was the founder and president for nine years of the Denver Free Kindergarten Association, and through her untiring energy and liberal donations the building for the Y. W. C. A. was constructed. She was its president for eight years. While her husband was senator she made their home one of the social attractions in Washington by her generous and elegant entertainments.

She represented Colorado as vice-regent of Mt. Vernon Association from 1889 until her death in 1908, and ranks among the notable women of her day.

Senator and Mrs. Hill had three children: Mrs. Franklin Price Knott, elegant and accomplished; Mrs. Lucius M. Cuthbert, who is a woman with strong personality and fine executive ability. She is deeply interested in the problems of today. Since early womanhood Mrs. Cuthbert has been identified with numerous charities and philanthropies.

Mrs. L. M. Cuthbert

Her sympathies and practical aid have been especially devoted to the cause of women and children. In June, 1915, Mrs. Cuthbert was chairman of a campaign committee to raise funds with which to build a hospital for sick and crippled children. This was the most interesting and lucrative campaign ever conducted in Denver, which resulted in the splendid sum of $210,000 being subscribed during a period of twelve days.

Mrs. Crawford Hill

Mrs. Cuthbert has always been a zealous advocate of political freedom for women. In the autumn of 1911 she served as vice-chairman of the "Republican State Central Committee." As a member of the advisory council of the Congressional Union and a national vice-chairman of the Woman Voters' convention, held in San Francisco in September, 1915, Mrs. Cuthbert's attitude toward "Woman Suffrage" is clearly defined.

Senator and Mrs. Hill's only son, Crawford Hill, was associated with his father in business, and inherited many of his fine qualities. He married Miss Sneed of Tennessee, who possesses that indefinable something called charm, which makes her the leader of Denver society.

CHAPTER XVIII

RAILROADS

How the Pioneers Kept Denver From Being Side-tracked

While the great industry of mining brought about the founding of Denver, the railroads have rendered a mighty work in the development and upbuilding of the city and State.

In 1862 Congress passed the first Pacific railroad bill, and the sanguine, enthusiastic pioneers could see Denver's railroad communication in the near future a positive assurance.

They argued, with the pride of the pioneer, that Denver was the only town of importance in the Rocky Mountain region. It did not seem possible to them that a railroad to the Pacific could be built anywhere except by way of Denver.

In 1865 the scheme of W. A. H. Loveland to make Golden a railroad center caused a great disturbance in Denver. Golden was then the Territorial capital, and was boastful and arrogant in regard to its supremacy over the town at Cherry creek. The competition between the two places became fierce.

In 1865-66 the construction work on the Union Pacific and the Kansas Pacific was pushed with great activity. John Evans and other enterprising men began laboring with the Union Pacific directors to bring their road this way.

They mapped out a route through Denver, up Clear Creek canyon, and thence by way of Berthoud Pass, across Western Colorado to Utah. In the mid-summer of 1866 the news came that the Union Pacific would pass one hundred and twenty miles north of Denver.

In looking about for a pioneer to tell of the building of the first railroad, I called upon Mr. John Sidney Brown, a man whose strict attention to business and clear commercial insight had made him a multi-millionaire. Mr. Brown threw himself back in his chair, and his eyes seemed to be looking into the history-making past.

"That road had to be built," he said, with a quick toss of his head that was characteristic of him. "Only those who lived at that time can appreciate the danger that threatened the city. People were leaving, going to Cheyenne or some other place along the line of the Union Pacific, which was being thrown across the continent, linking the East and the West. Business was brisk in Cheyenne and deadly dull in Denver. We were at the fag end. Transportation facilities retarded the development of mines and of agriculture.

We sat here during the middle of the '60's contentedly confident that the Union Pacific would build its main line through Denver. But it did not; stage coaches dropped down from Cheyenne; we were side-tracked. No one felt certain of remaining here. While the railroad question was in doubt, I was among the many who visited Cheyenne, with a view of locating there. The First National Bank of Denver had a branch in Cheyenne; the Kountze Brothers had a branch there; George Tritch opened a store there. It looked for a time as if Cheyenne would be the one great distributing point of the Rocky Mountain region.

In the evenings the men collected around the doorway and in the halls of the old Broadwell house to discuss the situation, and they decided to create a Board of Trade for unity of action. It was organized November 13, 1866.

W. A. H. Loveland, always enterprising and vigorous, was pushing forward his railroad project to make Golden the chief city of Colorado. Colonel James Archer of the Kansas Pacific had come to Denver in the interest of that road. The condition of Denver was nearing a crisis. Colonel D. C. Dodge, representing at that time the Chicago and Northwestern, realizing that something must be done immediately, telegraphed General Grenville M. Dodge to send someone here to discuss the railroad question on some basis within the reach of the people of Denver. Promptly in reply to the telegram came George Francis Train. He was known to be erratic, and the people were disposed to be indignant that he was sent to counsel and guide in this dark hour.

The new Board of Trade called a meeting, and the house was packed with serious, thoughtful people. General Bela M. Hughes addressed the audience in his forceful manner, urging the importance of standing loyally by the organization of business men, and the imperative necessity for immediate action upon the railroad question in order to maintain the supremacy of Denver in Colorado.

Colonel Archer, in a brief speech, stated that the Kansas Pacific would build to Denver if the people would give a bonus of $2,000,000; otherwise it would not. There were many in the audience who had not been told of the proposition Colonel Archer had been authorized by his company to make, and it fell like a thunderbolt among them; they were simply stunned.

George Francis Train followed with a sensible, vigorous and logical address; he outlined a plan for Denver to build a line of her own to connect with the Union Pacific at Cheyenne. "Colorado is a great gold mine, Denver a great fact; make it a railroad center," said Train. The town builders were thrilled and filled with courage.

The new Board of Trade immediately acted upon

Train's advice. A mass meeting was held in the old Denver theater, with W. F. Johnson as president, John Walker, of the Denver Tribune, secretary. John Evans was the principal speaker. He had such a mighty faith in the future of Denver that one stood appalled at its mightiness. At this meeting he predicted that within fifty years Denver would be the bullion center of America, and it would be made an important railroad center. Within twenty years thereafter both of his prophecies were fulfilled.

Talk gave way to work. The Denver Pacific Company was incorporated. The officers were: Bela M. Hughes, president; Luther Kountze, vice-president; D. H. Moffat, treasurer; W. F. Johnson, secretary; F. M. Case, chief engineer. The board of directors were: Joseph E. Bates, Wm. M. Clayton, John Evans, Bela M. Hughes, W. F. Johnson, Luther Kountze, D. H. Moffat, John Pierce and John W. Smith. All names of importance in themselves. "We knew with these men at the front the road would be built," said Mr. Brown in conclusion.

How it was announced in the old Denver Tribune:

THE BIGGEST KIND OF NEWS!!

Building of the D. P. Railway. The Contract Made at Cheyenne

A Dispatch From the Directors

Fire the Guns—Bring Out the Music

Cheyenne, April 27.—Have contracted for the building and equipment of the Denver Pacific Railway. Nine cheers. Music, Fire, Cannon.

J. W. SMITH,
A. B. DANIELS,
F. Z. SALOMON,
Directors D. P. R. Company.

Denver was a little town on the edge of civilization; Cheyenne, as the headquarters of railroad construction, was throwing a long dark shadow over Denver; hard times were a reality. Yet in four days $300,000 in stock had been subscribed. This was not sufficient to complete the road. Arapahoe County issued $500,000 in bonds. They had difficulty in disposing of them. A committee went to Chicago to sell them, but Chicago bond dealers did not think they were of much value. Arapahoe County was a wilderness, and Denver was just a rag of a town. But when John Evans, bearded and big bodied, put his shoulder to the wheel, it moved. He determined to go ahead.

The breaking of the ground for the Denver Pacific was the occasion for much rejoicing. Two women, Mrs. Frederick J. Stanton and Miss Nettie Clark, held the plows that turned the sod. A large number assembled to witness it; a brass band filled the air with music, and Governor Gilpin made one of his famous prophetic speeches.

When the building of the Denver Pacific was an assured thing, the inhabitants of Denver politely informed the Kansas Pacific railroad officials that they could bring their road into Denver if they so desired, but no bonus would be paid. Then commenced a lively race in railroad building, and the Kansas Pacific reached Denver August 15, 1870, two months after the Denver Pacific.

It was the custom in those days to paint the name of some individual on the locomotives. The first locomotive, named D. H. Moffat, arrived with the construction train on June 15.

This engine, previous to its purchase by this company, had been known as number 29 of the Union Pacific road, and had a history. It was the first to enter the town of Cheyenne, the first to cross the Black Hills (west of Cheyenne) and the Rocky Mountains, the first to signal its presence in the valley of Salt Lake, and finally, with the veteran engineer, Sam Bradford, the first to announce to the people of Denver the completion of their first railway.

June 24, 1870, the first passenger train came in; Governor Evans drove the silver spike, which was a present from Georgetown. On one side of it was engraved, "To the Denver Pacific Railway;" on the other side, "John Evans, president." The event was celebrated with music, processions and speeches.

These two railways formed the nucleus around which Colorado's present railroad system was built. Only the group of railroad builders of that time know of the difficulties, the uncertainties, the haltings, the sanguine hope and the utter despair that attended the pioneer railroad enterprises. They had many trying situations to meet and great obstacles to overcome; financial and political difficulties clogged their way, and litigations beset them on every hand.

While these heroic men were struggling to build the Denver Pacific, they were also planning the construction of various other roads in Colorado.

Governor Evans

There were five master leaders among the men who laid the foundation of Denver's great railroad system: Governor John Evans, W. A. H. Loveland, W. J. Palmer, Jerome B. Chaffee and David H. Moffat.

After John Evans retired from the office of governor he gave his energy and constructive power to the development of the resources of the Territory, particularly concerning railroad transportation facilities.

He outlined a system of railroad for Colorado extending from Denver to Golden, Central, Georgetown, Boulder, up South Platte canyon to South Park and beyond into the valley of the Blue river.

It seemed like flights of fancy at that time, yet they were built with marvelous swiftness.

Governor Evans was a shrewd, energetic and farseeing business man. He was active in the many affairs of the fast growing city; founded Colorado Seminary, out of which grew the University of Denver; a philanthropist, a church builder and a great Denver builder. To the prophetic vision of Governor Evans Colorado owes much.

Mr. William G. Evans, the son of Governor Evans, has been connected with some of the greatest enterprises which have made for the greater development and the building up of Denver and the State. He was the chief lieutenant of Mr. Moffat in the construction of what is known as the Moffat Railroad to connect Denver with Salt Lake, was one of its board of directors; he was one of the builders of the Denver Tramway, and its president for many years. He is interested in real estate and has been, in part, the means of constructing some of the large business blocks of the city.

Mr. Evans is a man of courage, indomitable will and a marvelous grasp of affairs; he has been a vital factor in shaping the destiny of Colorado; and, as he is yet in middle life, much may be expected of him in the future.

General Bela M. Hughes

Among the really great men in the history of this western State, not one stands forth with more distinction than General Bela M. Hughes. His efforts in the construction of the first railroad and several later railroads, and his participation in many affairs of the fast growing city placed him among the Colorado State builders.

He was a brilliant lawyer, and what he did in carrying forward the pioneer enterprises, by his eloquence and convincing speeches, cannot be estimated in words and figures.

With a personality distinctly individual and a fine flow of language he could command and hold attention at any time, at any place, and inspire his audience with hope and courage to face the problems of the day.

It was my privilege to know this distinguished gentleman from Kentucky, whom Colorado claims as her very own. His manners were those suggesting a courtly ancestry, he impressed all with his ability and with his breeding. He was naturally retiring and modest, never a seeker of fame, but his scholarly attainments caused men to seek him out. To avarice he was a stranger, valuing money only for the enjoyment it gave him in providing pleasure and happiness for his family and his friends. He was a financier of brains and at the same time a man of heart, which marks the rarest blending in human nature. While carrying forward his work in life, he climbed to fame and wealth, but not at the expense of his fellow creatures.

His wife was a woman of the old Southern school, refined and modest, and in her quiet way became one of the best known and best loved women in Denver; her home was open to everyone, both in a social way and to those needing assistance. Their children are Mr. Andrew S. Hughes, Miss Mary Hughes, Mrs. Sewell Collins, Mrs. Charles E. Roberts, Miss Georgia Hughes and Dr. Tandy Hughes.

Mrs. Peter Randolph Morris, the granddaughter of General Hughes, has inherited many of his fine characteristics, and is today an important personage in the social world of Denver.

David C. Dodge

David C. Dodge

David C. Dodge is a highly respected citizen of Denver. He began life as a civil engineer, and while he was competent and successful in that line, it did not offer a field large enough to satisfy his ambitions. He came to Denver in 1865, and engaged in mercantile business. In 1867 he entered the employ of the Chicago & Northwestern railway as general agent for Colorado and New Mexico, and became associated with other railways. While in the service of these companies his worth was recognized by railway officials and other positions were open to him. He was chosen vice-president and general manager of the Rio Grande Western railway, and the rapid development of that pioneer system under his management forms an important chapter in the history of the State. He is a man of sound common sense, quick perception and fine executive ability.

He is public spirited and always interested in movements which tend to the material and social benefits of the State. In Denver he is known to almost everyone and has many personal friends. His second wife, Miss Nannie O. Smith, was an educator of high standing in Denver for many years. She is a woman of generous impulses and fine culture.

The first telephone installed in Denver was part of a system which operated between the offices of Colonel D. C. Dodge, then manager of the Denver & Rio Grande railroad, and the company's passenger station in this city. The first telephones were operated by a battery which was usually placed in a box in some out-of-the way corner of a room and which was unsightly and unsatisfactory. A Denver grocer conceived the idea of putting a small box under his telephone on which he could write orders from customers. He had the battery placed in this box because it was the most convenient place. Mr. Bell happened to be passing through Denver and was the guest of Colonel Dodge. The box arrangement came under his observation and out of that grew the combination wall instrument which was in standard use for many years.

COLONEL JAMES ARCHER

After the coming of the railroads in 1870, there was a change in the feelings of the people. All doubts of the future vanished and Denver's position as the metropolis of the region was assured. While there was no boom the hotels were crowded, and men were discussing new enterprises.

Colonel James Archer, who was identified with the building of the Kansas Pacific, became one of Denver's forceful and valued citizens. He proposed to the city the construction of gas works. The people approved of his proposition, and the city entered into a contract with Colonel Archer's company for lighting the streets. The gas service was ready January 22nd, 1871, and it was a delightful change, for the artificial lights up to this time had been chiefly stearin candles and coal oil. The maximum price of gas to private customers was five dollars per one thousand feet. Simultaneously with the forming of the gas company, Colonel Archer organized the Denver City Water company, composed of Denver men, to construct water works, on the Holly direct-pressure system, using steam power, to distribute through three or four miles of street mains, supplied from the Platte river.

The people received this proposition with some incredulity. However it was agreed upon, and a contract was made with the city for fire protection by fire hose hydrants on the streets.

In 1871, construction work was begun and rushed to completion. Up to that time domestic water was supplied from wells in door yards.

With these two public utilities Denver started on its way to be the beautiful city of verdure and lights that it is today.

Colonel Archer lived in Denver to the day of his death and was an enterprising and highly respected citizen.

John L. McNeil

Mr. John L. McNeil came to Denver May 1, 1870, and upon the advent of the Denver Pacific railway, became chief clerk and cashier in the freight office, which gave him a wide acquaintance with Colorado business men. He entered the Colorado National Bank early in 1871, serving as paying and receiving teller until January, 1876. At that time he opened the Bank of San Juan at Del Norte, in company with Alvin B. Daniels, Junius F. Brown, J. Sidney Brown and William Moritz Barth, under the firm name of Daniels, Brown & Company. The bank was later moved to Alamosa. A branch was established at Durango in 1880, now the First National Bank of that city with Mr. McNeil as its vice-president.

John L. McNeil

While connected with the banks at Del Norte and Alamosa, Mr. McNeil began to make investments in the San Luis valley and the southwest, developing many interests in that part of Colorado.

In 1883, at the request of prominent business men in Leadville, Mr. McNeil went to that city, where he established the Carbonate Bank, which is still in successful operation.

In 1887, Mr. McNeil removed to Denver, where he represented the Pennsylvania Lead Company of Pittsburgh, purchasing silver and other bullion to the extent of millions of dollars annually. He was president of the Denver Clearing House Association in 1891; was one of the organizers and a director of what is now the Globe Smelting plant of the American Smelting & Refining Company, and was one of the organizers and builders, also the secretary of the Rio Grande Southern railroad. In 1909 he organized the Durango Trust Company of which he is president.

During forty-five years, Mr. McNeil has been connected with the banking, smelting and mining interests of the State. Sterling integrity, good business judgment, combined with firmness and tact, are qualities that have enabled him to become a successful and prosperous business man. His genial disposition makes for him a host of friends.

Mrs. John L. McNeil

Mrs. John L. McNeil has had a public-spirited career; both as club woman and patriotic citizen, she has been prominent in many circles of activities which entitle her to a place among Colorado State builders. As charter member and life member of the Woman's Club of Denver she has rendered vital assistance to that organization. She was the club's first treasurer, and her active work in building up the organization has been rewarded by many honors at the hands of her fellow-members.

Mrs. John L. McNeil

She was chairman of the committee appointed to secure the first appropriation from the Legislature for the support of the State library; the object was accomplished, which attested the efficient work of the committee.

Mrs. McNeil was member of the committee that secured a National Charter for the General Federation of Women's Clubs, 1901. She was chairman of Emergency committee, Colorado Soldiers' Aid Society, 1898, Spanish American war. Charter member of the George Washington Memorial Association October 31, 1898. A member of State commission to mark Santa Fe Trail in Colorado, 1908-09.

Her work as State Regent for Colorado of the Society of the Daughters of the Revolution is an interesting story of itself.

She has been a loyal member of the Denver Fortnightly club for many years.

In local philanthropic work Mrs. McNeil has always been active, serving a long time on the Board of Managers of the Denver Orphans' Home and on that of the Woman's Christian Association.

Her interest in the manners and customs of the Indians led her to become the first Colorado member of the American Folk-lore Society. Her collection of Navajo blankets, gathered from many Indian tribes, before the market was gleaned by tourists, is probably the finest in Colorado.

Yet with all these many phases of active service, Mrs. McNeil finds time for the graces of social companionship and has gathered around her a large circle of delightfully interesting people.

D. H. Moffat

Denver will always place David H. Moffat high among those who labored for the foundation of its greatness.

His career is romantic and full of interest: A poor farmer boy in New York; at the age of twelve, he left home for the city and obtained employment in the New York Exchange Bank as a messenger boy. His promotion was rapid; at the age of sixteen he was assistant teller, and soon after, he accepted the position of teller for the firm of A. J. Stevens & Co., in Des Moines, Iowa.

D. H. Moffat

When he was eighteen he was offered the position of cashier of the Bank of Nebraska, in Omaha. He filled this responsible position satisfactorily for four years.

The Pioneer State Builders

At this time the Pike's Peak gold excitement was beginning to arouse interest in the east, and Omaha was the starting point for many overland parties. David Moffat became enthused with the spirit of adventure; he formed a partnership with C. C. Woolworth, and together they loaded four wagons with books and stationery. Woolworth remained at home and forwarded supplies, and Moffat, the master builder, started on his pioneer journey, which was to end at the summit of the world.

DAVID H. MOFFAT 1860.   DAVID H. MOFFAT 1865.

He arrived in Denver March 17, 1860, and immediately opened a book and stationery shop in Auraria, now called West Denver. Later he moved to the corner of Blake and Fifteenth streets in Denver City. His business venture proved successful and he was soon at the head of one of the largest hardware houses of Denver.

In those days David H. Moffat was a slender youth weighing only one hundred and ten pounds. He appeared to be in delicate health, but the life-giving air of Colorado developed in him a robust constitution, which enabled him to undergo the most active and unceasing labors. Two years after his arrival in Denver he mar-

Mrs. D. H. Moffat and Daughter

ried Miss Fannie A. Buckhout, of Saratoga, New York. There was only one child, now Mrs. Marcia McClurg, widow of James A. McClurg.

A. W. Bailey, who came to Denver about the time Moffat arrived here, tells the following story: It was a custom of young married couples to meet at the homes of different friends once a week. One evening we met at Moffat's cottage home in West Denver. Dinner had been served and the men sat together around the table smoking and talking of our business and our ambitions. Moffat had been silent several minutes, listening to the conversation. Suddenly he turned and looked me squarely in the eye—a way that was characteristic of him,—"Billy," he said, "did you set a stake for yourself when you came out here?" "I did not think much about what I would do here," I replied, "except to make a living, and lay up a little money."

"Well," he said, "I set my mark before I started for Colorado. I determined to make $75,000. When I have done that I will go back to New York and enjoy myself."

His real climb to fortune began when he became engaged in the lucrative business of buying bullion from the miners, and shipping it to the east. It was then that he forgot his stake of $75,000 and set out to make himself one of the big financiers of the country.

His early experience as well as his natural abilities

The Pioneer State Builders

inclined him to banking. Experience had secured him a position in Denver's first banking house, that of Clark & Company, on Blake street, which was swallowed by the First National Bank.

In 1865 the First National Bank of Denver was authorized by the comptroller of the currency. It opened for business May 10, with Jerome B. Chaffee, president; H. J. Roberts, vice-president; George T. Clark, cashier.

In 1867 Moffat's ability as a banker was recognized and he was elected cashier. He became its president in 1880, and continued to hold that position to the time of his death, March 18, 1911.

Moffat had the Midas touch, he became a banker of nation-wide recognition, and during the time he was making a success of the institution with which he was identified, he contributed largely to the upbuilding and the maintenance of the general business of the City and the State. The history of Colorado's progress for forty years carried his name in every chapter. Men regarded him as a brave, far-seeing, aggressive citizen; they admired him as a leader, and loved him as a man.

Other men have been content to succeed as bankers, but Moffat was driven by an inexhaustible energy and purpose. He became engaged in mining, and either alone or in association with some of the best mining men, he was interested in many of the largest gold and silver mines in the State. He dug millions from the ground.

A story is told that in a big Leadville mining deal he set aside an interest for Sylvester Smith, an old associate. Smith's profits amounted to $75,000. Smith was in New York and did not know of his good fortune. One day the cashier of the First National Bank went to Moffat and said, "What do you suppose that fellow Smith has done? He has drawn on us for $50,000." "Well," replied Moffat, "his account is good for it, isn't it?" "Yes," replied the cashier, "but he does not know it." "Don't suppose he does," returned Moffat, "but he knows I am here. He is probably helping a good fellow out of a hole, and knows I'll not go back on him." This was characteristic of D. H. Moffat. He was constantly letting friends in on his good fortune.

Simplicity marked his home life; display was at all times distasteful to him; wealth had a tendency to enlarge his sympathy and good will for his fellow man. No old friend of pioneer days ever went to him for help, who did not receive it. In the panic of 1893, he saved from ruin more than the public will ever know.

Not a State bank, connected in any way with Moffat's bank, went down in that panic. Their credits were extended and money was advanced to tide them over. With his help, tottering mercantile houses weathered the storm. It is said that he dumped $2,000,000 of gilt-edged government securities, his personal property, on the market to save those with whom he had labored through the hard frontier days.

He was often urged to accept the office of United States Senator, but he as often refused, saying he would not have the position if it were handed to him on a silver salver.

Though he never cared for political honors, his influence in politics was powerful. He was a Republican and stood by his party whenever he felt that he was needed.

He was democratic in his ideas; while his friends rode in elegant carriages, he spurned vehicles, and walked. He became a familiar figure on Seventeenth street, strolling along, usually alone, from his home, on Seventeenth and Lincoln, to his bank.

Moffat Held Up

May 28, 1888, the banker had just entered his private office, when a card was brought him. He did not know the man who sent the card, but, as was his custom in

The Pioneer State Builders

those days, he directed that he be admitted. A young man with brisk air, entered. He was well dressed and seemed excited. When Mr. Moffat asked him his business, he pulled a small vial from his pocket and said:

"I come for money. I want $21,000, and if I do not get it at once, I will hurl this vial against the wall; it contains nitroglycerine; you and this building will be blown to pieces."

Moffat looked the young man in the eyes, and said not a word. Then wrote a check for $21,000, and escorted the man to the cashier's window where the money was paid. The young man, after receiving the money, vanished, and never a trace of him was found.

"I felt," said Mr. Moffat, "the moment I looked him in the eye, after he told me why he had come, that he was in earnest."

After that time the banker never admitted strangers into his private office.

Mr. Moffat was also one of the great railroad builders of the State. In 1869, after he had made some money in mining and in banking, he co-operated with Governor Evans in building the Denver Pacific, and later became identified with the construction of many railroads in the State. When he was unable to raise the money from capitalists for a railroad, he would say, "Very well, I'll build it myself." For this expression he was called the conqueror of the mountains.

He built the Boulder Valley railroad to the Marshall coal fields with his own money and first used that expression. When the Rio Grande refused to build a branch of its road from Florence to Cripple Creek, Moffat built that line, and it was afterwards taken over by the Rio Grande system.

For many years he studied the possibilities of Routt County, and the idea of a direct line connecting Denver with Salt Lake gradually took possession of him and became his life dream.

When the financiers of Wall street, with the money market at their command, refused to advance money for this enterprise, he answered, "I'll build it myself."

The enterprise required millions. Railroad men of long experience laughed at Moffat's dream of opening new empires. This aroused his fighting blood, and made him more determined. It is said that he converted nine millions of personal securities into cash, and began the construction of the Denver, Northwestern and Pacific.

This was the last of Mr. Moffat's great undertakings. The opposition of powerful business and commercial interests was met by him single-handed and alone. Many of the trials and tribulations connected with the feat have gone to the grave with him; he never told half the story. The public saw only the result. As an engineering feat it is one of the wonders of the world.

The ambitions of David H. Moffat were more than personal. He loved the State which he had helped to build, and often remarked, "If I succeed in putting Denver on a trans-continental line, I will then think that I have done something for my State."

He lived to see railroad trains running across the Continental Divide, and the pathway to the Pacific ocean opened. But the much desired tunnel through the mountain, which was to make this line the competitor of others, had failed to materialize. His inability to secure the necessary funds for this enterprise, and the entanglement of his own fortune in his work for the public good, undoubtedly hastened his death, which occurred in New York City, while there on business connected with the Moffat tunnel.

He grew with Denver from the beginning; became a promoter and constructor of public utilities; a millionaire mine owner, a railroad builder; and all combined to make him a State builder. He came in 1860 intending to return when he had made $75,000, but he remained more than fifty years, and won a fortune estimated at millions, which in the last years of his life sadly dwindled.

CHAPTER XIX

SETTLEMENT BY COLONIES

The Union Colony

A movement towards settlement by colony closely followed the arrival of the railroad in Colorado.

N. C. Meeker was for many years agricultural editor of the New York Tribune, which position he resigned in 1869, to found a colony on the Cache la Poudre, under the patronage and hearty support of Horace Greeley, whose name it bears.

N. C. Meeker

An organization was perfected and named the Union Colony. A constitution and by-laws written by Meeker was adopted. Meeker was elected president of the colony, General R. A. Cameron, vice-president, and Horace Greeley, treasurer.

They had their share of hardships the first four or five years. There were continual Indian scares. The winter of 1873 was the worst Greeley has ever suffered. Antelopes, nearly starved, came into town by the hundreds.

"When speaking of the 'Union Colony' now, they say 'it was a great success, and people should always immigrate in colonies.' But at that time there was much dissatisfaction, and the colony officers were obliged to bear a great deal of abuse. Still they never lost courage. Poor Mr. Meeker, who was as sensitive as a woman, would have been made very unhappy at that time if his fellow-worker, General Cameron, had not taken the brunt of the work in guiding the people, and explaining continually that the project was bound to succeed. Curses and sneers rolled off his broad shoulders like water off a duck's back.

"When he would say cheerily, 'My friends, it is all right, this thing is bound to succeed, and Greeley will be one of the finest farming regions on the face of the earth!' some one in the crowd would retort, 'O, yes, I bet that "feller" gets four dollars a day for lying.'

"Greeley has never had a whisky saloon. It was long known as Saints Rest, and is often so called now. The name arose from the fact that they had no wickedness and no need of police.

"Many left Greeley declaring it was a fraud, there was no chance to sell whisky, the soil was not good for anything, and Horace Greeley and Mr. Meeker were fools. After the 'soreheads' had taken their departure there was less talking done and more work. Men adapted themselves to their new surroundings, and a man in overalls, shirt sleeves and old straw hat, was as likely to be a minister, doctor or lawyer as a common workman. It was as if people were going about in disguise, for men cannot wear fine clothes while making adobe bricks, and that was the occupation of many during the first summer."

Meeker started a paper, which he called the Greeley Tribune. The first issue appeared two days before Greeley's arrival. The paper is still in existence and has, perhaps, the most unique headline of any paper in the country. Greeley wrote the headline for Meeker and a photo-engraving was made of his writing. It is still used. When the paper was changed from a weekly to a daily, the postoffice authorities ordered that the word "daily" be inserted in the title. So the historic old headline was taken off and replaced with plain print. The community arose in arms and demanded the return of the headline. To satisfy both government and the citizens, the word "daily" was "faked" to resemble the rest of Greeley's almost illegible writing.

Few pioneer communities have been blessed by more forceful individuals than those of the Greeley Colony.

Jared L. Brush crossed the plains in an ox team during the P. P. excitement of 1859. In 1870 he became a member of the Union Colony and located at Greeley. He was a freighter, a farmer, a "cattle man" and a banker. In the course of time he became one of the best known and most prominent men in the history of the State. He was elected to the first State Legislature and re-elected. He was elected Lieutenant-Governor under Governor McIntyre and re-elected under Governor Adams.

Mr. Brush took an active part in educational affairs and was influential in securing the location of the State Normal School at Greeley.

Benjamin H. Eaton was attracted by the gold excitement and reached Colorado in an ox-team in 1859. He immediately commenced to farm.

It is related of him that "his first crops were snakes from sand dunes, while grasshoppers and other pests thrived better than wheat or potatoes, and there was little promise in the land." After he joined the Greeley Colony he became one of its greatest moving powers. In connection with farming he early became a large contractor and constructed the first irrigating ditch from the Cache la Poudre, which was the beginning of a splendid system of irrigation.

He became the largest individual holder of land and the wealthiest farmer in the State. His principal crops were wheat, alfalfa and potatoes.

The Pioneer State Builders

He had many fine characteristics and many warm friends. He was elected to the Territorial Council and later made Governor of Colorado.

The sad fate of Mr. Meeker will be found in the following brief sketch of the Ute War:

Naturally philanthropic, among other things he made a careful study of the condition of the Indians, and believing that, with the earnest support of the government, they could be made to accept civilization, he applied for and obtained the agency for the White River tribe of Utes in 1877.

Arriving at the agency he found that many of the Indians had left the reservation, and great dissatisfaction existed among them, because of alleged ill-treatment by former agents. True to the main purpose of his mission he soon succeeded in restoring quiet among the malcontents.

It was a favorite theory with him that it was possible to make the agency self-supporting by teaching these savages to adopt stock raising and agriculture. He also thought the young might be induced to attend school, and grow up educated in the English language and trained in the manner of civilized society.

The agency was removed during Mr. Meeker's administration twenty miles from White River to Powell's bottom, one of the most beautiful tracts of land on the continent. Here he began to teach the unsophisticated children of nature how to cultivate the soil. The experiment worked well until the spring of 1879. Mr. Meeker fenced the ground, dug wells, and built irrigating ditches. The Indians made serious complaints of these innovations. To the fence they objected strenuously, because it injured the feet and legs of their ponies.

They made frequent protests to Mr. Meeker, and finally sent a delegation of four to lay their grievances before Governor Pitkin.

These commissioners bewailed bitterly the agent's effort to cultivate the ground, and his daughter's attempt to teach their children the ways of the white man. They wanted him restricted to supplying them with food, and compelled to allow them to live their lives in their own way. They assumed a hostile position during the entire summer, at times committing horrible depredations on the white man's side of the line, and the miners or prospectors who ventured on their reservation to dig for gold, were shot down like dogs. They wandered up and down the country, burning the forests and grasses, leaving a trail of fire from the Wyoming line to the boundary of New Mexico.

Meanwhile, certain members of the tribe became very troublesome to Meeker. On one occasion he was brutally assaulted by Chief Johnson and quite seriously injured. Immediately after this occurrence Mr. Meeker applied for troops for protection, and Major Thornburg, commanding at Fort Steele on the Union Pacific railroad, was at once ordered to use all dispatch in reaching the Indian country.

During this time the Utes were secretly preparing for a massacre. They purchased, at exterior points, arms of the most improved pattern, and ammunition in large quantities.

Everything being in readiness, Chief Douglass visited the agency on the morning set for the massacre. He made some remarks about the soldiers coming. Mr. Meeker assured him that their coming did not mean war. Apparently convinced, but at heart resolved to do murder, Douglass ate dinner with them, and lingered long after the meal, laughing and talking in a very pleasant manner with Mr. Meeker, Miss Josephine and Mrs. Meeker. Suddenly he left. He was thought by the people of the agency to possess many good qualities, but he proved himself to be one of the most cruel and heartless, as well as one of the most treacherous of the band. A few minutes after his departure the firing began. The women and children, in great alarm, sought a hiding place, and when they were driven from their shelter the cruel work had been accomplished. The agent and his employees were murdered, and no white person survives who witnessed it. Mrs. Meeker, after emerging from concealment, in passing across the grounds, came close to the side of her dead husband, with whom she had passed twenty-five years of contented married life. She stopped to kiss the cold blue lips, but was rudely ordered by Douglass to pass on.

The men were dead. Miss Josephine, young and intelligent, and Mrs. Meeker, sixty-four years old, one of the gentlest, most motherly of women, were in the hands of the barbarians.

The Six Days' Siege

Major T. T. Thornburg, in obedience to orders, left Rawlins immediately for White River agency. When his command reached the point where the road crosses Milk river they were attacked by about three hundred warriors lying in ambush. Major Thornburg, at the head of twenty men, made a bold charge upon the enemy. In this valorous dash the gallant leader was killed and Captain Payne came into command.

The third day of the siege they were reinforced by a company of colored cavalry, under the command of Captain Dodge, who had been notified by a Rawlins courier of the distress of their white brethren in arms.

And still the murderous work went on, ceasing at night, but with the first dawn of day the alert foe, securely hidden behind the sheltering bluffs, renewed their fire. On the fifth day General Merritt came to their rescue with a considerable body of troops.

Observing the strong reinforcements, and realizing

their inability to maintain the fight any longer, the hostiles withdrew, leaving the field to General Merritt, who immediately marched to the agency, where he found the bodies of the unfortunate men, who were slain at the beginning of the outbreak, and buried them in a beautiful spot near the crystal waters of White river.

He then started at the head of seven hundred men for the camp of the hostiles who held the captive women, and which he had every reason to believe was located on Grand or Blue river. After a march of about six hours he received orders to suspend operations against the Indians, as negotiations for peace were in progress, and it was believed they would agree to surrender the captives and deliver the warriors who had led the outbreak. The military and the country generally considered this a disgraceful termination of the campaign, but were, of course, powerless to prevent it.

Ouray, the head chief of the Utes, had started on a big hunt which was to have lasted three months, but news of the trouble at White river caused his speedy return. He sent a positive command to the hostile Utes to cease fighting.

The Rescue by General Adams

General Adams was agent for the White River Utes in 1870-71. At the time of the Ute war he was special agent for the United States Postoffice Department, with headquarters at Denver. He received telegraphic notification that at the request of Secretary Schurz he had been detailed for special work as representative of the Interior Department among the Indians. This was soon followed by another dispatch conveying specific instructions as to his mission and how to proceed.

General Adams arrived at Ouray's camp on the night of the 18th, and the chief of the Utes confirmed his reputation as a friend of the white man, by giving his aid and advice in perfecting the plans for the trip to the Grand river, one hundred miles north, where the captives were then known to be.

The following morning the general started on his journey, accompanied by three chiefs and ten other Indians. There was also in the company a special correspondent of the Denver Tribune and Captain Cline, an experienced scout and frontiersman, with two men to drive wagons and take care of the camping outfit.

The chiefs who escorted the general were named, Sapavanaro, Shavano and Colorow.

When the general reached the Indian camp he made Chief Douglass understand that he had been sent by the government to say "it did not want to fight, but the white squaws *must* be returned to their friends."

Then commenced a council which lasted five hours. Chief Sapavanaro stood by the general, who formally made known his errand; then one after another of the hostile chiefs spoke, the majority of them refusing their consent to the surrender of the prisoners. The pipe was passed around, but Adams refused to smoke with them until they should agree to his request. Sapavanaro also refused to smoke. Shavano became angry and withdrew from the council. At this Sapavanaro strode resolutely into the circle and made a powerful speech. He told them he bore the mandate of Ouray; that unless the Indians surrendered the captives to General Adams they would be cut off from all communication with their head chief, who would join with the whites in forcing them to terms.

During the speech there was a great pow-wow and considerable excitement in the council, but it had the desired effect.

The captive women were surrendered to General Adams. They were escorted to Chief Ouray's house and there met by Ralph Meeker, eldest son of the murdered agent. He took them to their home in Greeley and the poor sorrow-stricken women were once more among loving friends.

The Growth of the State Teachers' College of Colorado

Twenty-five years ago the State Legislature established the State Normal School at Greeley. The school began on a very modest basis. There were four teachers and about eighty students. They occupied what is now the east wing of the administration building, in which there were five or six class rooms. The campus of forty acres was little more than a sand waste where sage brush, cacti and jack-rabbits were plentiful.

In 1891 President Snyder assumed charge of the school. He began at once to develop a unit plan of building and campus improvements. As a result no State institution in Colorado presents a more useful and pleasing arrangement of its buildings and other improvements. The campus has become one of the beauty spots of the State. In it is found growing every tree and shrub that will grow in this climate; and what was once a sand waste has been converted into a great outdoor museum and laboratory for the use of Colorado's citizens.

Z. X. Snyder

Because of the standard of work done at the Normal school at Greeley, the Legislature in 1911 changed the name of the school and it is now officially known as the State Teachers' College of Colorado.

The State Normal School faculty of four in 1890,

instructing a student body of eighty, has grown from year to year until in this year of 1915 the State Teachers' College of Colorado has a faculty of ninety-six, instructing a student body of fifteen hundred students. In 1891 there were twelve persons graduated from the school; in 1914 the college gave four hundred and fifty-nine diplomas to its graduates. From 1891 to the present date the school has graduated 3,419 teachers and sent them into the public schools of this and other states, where they have done and are now doing great service in the cause of education.

For a quarter of a century Dr. Z. X. Snyder has labored diligently to make the State Teachers' College of Colorado one of the foremost schools of its kind in the United States. He has given the best of his life to the cause.

As a result of his masterful teaching thousands of young men and women have come to a realization of the true values of life. His name will go down in our history as one who has had a powerful influence upon educational thought and practice in this country.

The success of the Greeley Colony led the Chicago-Colorado Colony to select the site of Longmont, environed by splendid agricultural lands. The town was established in 1871.

Mr. H. D. Emery, then editor of the Prairie Farmer, was chairman of the locating committee.

Longmont is one of Colorado's towns made prosperous by sugar beets. It is a busy city with prettily kept streets and parks and is one of the best known gateways to Estes and Rocky Mountain National parks.

Loveland is a beautiful city of 6000 people; it is the hub of an agricultural district where many of Colorado's superlative achievements have been made.

Fort Collins was a rallying point, used by the United

States military for protection to settlers during the Indian wars. In 1872 the town was settled by a colony similar to that of Greeley, under the superintendence of General R. A. Cameron. W. E. Pabor was secretary and treasurer. It is situated in a beautiful valley, which has become one of the most important agricultural regions of the State.

The State Agricultural College is located here. This college had its beginning in territorial days. Three citi-

LONGMONT SUGAR BEET FACTORY

LOVELAND

zens of Fort Collins donated to the Territory two hundred and forty acres of land adjoining the city and later handsome buildings were erected, fully equipped for the work of the institution. Here thorough instruction is given in agriculture and the natural sciences connected with that pursuit. The college maintains four experiment stations which are in active operation.

An interesting relic of pioneer days is the "Aunty Stone cabin," which the pioneer women of the Cache la

Poudre Valley have repaired. It is the only building left in Fort Collins to tell of the days when the savages roamed the plains searching for plunder and the scalps of the hated white people.

The cabin was built by Lewis and Elizabeth Stone in 1864. The logs were brought from the mountains, six miles distant, with ox teams.

After the United States troops were withdrawn, Mrs. Stone, whose husband had died, converted her home into a hotel, and was hostess to many distinguished men of the Territory and Nation.

Aunty Stone Cabin

The first school in Fort Collins was opened in this building by Mrs. Stratton, the mother of Mrs. P. J. McHugh, who is prominent in club circles and widely known throughout the State.

Mrs. Stratton, at this writing, is a frail little woman with snow white hair and pleasing personality. She talks interestingly of the early days. "A band of friendly Indians camped here," she said, "and one day it suddenly grew dark in my school room; I looked up to find the two windows filled with Indians. They looked on quietly for a time, and left quietly." This school inspired the people to form a school district, the first one on the Cache la Poudre.

Within the walls of the Aunty Stone cabin, the pioneers hold their pleasant re-unions.

One of the most important manufacturing industries in northern Colorado is canning; vegetable products, of many kinds, peas leading in value, are canned in the northern Colorado towns. Here are located great lignite coal fields which supply the manufacturing establishments. Greeley, Fort Collins, Loveland, Longmont, Fort Morgan, are full of opportunity for the merchant or manufacturer.

Every year sees some new manufacturing enterprise, a canning factory, a creamery, a milk condensing plant, a flour mill, placed in operation in these towns of the Platte valley.

CHAPTER XX

STATEHOOD CONSUMMATED

JEROME B. CHAFFEE

During the fifteen years that Colorado was a territory, there were eight different administrations. These frequent changes in the Territorial executive and the political conditions, proved unsatisfactory to the pioneers. In 1864 a movement was made for the admission of the State—a constitution was framed, submitted to popular vote and defeated. In 1865 another constitution was framed and adopted by a small majority. The act passed by Congress providing for our admission under this constitution was vetoed by President Andrew Johnson. A third attempt was made, when Congress met in December, 1866, and at this time a bill for an enabling act was introduced early in the session; it was amended by the House, passed the Senate and was promptly vetoed by President Johnson, and the hopes of the State workers in Colorado were again cast down. But they did not give up. February 12, 1868, a bill for the admission

Jerome B. Chaffee

of Colorado was introduced by Senator Yates, of Illinois, but it did not progress beyond its introductory stage. Each failure was to some extent the result of jealousies and contentions of politicians, who in seeking a comfortable place for themselves, did not hesitate to forward their own interests.

The popular judgment here had been opposed to forming a State, giving as one reason the small population. But the marked advance made by the number of new railroads, the development of new mines, the increase of agriculture and rapid accession of population, led the politicians to hope that the people would be willing to assume the responsibilities and burdens of State government.

In the Forty-third Congress, 1873-75, Jerome B. Chaffee, our delegate in Congress, again worked for Colorado's recognition. He was a pioneer in legislation and gold mining, and one of the greatest political party leaders of his time.

The following is quoted from Frank Hall: "Chaffee was the father of the State." In 1873, President Grant, inspired by Mr. Chaffee, urged the passing of an "enabling act" for Statehood. The attachment between these men was exceedingly close, and it was due unquestionably to Mr. Chaffee's earnest entreaties that the recommendation was made.

When a bill was introduced nearly all the influential newspapers of the country were bitterly opposed and many of the Senators and Representatives of the older States were openly hostile, largely on the ground of insufficient development and population.

Long prior to his election as a delegate to Congress, Chaffee had acquired a moderate fortune in mines and held the presidency of the First National Bank of Denver. He formed intimate personal relations with leading men in Washington, he dressed well, lived well, was extremely companionable, and what is more to the purpose, played poker with the skill of a veteran; there was no form of entertainment that the big men of that period loved more passionately than a pleasant quiet game of 'draw,' at night after the arduous labors of the day were over. The fight for Statehood proved a long, costly battle for Chaffee, lasting ten solid years, and absorbing the greater part of his fortune. He expended in his several campaigns more than $150,000 of his private means. To convey a clear idea of local conditions, take a backward glance and briefly epitomize the situation as it existed when President Grant wrote the message which inspired the successful movement for Statehood.

In 1870, Denver had a population of 4,000. Three railroads had been constructed; the Denver Pacific to Cheyenne, Kansas Pacific, and the Colorado Central to Golden. The entire population of the Territory did not exceed 40,000. The assessed valuation of property in 1873 was $35,582,438. There was no Leadville, Cripple Creek had never been heard of, Gunnison and San Juan countries were occupied by Indians, Colorado Springs and Manitou had no existence until 1871, Pueblo was a small village and the only productive mining sections were Gilpin, Clear Creek, Lake, Park and Summit Counties, whose yields of precious metal were limited.

During the pendency of the bill for the "enabling act" and the debate thereon, a leading journal of Pittsburg, Pennsylvania, said: "Colorado is one of the most intelligent manifestations of the spirit of territorial enterprise we ever had. The discovery of gold and the profligate scenery of the spot is its entire fortune. Colorado consists of Denver, the Kansas Pacific railway and scenery. The agricultural resources do not exist at all."

A New York paper said: "The population, such as it is, is made up of roving hordes of adventurers, who have no settled homes, there or elsewhere, and they are there solely because the state of semi-barbarism, prevalent in that wild country, suits their vagrant habits. There is something repulsive in the idea that a few handfuls of rough miners and reckless bushwhackers numbering less than 100,000, should have the same representation in the Senate as Pennsylvania, Ohio and New York, and that these few thousand should have the same voice in our legislation and administration of the government as the millions of other States. A territorial government is good enough and effective enough for such unformed communities, and to that they should be confined for a generation to come."

Then came the awful "Black Friday," that paralyzed the country, followed by a rush of population to the new gold discoveries in the Black Hills of South Dakota, which took away thousands of our people. Add to this a still greater calamity, the appalling devastation by grasshoppers, that appeared in countless millions from 1874 to 1876 inclusive, and laid waste all the agricultural sections and reduced our farmers almost to the verge of destitution, and you have a tolerably complete epitome of the conditions under which we made our last appeal for a place in the American Union.

Impelled by the friendly attitude of President Grant's message, Chaffee, on the 8th of December, 1873, introduced a bill for an act to enable the people of Colorado to form a State government. It was referred to the committee on territories of which he was a member, then it was reported back to the House and passed by that body without serious opposition, on the 8th of June, 1874.

Mr. Patterson relates a very interesting incident connected with the State's admission.

"It was the plan of the managers in the House to admit Colorado and New Mexico at the same time," says

Mr. Patterson. "New Mexico then had a larger population than Colorado, though of a different character." The bills for their admission were introduced at the same time, and they passed the House at the same time, by the same vote, and they went over to the Senate, where both were hung up. At length the Senate passed both bills by the same identical vote, but with a number of inconsequential amendments, tacked on by the enemies of statehood, to ultimately defeat the measure.

It was a period of great political bitterness, and was associated with reconstruction measures for the South, all of which the South fought with unswerving steadfastness. What was denominated a "force bill" was before the House during this short session, and debate upon it occurred after the statehood measures had passed the Senate and been returned to the House for concurrence in the amendments. During the discussion of the force bill, Hon. J. C. Burrows, then a new member from Michigan, and later a senator from Michigan for a good many years, made a speech favoring the force measure. His speech was conspicuously bitter and eloquent. The House rang with his rounded and vitriolic periods. Before its conclusion the Republican members had gathered about the speaker and were carried off their feet by the splendor of Burrows' peroration. On its conclusion there was a general rush by the Republican members to congratulate Burrows. The very first person to reach and shake his hand was Mr. Elkins, then the delegate in Congress from New Mexico. The Democrats, and especially the southern men, looked on this scene with grim remonstrance, and they noted the celerity with which Elkins rushed up to congratulate Congressman Burrows. Many of them who had voted for the admission of New Mexico, as well as of Colorado, gritted their teeth, and then mentally resolved they would repay Delegate Elkins for his unwise enthusiasm, and the display of it which he made, and they bided their time until the bills for the admission of the two territories were finally voted upon.

It was the last night of the short session of the Forty-third Congress. Mr. Blaine had been attending a social function, and entered the chamber a short time after midnight, dressed in evening clothes. He took the gavel to direct the House business during the rest of its closing hours. Very soon thereafter the Colorado and New Mexico bills were reached, and Mr. Hoskins, who had them in charge, being recognized by Speaker Blaine for the purpose, moved that the bill for the admission of Colorado, with the Senate amendments, be taken from the speaker's table, that the rules be suspended, the amendments concurred in, and the bill placed on its final passage. Owing to the parliamentary situation of the measures, a two-thirds vote was necessary to carry the motion. But the Colorado measure received the requisite two-thirds by a very small margin and Colorado's statehood was assured. Immediately, Mr. Hoskins, the same member, being again recognized by Speaker Blaine, made the same motion with reference to the bill for New Mexico, and the roll-call immediately followed. The whole House was watching the progress of the roll-call with intense interest, and it was noticed that here and there along the line some Democratic member who had voted for Colorado voted against New Mexico. Some of the southern men who were incensed with Elkins for the Burrows episode were getting in their deadly work, and when the roll-call was concluded and the result announced it was found that New Mexico's statehood had been defeated—lacking seven or eight votes of the requisite two-thirds. Colorado became a full fledged State by the proclamation of President Grant in the Centennial year of 1876, while New Mexico was compelled to struggle in the bonds of territorial vassalage until 1911, when the long delayed justice of admission was given it. Every member and senator in those days knew that it was that unfortunate and ill-timed enthusiasm of Delegate Elkins that prevented New Mexico from being made a State in the Union at identically the same time with Colorado, and that it was the slip of Mr. Elkins that kept it out of the Union for thirty-four long hungry years, and Mr. Elkins was to have been one of New Mexico's senators, as Mr. Chaffee became one of Colorado's. Elkins, disgusted with the failure, moved from New Mexico to West Virginia, and became a senator from that new-made State, which position he held until his death—not so very long ago.

THE STATE CONSTITUTION

On the 14th of September, 1875, Governor John L. Routt issued his proclamation to the sheriffs of the several counties, notifying them that an election would be held for delegates to the constitutional convention on Monday, October 25th, in the city of Denver. The Republicans elected twenty-four and the Democrats fifteen. Each party had nominated some of its ablest men. But in a number of counties of the State, delegates were not nominated nor elected as members of any political party, since a constitution is in no sense a party measure or instrument, but for all the people of the State. The convention met in Denver December 20th, 1875, and conducted its labors to final conclusion under the presidency of Joseph C. Wilson, of El Paso County. No more honorable, patriotic or efficient body of men has ever been assembled in Colorado during any period of its history.

The convention completed its work March 14, 1876, and after drafting an admirable address to the people, adjourned.

The next step was to procure its adoption by the people; many were openly hostile to the State movement, owing to the depression from causes already cited and the fear of increased taxation. The few newspapers advocating the cause brought to bear every convincing argument that the editors could think of, and the members of the convention took the platform in their several communities and argued eloquently in its behalf.

On the 30th of June a mass meeting was held in Denver; the speakers were Governor Routt, Hon. G. S. Symes, H. P. Bennet, Judge Blackburn, W. B. Mills, W. S. Decker, Gen. Bela M. Hughes, Alfred Sayre, Gen. S. E. Brown, Maj. E. L. Smith, A. P. Hereford and others. The meeting was arranged by Dr. R. G. Buckingham as mayor and chairman of the special committee appointed for the purpose. These men by their arguments and eloquence succeeded in stirring up a feeling of activity for the measure.

Mayor Buckingham issued a proclamation earnestly requesting the business men of the city to close their places of business on July 1, between the hours of one and four that their employes might have the privilege of casting their votes on this glorious occasion.

The election occurred on Saturday, and Sunday morning the newspapers gave the news of a gratifying result.

Fourth of July

That same week the Fourth of July was made a day of great celebration. A large procession was formed of people from every walk in life, and stout-hearted pioneers whose pulses beat true to the best interests of the new State, were conspicuous in the streets and shouted themselves hoarse with enthusiasm at the glorious pageant.

May Butler Brown, who had been officially recognized by the pioneers as the first female white child born in the territory, represented Colorado and carried the flag in the "Procession of States." She was born October 15, 1860, on the site of the old Charpiot's Delmonico hotel, Larimer street, between Fourteenth and Fifteenth streets.

The procession, keeping step to patriotic music, marched to Denver Grove, where a number of orations were delivered.

That year having brought the one hundredth anniversary of the founding of the National government, Colorado was familiarly called the Centennial State.

May Butler Brown

The following interesting telegrams were received:

Philadelphia, July 4, 1876.

To Governor Routt:
  Are we a state? Answer.

STEPHEN DECATUR.

We are. The Centennial State and 20,000 here assembled send joyful greetings to the sister States of the American Union at Philadelphia on this our Fourth.

ROUTT.

Washington, D. C., July 4, 1876.

To Governor Routt:
  Through you I greet the Centennial State, the latest but the brightest star in the political firmament. I am proud of the consciousness of representing the grandest State, the bravest men and the handsomest women on the continent.

T. M. PATTERSON.

On Tuesday morning, July 28th, John M. Reigart, private secretary to Governor Routt, left Denver for

Washington, bearing a duly authenticated copy of the constitution, ordinances, an abstract of the votes, copies of proclamation and other documents, to his excellency, U. S. Grant.

Colorado Day

August 1st, President Grant issued his proclamation, declaring the fact that the fundamental conditions imposed by Congress on the State of Colorado to entitle it to admission into the Union had been ratified and accepted and that the admission of said State into the Union was now complete.

That is why the Sons of Colorado celebrate August 1st as "Colorado Day."

T. M. Patterson

T. M. Patterson says he was first attracted to Colorado by reading Bayard Taylor's thrilling and charming description of its mountains, its mining camps, and Denver. This was in 1868, and later in 1869 he made up his mind to see the country for himself. He only got as far as Wallace—the last station on what was then called the Kansas Pacific railroad—which had just been extended beyond the western boundary of Kansas into Colorado. The Indians were then on the warpath between that point and Denver, and no stages were running, and other overland travel had entirely ceased. He reluctantly turned back, but determined to try it again as soon as conditions would permit. But his affairs prevented him from turning towards Colorado again until 1872, when he got here by "all rail," and was soon satisfied that Taylor's description of the country had not overshot the mark. Mr. Patterson says he found that he had decided inclination towards politics, and wished in coming west to locate in a country where the Democratic party could

SENATOR T. M. PATTERSON

MRS. R. C. CAMPBELL

A WAR TIME PHOTO

AT THE AGE OF 20

offer an ambitious young man no inducements to enter political life, and he thought Colorado was that place—for no Democrat up to that time had been sent to Congress, nor had been otherwise favored by the voters of the Territory. Colorado was considered dead safe for the Republican party for all time. How Mr. Patterson succeeded in avoiding the temptation of politics is shown by his career after getting here. He was elected city attorney in the early spring of 1874, when he had been in the Territory less than fifteen months, and was elected delegate to Congress in the summer of the same year, when he had lived here less than twenty-two months. It may not be amiss to relate that Mr. Patterson was elected city attorney because he demonstrated during his first year in Colorado his brilliancy and efficiency as a lawyer.

The bill for the admission of Colorado as a State was pending in Congress when Mr. Patterson was elected to that body. It had already passed the House, but was water-logged in the Senate. The Senate in those days was very much opposed to the admission of new States, for every new State added as many senators to that body as the great State of New York had or any other of the older States, and it was that feeling that caused the Senate to hang up Colorado's admission. Mr. Patterson felt that he could materially assist in getting the Senate to let go, so as soon as the short session convened in December, he went to Washington. His efforts with Democratic senators soon bore fruit. The bill was gotten to a vote in the Senate, and the great obstacle to statehood was overcome.

Following the admission of the State, Mr. Patterson was elected to represent it in Congress. By that time he was recognized as one of the few great leaders of the western bar. While in Congress he was recognized as a leader in his political party, and through his profound legal knowledge and brilliant oratory he won national fame. He was elected to the United States Senate, and succeeded E. O. Wolcott in 1901.

Recalling the struggle for State admission Mr. Patterson referred to Hon. Jerome B. Chaffee, whom he succeeded as delegate to Congress in 1874: "Mr. Chaffee," he said; "was one of the most influential and best equipped men who ever represented the West in Washington." His enemies frequently denounced him as a corrupt politician. The ground for this was that in one of his campaigns Mr. Chaffee caused hundreds of sacks of flour to be distributed among the Mexican voters, of which he made no concealment. That was considered terribly corrupt in those early days, but since then corruption in politics has taken a different and wider scope.

Speaking of the primitive state of society in Denver even as late as 1873, Mr. Patterson recalled that in that year a band of the Ute Indians passed through Denver bound for the plains to meet their ancient and implacable foes, the Cheyennes. A battle between the two bands occurred not far to the east of Denver. The Ute band, several hundred in number, returned to Denver, carrying on the ends of long poles the bloody scalps of Cheyennes they had slain. They paraded through Denver's principal streets on horseback, single file, their bodies naked except the usual clouts, and covered with war paints, with the bleeding scalp trophies waving aloft. They went into camp across the Platte near Barnum and were there for a week. Every day and night they gave their scalp dances, which were witnessed by thousands of Denver's people.

From Mr. Patterson's first arrival in Denver he thoroughly identified himself with the development both of Denver and the State. He has erected a number of Denver's finest buildings; he has been a large employer of labor, in the working of mines, both coal and the precious metals. In 1891 he bought a controlling interest in the Rocky Mountain News, and later the whole of it; he bought the Denver Times from D. H. Moffat, and how he built those papers up and made them a power for reform in government and the State's general welfare is now part of Colorado's history.

His daughter, Mrs. Richard Crawford Campbell, is actively connected with some of the most important charity organizations in Denver, and is prominent in the city's intellectual activities.

The Centennial State

The last Legislature of the Territory met January 2, 1876, and owing to the State movement that was under way they decided to do very little business and get along without a chaplain, for which it has passed down in history as the "Prayerless House."

The constitution provided that the territorial officers should continue in their respective positions and in the discharge of the duties thereof, in the interval between the State's admission and the inauguration of the duly elected State officers. The first election of State officers and members of the Legislature was held according to the constitution on October 3, 1876. Two tickets, Republican and Democratic, were in the field, and the contest was a lively one. Governor John L. Routt led the Republican, and General Bela M. Hughes the Democratic. The Republicans won by a narrow margin.

The last House of Representatives of the Territory of Colorado and the first of the new-born State convened November 1, 1876, and in spite of it being called the prayerless house, it was one of the most harmonious legislative bodies that either the Territory or the State ever had. By act of Congress this House was allowed to sit only forty days, as it was the first House that ever sat for the State of Colorado. Even though the time was short, the prayerless house did such work in organizing the business of the State that it cannot be forgotten. In this gathering were many of the builders of the western country, men who went through all kinds of hardships and emerged the stronger for their experiences. Alfred Butters was speaker of the House. He had been, and continued for years, an important factor in the affairs of the West.

The State executive officers elected were inaugurated November 3. Herman Beckhurts, Otto Mears and W. L.

Hadly were chosen presidential electors. Jerome B. Chaffee and H. M. Teller were elected United States senators. January 9, 1877, Moses Hallett was appointed United States district judge, and Westbrook S. Decker United States district attorney, by President Grant. So, after a hard struggle, the victory was won, and Colorado entered upon her brilliant career as the "Centennial State."

PART VII
THE MOUNTAIN TOWNS

CHAPTER XXI

PROSPERITY OF THE COUNTRY

THE RANCHMAN'S STORY

I have dwelt somewhat minutely on matters and things connected with the settlement of Denver, for its rise and progress is a marvel of modern civilization, and, in a measure, its history is the history of Colorado. Never before has there been such a city built up under so many conflicting circumstances, particularly in its first decade.

The establishment of new mining camps was in general a repetition of the scenes enacted at Cherry creek. To trace this movement throughout the pioneer camps down to when Colorado became a State would be a task impossible without repeating the facts that make up the history of Colorado.

Each town, in its own history, forms an integral part of the whole, and while it is not my purpose to go into the details of the settlement, my stories will show the up-building of the great industrial mosaic of the State.

One bright morning in August I took the Colorado Central, in company with a party of eastern tourists, to "do" the mountains, and gather stories of history, adventure, life and scenery, which I hope will prove more interesting to my readers than a prosaic array of statistics and of repeated rigmaroles about big mills, big leads, rich tailings and astonishing sales of interests in Tom, Dick and Harry's mines.

August is the very month to travel in the mountains. At this season the halcyon days begin, and continue for weeks and even months, with but little variation, making it a physical luxury to live and breathe the pure transparent atmosphere.

While the train moved over the great valleys I fell into conversation with a ranchman, who said: "When the grazing advantages and productive qualities of this soil were discovered, there was a great rush for land, and the country all around, far and near, was pre-empted.

"According to law, a house must be built on the pre-empted claim, the party must live in it a stated period and cultivate the land. Often a rough, unpainted board shanty was built, after which the pre-emptor would not see it again until, with the growth of the country, the land had become valuable, when he would 'bob up serenely' to claim his property. His perjury never occasioned any pricking of conscience, for, don't you see, it was one of the customs of the country.

"About twenty-five miles below Denver a party had taken up a certain tract of land in that way. Subsequently a man, tramping about there on a tour of observation, found the empty house and took possession of it.

"The pre-emptor heard of it, and, upon inquiring what he must do to secure possession, was advised to work the land.

"He bought a plow, went to his ranch, turned the interloper out and commenced plowing. Not being accustomed to farm labor, he was greatly fatigued by his day's work, and slept late the next morning. The first sight that greeted him was the man who had taken possession of his house, with a bag swung over his shoulder, dropping something in the freshly broken ground. Upon being interrogated as to what he was doing, he replied: 'I am planting a little corn.' "

At this point the ranchman laughed heartily. I was anxious to know how the affair terminated, but before he recovered his mental equilibrium we arrived at Golden.

Golden

The castellated cliffs surrounding this pretty town, planted just between the foothills and the plains, appeared so like real castles with towers, buttresses, battlements and moats that had the sound of a warder's horn from the walls been heard, a great gate swung open, a drawbridge lowered, I should scarcely have been startled.

The town of Golden was organized in the summer of 1859. It was named for Thomas Golden, who, with James

Saunders and George A. Jackson, camped upon its site while prospecting for gold. The town company was composed of George West, David K. Wall, J. M. Ferrell, J. C. Kirby, J. C. Bowles, Mrs. Williams, W. A. H. Loveland, H. J. Carter, Ensign B. Smith, William Davidson, I. W. Stanton, C. A. Clark, F. W. Beebe, James MacDonald, E. L. Berthoud and Garrison. Irving W. Stanton was elected the first mayor in 1860.

Here is located the reform school and the School of Mines, which is a thorough technical school, and prepares its students for intelligent practical mining of every kind used in the treatment of mineral ores the world over.

While our party visited the School of Mines I talked with Mr. George West, who has been a prominent and interesting figure in Colorado, as editor and publisher of The Transcript.

"Tell me something of the early days of Golden," said I.

His eyes twinkled with merriment as he gave me the following incident:

"After the town was laid out, in July, 1859, the erection of houses here and there was at once commenced. As sawed lumber was scarce and commanded enormous prices, most of the dwellings were built of logs. The company with which I was connected, known as the Boston Company, commenced a huge log building calculated for a store and dwelling combined. Soon after Mr. Loveland began a rough log structure for a store, and as work progressed considerable rivalry was engendered as to which should be first completed. The rafters were put on both about the same time, and the strife to get them shingled became quite animated. All the neighbors were interested in the contest, and who would prove the victor became a lively topic of conversation. By a lucky trade we had secured sufficient shingles to cover our roof, and all but three or four bundles had been put on when night interrupted our work.

"Mr. Loveland had also obtained some shingles, but not enough to complete his roof, which left him in a bad fix. We went to our downy couches that night feeling much elated at the prospect of beating Loveland in the race. But fancy our astonishment in the morning on discovering that he had come over with his men, stolen our remaining shingles, and was at that very moment nailing the last of them on his own roof.

"During the forenoon, however, he sent us over the

same amount of shingles he had surreptitiously appropriated, with his compliments and a five-gallon keg of the best whisky in his stock. He had beaten us in the race, and that was all he cared for."

West's Duel

*Hon. W. A. H. Loveland is one of the heroic figures in Colorado history. As pioneer road builder and a projector of great undertakings his name is mentioned often in these stories. There is also a delightful social side to him. He was on a visit to Golden at this time and had quietly taken in the story; then, in a good-humored way, said: "Turn about is fair play, so I'll tell you of West's duel.

W. A. H. Loveland

"In the fall of 1859 West established a paper at Golden called The Western Mountaineer, publishing the same during the following year, when he sold out to enter the Union army. A rough element had gathered here during the winter of '59-'60. There were many southern sympathizers in this locality, most of them good fellows, but quite free, in the vernacular of the period, 'to talk with their

---

*Hon. W. A. H. Loveland passed away since this writing.

mouths.' Among them was a young fellow known as 'Dick Turpin,' from Western Missouri, a rabid secessionist, and somewhat addicted to drink. When full of 'tangle-foot' he was particularly loud-mouthed and reckless. One day he mounted his horse, and, pistol in hand, rode through the streets, cursing all who claimed to be 'Yankees.' In the next issue of The Mountaineer West gave him some pretty severe taps for his recklessness and general cussedness, at which he took umbrage, and called at the office to demand satisfaction.

"He had taken the precaution to 'brace up' at the liquor saloons en route, and by the time he arrived was pretty full. He demanded to know if West was the author of the attack, and, being assured with great urbanity that such was the fact, he issued a peremptory verbal challenge to mortal combat. In fact, blood seemed to be the only fluid that would satisfy him and heal his wounded honor.

"Taking in the situation, West thought best to humor him in his sanguinary desires, and, after much talk, said: 'Why, Dick, don't you know that this is not the best way to get at the business? I'll fight you, of course; but you ought to send a friend with the challenge; then I will refer him to my friend, and let them fix it up for us.'

"'Well, Cap,' said he, 'I'll be dog-goned if that ain't so. I didn't think about the 'forms.'

"They joined in a little 'O-be-joyful,' to bind the bargain, when Dick departed in search of a second.

"He selected Jim Watson, who was a particular friend of West's, and who soon presented him with a challenge, properly made out. West chose George Jackson as his second, and between them they fixed up a scheme to sober Dick, a difficult matter at all times; but they concluded if he could be brought to that condition he would not care to fight any more than West did. His second found him shortly afterward fuller than the legendary goat, informed him that his challenge had been accepted, and endeavored to impress upon his mind the necessity of sobering up in order to do justice to himself in the approaching combat. He succeeded in shutting him up in his room, and refused him any more liquor.

"As the effects of the liquor gradually wore off, he was informed that the challenged party had the choice of weapons, time and place of meeting, and he had chosen bowie knives.

"This suited him exactly; he said bowie knives were his favorite instrument of death.

"Finally Watson and Jackson had West's antagonist in a proper state of mind to receive his ultimatum.

"They presented the cartel to him for his signature. It had already received West's, and ran to this effect:

"The parties were to be on the ground at sunrise on the following morning; the instruments to be bowie knives of equal length and sharpness; the blade to be not more than eight inches long and one and one-half inches at the widest part; the combatants to be placed back to back, one on the south edge of North Table Mountain, the other on the north edge of South Table Mountain, and at the words 'one, two, three,' to turn and fight across the intervening gulch!

"The chasm over which the fight was to take place is fully a half mile across. Dick, of course, saw the joke, the very ridiculousness of the proposal acted upon him as expected, and he declared himself satisfied, accompanied the seconds to the Mountaineer office, and compromised it over a bottle of 'old cherry bounce.'

"'Yes,' said Mr. West, 'that was one of the duels I didn't fight, and I assure you it was decidedly a 'satisfaction' affair."

I was deeply impressed with the danger of early journalism in Colorado.

From Golden sprang the first railways, developing

The Mountain Towns

the great mineral resources of the State. Even as early as 1861 the project of a Pacific railway had taken form. Mr. Loveland and others were ambitious to establish the route via Golden to Salt Lake, and the agitation of the question resulted in a survey being made by Captain E. L. Berthoud to determine the feasibility of a stage and wagon road through the mountains between the two towns. The survey demonstrated also that a railroad could be built over the same route.

The greatest achievements in early railroad construction are justly accredited to Captain Berthoud. While chief engineer and secretary of the Colorado Central Railroad Company he designed and built lines from Golden to Cheyenne and Denver; the famous Central City switch-back and the still more remarkable Georgetown Loop. He discovered the pass that bears his name.

We took the cars again and were whisked into a valley of scenic wonders. Fantastic turrets, crowned with lofty pines, towered above us, and below the angry, foaming torrent of Clear creek coursed down toward the sea.

John Gregory

May 6, 1859, John H. Gregory of Georgia discovered gold in Gilpin County. He followed Clear creek until he reached a point about where Black Hawk now stands. Indications of gold caused him to go up a tributary gulch. He was alone, and, being caught in a heavy snow storm, nearly perished. After the storm he had to return to the base of the mountains for supplies, and there he met Wilkes Defrees, whom he induced to go with him. They reached the gulch after three days of tedious climbing. Gregory scraped away the grass and leaves that covered his pan, which he had filled with dirt; he panned this out, and it produced about four dollars' worth of gold. The sight of the gold in the bottom of the pan caused a mercurial nature like Gregory's to effervesce fluently, and his expressions of delight, if given, would be pronounced very profane history. It is recorded that the first forty pans of dirt from the Gregory lode, taken in 1859, the year of its discovery, yielded forty dollars. And Gregory talked all night. Defrees fell asleep about three o'clock in the morning and awoke at day-break to find Gregory still talking. That day they started for Auraria, and reached the town just in time to stop the stampede for the East. This is today one of the richest gold mining districts in the world.

During the summer of 1859 the district at first known as Gregory's Diggings was subdivided, and new mining camps were opened for miles around. Curious laws prevailed at that time.

Mining Laws

Mr. Harper M. Orahood* said: "Whenever a prospector discovered a mine of sufficient richness to attract a number of people, the next thing in order was to organize a mining district. Such a district was a democracy pure and simple." After the district was organized, some qualifications were required for citizenship—usually a residence of ten days in the district, and often that a claim of some kind should be owned. This last could be complied with if the applicant had half a dollar in gold dust to pay the recorder. But there was no such thing as representative government in the mining districts. Every man took part, or had the right to take part, in the government of the district.

To organize a district a miners' meeting was called. This was usually done by posting notices, giving the time and place for the meeting. Thereupon a chairman was selected and a secretary appointed. The chairman, with

---

*Recently passed away.

JUDGE W. L. KUYKENDALL

CLEAR CREEK CANON

HARPER M. ORAHOOD

the approval of the meeting, appointed judges of the election, and they appointed clerks. At the first election, as a rule, there was not much of a contest. Subsequent elections, however, were often as closely canvassed and contested as they are now. The officers usually consisted of a president, a recorder, a judge of the miners' court, and sheriff, sometimes a treasurer, but he was more ornamental than useful. A district, as such, seldom had any funds.

It is a curious fact that these laws, however small and insignificant, have, by subsequent legislation, been recognized and been made valid by the laws of this State and acts of Congress of the United States. By the same high authority the judgments of the highest miners' courts have been recognized and made as binding as a judgment of the supreme court of Colorado or the United States.

A friend introduced me to Judge W. L. Kuykendall, the father of John M. Kuykendall, one of Denver's well known and highly respected citizens.

"What changes the whirligig of time brings around!" I said, by way of opening the conversation. "Years ago John Gregory fought his way through this gorge in a blinding snow storm. Twenty yoke of oxen were required to haul a small boiler over the precipitous declivities of the toll road that was opened later, where now we glide in luxurious coaches."

"Yes," he answered, "and steam, science and stock companies have taken the place of pick, pan and shovel. I became a citizen of Colorado early in 1865, when it was in its infancy, during a time of great financial stringency and general stagnation of business in all lines. I reached Denver thinly clad, with a dollar and twenty-five cents as the amount of my cash capital. I had served four years as a soldier of the South, and although the war was over, and I had accepted its results in good faith, I could feel that with many I rested under the ban of ostracism. Seeing nothing in or around Denver by which I could obtain employment, I journeyed to an old friend's place near Black Hawk, who had known me from the time I was a small boy, and he offered me two dollars a cord for all the wood I could cut, which was gladly accepted, for I was an expert with the axe. After a few weeks I went into the pinery of dead timber on my own account, chopped a large amount of wood and put up my charcoal pits for future burning. Running out of money and provisions, I worked at five dollars a day, excavating a pit in Russell Gulch, near Central City. With the capital thus secured I bought horses and wagons, and engaged in freighting from Denver to Black Hawk and Central. Charcoal then ranged in value from twenty cents to sixty cents a bushel. I soon had from two to four pits burning at the same time, to which I gave my personal attention. It necessitated sleeping in my blankets near the pits to save them in case of explosion from gas, which sometimes occurred, requiring swift and awful hard work with the shovel. During this time my most intimate friends would not have recognized me if they had met me in the road, because my face was black from the charcoal. I felt a pride in my work, owing to the fact that in that humble way I was aiding in the attempt to revive the languishing mining industry that was everything to Colorado at that time, and my labor was a factor in trying out experimental mining plants then in course of construction for working the refractory ores of the Black Hawk and Central districts."

I soon discovered that Judge Kuykendall was a man of superior mental attainments. He left Colorado in the winter of 1865, and made his home in Wyoming, where he became a man of influence, was elected to the Legislature and ably filled many important positions. In fact, he was one of the builders of Wyoming.

BLACK HAWK

The shrill whistle of the little engine announced Black Hawk. We were just one mile from Central, but the train must travel nearly four to overcome the intervening grade. We move forward awhile, then back, and change places in a dance on the giddy slopes overlooking the gulch, where private residences, stores, saloons, quartz mills and reduction works are crowded in, helter skelter, as if dropped from the clouds. And way down deep "in the earth beneath" hundreds of men are toiling in the mines. We could step from the car into the notable Bobtail lode, which derived its euphonious title from the fact that the first pay dirt from this magnificent gold-bearing fissure was hauled down to the gulch for sluicing by a bob-tailed ox in harness, the quartz wagon being a forked limb with a rawhide stretched upon it. This unique vehicle caused the miners much merriment, and suggested the name "Bobtail."

Pat Casey

Many amusing stories are told of that early gold excitement. Among the prospectors who poured into this gulch in 1859 was one from the Emerald Isle, Pat Casey, who came in the capacity of a general roustabout to a wagon train, and soon after became Colorado's first bonanza king.

Being young, able-bodied and accustomed to manual labor, he found employment as a miner on the Ben Burroughs lode at "$2.50 a day and feed himself." After awhile he did some prospecting for himself on Sundays and evenings after working hours. It was not long before he uncovered a vein which proved to be very rich. Qutting his employer, he devoted his entire time to his own shaft, and a few wagon loads of quartz made him a capitalist. He threw off his ore-stained overalls, bought the best clothes he could find in Central City, and his amusing peculiarities became the talk of the entire region.

As Casey's fortune developed he employed more hands. On one occasion Pat, having use for some men

The Mountain Towns

at the surface, went to the shaft and, yelling down, asked, "How many of yez are there?"

"Five," was the answer.

"Well, half of yez come up here; I want ye."

This story has been often used, but it originated with Pat Casey.

Riches poured in upon him like a stream. Walking and horseback riding were discarded. He bought a span of beautiful black horses, a fine buggy, and drove up and down the gulches, attracting wild-eyed attention and shouts from the miners. He stopped and held animated conversations with the better dressed and more important merchants and mine owners, and never tired of telling the people he met of the money he was making and the number of night and day hands in his employ. Casey always carried, conspicuously displayed in a side pocket, a leather covered memorandum book, with a lot of pencils. When a trade was concluded he made a bluff of entering it after the fashion of business men, but everyone knew that he could not write a word, not even his name. It was his boast, "I use up tin pincils a day and thin don't get half through me business." One day Sam Buell, who kept a book store, called out, "Hello, Pat!"

Swelling with indignation at the familiarity, Pat replied, "I'd have yez to know that me name is not Pat at all, but P. Casey, Esq."

Frank Hall tells the following: "The principal place of amusement was the old Montana theater. Pat Casey's night hands, a large body of reckless, turbulent fellows who dominated Quartz Hill and every other place they entered, were the talk and terror of the whole region.

"Mike Dougherty, a fine comedian, was in the habit of writing and singing topical songs. On one occasion he produced a cutting satire on Casey's night hands, which created no end of amusement.

"Next day Casey rode into the town in a white rage

against the Montana theater. He swore that if Langrishe and Dougherty made fun of him again he would bring down his men and clean out the town.

"This was during the heat of our Civil War, and Sergeant Pepper had a recruiting station in Central. Attracted by Casey's boisterous talk and threats, Pepper said to him: 'Mr. Casey, I represent the United States government, and you must be quiet or I will have to arrest you.'

"Quick as a flash Casey roared out, 'To hell with you an' the United States government; I tell you I'll bring down me men and clean out the town, and you can't stop me. I won't have Langrishe and Dougherty slanderin' me and mine.' Continuing in this strain, uttering all sorts of vituperations and refusing to be pacified, Pepper arrested him, and put him under guard in the recruiting station, and then called on the sheriff for assistance. The sheriff put Casey in jail. A riot was feared. The night and day hands, who were devoted to Casey, organized. After making a great deal of noise and loading the air with imprecations, better counsel prevailed and the force dissolved.

"Reports of these occurrences were telegraphed to Governor Evans, who directed the military to act under the order of the sheriff, and endeavor to preserve the peace. He then took a carriage and drove to Central to take further action of it might be deemed necessary, but the riot was ended before he arrived.

"The redoubtable Casey was held in jail until he promised to behave.

"P. D. Casey, at the height of his prosperity, was worth $200,000, subject to many fluctuations growing out of his reckless extravagance.

"In 1863 the property was sold to Warren Hussey and W. H. Russell. Casey received about $60,000. He left the mountains, went to New York, where he was persuaded to invest his capital in a wholesale tobacco commission house. Through mismanagement it was soon lost, and he ended by opening a saloon and tending the bar himself."

CENTRAL CITY

When President Grant visited this elevated mountain town, a walk, composed of solid silver bricks, was laid from the carriage of the Teller house for him to step on. No such ostentatious display of wealth was made in honor of our arrival. However, as we are to linger here awhile, I shall turn public interviewer and tell my readers all that I find of interest.

It was my good fortune to meet General Frank Hall, who is a walking encyclopedia of Colorado lore. He was one of the most conspicuous characters in the early history of the Territory and State. During the territorial period there were three territorial secretaries; the term of General Hall covered more than half of the period. He was lieutenant-governor when McCook was governor, and acting governor in his absence. General Hall has written a comprehensive history of Colorado, which will always be valuable as a work of reference. He is in the highest sense a literary man, and is now filling a position on the Denver Post. He walks with a military air which gives the impression that it was only a few years ago when he wore the epaulets. Though forty years have come and gone since then, his eyes and his intellect are as bright as then, and I said to myself, surely this man has found the fountain for which Ponce De Leon searched.

We were soon conversing about the pioneer days.

"Gregory gulch may be aptly called the hall of fame," the general said; "no spot of the same dimensions on the face of the earth has ever turned out so many men

of distinction in the political and the financial worlds. At one time the political destinies of Colorado, both at Washington and at Denver, were in the hands of men who had lived and toiled together in this teeming camp, then divided into three municipalities, Black Hawk, Central and Nevada, and they remain so to this day. In this picture gallery were Henry M. Teller, United States Senator and Secretary of the Interior. Teller was a noted lawyer; he untied more mining knots than any other man who made mining law a specialty. He received more honors than usually fall to the lot of men. He was returned to the Senate again and again as a Republican, and served twenty-nine years, and was further honored by being made one of President Arthur's cabinet as Secretary of the Interior.

"Jerome B. Chaffee was in the first rush to Gregory gulch; here he laid the foundation for a fortune, erected a quartz mill, which he operated three years, then, with the profits in his pockets, he went to Denver, the principal trading point of the mountain section, and organized the First National Bank. Jerome B. Chaffee and Henry M. Teller were the first United States Senators elected from Colorado, when admitted to the Union in 1876.

"Then there was James B. Belford. It required the towering Rocky Mountains to form a fit background for big-boned, rugged, square-jawed, square-brained James Belford. He was called the 'Red-headed Rooster of the Rockies.' He received the appointment from President Grant as one of the judges of Colorado Territory Supreme Court, and he went direct to Gregory gulch. Central was his home for thirteen years. At that time Colorado was divided into three judicial districts, and the three judges of the court traveled from one court town to another on horseback or in stages, much as the old Methodist circuit riders used to do.

"It was Belford's custom to devote a certain period of time every day to study, and he took up mining law because it had a mysterious fascination for him. His friends laughed at him for wasting his time, but his wife, who was his good genius, encouraged him in his fad. She said her husband had never stored up any knowledge that had not come into good use. It was the knowledge gained at this time that enabled Belford to deliver sound opinions and decisions on the bench, and later, as a member of Congress, to take a prominent and wise part in shaping the mining laws of the nation. In 1878 Belford was elected to Congress. After serving his term he retired from politics and devoted himself to literature until he died, honored and lamented.

"Joseph Standley, Joe Thatcher's partner in Central, is with him in the Denver National. Standley owned the California mine, with its shaft 2,200 feet deep, for many years the deepest mine in the United States.

"Henry R. Wolcott, assistant manager of the Boston and Colorado smelter, became State senator, and was long a Republican leader in Colorado, now retired, and lives quietly in Honolulu, where he has bought a magnificent estate.

"Still another United States Senator who lived in Gregory gulch long enough to feel the Midas touch was W. A. Clark. He too worked the Bobtail, but never identified himself with the camp life. He took his money and went to Montana, where he became a copper magnate and millionaire.

"George M. Pullman made a brief but busy stay here. He took out the money which enabled him to build sleeping cars and give to the world a degree of luxury in travel never dreamed of before. When he made enough money to float his sleeping car project he quietly sold his interest and disappeared, to be heard from again when his fame as an inventor had girdled the earth.

"Eben Smith! Ah, that is a name to conjure with!" said General Hall. "He formed a partnership with Chaffee, and was very successful. He and Chaffee were among the first to make a success of the Bobtail mine. When Chaffee died, Smith formed an alliance with D. H. Moffat, and they opened up many mines in Leadville, Cripple Creek and other camps.

MAJOR HAL SAYRE

"Major Hal Sayre was the pioneer surveyor and civil engineer of Gilpin County, beginning in 1859. In his duties of civil engineer he had much to do with the earliest definition of mining claims under the miners' law. Subsequently when Congress passed the first act fixing the boundaries of claims and defining miners' rights, his duties were materially enlarged. As a consequence he became one of the busiest men in all that region. In due course of time he fell in love with a Miss Elizabeth Dart, and, after a swift courtship, married her. Of this marriage three children, two boys and one girl, were born. The girl became the wife of Wm. B. Berger, cashier of the Colorado National Bank. The elder son, Hal, went into the United States army of the Philippines, and later met his death in New Mexico; the other son, Robert, is now at the head of some important mining enterprises in Gilpin and Clear Creek counties. Robert is a graduate of Harvard. Hal Sayre, Sr., is a highly educated man and delightful in conversation. His wife is refined, with gentle manners, and they contributed much to the social life of Central City, while they resided there. He built, and now occupies, a fine residence, in the Moorish style of architecture, at the corner of Eighth avenue and Logan street, Denver. Here Mr. and Mrs. Sayre have established one of the most charming home circles to be found in this municipality, where it is always a delight to visit.

"E. O. Wolcott," Mr. Hall went on, "was a picturesque character, a handsome man, with a commanding presence. He possessed a brilliant intellect, and was a born orator. Mining and milling did not appeal to him, so he taught school; he became a member of the local lyceum and gave his oratorical powers full play. He was naturally inclined to politics, and when the opportunity came he crossed over to Georgetown, where he lived for many years. In the course of time he was elected district attorney, and then his progress was rapid. He became leader of the Republican party, and in 1889 was elected to the United States Senate—the fourth Gregory gulch man to attain that honor."

I had listened with bewilderment to the long catalogue of distinguished men, and made rapid notes while the general talked.

"It seems to me," I said, "that everybody of note lived in this narrow little gorge at one time."

"That is true," he replied, "and when they found themselves in this happy canyon among the everlasting hills, at an altitude approximately 9,000 feet, and seven hundred miles away from the end of the nearest railroad, life was not so intolerable as some might suppose. The camp had its society, with lines not so clearly drawn as in New York, still well defined. There were wholesome amusements of various kinds. The theater was managed by Jack Langrishe, who gave everything from East Lynne to Othello. We had a lyceum, a singing school, spelling bees and church sociables; men and women of culture were there," he said in conclusion, "and, you know, refined brains are always at a premium."

Joseph A. Thatcher

While I sat in the rotunda of the Teller house, Joseph A. Thatcher came forward to greet me. His name will ever be associated with the early days of Central City, and it is picturesquely interwoven with Colorado's banking history. His strong, clear-cut features are touched with a benign expression and ennobled with white hair, white mustache and imperial. He is a native of Kentucky, and, although fifty-five years in the West, his accent and bearing are distinctively southern. He is a man of keen intellect, quick wit and a broad view of life.

Joseph A. Thatcher

Mr. Thatcher is delightful in conversation; bright thoughts and words leap from his brain. A lady once asked him, "What keeps you so young?" "Flattery and vanity," he replied. "When I am told that I look young, I always straighten up my shoulders and step quicker."

"How did you get into the banking business?" I asked. "Through failing," he replied, with a laugh, as he seated himself in a chair. "My chum, John Ralston, wanted me to go in partnership with him, and bring a stock of goods to Colorado. He had some money; I did not have any, so I was willing to go in partnership with him. He was a fine fellow, but he stuttered, and it took him a long time to say 'damn,' but when he did succeed, it was expressive." Mr. Thatcher laughed as if in his mind's eye he was looking back on those days. "We started from Kansas City with ten wagons, loaded with merchandise, and drawn by oxen. We had bought the merchandise and the oxen, too, mostly on credit. A negro cook prepared the meals for the caravan.

"Among the team men I hired was one from Massachusetts. All the men were armed, and the Bay State man carried a gun big enough for a piece of artillery. One day as dark came on I, as was my custom, rode ahead to find a camping place. When I had selected a place about three hundred yards in advance of the teams, I heard three shots in rapid succession. I turned my pony and galloped back. Behind the last wagon sat this man in the middle of the road, and Ralston was standing by him. Colonel Bent, with his Indian wife and two men from Georgia, were traveling through to Bent's Fort in an ambulance. They had a lot of loose horses, and this fellow, in his excited fear, had fired off his piece of artillery at them. Two of the bullets went through the bottom of the ambulance, and Bent and his Indian wife tumbled out. Colonel Bent was mad and the squaw was furious; she wanted to kill the man there and then, and insisted upon it.

" 'What is the matter?' I asked.

"Ralston explained that the hired men had practiced upon the credulity of this fellow; had told him extravagant stories about Indians, which had upset his reason.

" 'He is an infernal scoundrel,' said Bent, 'and should be hung; for your own safety you ought to hang him.'

"Colonel Bent then looked us over.

"'What are you kids doing out in this country, anyhow?' he demanded. 'You are a pretty looking pair to be on an expedition like this.' The whole affair seemed to fill him with disgust. We finally succeeded in appeasing him, and he went on his way.

"I decided to go ahead of my teams, and three days before reaching Denver I fell in company with a deserter from the troops stationed at Santa Fe; we became fellow travelers. The deserter's great fear was that someone would steal his horse, but after looking him over carefully I quieted his fears, for his horse and mine were equally no good. When we stopped for supper we took an inventory of our supplies. He had ground coffee, and nothing else, and I had stale bread and uncooked bacon. We drank our coffee from the pot it was made in, and varied our menu by having coffee first for breakfast and last for dinner. On July 17, 1860, I rode into Denver on my little old pony, after forty-seven days out from Kansas City. The pony could not go any farther, so I took off the bridle and saddle and turned him out on the plains now called Denver. I never saw him again. No doubt some undesirable citizen who had received peremptory orders from the People's court to leave the city used him in complying with the notice.

"Five days later my wagons and teams arrived in charge of my partner, John Ralston, and we turned our cattle out where the Brown Palace now stands. In Denver there was a mixed, straggling, excited, unsettled population; doubt and uncertainty were in the minds of most of the people, and the principal business was done by saloons and gambling houses.

"After a few days we hitched up and struck out for Central, and reached here in nine days, encountering accidents, floods and breakdowns. At Golden we had to unload our wagons, and were half a day getting up the side of the first mountain, the oxen pulling the empty wagon. Then, packing our stuff up, we reloaded, and in going down the other side we cut a tree and fastened on behind as a brake. One of my drivers left on the second day out, and I whacked his team of bulls into the camp myself. We reached Central in nine days.

"In the spring of '61 the placer or gulch mines ceased to produce gold. The people thought there were no other industries in the country, and made their way out as fast as they could. The merchants had no one to buy goods; as a result I failed. The people who could not get away began the erection of mills for the treatment of gold ores. In 1862 I sold out my stock, mainly on credit, and closed my career as a 'merchant prince.' I took the money I got for my stock and bought a stamp mill. I moved it to Buckskin Joe, and in a short time I had nothing left—except mountain fever. Then there was a gold excitement at Montgomery. I hauled my mill over seven feet of snow to that camp. There were from eight to ten thousand people there, but in a short time the camp was deserted. I failed again, and my mill rotted away.

"I would not allow myself to become discouraged. I made a study of ores, bought and sold mines, and in a short time paid off my debts. In 1862-63 the government issued a large amount of greenbacks. Mr. Warren Hussey established a bank office for the purchase of gulch gold and placer gold. Owing to the fact that I had acquired a knowledge of mill gold value, retort and any kind of gulch gold, Warren Hussey engaged me to manage his bank.

"With the enormous issue of greenbacks by the government, and the immediate difference between gold and currency, the banker found it profitable to purchase gold bullion and have it coined. Gold went up until it took two dollars in currency to buy one in gold. I worked for Warren Hussey for seven years, and then I bought him out. Why run a bank for another man for seven years, and not be able to buy him out?" asked Mr. Thatcher, with a glint of humor in his eye.

"I organized the bank of Thatcher, Standley & Co., and during the panic of 1873 I bought gold in the daytime, made the trip to Denver every night for currency. and returned the next morning to Central City to open the doors of the bank. In 1874 I organized the First National Bank of Central City, and was made president of it. I remained at Central City banking until 1884, when I moved to Denver and organized the Denver National Bank, in company with Dennis Sullivan, Joseph Standley and others. I was made president of the Denver National, and occupied the president's chair for twenty-nine years."

Mr. Thatcher's banking career is one of the most interesting in the State, because running through it all is the beautiful human element. But he refused to discuss any of his benefactions. However, it is well known that Joseph A. Thatcher never pushed anyone financially who he knew was doing his level best, yet was unsuccessful. In his bank he has cancelled the note of many an unfortunate friend. His name and his money have been factors in everything of a cultured and artistic nature in the progress of Denver. He carries into his business and his home the spirit of fairness and benevolence, and in his quiet, unostentatious way has opened the doors of education to many young men and women; his timely help to friends in his own circle has paved the way for their success. He aided in building St. John's cathedral, St. Luke's hospital and the Young Men's Christian Association. When Mr. and Mrs. Thatcher came to Denver the social doors swung wide to receive them. Mrs. Thatcher is a graceful, charming woman, averse to publicity or to securing attention through display, and has selected her friends at the dictates of her heart rather than from any motives of self-advancement. She has the distinction of writing the "social code" for Denver.

In speaking of the pioneer society, Mr. Thatcher said: "It's a sad thing to belong to that society; they are dying so rapidly. But I am interested in the society, and when I am a hundred I shall join it."

Mr. Thatcher assisted in establishing the Denver Union Stockyards, the Denver Electric Company and the Colorado Packing Company; he has also been connected with the water and gas companies. While his services have been useful in many undertakings that have contributed to the up-building of Denver, it has been in the management of the great banking institution of which he is the head that his well-trained financial genius is particularly manifested.

Mr. Thatcher is a great financier, a great philanthropist, and he is also a great "romancer"; indeed he may be called the Baron Munchausen of Colorado. From his interesting little book entitled "A Colorado Outing" I have taken the following:

Mr. Thacher's Bear Story

"We resolved to stay two or three days longer; and I concluded to try and bring some of my friends the results of my outing, and the day before we were to leave I started out rather early to a place about half a mile away from camp, where the stream was divided by a small island covered with willows. I carried, beside rod and creel, a hunting knife in the leg of my long boot and a lariat around my shoulders, which I used sometimes in dangerous places, where the stream was very deep and swift and the bank too steep to fish from with safety. I had stopped at the head of the pool and had taken eight or ten fine trout, and thought I would cross over to the island and see what the other arm of the river looked like. I had walked a few rods through the willows when I saw quite a disturbance ahead of me, and stopped. Not more than thirty rods away a huge brown bear rose up out of the willows; he stood on his hind legs and looked directly at me. I turned and made for the stream with all the speed that paralyzed fear could make. I crossed and, turning, saw the bear following me through the water. I rushed through the low brush that lined the bank and out into the open stood a fair sized tree two hundred yards away that I thought I might reach. I glanced back, and the bear was coming out of the bushes right on after me—somewhat faster, it seemed to me, than I was going. When within fifty yards of the tree another look at him convinced me he would get there about the same time I did, or probably before, so, to lighten my load and increase my speed, I dropped my rod, threw off my creel and my hat and I hastened my efforts to the utmost. As I got to the tree the bear got to my creel and stopped. I scrambled up the tree and reached a dead limb ten feet above the ground, and from there I could reach the forks of the tree about fifteen feet from the ground. When up there I saw that the bear had shaken the fish out of my creel and was eating them. He then came on to the tree, walked around it several times, then started to climb up. Seizing the dead limb with his arms, he tried to pull himself up, when the limb broke off close to the body of the tree, and he fell to  the ground on his back and head, the wind knocked out of him. He got up rather slowly and commenced walking around the foot of the tree, acting as though he thought I had played a trick on him. I could have

laughed outright at his sheepish look if I had not been
so scared I could not open my mouth. After walking
around the tree some time he went back to the creel,
smelled all around it, went to my hat, took it in his
mouth and shook it like a pup would an old slipper. I
suppose he thought I carried trout in my hat as well as
in my creel. There was no doubt but what he was hungry, and, not getting any fish out of the hat, he came
back to the tree again, and stood on his hind legs and
reached up toward me as far as he could reach. I made
up my mind I must cut his paws off if he came up that
tree, but he made no attempt to climb up again, and continued to walk around and around, and would then stop,
stand on his hind feet and reach up as far as he could.
All at once the thought struck me, why not try to lariat
him? I acted on the thought at once, unwound the lariat
from my shoulders, fastened one end around a near fork
of the tree, got the noose ready and waited for him to
come directly under it, and when next he stood up I
dropped it down over him and pulled with all the
strength of desperation, and caught his forearms just
behind his big paws. I tightened the rope to the utmost
upon the limb, and found I had him standing on his toes,
and unless he could spring up and bite the rope, I was
safe, his neck being so much shorter than his arms he
could not possibly reach the lariat. He jumped until he
was worn out and spent from the exertion. Then I
looked over the situation and found that if I climbed
up some ten feet higher I could go out on a big limb,
and by a good drop reach the ground. I did this, and
found myself safely on the ground; then, convinced in
my own mind that he could not get loose, I said to myself, 'Old fellow, you have scared me out of ten years'
growth; I would like to take your hide or your claws
as a trophy.' So I pulled my long knife and approached
the tree cautiously. keeping it between me and the bear.

He seemed to be swinging helplessly, and I got squarely against the tree and gave a lunge with my knife around it, aiming at his heart. As I did so, the bear gave a last struggle and his head fell over to one side, and he was as limp as a rag, and did not move. I waited for about ten minutes, and as he did not move I felt sure that he was dead. I then went up close to him, and certainly he was a dead bear. I concluded to cut his claws and take them to camp and get Dick to come out and help skin him. I reached up and cut the rope, and the bear fell over on the ground, not moving a muscle; but the suspicious thing was that he was not bleeding at all, as far as I could see, and after studying over the situation for some little time, I concluded it was safer to run into camp and get Dick to come out and help skin him. I had never had any experience in that line. I struck camp pretty quick, and told Dick with great excitement all about it. He was very incredulous, and started out with me at once; and as I went along he roared with laughter at my account of the whole affair. When we came in sight of the tree I did not see anything around or near it. We went on to the tree, but no bear was there. My rod, creel and hat were gone. I said, 'Why, here was where I left him.' We turned and looked around about everywhere, and directly down a narrow path, leading to the water, we saw the most astonishing sight that I ever beheld. We saw that bear walking on his hind legs toward the water, with my creel over his shoulders, my rod in his hand and my hat on his head.

"Dick turned to me and said: 'Look! Yes, you slaughtered him, Joe; no doubt about that!' and then fell upon the ground and roared with laughter, until I thought he would die. I turned and started for the camp, saying: 'Come on, Dick; don't be a fool!'

"Well, having lost my fish, rod, creel, hat and bear,

we packed up and left for home. But as to whether that bear was possuming, or fainted from exhaustion, or had heart failure for the time being, I could never determine."

Frank C. Young

Mr. Thatcher introduced me to his old-time friend and associate, Mr. Frank C. Young, who is a man of rare culture and literary taste. Had he given his time to literary work instead of to bonds and stocks, he might be the Washington Irving of the West. He has written two charming books, "Across the Plains in '65" and "Echoes from Arcadia." The latter is a story of Central City.

Mr. Young, with his usual modesty, refused to talk about himself, but he soon became enthusiastic in talking of the early days of Central.

"In the fall of 1865 there was little doing in a business way, but there was great activity in politics. We had three distinct elections here, one of them for State affairs, and one for the Legislature, which was to meet in the winter and choose United States senators for the State that was yet to be.

Frank C. Young

"The contest was, in the main, a good-natured one, and the continuous diversion it created proved a Godsend to the depressed colony. In the third election, whatever their earlier attitude towards statehood, all parties came into the field to compete for a share of the spoils, if the fates should decree our admission, and many and curious were the tickets and platforms which were offered to the consideration of the electors. Deacon Walker presented himself for Congress, as an independent candidate, and in support of his claim upon the suffrages of his fellow-citizens declared himself 'in favor of women's rights, gold-bearing lodes, free drinks and Freiburg pans; also all disintegrating and desulphurizing processes without let, hindrance or remorse, and without regard to smells; and 'most of all I will insist upon the substitution of an automatic wheel-barrow for the ox now employed in transporting the mails to and from the States.'

"There was no difficulty in marshalling voters to the polls. Everybody voted at all the elections and without the officious or fussy restrictions of an Australian ballot or other impertinent modern inventions. Whoever got the most ballots in the box was the best man, whether his supporters were those of a "local habitation and a name" or just arrived today with a bull team from off the plains. All were independent Americans, who were not to be defrauded of their rights, and meant to exercise them how and when and where they pleased. Black Hawkers voted in Central and Centralites, not to be outdone in courtesy, returned calls and voted in Black Hawk; and when the results were declared, he was a rash man indeed who would suggest a contest.

"The pioneers of various religious societies followed close upon the trail of the placer miners in their first

B. T. Vincent

invasion of Gregory gulch; among them were the aggressive Methodists. Brother B. T. Vincent, their shepherd, was active, genial and extremely popular among all classes, whether in or out of his own sect. To him is due the honor of creating a Library Association, from which much intellectual activity developed for the public benefit.

"In our little community," continued Mr. Young, "everyone knew and recognized everyone else, whatever might be the positive differences of social position. In this connection I might speak of Aunt Clara Brown. She was raised in old Kentucky, and with her own freedom secured after years of persistent, patient toil, when well along in life she joined the procession of gold-seekers to Gregory gulch. Through the unusual returns of a mining camp for labor such as hers, she was able to bring out from the old plantation her children and later her children's children; and with them, whether aided by her efforts or stimulated by her example, have, year by year, come many others of her race, worthily represented by the Poynters, the Lees, the Nelsons and other families who are as tenacious of recognition as subjects of the 'little kingdom' as you or I may be.

"I must not forget to speak of the old stage driver. It is hard to suppress one's regret at seeing everything that invested the old-time journey with a bit of the picturesque and the romantic, and enlivened it occasionally with a spice of adventure, so ruthlessly and abruptly driven off the scene, even though the displacement represented the march of progress.

"It was Bill Updike's love of the manly art that travelers were indebted to for a radical shortening of the time schedule of many a journey between Denver and the mountain town, where there chanced to be a boxing match of an afternoon at either end of the route; the timid 'tenderfoot' whose luckless fate it was to be a passenger on such an occasion, would get an experience of lively mountain coaching, the recollection of which made his hair resist the brush for many a week afterward.

"Oh, I must tell you about our 'sleighing fete,' " Mr. Young went on, seeming to enjoy telling reminiscences of the early days. "In the winter of 1868 the first snow came in October and there was not a thawing day through the long dreary winter. By holiday times, the roads, which were constantly used, had become firmly packed, and as smooth as polished steel. We inaugurated a sleighing fete, which continued night after night for many weeks, and which was as notably comprehensive in its ensemble as it was crudely fantastic in its equipment, because of the many unique constructions that were forced into service, from the single seat, carved out of a drygoods box that served the youth and his girl, to the twenty-foot coaster, a combination of two rough wood sleds, that carried a dozen men down the steep grade with the velocity of a railway train. The course measured a fair two miles in its length, from its crown in Nevada to its foot in Black Hawk. Many were the sharp curves that called for the skill of the helmsman and many the luckless ones who were deposited, with small ceremony in the middle of the bordering gulches.

"On moonlight nights especially, the scene was one of hilarious excitement. At times a fair half of the colony were rushing down the crowded course, as voyageurs or looking on and cheering. And not by any means were these confined to the giddy youth or the reckless spirits of the mountains—the merchant, the banker and the professional man were there—jostling elbows with the toiler who had spent his day a thousand feet underground and was keen for a bit of relaxation in the crisp outer air. The parish priest, rosy and bubbling over with high spirits, waved a cherry salute *en passant* to the clerical brother of another sect, as he toils back up the long hill with the empty sled for a fresh start. The school master also was there, glad enough to accept the dauntless pilotage of the boy who that morning had cowered at his frown; and the young school ma'ams made up more than one sled load of laughing, shrinking, breathless figures, as they speeded down the slippery way. It was exhilarating, thrilling and often dangerous sport, for at times the roadway was badly jammed, and a fine mix up ensued when rounding a curve; but the sport was too good to be checked by trifles, and the opportunity too rare in our Italian climate to be allowed to pass unimproved."

Judge E. T. Wells

Judge E. T. Wells is another man of elegant military bearing, who was in Central in the early days. He has witnessed the development of Colorado in all its various interesting phases from 1865 to the present, and taken an active part in much of its history.

The Judge said:

"When I came to Colorado in the Fall of 1865, the chief locality in which lode mining was being prosecuted was in Gilpin County; even there the industry was at a very low ebb. The only process in common use for the separation of the precious metals from the ore was the stamp mill, but many other processes were being proposed and experimented with. All of them without exception were failures, and for several years afterwards the iron used for the manufacture of new stamps, and for repairs, came from the establishments where these new processes had been installed, but in '65 every new man who came to Gilpin County was supposed to have an improved process for what they called the 'desulphurization' of refractory ores of the district.

"I took an office with the city clerk and police magistrate of Black Hawk and with Robert M. Clark, the city marshal, was joint tenant of a bed-room at the rear of the office. The office was warmed by a woodburning stove, about three feet in height. In order to procure hot water for the morning's toilet I devised and drew a sketch of a tin bucket to be set in at the top of the stove which should reach down to the fire. That it might not fall through the opening at the top of the stove I planned a rim round the top of the bucket which should support it. It was drawn to a less diameter towards the bottom so as to form a section of a cone, and looked a good deal like a soldier's hat of Civil War times. I took this sketch to a tin-smith and went to him after the lapse of a few hours to bring it away—everybody then did his own errands. He was giving the last blows to the invention as I went in, and, supposing it to be part of my process for 'desulphurization,' he handed it to me with the remark: 'There, that is the d——dst looking desulphurizer I have made yet.'"

E. T. Wells

Among the members of the bar of Gilpin County at that time was Ellsworth Wakely. He was a man of great learning in the law, but of quaint and whimsical manners. He regarded no law book as entitled to respect if published since the reign of Charles II. He told many anecdotes of the profession, always giving the stature and avoirdupois of each character. On one occasion he told me that the first court which he ever attended was in Connecticut; there were three judges, and "What do you think," said he, "One of those judges opened the court with prayer. I have often thought that Horace Atkins was about the size of that judge that opened the court with prayer, but Horace Atkins is a little heavier than that judge was. Sometimes I think that Sam Lorah is about his size, but Sam is a little taller. I have never seen but one man who was just the size of that judge. Five years ago I was going over to Empire, and I met on the roadside a man just exactly the size of that judge. I never saw him before, and never have seen him since, and I do not know who the h———l he was, but I thought at the time he was just exactly the size of that judge who opened the court with prayer."

Judge Gorsline, who presided in the District court in Gilpin County in those years, was not always in good health, and frequently when a long trial was coming on, he would ask counsel to agree upon some member of the bar to sit in his stead. Judge Wakely was often selected on these occasions, and delighted in the service. On one occasion an action of replevin had been tried, and when the verdict came in and was handed up by the foreman of the jury, Judge Wakely, instead of handing it to the clerk to be read, as the custom was, laid it upon the table, put his hand upon it while he searched through his pockets for his glasses. When these were recovered he read the verdict: "We find the issues for the defendant." "The verdict is not quite right, gentlemen of the jury," he said, in a mumbling, indistinct voice, "It should be, 'We find the defendant not guilty;' but that doesn't matter, jurors are not expected to know these things, some lawyers don't know them. As our judge in Iowa used to say, Judge A. W. Hubbard—I suppose the jury have heard of Judge Hubbard,—a very excellent judge,—had a very excellent clerk,—I have forgotten the name of the clerk." Then he wandered off upon the avoirdupois of the judge and the clerk, and forgot the intended communication of the sayings of the judge.

At that time, as it may be imagined, we had no theatres, concerts, or other diversions, in this remote community, and the ladies one winter organized a lyceum, or what irreverent young men sometimes call a "spout shop," and detailed the lawyers, preachers, and doctors to deliver lectures. I believe I was the first victim. I had been reading then Buckle's History of Civilization in England, and delivered a sort of a lecture upon that book, presenting the idea that civilization and the progress of humanity depend largely on soil and climate. I remember that my most excellent and respected friend, Rev. B. T. Vincent, then, and still a noble ornament of the clerical profession, congratulated me, but he added, "I thank God that is not my idea of civilization." The lecture was noticed in the local paper the next morning, the notice ending with the equivocal compliment,—"At the conclusion of the lecture the audience seemed very much gratified."

Mrs. James B. Belford was as popular in Central in the early days as she is in Denver today. She is a rare woman. Her general information covers a wide range of literary and historical subjects; her quick wit, delightful humor and forceful personality place her among

Mrs. James B. Belford

the foremost women of Colorado.

With a smile in the corner of her mouth, which always plays there when memory calls a pleasant incident out of the past, she said: "I can tell you about a mother who didn't know her own son.

"In the early 70's I was returning to my home in Central, and on the seat beside me in the car was a sweet faced little woman who said she was going to her son who lived on a ranch near Golden; she had not seen him for seven years. He graduated from a law school and came to Colorado to recruit from exhaustion of protracted study. He regained his health and had determined to make his home here. 'God is so good to me,' said the little woman, in a spirit of thankfulness, 'to be under the same roof with my son is happiness enough for me.'

" 'I wonder if you will know him?' I asked.

" 'Certainly,' she replied; 'it has been a long time, but I will know my son.'

"She talked of him all the way. Every cell of her brain seemed filled with memories of her son.

" 'I hope the train is on time,' she said, anxiously.

" 'I think it is, and there is your son,' I said, pointing to a man who was making long strides in the direction of the station.

"She looked eagerly out of the window and said:

"'Oh, no, that is not my son—my son is tall, and slim, and white—so white.'

"As we neared the station she took up her valise, smoothed out her dress and stood in the aisle waiting in thrill of expectation.

"Presently the door opened, and a tall, broad-shouldered, sun-burned man—the same that I had seen making long strides for the station—opened the door and stepped in. He gave a searching glance through the car, rushed to the little woman and gathered her in his arms. She drew away and said: 'How dare you, sir?'

"'Why, mother,' he exclaimed, 'don't you know me?'

"'Yes,' she cried out joyously, 'I know that voice—it is the voice of my son. How big and strong and well you look.'

"'That is what Colorado has done for me, mother,' he said.

"They went away chatting, the little mother encircled by the arm of the big son to whom Colorado air had given health and strength."

The Bonanza Tunnel

Believing that "familiarity breeds contempt," we concluded not to return by way of the switch-back, therefore took a carriage to the depot at Black Hawk, stopping on the way to see the renowned Bonanza tunnel. As we entered it, the air that greeted us was like a vagrant breeze from the North Pole. Our lips turned blue, and teeth chattered so as to make conversation unintelligible.

A gallant Boston man threw his linen duster around me. It was as cold as the "mantle of charity;" but I appreciated it, for it was something after the style of the widow's mite—"all he had." He, like many others who come from the "benighted east" to "do" the mountains, had no heavier wrap than a linen duster.

The tunnel pierces the solid mountain twelve hundred feet, and crosses twelve veins glittering with mineral. As we explored its darkness by the light of our flickering candles we resembled a procession of spooks haunting the underground workers of earth.

It is solid comfort to travel with a company. When one is brimful, "shaken down and running over" with enthusiasm at some beautiful, grand and glorious freak of nature, it is delightful to have some one to nudge, and see the eyes sparkle and faces brighten up with the same pleasure; and it is superlatively agreeable to have some one around when one feels afraid.

"Of all the ghostly habitations I have ever seen this takes the 'confection.'"

When we returned from our subterranean tour we were met by an army of little boys with specimens to sell. The rapid reduction of prices in these wares was something astounding. Rocks that were offered at first for fifty cents apiece fell to ten; and after I had bought all that I felt able to carry, a little boy emptied his box in my lap and said: "You can have them all for five cents."

The driver informed us that we had barely time to "make the train," and away we went, at a hair-lifting speed, over a road that was ploughed into gullies by the late rain storm.

We left this focus of gold-bearing veins for silvery Georgetown, and again we are in the grand old canyon. I can hardly believe it is the same, for, viewed from the other side, every curve, rocky dome and spire seems new. There are two sides to a canyon as well as to a quarrel; I am convinced of that, but my readers must be satisfied with a one-sided view, for I have not command of superlatives sufficient to describe the other view.

CHAPTER XXII

SCENERY AND STORIES

CLEAR CREEK CANYON

While waiting for the up train at the Junction we had a delightful lunch, not like the usual fare at railway stations when you "ask for bread and receive a stone," but nice fresh rolls, genuine butter and savory coffee.

We started again eager for the ride through Clear Creek canyon, which is almost the perfection of pleasuring. There is a beauty and charm about this canyon that pleases, but never awes the beholder. The mountains are an unceasing wonder; none of them snow-clad, yet they mount high enough towards the sky to veil their heads in the clouds; they are not barren and repulsive, but clothed in green, with occasional cascades breaking over them, forming pictures restful and pleasing to the eye.

While rolling dreamily along, a castle with turrets, battlements and quaint windows loomed up before me. I started and rubbed my eyes, thinking it possibly arose from the heat of an over-wrought imagination. But it was a real castle; we had reached Idaho Springs, and this was the dwelling of the Honorable Thomas B. Bryan. It is so situated as to command a view of the valley, with its picturesque brown-roofed houses and rustic bridges that span the stream. Back of it are great dome-shaped hills, covered with evergreens, and beyond tower lofty mountains.

IDAHO SPRINGS

The hotels in this quiet little town, shut out from the world, were crowded with people, and many of them were there for a purpose, too, for they are racked with rheumatism and other ills, and just across the way are the famous "hot springs," which form, perhaps, the most important feature of this noted resort. The water issues from the ground boiling hot, and strongly suggestive of being sent up from the kitchen of Pluto. However, the temperature can be arranged to suit; "you pay your money and take your choice," whether you will be parboiled or well done.

Radium Cave Baths at Idaho Springs

Idaho Springs, sheltered in the hills, is now Colorado's famous resort for "radium water" cure.

George A. Jackson, of Missouri, while on a hunting expedition through the mountains, discovered these springs, and a little farther on he reached a point on Chicago creek, now within the limits of Idaho Springs, where he thought the indications favorable to mineral. He built a fire of logs and thawed the ground to enable him to dig with a knife. His tin cup served as a pan, and with these implements he began digging and washing. His first cupful of sand yielded him one dollar, and after working awhile he found he had washed out about nine dollars in shining gold dust.

The discovery was made on January 7, 1859.

After carefully marking the spot, Jackson returned to Golden and then to Auraria to await the coming of spring. In April, he went with twenty-two men to his find and later developments caused a great rush to the mountains. Jackson sold his interest in the claim and in 1860 joined the Confederate Army. His discovery marked the starting point of the mining history of the state.

About three miles above Idaho Springs are Chicago Lakes, where it is said that Bierstadt found the subject of his grand painting, "A Storm in the Rockies." The lakes are at an elevation of 11,500 feet. When anything as unstable as water can attain that eminence, it arouses reflection upon the enormous possibilities of this world.

The time passed pleasantly at Idaho. We were pleased with the baths and *more* than pleased with the water. It has a flavor that I shall not soon forget. Soda mixed with sulphur is never a palatable beverage. It is a "cultivated taste," so they say, and grows upon one, but we didn't stay long enough to acquire it. It is said to cure all the ills flesh is heir to, and many old habitues seemed to take to it like ducks to water and drank it, to all appearances, with perfect enjoyment.

BISHOP RANDALL

As we moved along through this wild, beautiful canyon, with the evening sun bathing mountain top and valley in a dreamy, mystic light, I thought of the good man who aided in shaping our social, mental and Christian developments, Bishop Randall.

He was an untiring worker in the cause of Christ. "I accompanied him through one day's labor in the mountains," said a lady member of his church. "We left Trotter's station early one morning and reached Idaho in time for service. I rang the bell while the Bishop opened the church, dusted the pews and books, and arranged his robe. After service, without stopping for dinner, we drove to Empire, where we had dinner, and the Bishop preached again. We then went to Georgetown, where he held service in the evening. The next morning we left Georgetown before breakfast, in fact before there were any signs of life on the streets. I shall never forget the beauty of that morning, as winding our way through the deep canyon, the sun peeped over the mountain tops, gradually growing brighter, until all the world seemed glorified by the splendor of its rays.

"We took breakfast at a station on the way, and continued our journey, for the Bishop had an engagement in Denver that day which he felt compelled to meet."

That is only a trifling incident in his laborious life, but it was suggested to me by the trip being made in a single buggy, without brakes, over this very road, then rugged and precipitous, which the skill of the engineer has since converted into a solid bed for the steam car. While others were building roads, developing mines, encouraging agriculture, creating commerce and giving impetus to our material advancement, Bishop Randall was building churches, establishing schools and setting in motion those varied regenerating influences without which there can be no civilization, no society. The "General Convention of the Protestant Episcopal Church" elected him Bishop of Colorado December 28, 1865. Twenty-two years he had labored as a parish priest in the City of Boston. His heart was bound to his people in those sacred ties of pastoral relations, and he had reached the time of life when most men feel the advance of age and begin to think of rest. His call was to him as the call of God to Abraham. He suffered the same trial of his faith. It seemed to him a terrible summons to uproot those firmly bound relationships and exchange his peaceful, happy home for the trials and harassing anxieties and homeless wanderings of a missionary bishop. He was a man and could not easily sunder ties so dear.

After prayerful consideration he decided to take the staff and go forward in fear and faith, believing it was the voice of God calling him to this work. He arrived in Denver June, 1866, making the journey across the plains in a stage coach. At that time there were but two parishes in the Territory, St. John's, at Denver, and St. Mark's, at Central. The Territories of New Mexico and Wyoming were also added to this diocese. The field was a large one and the work to be performed laborious. He traveled annually over his entire diocese, from Silver City, eight hundred miles to the southwest, on the farthest borders of New Mexico, to the out-posts of the Wind river valley, five hundred miles to the northward, enduring hardships, encountering dangers, suffering deprivations, preaching the gospel, establishing schools and performing the various sacred duties of his high office. Never was there a more faithful or devoted worker.

In the midst of his great labors, seven years from

the time he arrived in Colorado, the Master called him home.

The greatness of his success is best told by a brief review of the results. Parishes were organized and churches were built at Golden, Nevada, Georgetown, Pueblo, Canon, Colorado Springs, Idaho, Littleton and Baldwinsville, at Cheyenne and Laramie in Wyoming Territory, and at Santa Fe and Albuquerque in New Mexico. Wolfe Hall, a school for young ladies in Denver, was opened in 1867. He was a pioneer in the highest sense of the word, and possessed the qualifications which fitted him for the tasks thereby imposed. As an able, learned and eloquent divine he had few equals.

Georgetown

Georgetown is picturesque and romantic, nestled amid the eternal mountains, that stand like gloomy sentinels guarding it from the world, and guarding at the same time with morose and forbidding exterior the shining glories in their own deep hearts. As they stretch away in their mighty upward slant, they are dotted with cosy little cottages that lend an additional charm to the landscape. Along the principal streets the houses have a comfortable, home-like appearance; the windows are garnished with boxes of blooming flowers, and vines climb in graceful beauty around them.

We telegraphed ahead for a carriage to take us to Green Lake, and we found it waiting—a large, overgrown spring wagon, "lined and bound" with buffalo robes; the finest type of a mountain vehicle. It was drawn by four very handsome horses, and the driver was Hiram Washburn,* who drove the first stage into Central City, Black Hawk, Idaho Springs and Georgetown. He told wonderful stories of how he made the hair of dis-

---

*It must be remembered that these mountain stories were written in 1884.

tinguished passengers stand on end, by causing the rattling old coach to roll along first on one wheel and then on another; in fact perform any kind of acrobatic feat save that of a complete somersault, as the six horses dashed wildly along the precipitous mountain road.

Green Lake is only two miles from Georgetown, yet two thousand feet above it, reached by what is called a good mountain road.

It was the most remarkable road I ever saw. We wound in cork-screw curves, with only the road between imposing precipices above and yawning chasms below. It was "grand, gloomy and peculiar." Unlike Lot's wife, I had no disposition to look back to where I came from—it made my head swim, confused my ideas, and left an unpleasant sense of uneasiness and distress.

For the first time I lost interest in the summits, and became deeply absorbed in thinking how we were to get out of it.

Finally we switched around a deep curve and entered a trail, heavily fringed with dense and fragrant pines. I cannot describe the feeling with which it inspired me. It suggested both mystery and supernaturalism, and the peculiar sombre tint of the prospect intensified the feeling. We seemed to be winding through a resting place of the dead. Soon the awesome feeling was succeeded by a sweet religious ecstacy.

The busy work-a-day world was shut out and "peace on earth, good will to man" pervaded this great cathedral of nature. The emerald lake, with its placid water, the petrified forest at the bottom, and speckled trout that skimmed near its surface, was entrancing. The tall, trim evergreens that surrounded it, were perfectly mirrored in the water, and seemed to grow both ways, while the sun's rays, that fell through them, was like the dim religious light that shimmers through monastic windows.

There were no exclamations, but everyone seemed to quietly and meditatively take in the divine picture.

But we were out for pleasure, and we thought the greatest sport of all would be to catch some of the beautiful fish, that stuck their heads up out of the water and made mouths at us in the most tantalizing way. The warder supplied us with rods, and the way we caught fish would have given pleasure to any lover of the Waltonian art. A lady, in great excitement, went around inquiring for a bucket, she wanted to fill it, and take it home to her dear husband, in Denver. But buckets were scarce up there, and none could be had for "freighting purposes." She was dreadfully disappointed, and said she intended to suggest to the proprietor of the hotel the advantage of keeping a stock of buckets for the accommodation of tourists. But when we came to settle our bills, and found we were charged fifty cents apiece for every fish caught, she forgot to make the suggestion.

After one sweet hour of heavenly quiet and calm in that beautiful spot we began our descent.

The driver, who plumed himself upon his skillful manipulation of the ribbons, seemed intoxicated with pleasure and we went down that steep and rugged path, past the everlasting procession of tourists, at an alarming rate. A broken vehicle lay up against the side of the road, awaiting repairs. "Just watch me take the wheel off that," said he, cracking his whip and augmenting his speed. I felt myself turning pale, and closely embraced the arm of a gentleman who sat beside me.

Off came the wheel, throwing our wagon against a huge stone on the edge of the road; that being thus rudely knocked from its resting place, stopped not to "gather moss" on its way downward.

He laughed, almost shouted over his exploit, and turning deliberately around in his seat, said, "Don't get frightened, I have driven over this road a hundred times and have never met with an accident;" but I would have felt vastly more comforted if he had kept his eyes on his horses.

It seemed natural to rush by the "Devil's Gate," but we would have preferred a more lingering look at the "Bridal Veil Falls." Strange the fascination attached to that veil, whether it be of tulle, lace or water! To my agreeable surprise I reached Georgetown with my head on my shoulders, and, on the whole, delighted with the trip.

In the parlor at the hotel a mining expert told us a very amusing incident. A negro had been importuning him for weeks to look at his mine. He finally brought a specimen and said he had four feet of just such ore as that. Upon looking at it he thought if the negro's story was true, he had something worth having; so he hired a buggy and started off with the dusky miner. When he came to examine the mine he found a little vein about one and a half inches thick.

"What do you mean by fooling me in this way?" he said to the darky, rather roughly.

The negro turned his head to one side, and in a dazed sort of way said: "Ain't da fo' foot da, boss?" Then he examined it himself; "Well," said he, "if it aint jes like it was when I left it; but de closer I got to Georgetown de bigger it growd, and when I got da, I d'clar fo' de Lawd it was fo' foot."

The expert said the sell was so complete and ridiculous he couldn't get angry.

Gray's Peak

The following morning, refreshed and in good spirits, we started for Gray's Peak, the dome of the continent. It is 14,351 feet high. Nature is built on a grand

GRAY'S & TORRY PEAKS

GEORGETOWN LOOP

scale around here; "there is nothing little" about Georgetown, I'm sure.

One can ride to the summit of Gray's Peak in a carriage, but we preferred to go on horseback. The morning was breezy and cloudless, the ascent gradual, and as we mounted higher and higher toward the clouds, the green valley with its shady nooks and silvery streams was as charming as glimpses of fairy land.

About half way up we stopped to rest and talk to a returning party, who had been to the summit to see the sun rise. They were so enthusiastic over the marvelous view that we took out our guide book to see if their *far stretching* yarns were true. It corroborated their assertions as follows: "From this point are plainly discernible Pike's Peak, eighty miles away, Mount Lincoln, fifty miles, Mount of the Holy Cross, eighty miles, Long's Peak, eighty miles, the City of Denver, sixty-five miles, and even the summits of the Spanish Peaks, two hundred miles southward, and the highest ranges of the Uintah mountains, three hundred miles westward. The total range of the vision is not less than two hundred and fifty to three hundred miles."

After reading this, our desires were greatly increased to take the "tip-top" view. Toiling up, up, up, we at last reached the summit. Surely this must have been the great play-ground of the Titans, when in a game of pitch and toss with mountains, they left them as we find them, heaped in stupendous confusion to commemorate the occasion. There were mountains, mountains everywhere, seemingly without bound or limit. Far away hung the emblem of the Christian faith, the Holy Cross. There was something subduing and awe-inspiring in the sacred symbol that above all and over all stretched its arms in mute appeal to man's reverence for the Creator. One had the sense of standing before the visible throne of God waiting for the words, "depart from me," or, "ye are the chosen of my Father."

I sat down to contemplate and thoroughly enjoy the stupendous scenery, when the party gathered around and listened to

The Legend of the Mount of the Holy Cross

Many years ago, when the Franciscan Friars were earnestly engaged in the grand work of converting the inhabitants of Mexico to the worship of the true God, a monk in Spain yielded to the tempter and committed a great sin. Day and night, with contrite heart, he sought in prayer expiation for his sin. It was revealed to him in a vision that when he saw a cross suspended in the air, it would be a token of his forgiveness.

Then he became filled with a feeling of unrest and longed to travel. He joined an expedition to Mexico, and wandered over the country in search of the sacred symbol, until his hair was frosted and his limbs were infirm with age.

Finding no rest for his soul, he joined an exploring party going north. By winding ways they traveled; from mountain summit, where the sunshine lingers to valleys barred with light and shadows; through deep defiles robed in verdure, to mountains girdled with flowers and crowned with snow; onward they went.

Arriving one day on the summit of a lofty mountain, they pitched their tents. It was not the hour to camp, but their further progress was prevented by a dense fog, that with the morning sun rose from the ground and gradually grew thicker and higher until it mingled with the clouds and enveloped the whole earth.

The pious man wandered away from the sound of human voices to pray for the removal of his burden of sin. Kneeling in deep humility he raised his hands and voice to God; when lo! the cloud was lifted; and suspended before him, resplendent with the rays of the glorious sun, was the "cross."

Wondering at his long delay, his companions went to search for him, and found him in the attitude of prayer.

The Great Spirit had breathed forgiveness, and illumined with divine light, the face turned toward the "Mount of the Holy Cross."

The mountain is located near the town of Red Cliff, Eagle County, on the Denver & Rio Grande. The distance by rail from Denver is 294 miles. It is formed by great transverse canyons of immense depth filled with eternal snow. The symbol is perfect. From the crest of Fremont Pass and from Tennessee Pass this snow white banner of Christian faith, set high against the brown brow of the mountain, is clearly visible. Holy Cross creek, which flows at the base of the mountain is a picturesque and beautiful stream.

This world-famed peak is one of Colorado's great scenic points and the cross is as perfect today as it was in the time of the early Franciscan Friars. Russel A. Chapin and Mr. Schmidt are among the few who have had the temerity to climb to the peak of the Mount of the Holy Cross.

During the recital of the legend the air became suddenly colder, clouds shut out the sunlight, and it was evident that a storm was brewing. With all possible haste we started on the downward march. The roads were good, and as it was all down hill, we hoped to out-travel the storm.

Mt. of the Holy Cross

Angry nature fumed, fretted and threatened for an hour or so, and then rain came down in torrents. The thunders rolled, the winds lashed us, and all the elements seemed pretty busy for a while; but no matter, we had made the ascent and were happy, a new picture was hung in the gallery of memory, that time could never efface. We had something to think of and talk about, not for a day, but for many days.

The forlorn and bedraggled party which entered the hotel that evening bore no resemblance to the one that left it in the morning. We looked as if we had been attending a Baptist revival and become converts to the "dip theory." One complained of toothache, another of sharp rheumatic pains, still another of neuralgia, but such minor damages count as nothing when we take into consideration the magnificent view.

The Mining Expert

The next morning found us on the train for Denver, well and happy. Here again we met the mining expert.

As my mission was to gather stories, I endeavored to improve each shining hour, so commenced a lively conversation with him.

"I was sitting in my office one morning," said he, "reflecting over the old adage, 'all that glitters is not gold,' when I was suddenly awakened from my reverie by the salutation, 'Well, boss, how does you do?' Looking up I recognized the intruder as my old colored friend, Jim Boyd. Jim came to the country in an early day, and cast his lot with thousands of other fortune-hunters of the then wild country of Colorado, and being from the South myself, Jim often came in to talk about the old home, the fried chicken, sweet potatoes, and the many good things to us then 'non-come-at-able.'

"'Well, Jim,' said I, 'I'm glad to see you; sit down. What can I do for you?'

"'Golly, boss, struck it rich; no, I thank you, boss, drudder stand up.' Pulling out of his pocket an old dirty handkerchief, with something heavy in it, he produced from it some specimens of rocks. 'Here it is, boss; right out of de bottom of de shaft. Here's de wealth for you, sho'!'

"'You are excited, Jim. Sit right down and tell me all about it.'

"'De fact is, boss, I want to sell you dis mine.'

"'How deep are you, Jim?'

"'Down forty feet; dug de hole myse'f.'

"'How much ore?'

"'Eighteen inches pure stuff, boss.'

"'How does it run? Had any assays?'

"'Better den dat, boss, had a reg'lar mill run; $170 a ton and plenty of it.'

"'What price do you place on this property, Jim? I don't want to buy, but perhaps I can sell it for you.'

"'Now you struck me, boss. You can sell dis mine for $500; all you gets over—dat's yo' money.'

"'But, Jim, I wouldn't sell such a mine as that for so little; you can work it, if it is as rich as you say, and make from twenty to fifty dollars per day, which would soon make you a Bonanza king. Then you might be governor, or perhaps senator, who knows.'

"'Now, boss, I'se a colored man, a po' man, and all dat, but I'se honest, and I'se never done anything yet to qualify me for dem positions you speak about—sides all dis, I'se never harmed you, and I doesn't think you ought to cast such insinuations at me.'

"'Well, well, Jim, beg your pardon, but about the mine. Hadn't you better work that mine? I dislike to see an old friend who has struggled in these mountains so long and worked so hard, throw away such a good thing for a few hundred dollars.'

"'At this Jim came forward, and laying his big, black hand on my shoulder, sunk his voice to a whisper and replied: 'De fact am, boss, dar's many a good mine in dis country *spoilt by working it*. Sell de mine, boss.'

"Since that morning I have frequently had occasion to call to mind Jim's remark, 'dar's many a good mine spoilt by working it.'"

Georgetown is a great place to get a pocket full of rocks; the windows are full of specimens, views, etc.

An expert had a valise full of mountain souvenirs. A specimen is an expert's jewel, treasure, sweetheart, and everything that is delightful. He talked rapturously of the auriferous, cupriferous, galenous, argentiferous and ferriferous, and seemed delighted to find a sympathetic ear. His metalliferous voice softened into mellifluous undulations as if speaking of his first love, when he showed us a beautiful specimen of smoky quartz. Holding it at a proper angle to catch the sun's rays he said: "Quartz is an essential constituent of granite, and abounds in rocks of all ages." He had beautiful amethysts, carnelians, jaspers, agates, and so on, and he lingered affectionately on the perfections of each and every one. A friend of mine smuggled a wink to me and asked him, "What makes quartz?"

He contemplated her contemptuously and replied: "Twice as many pints, Miss."

Then, feeling, perhaps, that he was casting pearls before swine, he drew himself away and looked dreamily out of the window.

I took her to task for it, but she said it provoked her to see me looking as wise as an owl, absorbing that man's knowledge, when I didn't know or care anything more about rocks and minerals than I did about Sanscrit.

I reminded her of the trite adage, "it is never too late to learn," and accused her of spoiling my golden opportunity. We didn't have time to quarrel long, for our attention was attracted by the rocky sides of the canyon, where great masses of granite rocks, like Ossa on Pelion piled, seemed to pierce the very heavens, and in striking contrast to the blue sky above was the turbid stream below, beating itself in mad fury against the boulders in its course. Clear creek, so called, from the original transparency of its water, now turgid from the dust and other residuum of many quartz mills, is a self evident misnomer.

Luxuriant evergreens grew straight up out of the rocks. The same evergreens, if taken to Denver, carefully tended, watered and petted, would be sure to die. Just so with some people, they droop and die, or are dwarfed—which is worse—amid the luxuries of life, and the hard paths develop them into bright and shining lights.

The conductor put a stop to my sermonizing by inviting me to the rear end of the car to see the "Old Man of the Mountains."

When viewed from that distance he looked natural

enough to flirt with. We cheered him and waved our handkerchiefs as we glided by, but the *stony-hearted* old fellow did not even smile in return. How long he has been there none know. In ages past the earth, rocked with volcanic fires, in frenzied throes, gave him birth, and there he stands a relic of past grandeur, watching the roll of years.

I have spun so many yarns on the way this seems like a long trip, but it can be done satisfactorily in two days at a trifling expense.

Upon reaching Denver, the natural key to all points of scenic interest, we expressed a great desire to turn right around and go over the same route again, but our plans were mapped out and we had no time to repeat.

PART VIII
THE WESTERN SLOPE

CHAPTER XXIII

OVER THE MAIN RANGE

Platte Canyon

Touring in the mountains of Colorado is attended with none of the fatigue and weariness that generally accompanies excursions elsewhere. The distance from one place of interest to another is short, the air bracing, the hotels comfortable, and the trains start from all points at such seasonable and reasonable hours one is not afflicted with nervous excitement in a frantic effort to be on time for the cars—or sick headache.

We took the South Park railroad line for a trip over the main range.

Twenty miles from Denver we entered Platte canyon through an imposing gate-way of rocks, rising fully one thousand feet above the stream on either side, and breaking into all sorts of fantastic shapes at the top.

Our train makes some marvelous turns. Suddenly a projecting angle seems to threaten ruin and destruction, and while this thought is upon one the engine glides gracefully around it into new surprises. On the opposite side from the roadbed an English company has constructed a flume which conveys water to an irrigating canal, that waters and fertilizes countless acres south of Denver. This ditch is so large, and involves consequences so vast, one irresistibly cranes the neck to catch a glimpse of the boats and sails which should ride its waters like those of the rivers we knew in former times.

Platte river, which gives the name to this canyon, is as clear as crystal. Its waters have not yet been soiled by the working of mines and stamp mills in the mountain camps beyond. It rushes over miniature falls, breaking into feathery foam as it dashes against rude boulders, and leaps on as if flying from some mighty pursuer. This stream is full of speckled trout, the gymnast of the cascade, the most beautiful of the finny tribe, the delight of the epicure.

The conductor said, "they had only to throw out a line while the train was rolling along, and haul them in as fast as they could count."

That seemed almost as miraculous as some fish stories told by Matthew and Mark.

Platte Canyon

On looking up, I saw coming toward me, with his hand extended in a pleased-to-see-you manner, Mr. Jake Scherrer, one of Colorado's cattle kings. I told him I was gathering romances of the mountains, and should levy a contribution upon him. He immediately proceeded to tell me of

"Meeting An Old Acquaintance"

"Many years ago I was engaged in freighting to and from the mountains. While following a grapevine road through a wild and awesome canyon, using vigorously the usual ox-persuader in my intense anxiety to reach a human habitation before night-fall, suddenly clouds gathered and filled the canyon with gloom. They whirled and tossed and swept through the heavens, and presently the mist and wind enveloped my path in a mass of foam, often lulling for a moment to let a ray of sunshine through to delude me with false hope, then returning with a force that made my covered wagon writhe and tremble. One false step would have sent me and my little cargo to certain destruction. I shall never forget that experience.

"Coming at last to a small log-cabin, the outlines barely visible through the fast falling snow, I stopped to 'turn in' for the night, feeling grateful to find shelter from the storm.

"Tall, dense, dark evergreens surrounded it, wrapping it about like a pall. I pushed back the blanket which served as a door to the establishment, for doors on hinges and window glass were luxuries not to be had in those days. I looked around, but there was no one in. As the pioneers, like the ancient apostles, had everything in common, I took possession, and proceeded to make myself at home.

"Taking down a carcass of deer that hung on the wall, I cut some fine steaks from it and cooked my supper. While eating, I heard approaching footsteps. The blanket was drawn aside, and a large man, with unkempt hair and long gray beard, stepped in and glanced fiercely around.

" 'Hello, Cap.,' said I; 'do you live here?'

" 'I thought I did,' was the curt reply.

"Not a very hospitable greeting, but the weather outside trampled upon dignity, and forbid bowing out with, 'I beg your pardon, I did not intend to intrude.' So I said again, in an off-hand way, though I was conscious of a shudder, 'splendid steak this, sit down and have supper, Cap.'

"He hung his hat on a peg sullenly, and took his seat.

"His manner was darkly suggestive.

"We ate the meal without another word. The wind was sighing and wailing—shrieking sometimes—and ending in fearful hisses. As I sat there with that grum stranger confronting me, I thought of the loved ones at home, of my own sweetheart, joyous and happy in fresh and dewy girlhood. If I should fall a victim to this border ruffian, my death would be her first grief. Men think swiftly when their lives are in danger.

"After supper I pulled my pluck together and said, 'let's have a smoke.'

"Producing an old, deeply blackened and strongly odorous brier-root, the pioneer's meerschaum, and lighting it with a coal, he opened the conversation by asking:

" 'Where are you from, stranger?'

" 'From S———, a town in Iowa,' I replied.

" 'Why,' said he, 'that was my old home, I always made ——— hotel my headquarters there.'

" 'You ought to remember me, then, for I was an errand boy in that hotel.'

" 'What,' said he seizing my hand with a hearty grip, 'is this little Jake Scherrer? Why, of course I remember little Jake. Pardon my inhospitable treatment, but I thought when I found you here that your purpose could only be murder and robbery.'

"I replied that I, too, considered my life in imminent peril from his threatening appearance. We had both contemplated each other with suspicion, and were quite pleased at the agreeable termination.

"He laid his hand fondly on my shoulder, stroked my head, as if I were still a boy, and said: "Ah, you resurrect a thousand memories of better days. Then I had money, friends and hope. But the woman I loved deceived me. Our wedding day was set, and when I arrived to claim my bride, the words had just been pronounced which made her the wife of another. Disconsolate and forsaken I left the country and have never given anyone the slightest clue to my whereabouts. I could not endure the humiliation in the presence of old friends, and so for twenty years I have been a wanderer in these mountains, never seeing a familiar face. Yours is the first.'

"We sat up late that night talking of the old times. When bidding me good-bye, he said, 'we shall never meet again. I shall quit this spot and leave no trace of my further wanderings.'

"A few months afterward I passed over the same road. An enormous boulder had fallen from the mountain top and torn out the logs on one side of the cabin. I searched carefully among the ruins, thinking he might have been crushed beneath them, but he was not there: the hut was deserted and a wreck; strangely typical of the life of its occupant."

The varied beauties of Platte canyon form a constant succession of surprises. From beginning to end it is a prodigious art gallery, hung with the works of the Great Master.

After reaching the parks the mountains were beautiful and verdure-clad, but not on so grand a scale as at the entrance of the canyon. At Webster we took an observation car and our train was off again. Having seen it circumvent so many mountains which persisted in not getting out of the way, I supposed it was bent on some sort of strategy calculated to dodge the next one. But there I was again deluded, for it turned suddenly to the right and seemed to be making a straight, short cut for the summit. From the car windows we could look down the chimneys of the little village left at the foot of the ascent.

Another half-hour of persistent steaming brought us to the top of Kenosha Hill, 10,300 feet above the sea. There was an explosion of opinions. The charmed tourist said "excelsior"—the hurried man of the mines, to whom this hanging on the selvedge edge of the mountains was an old story, gave a disgusted "umph!"

South Park

Swinging dizzily around a sharp curve—what a vision! Stretching out beneath the summer heaven's delicious blue was a landscape unlike any I had ever seen before. A natural park of magnificent proportions, watered by sparkling streams, and dotted with mounds and hills, fringed with dark clumps of pine, spruce and balsam, and protected by mountains that stand like giant warders to this enchanted land. The whole so wondrously wild, yet so serene and peaceful, one could scarcely realize that the adjacent fastnesses were ever used to shelter bands of guerrillas, thieves and robbers.

Fate of the Guerrillas

In 1864 there came from Texas a troop of cutthroats, who claimed to be Confederate soldiers, but were nothing of the kind. Their leader, Jim Reynolds, was one of the earliest gold-seekers of Gregory diggings, and knew the country well. He came to plunder the miners, and excited his followers with marvelous tales of the riches to be had. One pleasant day in July, 1864, as the coach that maintained communication between Buckskin Joe and Denver was nearing McLaughlin's ranch, where Como now stands, these guerillas, mounted, spurred and armed to the teeth, appeared before it, and roughly commanded the driver to halt and surrender, declaring themselves to be Confederate soldiers, capturing all such outfits. The line was owned and conducted by Mr. W. G. McClellan, a small, gentlemanly man, who was seated by the driver, Ab. Williamson. They were ordered down, and their money demanded. Ab. said a stage driver was never before suspected of having any; but this little piece of raillery did not prevent their searching him. They then snapped his whip under his nose, which is the greatest indignity that could be offered a driver, and proceeded to business.

With a pistol aimed at the head of Mr. McClellan, they demanded the express box, the mail bags and his watch. Fearing the weapon might be accidentally discharged, he gracefully handed them over without any parleying. It was then about noon, and they were only a half mile from McLaughlin's ranch, which was a stage station. They went there and ordered dinner. A guard was placed over the occupants of the coach, and while the meal was being prepared the guerrillas opened the express trunk, took the treasure, amounting to several thousand dollars in gold dust, ripped up mail sacks, opened the letters, and appropriated what money there was in them, chopped up the coach wheels, remarking that they wanted to do the United States as much damage as they could, then mounted their horses and proceeded on the road towards Denver.

McClellan and Williamson returned on foot to Buckskin Joe, over the short trail via Montgomery, where their story was told, and a party organized at once to pursue the fugitives.

After several days' raiding along the road, when near to Central City, the guerrillas retraced their course, and one night camped in the thick woods of the canyon, about a mile above where Webster is now built, and while some were cooking, others playing cards, a party of twelve or fifteen from Gold Run, under the leadership of Jack Sparks, came suddenly upon them and fired, killing three and wounding the leader, Jim Reynolds, in the arm. The party scattered in the greatest confusion, and took to the bushes, leaving all their arms, plunder and camp equipage on the ground. One of the slain was the next day beheaded, the ghastly trophy placed in a sack and carried to Montgomery by a doctor of the party.

Two days afterwards one of the band was captured alone, and several days afterward all except two were captured and taken to Denver by Lieutenant Shoup, with a detachment of the First Colorado Cavalry, Governor Hunt, then United States marshal, and Wilbur F. Stone, assistant United States attorney, of the Park County forces. At Denver the prisoners were turned over to the military authorities.

Colonel Chivington, commanding the district, ordered them to Fort Lyon. They were placed in charge of Captain John Cree of the Third Colorado Cavalry. When near the head of Cherry creek, in Douglas County, the prisoners, as afterward reported, attempted to escape, and were all killed by the troops in charge of Captain Cree.

The troops returned to Denver, leaving the bones of the robbers to bleach and whiten on the plains.

While following the guerrillas to their fate the train has arrived at Como.

Naming Fairplay

Arriving at the hotel, we were ushered into a large, square room, called the parlor. The only articles of furniture visible were a round table, as large as King Arthur's, and a few chairs. When the proprietor became aware that I was gathering material for a book, he kindly brought in the pioneers to see me.

One of them told me of the naming of Fairplay. "In 1859," said he, "certain parties made a discovery of rich placer diggings in the South Park, at or near what is now called Hamilton. These diggings were so rich that it was said one ordinary laborer could dig a pound of gold per day. The name Tarry-all was given by the discoverers, who laid claim to all the valuable ground, or, to use a frontier phrase, 'gobbled up' everything, so that later comers could not secure any mining ground without paying exorbitant prices for it. By reason of this the place was called 'Grab-all' by those who failed to get a show in the diggings.

"The disappointed fortune-seekers subsequently pushed further on along the middle branch of the Platte and there made other valuable discoveries. Among the number were four men from Central, then called Gregory, who, having heard the fabulous stories in circulation respecting the new mines, clubbed together, and loaded a mule, that belonged to one of the men, with all their earthly possessions, and started for the new mining camp.

"They had stopped at the above mentioned camp and panned out considerable gold, making one of the men, by the name of Hill, banker. Their provision gave out and

Hill refused to let them have money to buy more, which immediately aroused their suspicions.

"One of the party, a man named Tom Payne, laid their complaint before Reed, Mills & Company, who had a provision store. They called the miners together to arbitrate on the subject, and after patiently hearing the evidence, it was decided that Mr. Hill must weigh the gold and give every man an equal share. While they were talking around the camp fire Hill plunged out of the cabin into the dark, and the miners started in quick pursuit, keeping track of him by the cracking of the grass and dry branches under his feet.

"Finding it impossible to escape them, he made a wide circuit and entered his cabin, where they found him in bed, covered up head and heels. They dragged him out, took the gold dust, and, in the presence of the arbitrators, weighed it and gave each man his portion. Hill refused to receive his, but they held him, and while he struggled in resistance, they put the money in his pocket.

"James Reynolds, who afterwards became a notorious guerrilla, stood by, with his hands in his pockets, quietly watching the transaction. When finished, he exclaimed: 'Thar, b'gad, if one is the devil and t'other Tom Payne, they shall have '*Far play!*'

"Shortly after this a committee was appointed to draft rules for the district and give it a name. Captain Charles Nichols, John Reed and Sydenham Mills were the committee. After drafting the rules, it was agreed that Mr. Mills, being the oldest miner, should give the name. He had taken an active part in the incident above narrated, and with his mind strongly imbued with the idea that everyone in that camp must have justice, named the town 'Fairplay.'

"Yes," said Mr. Stansell, "that is how the name was given, and hearing it related brings to mind a romance that occurred there a year later, which I will tell you. It is now called

THE LEGEND OF FAIRPLAY

"In the summer of 1860 a solitary man was industriously at work sinking his 'prospect hole' and trying to reach bed-rock, when suddenly there appeared at the top of his shaft a man, rifle in hand, who remarked, 'I have you at last.' The miner looked up from his work, recognized the individual at the top, and responded, 'Yes, you have, but you will give me fair play, won't you?' To which the other replied, 'Yes; meet me at sunrise tomorrow, at a certain point,' designating the place. The man in the shaft said, 'I will.' Whereupon the one on the surface swung his rifle over his shoulder and walked off.

"The next morning dawned bright and beautiful, and at sunrise the two met, without friends, surgeons or the usual parade of meetings 'of honor,' and, with their rifles, took positions fifty paces apart, and commenced the combat. At the first fire the miner fell, mortally wounded. The stranger deliberately shouldered his rifle and walked away, no one knew whither. The miners buried the dead man at the spot where he fell.

"The explanation of this tragedy was subsequently learned to be this: The two men had formerly resided in Texas, and had been comrades since boyhood; had played, studied, traveled, planned, enjoyed and suffered together until their attachment had strengthened into the love and trust of brothers. One of them had a sister who seemed to him an angel of truth and innocence. He was proud of her beauty, and introduced his friend, hoping that these two, the dearest upon earth to him, might love and be united as husband and wife.

"She fell a victim of his wiles, and her betrayer fled

the country. When the brother learned of the perfidy of his friend, he took a solemn vow to devote his life to avenging the wrongs of his sister. Arming himself, he started in pursuit of the fugitive, and for three years tracked him from place to place, without success, until he came upon him as above narrated."

Breckenridge

We spent an hour or so very pleasantly at Como, and enjoyed our dinners, for which the stimulus of the pure, bracing mountain air admirably fitted us.

Taking the Breckenridge branch, we immediately commenced the ascent of a succession of hills. Everyone sat in the open car and laughed and chatted and apostrophized the wonderful scenery.

As our train followed a groove in the mountain side, we looked down upon a green, exquisite little valley, several hundred feet below. A silvery stream wound through it, almost circling in its course a town. In proportion, as we mounted higher and higher, the houses diminished in size, so that this charming spot, surrounded with pine-covered mountains, seemed to us a fairy-land. I went to work building all sorts of air castles about it, but the conductor shivered them all by telling us it was the deserted mining camp of Tarry-all, one of the kind that spring up in a day, like "Jonah's gourd," and wither away as rapidly. This was the first dead town we had seen, and we thought it a rather attractive corpse.

The mountain sides were all aglow with rainbow-tinted flowers, and it seemed that we were being literally "carried to the skies on flowery beds of ease."

At Boreas, the summit, the train stopped long enough for us to gather bouquets and look down the valley of the Blue river, over which nature has thrown a beautiful blue mist, like a veil—the effect was enchanting. In our scramble for flowers I thought of Linnæus, of whom it is said that whenever he discovered a new flower he thanked heaven for the sight.

While arranging our flowers, George T. Clark, a "barnacle," joined our party. He was on his way to Breckenridge to look after some mining property, which brought up the subject of gold and prospecting.

He said that gold was first discovered on the Blue, near where Breckenridge now stands, in the summer of 1859, by a party of prospectors, one of whom was William Iliff, in later years the wealthy "cattle king." Since that time many millions of dollars have been taken out of the Summit County mines.

At Rocky Point, where we reach the acme of scenic glory on this line, the town of Breckenridge commences to play "Bo-peep" with the admiring tourist; first on this side and then on that, we see it—making another turn, a full view is obtained.

The pretty little frontier town seems only a stone's throw distant, but the train, as if in a frolicsome mood, with no other aim than to intensify our interest in the play, dashes away, making a short curve and surprises the town from another point.

The sudden change of temperature from the plains to the mountains forced us to don our heavy wraps, in lieu of which a gentleman put on his gossamer overcoat for warmth, and his linen duster over that for style. The gossamer hung below the duster, forming a border of black, which gave him the appearance of a bill distributer for a minstrel band. But he was dressed to life in good humor, which is, after all, the most becoming garb a man or woman can wear. We stopped at the Grand Central, an excellent hotel. Our party retired early, so as to be ready to ramble freely and extendedly the next day.

Immediately after breakfast I started out to find a gentleman to whom I had a letter of introduction.

"You want items," he said. "Ah, I see—and they have sent you to me because I am a sort of bookish fellow and have been a quill driver."

The man who thus spoke had a handsome head, well set on broad shoulders, a large soulful blue eye, and I wondered what trick Fortune had played on him to turn his hair as white as the snow-drift, for his face was yet young.

"You must see Judge Silverthorn; he loves to talk of the old times. He came here in '59, and was judge of the Miners' court. He is a diminutive man, almost dried to a crackling, and has such a strange, weird look that you couldn't help wondering to what age or order of human beings he belongs. His hair and beard are grizzly gray, and he chews continually. When he tells a border tale his little keen eyes twinkle with humor and intelligence, then he goes into convulsions of laughter and kicks up his feet until he resembles a jack-knife half open—forming a picture altogether grotesque. But he is the soul of honor and goodness, with a heart so large that it is continually running over with kind deeds and comforting words.

"His wife, who died recently, was called the mother of the camp, the good Samaritan to all in trouble and distress. How the boys loved her! She always spent her winters in Denver, and in the spring, when we heard Mrs. Silverthorn was coming, we put on our snow-shoes, met her at the top of the range and brought her down on a sled. That was fun, let me tell you. With loud hurrahs, and hats tossing wildly in the air, we heralded her arrival.

Duels

"There is nothing like a frontier town for thrilling events. We have had some very remarkable duels here. About twenty years ago two gentlemen, who were in every respect valuable citizens, quarreled about some trifle—I've forgotton what, but it resulted in a challenge to mortal combat. We were all greatly distressed, for they were good fellows, and we made every effort to pacify them, but without effect. They agreed to fight with hatchets, thirty paces apart. Mr. Bressler, that handsome blacksmith across the way, sharpened the hatchets, and the work was well done; they were as keen-edged as razors. The gentlemen practised so earnestly that almost every tree around the town received a scar from their weapons. The evening before the fight was to come off one of them received a letter from his mother, in which she informed him that his antagonist was the son of her dearest friend, and she hoped the boys would love each other like brothers. This letter brought about a reconciliation, and they are still living, both filling prominent positions in other States.

"Well," said he, "I started out to tell you about a duel, but that was a 'drawn battle' and doesn't count. Speaking of 'drawn battles,' I can tell you one that beats that one all hollow.

"Two fellows were mining over here in Galena Gulch, and they had a dispute about a girl, which resulted in a challenge. It was left to a meeting of the Miners' court to determine the manner of fighting. The miners had no confidence in their courage, and it was decided that they should stand back to back, walk off fifteen paces, then right about face and forward march, shooting and continuing to shoot until one was killed, or their revolvers emptied.

The Western Slope

"At the appointed time they met and were placed back to back in the presence of the entire population of the gulch. When the order was given to walk fifteen paces, they started off bravely. Upon reaching the line, instead of turning to face each other, they both walked on as fast as their legs could carry them, clear out of the country, probably thinking:

They Continued to Walk

"'He who fights and runs away
Will live to fight another day.'"

The conversation of this gentleman was a marvel of loquacity, and the friend with me, being familiar with the early incidents of the place, lost no opportunity in jogging his memory.

THE STAGE RIDE

Now arose a debate whether we should go to Leadville by way of Como or Frisco. We were informed that the coach left for Frisco every morning, and the road was level and smooth, through the prettiest valley that ever was seen.

The *stage ride*—that decided me. Mr. Smith, a walking embodiment of common sense, and the "brake and balance wheel" of the party, gave us the advice that Punch gives to people about to get married—"don't." But he might as well have said "do," for we immediately engaged passage in the stage, and I commenced to plan for myself a seat with the driver; for drivers are said to be living, breathing, talking encyclopædias of western lore.

Promptly at the appointed hour the horn blew; we gathered our traps and were soon on the veranda of the hotel. But where was the coach? We anxiously looked about for one of those gaily decorated affairs, like the chariots in the circus, where the driver and some favored passenger sits on top, entirely oblivious of who or what is caged in the box below. We waited. At last a fine looking man, in natty suit, broad brimmed hat, and bran new kids, politely inquired of us if we were going to Frisco. We replied in the affirmative. Whereupon he tipped his hat, and said, "Allow me to assist you into the coach." To our utter amazement "*the coach*" was a large three-seated spring wagon, painted in black and "old gold," and strikingly suggestive of an undertaker's rig.

I bounced to the front seat, eager that my chat with the driver should not prove a delusion also.

The pleasant-faced landlady invited us to come again, and the porch was crowded with new-made friends, who waved us good-by until we were out of sight. It was perfectly delightful to be treated that way; we felt at peace with the world and ourselves.

The driver swung around town gathering up his load, and when the last "all right" was given, he counted noses and found he had nine passengers. "A little too thick for comfort," said he, "but some of them will stop at the first station."

"How long have you been in this country, driver?" I ventured to inquire.

"Oh, I've been driving over these mountains, off and on, for over twenty years."

"I expect you have had many adventures?"

"You bet," he said.

I told him that I was gathering Colorado stories, with the intention of writing a book, and asked him to relate an adventure. He meditated awhile and said:

"I was driving a stage in the San Juan country several years ago, and among the miners at a little town called S——, where I always stopped for the night, was a young man named Robert L——. We called him Bob, because we liked him. He was an honest, hard-working chap, and as handsome a fellow as ever trod sole leather. One day Bob struck it rich, and with his face all beaming he told me he intended to start back home on my coach the next morning, to marry the girl he had been engaged to for seven years. 'I have served like Jacob of old,' he said, 'and I am at last to be rewarded. The old man objected, because I was poor, but now I have made my little "pile," and the hours don't go fast enough. I would like to fly to her, for during all the long, weary years she has been watching and waiting for me.' It was enough to make anybody feel glad just to see him and hear him talk.

"When we started the next morning his heart was full of joy, and he was cracking jokes and making the crowd merry. About three o'clock in the afternoon we reached a little stream that was heavily wooded, when several men, with their revolvers cocked, rushed out of the underbrush and commanded a halt.

"They compelled Bob to throw up his hands, and commenced searching his pockets. He had his dust in a buckskin vest worn under his clothing—there was $10,000 in it.

"When the robbers found it, Bob sprang to his feet and said, 'I have worked for that money with the hope of marrying the girl I love; if you take it, you will destroy my happiness forever.'

" 'We'll destroy you if you don't hand it over.'

" 'I'll never do it,' said Bob.

"Whereupon they blew his brains out. One searched him while the others stood with their pistols drawn on me and the other passengers.

"After getting the vest, they put spurs to their horses and were soon out of sight. To this day no trace of them has been found. Poor Bob—the villains had spotted him. I never drove over that road again; couldn't stand to pass the place."

The driver's voice grew husky and his eyes moist. Suddenly the horse to the right gave a plunge, and the driver gracefully curled his whip over his head and brought it down upon the flank of the refractory animal.

"You have handsome horses," I said, "what are their names?"

"Astronomy and Deuteronomy, 'Omy' and 'Duty' for short. Omy is always frisky when she starts out, but she soon breaks down. When it comes to the home-stretch, Duty knocks the persimmons every time."

Through the Fire

There was no more time for talking, for we were drawing near a "fire in the mountains."

The sight was grand; the long red tongues of fire were twining and lapping around the lofty pines up to the very top, and flying off in flags and sheets above. We began to feel their warm caresses, for the wind was in our direction. The flames had closed back of us, cutting off all retreat, and onward we must go.

I hoisted my sun umbrella to keep off the sparks. Vesuvius couldn't hold a candle to them. The "whole region 'round about" seemed on fire. My umbrella was reduced to a skeleton.

Finally we all curled down in the bottom of the wagon "like breakfast bacon in a frying pan," except the driver, for he had to bend his energies to keeping the frantic horses in the road; as it was they traveled considerable zig-zag country. He would occasionally tell us to "keep cool." But it was a difficult thing to do under the circumstances.

The Western Slope

We were a sorry looking outfit when we arrived at Frisco. O *my!* and "Duty" were minus mane and tail, and cooked in spots. It was a burning shame. The driver's face was so black with smut, he looked like a coal heaver. He said, "That takes the eyebrows off of any fire I have ever seen, and as soon as I can ascertain the origin I will send you full particulars. It will *illuminate* your book."

A Burning Shame

We invested in cold cream and anointed our faces until they looked like balls of butter in the sun. The facetious landlord remarked that we were the first *cremated* people that ever ate at his table.

Mining in San Juan

Taking the cars for Leadville, I was surprised and pleased to find among the passengers a number of successful mining men. As the San Juan country has for years attracted attention because of its fabulous wealth, I became quite interested in their stories of prospecting there, way back in '61, when it was known as Baker's Park, Baker being the first man to enter the country.

"It was in the winter of '61," said Mr. Curtis, "that a young friend of mine, knowing that I had some money, whispered to me of a 'new find' in the San Juan country, and said if I would 'go in' with them they would start immediately for the new Eldorado, build roads, lay out a town and by spring be ready for work. It was impressed upon me that 'mum' was the word. However, it leaked out as all such matters will, and there ensued a regular scramble for that country. Their provision and money gave out, and not finding a 'color,' they returned heaping abuse on the diabolical swindle.

"Speaking of the first rush to the San Juan country," said Mr. Cy. Hall, "I was at that time mining in California Gulch, but when I heard of the new discovery I grew dissatisfied with my 'pannings out,' and became restless for richer diggings. Distance lends a power of enchantment to a miner. He is always ready to follow any will-o'-wisp that happens to present an attractive story of rich mines found in some inaccessible country. It would be wasting breath to say, 'stay where you are,' for they won't do it. I know how it is. I've been there. I was doing well enough in California Gulch, but I heard such a world of talk that I clubbed in with some boys and followed the last excitement.

"Arriving at a point within a mile of where Durango now stands, we laid out a town, built seventy-five houses, and in a few weeks there were five hundred people there.

"Snow fell from three to four feet all over the country, and didn't melt an inch the whole winter.

"Many of us went there with our pockets full of glittering dust, but we all had to face starvation. We ate the oxen that carried us over, and even the entrails that had lain in the sun for days; lived on bullrushes for months. Those that went out hunting invariably got lost and starved to death.

"When the winter broke up everybody that could get away, went.

"I returned to California Gulch, suffering greatly on the way from hunger and cold, for moccasins and a blanket were about all the clothing I had.

"Arriving in sight of the cabin of my old partner, I called to him to bring me a hat and a pair of boots, I had a blanket, and I wanted to make a respectable entrance into the camp.

"Refreshed by my adventure I resumed mining in the old place with renewed vigor and determination."

"I can tell a story that will overtop that," said the Hon. Charlie Hall.

"In the winter of '61 I was attacked with the San Juan fever, and three of us strapped our provisions and blankets on our backs and started out to capture bushels of hidden gold. Our objective point was the present site of Ouray, the distance being comparatively short on an air line, we laid in a small supply of rations, which were exhausted after a few days out, and our luxuries during the remainder of the time consisted of a buffalo robe, leather pants and ants. We first ate the buffalo robe, singing the hair to a powder, which we ate, but when we came to masticate the skin, we found it as tough as a door mat. That lasted a day or so, and we then commenced on our boots. We went for the stew made of them with appetites that knew no limits. My leather trousers were the next thing tackled. We cut them into strips and ate with as much avidity as the Neapolitan would his long, luscious macaroni.

"Having now exhausted our mess-box, we went in search of ants, and peeled the bark of the trees and the old logs until they looked as if they had been struck by lightning. Ant lunch is pretty good when you can get enough of them. That sort of wrestling for life continued until there ceased to be any fun in it.

"A pedestrian tour over rocks and snow is not near so entrancing as watching the scenery from a car window.

"We subsisted for three days upon our vitals, rather expensive victuals, too—and there was an ominous wildness in the hungry eyes of the men that made me suspect they would soon be forced to cannibalism. As I was the smallest man in the party, I stood a fair chance of making the next meal.

"As night drew on this conviction preyed upon my mind, until every time I lost consciousness I had visions of drawn daggers and glaring, fiendish eyes, that startled me broad awake.

"After the camp-fire had died away, I gathered up my blankets and stealthily crept to another spot, but not to sleep, and as I lay there, I saw the two men approach the place I had deserted, feel around on their hands and knees, and foiled in their murderous designs, slink back to their blankets.

"The sun had scarcely awakened the sleeping world when I crawled out of my retreat and confronted the men with what I had seen, and announced my intention to leave them. One of them expressed a desire to accompany me, and take in the route we had decided upon the day before. The other man went alone.

"As we continued our tramp over the mountains, the days seemed like years, and the hunger-pain kept gnawing at our vitals until strength was gone. If we fell to the ground it was almost impossible to regain our feet.

"My friend was of robust physique, and could stand the 'racket' better than I.

"I had fallen off until my clothes were large enough for a dozen of my size.

"We struggled along for fourteen days, and I reached a pile of rock from which the snow had melted, and felt resigned to lie there and die; my lower limbs were already dead to my thighs.

"My companion, with painful effort, climbed to the top of what is now known in the San Juan country as Henson Mountain. He looked around at me with his face as bright as a Chinese lantern, and shouted, 'Brace up, Charlie! we are all right. Another outfit in the valley.' That was about the happiest moment I have any recollection of.

"The party in the valley came to our rescue. They carried me into camp, and I pulled the scales at forty-

eight pounds. They handled me as if I was a child; put my legs in boiling water, but I didn't feel it.

"It was Ben Eaton's party that rescued us. They fed me on water gruel for several days, but I didn't gain much fat on that kind of diet. Finally Ben made the awful announcement that I must die.

"He was absent a few days, and when he returned I told him they were starving me to death. He again gave me the pleasant information that I had to die, and I might as well eat everything I wanted.

"I did, with the appetite of an alligator.

"When I got on my feet again the boys would hardly have been more surprised if they had seen an Egyptian mummy rise up and walk."

The vast region of Colorado known as the San Juan country comprises the counties of San Juan, Rio Grande, Hinsdale, Ouray, Dolores, Montezuma, La Plata and San Miguel. Its principal mining towns are Durango, Silverton, Lake City, Creede, Rico, Telluride and Ouray.

Otto Mears was one of the earliest settlers in the San Juan district. In fact, when he built his house in 1865, at Saguache, his house was Saguache, and during the various Indian scares, it was a place of refuge.

Mr. Mears tells the following:

"In 1874, I made a trip to the Uncompahgre agency, where the city of Montrose now stands. Ouray was head chief then, and I wanted to see him. The distance was one hundred and fifty miles, and I went in a buggy with my wife and baby. When we were nearly to the place, we found that the river was badly flooded and we could not ford it. We had to get across, for we could not stay where we were. Finally, I thought of a plan.

"I had two empty oat sacks, for of course we had to carry all our provisions and fodder for the horses with us. I filled these sacks with rocks and tied one on each end of the back axle and drove my rig full speed. The horses swam, dragging the buggy after them. The buggy could not upset, because the two loaded sacks held it down, just as two anchors would. The water rose to our waists as we sat in the buggy. My wife held the baby up in her arms I tried to guide the ponies. When we reached the other side I heard the firing of guns and an Indian ran past me. Ouray came out and called to me to come into his house as quickly as I could.

"He lived in a 'doby' house and after we went in he barred the doors and windows. He said that the Indian we had seen had been sent out by the Northern Utes to try to induce his Indians to rebel and join with them in an insurrection against Ouray as chief.

"When Ouray heard this he ordered the Indian shot. He told us that there would be trouble during the night. We did not sleep much, but kept on the lookout, as Ouray felt that the Northern Utes would come down on him. We were not particularly comfortable in between these two fires, the Northern Utes on one hand and Ouray with his Indians on the other, but nothing happened that night.

"The next morning, all being quiet, I hitched up and drove on to the government agency, ten miles away. On the road we passed the dead body of the Indian we had seen shot the night before. We stayed at the agency ten days, and when we came back, the body still lay as we had seen it. It was badly decayed and covered with buzzards, who were eating the flesh, but not one of Ouray's Indians could be induced to bury it."

Soon after this, the Indians warned all of the white people out of the country. The San Juan was left undisturbed by prospectors until 1870, when the town of Silverton was founded and became a nucleus for the great mining development of the present day.

Until the treaty with the United States government, in 1874, all this country was the undisputed domain of the Ute Indian. Its settlement by white men form many thrilling stories of hardship and suffering.

OURAY

The town of Ouray is called the "Gem of the Rockies." It is set at the bottom of a perfect bowl—a Titanic bowl, lined with red granite. European travelers declare that Switzerland has no grander scenery than that around Ouray.

The town bears the name of the great Indian chief who made his summer camp here for many years.

He was renowned in his tribe for his wisdom, and his friendship for the white man made him very helpful in the material progress of Colorado. Up to the time of his death, in 1880, he lived at his home in the Uncompahgre with his wife, Chipeta, who, like Ouray, was kind and well disposed towards the whites. His home was a comfortable adobe built for him by the government. He took great pleasure in cultivating his farm and was anxious to surrender the reins of government to some younger man, desiring only to be known as Ouray, "the white man's friend."

Chief Ouray and Chipeta

He had but one son, who was stolen from him by the Arapahoes during a war many years ago between the Utes and that tribe. It was a source of great grief to him. The government made an effort to restore the boy to his home, and while General Adams was agent he accompanied Ouray to Washington, where, according to agreement, he was to meet the chief of the Arapahoes and receive his long lost boy. When the young Indian was brought in, he walked up to Ouray and asked him how much he was worth, and how many ponies he had to give him. The old chief eyed the mercenary young man sadly and said, "He is not my boy. If he was, I would feel it in my heart," and turned away grievously disappointed.

They never met again.

In the county of Ouray is the famous Camp Bird mine, which added the name of Thomas F. Walsh to the list of millionaires.

GRAND JUNCTION

The story of the precious metals of the Western Slope is enthralling and some may regard it in that light exclusively, but nothing could be farther from the truth. It is Colorado's banner fruit-growing district. The Grand Junction peaches have a more succulent flavor than the

The Western Slope

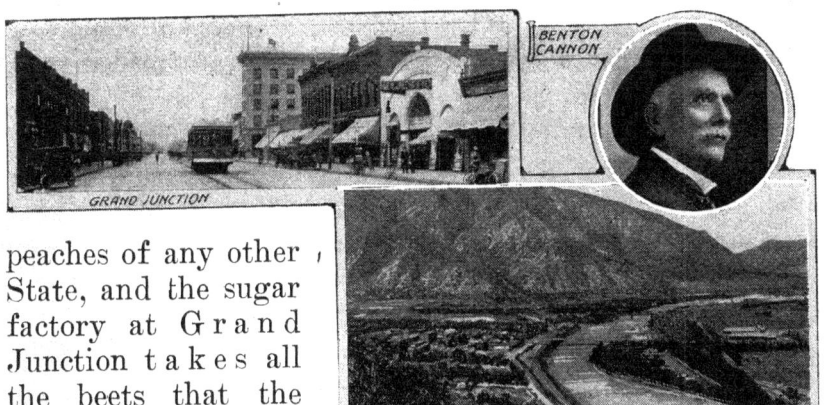

peaches of any other State, and the sugar factory at Grand Junction takes all the beets that the farmers can raise. The Western Slope apples bring the highest price of any apples in the nation. The Carbondale potatoes are grown on the Western Slope.

Grand Junction is the leading fruit-shipping point between the Missouri river and the Pacific coast.

Honorable Benton Cannon, who now resides at Grand Junction, is a Colorado pioneer, coming to Colorado when it was a part of Kansas, and settling in those early days down in Huerfano county. Mr. Cannon has been unusually active in the making of Colorado history. He accumulated a comfortable fortune while a resident of Huerfano county, and removed to Grand Junction before the coal mines of Huerfano county were developed, and before, if they were known at all, there was little knowledge of their extent or worth.

Mr. Cannon is now the treasurer of Mesa county, filling his third term. Whether the Democrats or the Republicans win at the election, Mr. Cannon has so completely acquired the confidence of Mesa county voters that he is retained in his position. Knowing that his statements could be relied upon, I asked him for information about the settlement of Grand Junction. He wrote the following:

"I located in Grand Junction in 1886 and engaged in the mercantile business first, and later in the banking business. In 1889 the Interior Department at Washington held up and refused to issue a patent on 640 acres of land that covered the townsite of Grand Junction. The town was growing rapidly and there was not a lot in town that could show a valid title.

"The homes and investments of the pioneers of our town were in jeopardy. There was war and rumors of war, and public sentiment was wrought up to high pressure. The good people of our community were divided in their opinions as to the best course to pursue in this emergency. One side wanted to petition the government to cancel the entry and file a new townsite. The opposition favored petitoning the department at Washington to issue patents to the original town company, thereby saving the homes and investments of our people. The emergency was pressing and something had to be done quickly and decisively to prevent serious results.

"I took upon myself the responsibility of selecting a committee of fifteen from the business men of our town and appealed to the citizens to endorse my action, which they did, and I was requested by the committee to act as their chairman. We met every day for three weeks and finally concluded to ask the property owners to join us in a petition to the Interior Department at Washington to grant patent to the original town company at the earliest possible moment, thereby preventing serious consequences to our citizens. The late Honorable Henry M. Teller was Secretary of the Interior at the time, and the patent was promptly issued and the controversy ended, with peace and happiness restored.

"The next dark cloud that appeared on the horizon of our desert valley and frontier town was in the autumn of

1889. A declaration of war was issued between the irrigation company and the landowners of the valley. Pistols and shotguns were quietly discussed on the streets of our town. The irrigation canal and its laterals covered about 40,000 acres of land and brought water for irrigation to the orchards and fields of our valley.

"This irrigation system was promoted by the late T. C. Henry and financed by the Travelers' Insurance Company of Hartford. The pioneer settlers had bought and paid for their water rights, but the expense of operation to the company was more than the income. The company wanted the annual charges increased and the landowners 'balked' and the 'devil' was to pay in general. I stepped into the breach again and named another committee of fifteen from the ranks of pioneer farmers and fruit growers of the valley. My action was endorsed by the people and I was requested to act as chairman. We met every day for a month and considered the matters in hand.

"The net result was that the Travelers' Insurance Company wiped off the slate their investment of about $1,000,000 and their equity fell into the hands of the late T. C. Henry and Mr. John P. Brockway, the Denver attorney, got it from Mr. Henry, and our committee of fifteen secured an option on the entire irrigation system for the water right holders in the old company for $40,000.00, and in due course the option was taken up, and there was not a gun fired or a man killed, and the clouds of depression passed away from Grand Valley, and sunshine and happiness took their place."

Glenwood Springs, the famous summer resort, is on the Western Slope.

Congressman Edward T. Taylor has resided in Glenwood Springs since 1887, and practiced his profession. For many years he has been associated in the practice of the law with his brother, Charles W. Taylor. In 1887 he was elected district attorney of the ninth judicial district; 1896 he was elected State Senator for the twenty-first senatorial district, and re-elected in 1900 and 1904, his twelve years' service ending December, 1908; was president pro tempore of the Senate one term, and was the author of forty statutes and five constitutional amendments adopted by a general vote of the people; he also served five terms as city attorney and two terms as county attorney of his home town and county. He is a Mystic Shriner and an Elk, and served two terms as eminent commander of the Glenwood Commandery of Knights Templar; has been president of the Rocky Mountain Alumni Association of the University of Michigan, and vice-president of the State Bar Association, and is now vice-president of the State Association of the Sons of Colorado, and has taken an active part in public affairs in Colorado for over a third of a century. He is now and has during the past six years, been the Colorado member of the Democratic national congressional committee. He is married and has three children. He was elected to the Sixty-first, Sixty-second and Sixty-third Congresses as Congressman-at-large. When the State was redistricted his home county was placed in the fourth congressional district, and

E. T. Taylor

he was re-elected from that district to the Sixty-fourth Congress. While in Congress he has secured the enactment of many laws of commanding importance to the State.

CHAPTER XXIV

LEADVILLE

How the Mining Excitement Started

Gold was discovered here in April, 1860, by prospectors from California, who had been prospecting along the Arkansas river. When they found the rich mineral, one man exclaimed, "This is California," and from that remark the region took the name of California Gulch, and the mining town was named Oro City. Then followed

Leadville in 1879

a mining excitement. The placer grounds were very rich in gold, and extended along the gulch nearly two miles on the north side of the Arkansas river, but as no gold-bearing ore was then found in the vicinity, the impatient fortune hunters began to prospect for more tempting fields, and in 1866 the camp was about depopulated, after more than a million dollars had been washed out of the gulch.

In 1876, "Uncle Billy Stevens" found the heavy sand known as carbonates, and then opened the marvelous carbonate era, which astonished the world with its riches. Owing to the lead carbonates, the name of the camp was changed to Leadville, and the little settlement of a few log cabins and tents suddenly arose to a city of 40,000 people.

The Greeks have enumerated seven wonders of the world, and Leadville, the magic city of the Rocky Mountains, deserves to be added to the list, for it grew to harmonious proportions and enduring strength in a few months. In 1877-78, it had gas and waterworks, telegraph and telephone lines, street railways, letter carrier system, fine public schools, several large smelting and reduction works, stamp and sampling mills, a fine opera house, several extensive wholesale and retail grocery, dry goods and hardware houses; three daily newspapers, the Chronicle, Herald and Democrat; corner lots worth $5,000 to $10,000, and everything that goes to form a full-fledged city, with a thick pine forest on three sides, and at an altitude of 10,000 feet above sea level.

The older districts, proud of their orthodox fissure veins, derisively called this camp the district of sand mines.

Many of these miners are still rich, but as in every other mining country, the majority of them are poor. Nine out of ten who made from five to twenty thousand spent it and philosophically returned to the pick and shovel as day laborers.

The men who invested in the carbonate belt and developed the rich blanket deposits are almost national celebrities; their names are household words throughout the country, and we felt privileged to talk about them. L. Z. Leiter, millionaire capitalist of Chicago, made his stake in Leadville; Meyer Guggenheim, founder of the house of Guggenheim; Samuel Newhouse. These are but a few of the men who are known nationally and who saw the inception of their prosperity in Leadville. Simon Guggenheim, son of Meyer Guggenheim, has been United States Senator from Colorado and has donated four large buildings to the colleges of this State.

Reminiscences of William R. Owen

While talking in a random manner, we were joined by Mr. William R. Owen, who is the only living member of the board of trustees of the town of Leadville, and I considered myself fortunate in having the opportunity of talking to an old-timer who, long ago, blazed the trail on these mountain tops.

"One who has lived in Leadville," said Mr. Owen, "always preserves a warm spot in his heart for the old camp and often returns. There is no doubt that Leadville has been the inspiration of thousands of men. While I was traveling for Daniels & Fisher I heard that this was a good camp and so I decided to come here.

"I reached the camp December 31, 1877, bought a lot at the corner of Chestnut and Pine streets, put up a building of logs twenty by fifty feet and opened a store.

"I started on $2,500, which was borrowed, and in ten months cleared up $20,000. I often sold goods from daybreak to one o'clock in the morning. Leadville was in its heydey, gold was pouring into the city in a marvelous stream and men were becoming millionaires over night. It brings to my mind the greatest struggle of strong men for wealth that this country has ever known. It is difficult for the people of today to realize that 40,000 people crowded within the city limits at that time. It was almost impossible to walk the streets, if going in an opposite direction to that of the crowd. Such a conglomeration of humanity has never been seen before or since. Representatives of every nation of the earth were here, except China. Leadville never allowed the Celestials within its limits. Millionaires, tramps, miners, ministers, gam-

W. R. Owen

blers, dudes and prospectors all jostled against each other. The buildings were not large enough to acommodate the gamblers, and some of us had to play on the streets." Mr. Owen gave a quiet sort of laugh and continued:

"There were one hundred and thirty saloons, all doing a thriving business, and all supplied thirsty customers with a substantial lunch; no matter how poor one was, he or she never went hungry. Money was made quickly and spent the same way. When a man went broke, all he had to do was to go to the hills, stake out a claim and sell it. Anything in the shape of a hole in the ground could be sold.

"When I came here, I took the train to Morrison and then staged into Leadville. I left Denver at eight o'clock in the morning and reached Leadville at six the following evening. H. A. W. Tabor had a general supply store here at that time. He sold everything from a tin pan to a suit of clothes, and made money. He was one of the men confident that Leadville would be a great camp.

"One afternoon, January 28, 1879, Tabor called the trustees of Leadville together in a log cabin, which served as a city hall, to receive formally the document from the Secretary of State that lifted Leadville from a mining camp into a city. Tabor was enthusiastic over the organization of a city; he declared that in ten years we would all be millionaires, which was considered an amusing statement. Besides myself, the trustees were William Nye, John Carrol, R. T. Taylor, R. J. Frazer and George Fryer. W. R. Kennedy as town attorney and Martin Duggan as town marshal were also present. Duggan had just received his badge of office. The man who had preceded him, George O'Connor, had been killed by James Bloodsworth, and this killing of O'Connor was the first of a long and bloody series that turned Leadville into a city of frenzy, where life counted for little and killings were common. Naturally, there was chaos, but out of chaos the better element brought order. The vigilance committee flourished and thinned out many and posted warnings that were heeded.

"While there was excitement in 1878, it was in '79

the great rush began. The Little Pittsburg mine had become known throughout the world; the R. E. Lee had turned out $117,000 in twenty-four hours. The Rio Grande had pushed in to Leadville, having a famous fight with the Santa Fe for the Royal Gorge. The Union Pacific, Denver & Gulf also pushed into the great camp.

"A. V. Hunter, with George W. Trimble, started the first bank in the city, known as the Miners' Exchange Bank. It is now known as the Carbonate National, with Hunter and Trimble still at the head. Hunter is also president of the Ibex Mining Company, the largest gold producer in the State."

I found Mr. Owen was in a reminiscent mood, so I asked him to tell me something about the churches and hospitals.

"When I made the first trip into the camp Parson Uzzell climbed into the stage at Fairplay. He said someone had told him that there was an opening for a church in Leadville. In a short time he laid the foundation of his spiritual usefulness by his religious activity, and was familiarly known as "Parson Tom." He was a man with unbounded love for humanity and broad religious tolerance. In 1879 he built the first church in the city, and its doors were wide enough to let in all. The simple doctrine of the golden rule was the religion he taught. The epitaph he wanted was, 'Here lies Thomas Uzzell. He did his level best.'

"Father J. Robinson, a pioneer Catholic priest, held the first mass in Leadville, with an anvil for an altar, in a blacksmith shop of the old Homestake mine. His congregation consisted of three, one a Catholic, one a Presbyterian and the other an atheist. He traveled in winter on snow shoes, over a trackless waste, to minister to the spiritual needs of the isolated mining camps, and while he was working to build a church in Leadville he was giving assistance to the Sisters of Charity, who were raising money to build the St. Vincent hospital.

"March, 1880, claim jumpers attempted to jump the grounds surrounding the building. One night the fence was torn down, and this so aroused the citizens that a guard was formed to protect the sisters and their property. About midnight two men appeared on the scene, and when told to halt, showed fight. The guard fired and one of the jumpers fell, shot through the leg. The wounded man was taken to the hospital and nursed to convalescence by the women he had tried to injure.

"A building that attracted attention at that time was the wigwam. It was built by Tabor in 1878 for the purpose of holding political meetings. A notable debate took place there betweeen J. B. Belford and T. M. Patterson, rival candidates for Congress in the fall of 1878. The night of the debate the immense building was packed to the doors; about 5,000 people were wedged in. Later on the building was used as a bunkhouse. The bunks were ranged in close tiers to the ceiling. It accommodated 1,000 sleepers at a price of $1.50 each, and every night it was full.

"Another historic building is one at the corner of State and Harrison avenue, known as Washerwoman's block. Mrs. Sarah Ray located the lots early in 1878, on which she built a slab shanty and put out a sign, 'laundry.' She did a 'land-office' business and in a short time erected a two-story brick building. Many a time she stood guard all night to protect her land from lot jumpers, and her only weapon was an old broom.

Broken Nose Scotty

"As you are seeking stories," Mr. Owen continued, "I will tell you one that is characteristic of the times, about James Ellis, better known as 'Broken Nose Scotty.' He was a prospector and was lucky beyond the average prospector, but his besetting sin was drink. One night he was arrested and placed in jail for being drunk, not having the money to pay the fine. While he was in jail a gentleman called and asked for James Ellis. The jailer said he had no such boarder, and when told that the man he wanted had a broken nose, the jailer at once brought out 'Scotty.' 'You own a claim on Carbonate hill,' said the stranger. 'Yes, sir.' 'How much will you take for it?' 'Thirty thousand,' 'Scotty' replied. 'Come with me to my lawyer, who will make out the papers and the money is yours.'

" 'The pleasant gentleman whom I first met when I entered this building,' explained 'Scotty,' 'thinks so much of me that he will not let me out of his sight unless I give him some money; as I have none, I will have to remain here.' The stranger paid the fine and 'Scotty' went with him.

"The next morning, when the bank opened 'Scotty' got $30,000 in cash. His first act was to go to the jail, where he paid the fine of all the chain gang, took them up town, bought each a complete new outfit of clothes from shoes to hat, took them to the Tontine restaurant, ordered the best meal the house could set up and before midnight every one of them was again in jail.

"A few weeks later 'Scotty' left for Scotland to visit his old mother. He gave her enough to keep her comfortably the remainder of her life, spent several months in the old country and returned to Colorado.

"One morning he appeared on the avenue without a penny in his pocket. He soon got a grub stake and was off to the hills and before the year was out sold several prospect holes for a good sum of money. Well," said Mr. Owen, after a little pause, "Leadville is still on the map, not having the same life and excitement as in her youthful days, but standing on a more solid foundation.

Four hundred million dollars have been taken out of these mines in the past, and it is my opinion that all previous records in production will be surpassed in the future."

Mr. Owen is now general manager and vice-president of the Denver Dry Goods Company, a man of fine business ability, who has been a factor in the success of that great mercantile house.

We decided to ring a change on the scene, and so we started back to the city, around which circled vast wreaths of furnace smoke, that looked as if it had been belched from the crater of a volcano. On reaching the hotel we found that we, like the dyer's hand, had taken our color from our surroundings. Indeed, during the whole of our stay there we were continually reminded of the sentence, "dust thou art." But while the lower world was shrouded in smoke and dust, the sky was a perpetual delight. The clouds were always experimenting and always getting up fine effects. The sunsets were superb.

Twin Lakes

The next morning our party visited "Twin Lakes," a pair of crystal beauties nestled among the peaks—a delightful resort for tourists, who camp and boat and fish there. The snowy sails that float over the silvery waters are nine thousand feet nearer the sky than those that fly the ocean. It cost me considerable of a pang not to go, but I had made a contract with myself to gather stories, and I could not fritter my time away in other pleasures. A woman is very conscientious about breaking an engagement—with herself! But one is always rewarded for resisting temptation. They had scarcely started when I was summoned to the parlor to meet a number of pioneers a friend had kindly brought to see me. They were a jovial set, and from them I gathered many stories.

John A. Ewing

John A. Ewing arrived in Leadville in 1881, from Pennsylvania, his native State, where he had been admitted to the bar.

He said, while on his way west, he stopped at Fort Wallace, Kansas; he was young, his resources were limited and he felt himself a stranger in a strange land. As he was about to enter an eating house at Fort Wallace, he noticed a sign which was in large letters, and which read:

"To trust is bust;
To bust is hell;
No trust, no bust;
No bust, no hell."

John A. Ewing

which was impressed upon his memory and was calculated to prepare him for many things which he encountered when he went to Leadville and began the practice of law.

He has continued in the practice of law, without interruption, in Leadville and in Denver, up to the present time.

He has never held any public office, although, as a Republican, he has always taken an interest in politics.

While following the practice of his profession he has found time to take an active interest in the development of mining enterprises. He backed with his credit R. R. Moore, who made the first shipment of zinc ore from Leadville to Antwerp, in June, 1899, which was, in fact, the beginning of the zinc ore business in Colorado.

From his advent in Leadville, in 1881, to the present time, he has been identified with the camp and its people, its enterprises, and is familiar and well acquainted with all the noted people which that wonderful camp has produced; he can recount many pleasant things, as well as tragedies, which have occurred in Leadville.

He is an active and enthusiastic citizen and is connected with numerous public movements for the State's welfare.

Mr. Samuel D. Nicholson located in Leadville in 1881. He had nothing but his own pluck and energy to rely upon, and soon obtained employment. He had been brought up on a farm and was entirely unused to the wild and strenuous life of the west. It can readily be imagined how a stirring mining camp appeared to a green country boy.

When in Leadville only a few days, he was one evening invited to dine with a Georgia gentleman, who found fault with the manner in which dinner was

Samuel D. Nicholson

being served by the colored waiter. The waiter protested, telling the host that if not satisfied, he could get another waiter; whereupon the host stood up and shot the colored waiter dead. Needless to say this ended the dinner. This incident was Mr. Nicholson's introduction, so to speak, to the far West.

In telling of his first mining experience, Mr. Nicholson said: "A Mr. Percival, of Texas, and myself located two mining claims in Little French Gulch, about eight miles from Leadville, and proceeded to sink a shaft regardless of formations. As time went on we discovered that we were sinking in solid granite, the only indication of ore being the mica contained in the granite. When we encountered a large bunch of mica, we thought that we were in close proximity to ore. We sunk the shaft about seventy-five feet in the solid granite, and it goes without saying that the venture was a complete failure. From this experience, however, we gathered a knowledge which became useful in future years."

From that time until the present Mr. Nicholson has been actively engaged in mining in the State of Colorado. His business instincts were keen, his judgment good, and he soon forged his way to the front. He has been connected with some of the largest mining and milling enterprises which have been carried on in the State. Mr. Nicholson is also interested in a number of other business enterprises in the State, including banking and the sugar industry.

Mr. Nicholson was twice elected mayor of Leadville, and was also a Republican candidate for governor of the State of Colorado in the primaries in the year 1914.

As a citizen, he is generous, patriotic, enterprising and honest, and participates in all measures designed for the advancement of the State. In his enterprising push and business ability he is one of the men needed for the prosperity of Colorado.

The leading journalists of the early Leadville days were: John Arkins, C. C. Davis, James M. Burness, R. G. Dill, Major Henry Ward and G. A. Leonard. These men wielded a strong power in shaping the destiny of the State.

While going from Leadville to Buena Vista, a newspaper man told me the following story:

Starting a Western Paper

"In 1878, when excitement ran high in Leadville, and fortunes were made with almost magical rapidity, Arkins, then foreman of the Denver Tribune, was struck, as he relates it, 'all of a heap,' with the idea of starting a paper in the Carbonate city. Friends advised him to let 'well enough' alone, and not go careering after the uncertainties of life. But he laughed at their arguments and ultimately invested every dollar he had in a printing press, which he shipped to the great mining camp.

"In those days the only railroad in that direction terminated at Webster, the rest of the journey being made in stages.

"So great was the rush of travel, only those who were in favor with the management could obtain a seat in the stage unless ordered long in advance. But our journalist, having an eye single to comfort, took the necessary precaution and secured it.

"While at Webster he saw the wagon trains heavily laden with bullion toiling on their way to the depot. He stepped around to see his freight safely transferred. The type had been packed in boxes, which, of course, were as 'heavy as lead.' A great, burly teamster, who seemed to possess Herculean strength, swooped down on a box, expecting to toss it with careless ease into the wagon, but somewhat baffled, he lifted it slowly, with a puff and pant, and said, 'Bullion both ways, by jingo!'

"There was but one of the gentler sex in the coach, and she carried a canary bird, a pet squirrel and a geranium in a pot; all of which she unhesitatingly deposited in the laps of the gentlemen that had not been previously converted into chairs for some one.

"They expected to arrive at Fairplay in time for supper, but before they reached the middle of South Park the wind and snow commenced a tussle, which was followed by a battle of the elements that was appalling. Arkins soon realized that the path to glory, like true love, seldom runs smoothly. He didn't more than half like the thought of having the snow for a winding sheet, even though it might be typical of purity; and had no notion of filling a grave far above the common world.

"When they reached the top of Red Hill, all above, beyond, and about was enveloped in Egyptian darkness. The snow didn't come down in eddying flakes that the poet talks about, but fell in blinding sheets.

"The driver said it was impossible to go on. The horses were bewildered by the darkness and the raging tempest. The leaders, as if thrust around by some irresistible power, doubled back on the wheel horses. There was no time to meditate; no time to be tender and comforting to the woman, who tearfully inquired if her household pets were in danger. They simply had to string their nerves to the highest tension and act promptly, or be frozen to death in that houseless solitude.

"There were a few scattering trees on the hill, but there was no ax; no way of kindling a fire. They dared not separate for fear of being lost in the darkness. So they joined hands and formed two lines, the first man in each line holding to the bits of the leaders, and made their way as best they could down the hill, the snow continuing to pelt them with relentless fury.

"They arrived in Fairplay at 2 o'clock in the morning. A crowd had assembled at the hotel and were vigorously discussing the feasibility of sending for the belated coach. They were received with a fever-heat of excitement, which so strongly resembled the stir and finish of a play that each particular man imagined himself the 'star actor on the stage.'

"Their moustaches and eyebrows supported little rifts of snow, and their limbs were rigid with cold; but, partaking freely of liquid refreshments, rapidly dispelled the freezing sensations, and early that morning they left for Leadville over the Weston pass.

"In process of time the Chronicle was established, with our hero in charge, in a little six by eight room, with a washstand for his editorial desk.

"All being in readiness for the first edition of the paper, Mr. A. seized a note-book and went in pursuit of items; when, attracted by a number of persons gathered around a little shanty, he bent his steps in that direction, walked in without leave or license and soon discovered the cause of the commotion in front. The air was stifling with chloroform. A woman lay stretched on a bed and a physician stood over her making active use of a stomach pump. The facts ascertained, he returned to his sanctum and dashed off an account of it.

"The next morning a large man with flushed face and bloodshot eyes entered his office accompanied by a woman. He demanded in stentorian tones to see the man who wrote 'that article in yesterday's paper about his lady,' and with a little frescoed swearing announced his intention to blow him into the warmest place in Lucifer's domains.

"The editor said meekly the reporter had stepped out, but if an untrue statement had been made, he, being the editor, would be pleased to correct it. He couldn't understand how it happened, for the merest glance at the lady was sufficient to establish her character, and, stepping forward with great suavity of manner, declared that she seemed to be the '*flour* of sulphur and the cream of tartar.'

"The caustic sarcasm of the apology passed unperceived by the enraged couple, and was received as the editor intended it should be. The woman smiled and bowed thanks; the man seized his hand, saying, 'Your head is level;' both united in an urgent invitation to 'Come, take a drink,' when all three waltzed into a neighboring saloon and—smiled unctuously."

Arkins later sold the Chronicle and bought an interest in the Rocky Mountain News, at Denver.

The Alpine Tunnel

The ride from Buena Vista to Gunnison is a wonderful, and in most respects, a delightful experience; there is nothing meek or humble about it, the clouds and mountains flirt and kiss each other right before our eyes. We continue to rise higher and higher until the Continental Divide, with its icy coronet, appears clear-cut and glistening against a background of blue sky. The r a i l r o a d, in its effort to outdo all rivals in feats of mountain climbing, has, in this instance, mounted to an altitude of 11,500 feet above the sea, at which point the trains plunge into the Alpine tunnel, and the next view we get of the light of day is on the Pacific slope.

About a mile farther on the e n g i n e dashes

Hell Gate

around a curve and stops at the "palisades," which rise almost perpendicular to a height of nearly five hundred feet. These towering rocks were beautifully embellished with beds of gauzy ferns. Graceful vines twined about their heads, and the ropes on which the men were suspended to carve out a roadway for the iron horse are still dangling there.

Quartz Creek, with its numerous tributaries, sparkles through a valley two thousand feet below. Raising one's eyes from this profound abyss, the range of vision extends over one hundred and seventy-five miles to the San Juan country, where the Uncompahgre peaks stand with haughty crests, and, lying between, softened by the light blue tint of this lofty atmosphere, are hill and dale in wavy line and sleepy rest. The eye drinks in such beauty as intoxicates the soul, then we are whirled away and the lovely valley, like all life's charms, slips from us, leaving a steel engraving in the picture book of memory, bearing the inscription, "Glorietta View"—yet it is called "Quartz Valley," which is, "of the earth, earthy."

And now we are carried swiftly through wonder after wonder of grand scenery. Keeping company with such lofty peaks makes one feel so insignificant; there arises an overpowering consciousness of being only a speck, an atom, an infinitesimal part of the great scheme of Creation. Such contemplations are not pleasant; I was glad when the neighing of the iron horse announced our arrival at Gunnison.

CHAPTER XXV

GUNNISON

Frontier Banking

The city of Gunnison was founded in the fall of 1879, by Professor S. Richardson, and now it has massive brick and stone blocks that seem to have sprung up with the swift and easy architecture of Aladdin's Palace. The La Veta hotel, a superb building, with accommodations equal to any in eastern cities, is entirely a native structure. The foundation rock and ornamental stone were all quarried at the edge of Gunnison; the brick was made there, likewise the woodwork. The iron castings are the product of their foundries; the lime for mortar and plaster of native manufacture. Adding to these products the gold and silver in the surrounding mountains, and we have the resources which are to maintain a constant growth.

How the Gunnison bank was established is a characteristic story of frontier life. In '79 Sam G. Gill, then living in Denver, conceived the idea that a bank would pay in Gunnison. Not until the spring of '80, however, was he able to organize it, then succeeded through the help of Governor Tabor and the late Colonel Jacobson. At this time the Rio Grande road was completed to Alamosa in Conejos County, Gunnison being distant one hundred and fifty miles. All freighting had to be done by mule and ox teams across Cochetopa Pass, a long, tedious haul.

When Gill left Denver he locked up the greater part

of his bank capital ($30,000) in his safe, and shipped it to Alamosa. Upon reaching that place he found such a vast quantity of freight en route to Gunnison that it was a week before the forwarding merchant could ship his furniture and safe.

All this time the latter, with its precious contents, stood upon the platform of the forwarding houses, passed daily by all the hard characters of a mining camp, who, had they known its value, would soon have wrecked it. Gill had it marked Alonzo Hartman, Gunnison, Colorado (the name of one of his partners), then purchased a suit of overalls and loafed around with the freighters so as to keep an eye on his treasure.

At length the valuable freight was loaded, and when ready to start, Gill stepped up to the driver and asked if he could secure passage with him. After some parleying the man said, "Yes, if you will do half the cooking, and buy all the supplies, tobacco and whisky, wash the dishes, hitch and unhitch the mules, you may go." Gill consented.

S. G. Gill

The fourth day out they were compelled to build a corduroy road, and were subsequently delayed a day by high water. In all, they were fifteen days en route. Gill performed his part of the contract to the satisfaction of his "boss." But it was rather a novel *role* for a bank cashier to assume.

Arriving in Gunnison, and having paid the freighter, he dropped his disguise and assumed his proper character, greatly to the astonishment of the latter, who then, for the first time, discovered the identity of his "cook and helper."

Adopting A Western Boy

The polite and obliging clerk brought the pioneers from the byways and highways to talk to me. One gentleman said: "Among the fellows who gathered around the camp fire and spun yarns in the early days was Dick Irwin. He was at once jovial, bright and witty, of large and varied experience, though his violet eyes did not speak of adventure, and his smoothly shaven face and small, graceful stature gave him the appearance of adolescent youth.

"Once upon a time he went to Philadelphia on a visit with Mr. Joe Watson, and while there was invited to a large and rather fashionable party.

"Out of courtesy to his host, rather than inclination, he went, but it had been many years since he attended a gathering of that kind, and he felt like a fish out of water. He took a seat in a retired corner and was enjoying the gay scene in his peculiar way, when the two beautiful daughters of the host timidly approached him and asked why he didn't dance.

"He told them that his early education in that direction had been somewhat neglected; indeed, he had never had any education; he was brought up by the rude savages, was stolen away from his parents when a child four years old. He was skilled in all the arts of the red man; could ride like a Centaur, dance the war dance and pitch the tomahawk, but was entirely ignorant of the graces of civilization. He related thrilling incidents, how he was stood up by a tree and the warriors shot their arrows around his head to see how near they could shoot and miss him; how he longed to be with his people, and in his effort to escape was apprehended and forced to travel, half-starved and foot-sore, over a rugged, mountainous country. He was finally sold to good Mr. Watson for a red blanket, a plug of tobacco and a jug of whisky.

"Their hearts and eyes were brimful of pity and sympathy for the poor young man, and before retiring that evening they related the sorrowful story to their mother, and begged of her to adopt him; they had no brother and they thought he would fill the bill to a fraction.

"The mother said she would sleep on the matter, but there came neither 'sleep to her eyes or slumber to her eyelids.' Like Miss Murdstone, 'generally speaking, she didn't like boys,' but this story harrowed up her soul, and her interest in this young fellow began to assume mammoth proportions.

"The next morning she called on Mrs. Watson and expressed her desire to adopt the young western boy. Imagine her astonishment when Mrs. Watson informed her that the 'boy' was the Honorable Richard Irwin, known throughout Colorado as a daring and adventurous explorer, that he was a leading member of the Colorado Legislature, and had a wife and four children!" Just as he finished the story a form darkened the door, and he exclaimed: "Dick Irwin—as true as I live! 'Speak of the angels and you hear their wings.' Where did you come from, old boy? We are having a sort of old-fashioned love-feast; sit down and give us a bit of your experience."

He declared he felt as embarrassed as if he had been called upon to speak in meeting, nevertheless his perfect repose of manner gave the contrary impression. His voice was low and his articulation so perfect as to render every word distinctly audible, which gave a peculiar charm to his conversation.

"Modesty forbids me to speak of myself," said he, "but I will tell you a funny thing that happened in the early days on the Huerfano."

How He Wooed Her

"A justice of the peace had been called upon to marry a poor Mexican to the object of his affections. The justice elevated his eyebrows in surprise to see such a handsome girl willing to link her destiny with the poor, shiftless fellow before him, but proceeded to declare them husband and wife according to law, and then demanded his fee—$5.00.

"The astonished Mexican exclaimed: 'Por Dios, I haven't it, Senor Judge.'

"'Well, then,' said the justice, 'I annul the legal contract until you get it.'

"While the fellow was hunting up his *compadres* and *amigos* (partners and friends) to raise the funds necessary to make him the happiest man on the creek, the justice said to the girl, 'Marcelina, couldn't you marry a more worthy fellow than that? He can't even pay the marriage fee.'

"'Por Dios,' she replied, 'it seemed the best I could do, and how miserable a poor girl feels away from her friends, without either home or husband. So when he asked me to marry him I couldn't say no, as I didn't know of anybody else who wanted me for a wife.'

"'Why, Marcelina, you could have done much better if you had only known it.'

"'Por Dios, I'd like to; who could it be?'

"'Why, you could have me, and as the fellow has not paid the $5.00, stand up and I'll marry you myself.' And he did so, thereby annulling the previous ceremony and clinching the final one."

Mr. Irwin then took his hat and bowed gracefully out of the room, saying:

"'Was ever woman in this humor woo'd?
Was ever woman in this humor won?'"

Later we were invited to see Dr. Jennings' large and handsome collection of specimens. He has specimens of the iron, coal, silver, gold, etc., produced in this region. Somewhat astonished at his list of the precious and useful, I asked, "Is that all?"

"Yes," said he, pulling his mustache in a meditative way; "we are only waiting for someone to suggest something that we haven't, and we will immediately send a prospector into the mountains to find it."

The Royal Gorge

It was with a sigh of regret that I left Gunnison and the many delightful people I met there.

We returned via the Rio Grande railway, and soon the little engine was panting and groaning in its toilsome ascent of the Marshall Pass. We were now approaching perilous heights; indeed, we seemed to be suspended, like Mahomet's coffin, midway between heaven and earth. Yet we had ceased to hold our breath to assist the locomotive, for one becomes accustomed to swinging on the ragged edge of the mountains in the course of a tour through them.

It was very cold when we reached the summit, and a tremulous inspection of the situation increased our chilly sensations.

The scenery along the Arkansas in its passage through the Rocky Mountains is varied and beautiful. At times the river glides smoothly through a wide valley, between vine-covered banks, and again rushes impetuously through a narrow defile, roaring and foaming over its rocky bed until again soothed to rest in a broad, open park.

The prospect becomes more and more sublime until the Royal Gorge is reached, where the towering rocks, thousands of feet above us, bend their heads together like the fabled Symplegades through which the Argonauts passed in their search for the Golden Fleece.

Our hearts seemed to sink and almost stop beating while contemplating this chasm, the supremest possible ideal of awe-inspiring grandeur. We may not see the face of God and live, but we can look upon His creation, learn of Him, believe and tremble. Soon we are whirled from this deep wrinkle in the dread frown of nature to the broad, smiling prairies. Earth, from the loftiest mountain tops and deepest valleys, the flowers that blossom over its wide plains, the stars that twinkle in the heavens, the elements that speak in thunder tones, or sigh in the gentle zephyrs, bids man join in the glad anthem:

Royal Gorge

"The hand that made us is divine."

PART IX
THE TOWNS OF THE PLAINS

CHAPTER XXVI

THE GARDEN SPOT OF COLORADO

Canon City

Canon City, called the "Gate City of the Rocky Mountains," and the "garden spot of Colorado," certainly makes excellent provision for tourists and—convicts.

The penitentiary, which is located here, surpasses any I have ever seen in the perfection of all its parts, and the hotel accommodations of the town are satisfactory. We were furnished a private parlor without extra charge, which is something unique in a traveler's experience.

We went to the mineral springs, just at the edge of the city, and found many invalids there, lolling in the rustic arbor, and drinking freely of the health-giving waters, which are said to cure chronic, cutaneous and blood diseases.

The next on the programme was Talbott Hill, where Professor Marsh of Yale College, and Professor Cope of the Academy of Natural Science, Philadelphia, exhumed bones of animals of enormous size.

Limited time prevented our visiting the orchard of Mr. Jesse Frazier, who succeeded in growing the first orchard in Colorado. He has now nearly three thousand apple trees bearing.

Canon City has been settled twice. In 1860-61 it was almost as large and important as Denver, but the diversion of travel to the South Park mines by another route, and a great many of her citizens having entered the army at the outbreak of the war, soon brought the place to ruin. In 1863 it was almost entirely depopulated, Mr. Anson Rudd and family being left its sole occupants. Any man who could remain in a frontier town while it was indulging in a Rip Van Winkle sleep of five or six years ought to be worth interviewing, and so, accom-

Sky-Line Drive, Canon City

panied by Judge Felton of the Record, I called at his residence, and found him to be a pleasant, genial gentleman, full of genuine wit and humor. He invited us to a rustic seat under the apple trees, that were literally breaking down with fruit.

In answer to my questioning he said: "I knew of the coal, iron and mineral springs in this vicinity, and saw that Nature had arranged things for a city, when the people should be ready, so concluded to 'bide my time.' I told them I was too poor to provide my family with provisions during a journey to some other place. Twelve others remained, but they were crippled or deranged, and as I was the only sound one, I was said to be the only man left. The loneliness and stillness were oppressive at times, and the large, empty stone houses that had been so full of noisy life intensified the loneliness. For a long time our existence as a community was ignored; we had not even the advantage of a mail; apart from an occasional visit from the Indians, there was nothing to break the monotony."

He then invited us to the house to see a picture presented to him by friends on his sixty-fourth birthday. It is called "Ye Old Timer," or "How I came to this Country." With a merry twinkle in his eye he said, "There is the buckboard to show how I came, and the rest of the picture is thus explained: Once, while out hunting with a party of friends, I saw the back of a jackass above the sage brush, and, taking it to be a bear, I crawled on my hands and knees until near enough, and fired—killing my jack—after which I sat upon a cactus, that caused me to take my meals standing for a week or two. This picture was presented to me by Judge Felton, in a very graceful speech, under the apple trees—a surprise party, they called it."

He escorted us through his fine orchard, plucking and presenting us in a hospitable manner with luscious apples and pears. There was no "forbidden fruit" in that garden.

The Religious War

The late Hon. Thomas Macon, in speaking of Canon, said: "The first settlement was made up of all classes. The second settlement began in 1864, and the settlers were of the highly moral order, and, like the Puritans of old, were determined to lay the foundation of social and sound moral principles, allowing everyone to worship according to the dictates of his own conscience, provided always the conscience was so far enlightened as to accept their theology.

"With this high and holy purpose, about twenty families arrived at Canon in July, 1864, and at once resolved, first, that the earth belonged to the saints; second, that they were the saints; and, proceeding to act upon their conclusion, took possession of the vacant houses in the town.

"They were of the old-fashioned orthodox Baptist creed; looked upon infant baptism as a sin against the Holy Ghost, and missionary enterprises as casting the children's bread to the dogs.

"They came without a shepherd, but they had a 'singing master,' who taught them to sing, and with his assistance they praised the Lord on Sunday.

"For a time all went on smoothly, but in an evil hour a wolf came to harass this flock of lambs, in the shape of a Universalist preacher, and they were sore distressed.

"The idea of taking from them their favorite hell was more than they could endure. One old lady, a sort of 'mother in Israel,' declared that fire was as necessary to salvation as water, and she would as soon give up baptism as hell.

"It was plain that they must have a shepherd, one who could fight with the weapons of faith. So, in process of time, they lit upon the very man they needed. He was fresh from Missouri, and rejoiced in the annihilation of all heretics. He arrived early in the spring of 1865, and at once began to prepare for war.

"He threw down his glove (buckskin, of course), and it was promptly taken up by Beelzebub, as the enemy was called, and for several months the entire community was agitated with profound discussions of original sin, total depravity, the efficacy of good works, the nature of faith and the mysteries of redemption, atonement, foreordination and election.

"At length Satan and his ambassadors were vanquished and fled the country, leaving our Baptist friends and their preacher master of the field. A great revival and many baptisms were the result of the victory, and it became necessary to court the favor of the church to gain or hold popularity.

"The politicians all became Baptists, and for a few years the church was omnipotent in Fremont County. But prosperity proved their ruin. Like Jeshuran, they 'waxed fat and kicked.' Having no external foes, they quarreled among themselves, and their preacher, or elder, as he was called, attempting to compose their differences, as is usual in such cases, incurred the hostility of both factions, and in a solemn assembly of the church he was put upon trial for slander, convicted, and in the presence of his weeping family dismissed, not only from his pulpit, but from the church.

"To the eye of flesh the good elder was lost, but the eye of faith saw further into the millstone. He was cast down, but not dismayed; discomfited, but not conquered. He bent before the storm, but did not break. His enemies boasted of their victory, and taunted him in his distress. He went on in the even tenor of his way, and devoted himself to making friends of the mammon of unrighteousness. They did not dream of the resources of one possessed of such unfaltering faith as he had. They forgot, if indeed they had ever known the proverb, 'Pride goeth before destruction, and a haughty spirit before a fall.'

"The good elder had taken the precaution to appeal or move for a new trial, and before the momentous day for that had arrived he was prepared. He had laid their grievances before the sinners of Canon City, and they were in the church in force, determined to see fair play.

"After the usual formalities, it came to a vote, and the sinners voted him back into the church and pulpit; his most active enemies were censured and suspended until they should repent and ask the good man's pardon, which they never did. When the elder placed an organ in the church, it caused further defections, and in the spring of 1868 all but four of the original families who entered Canon in 1864 sold out and removed to Missouri.

"In the summer of 1867 Bishop Randall of the Episcopal Church made his first visit to Canon, and his clerical garb at once indicated his sacred character. It was quite plain he was not a Baptist, and the beforementioned elder, in his zeal for the protection of his own, took the alarm, and after some inquiry, decided the bishop was a Roman Catholic priest. This was at once communicated to the faithful, and they were warned to keep away from him and his meetings.

"But they were assured by the bishop that he was an Episcopalian, and on the next day a few of the Baptist brethren, anxious to see the new form of worship, disregarded the warnings and ventured out.

"They were horror-stricken when the bishop appeared in his robes; but curiosity held them, and they sat with what composure they could command until the 'creed' was recited, and 'I believe in the Holy Catholic Church' was said, when with one accord they rushed out of the church, declaring the bishop to be a Roman Catholic, and proving it by the creed.

The Hunt

Taking the baby railroad* for Pueblo, we found ourselves in company with a party of Nimrods, who were

---

*These tiny toy-like trains went over the heights and down into the valleys for many years, till superseded by the standard gauge.

returning from a big hunt. They were enthusiastic on the subject, and talked freely of their exploits, as the following will attest: "We left Denver for a month's hunt in Southwestern Colorado, in the Ute country, from which the Indians had a short time previously been removed. The Rio Grande railroad was at that time building its Salt Lake line, and was just reaching the reservation. We arrived in Delta (now a flourishing town, but then the toughest place in the West) at midnight, and camped in the sand and sage brush. Talmadge said Leadville, in its booming days, surpassed anything he ever saw in the way of wickedness, but he should have visited a railroad camp when the graders and miners were making a night of it. We concluded the Utes had not been removed.

"We traveled up the wide valley of the Gunnison, thence up Tongue and Surface creeks until we reached the Grand Mesa, a country that can only be described by saying that ten by thirty miles in extent, it seemed like a tall range of mountains, from which the tops had been cut off, leaving a beautiful rolling mesa 5,000 feet above the surrounding country, and from the edge of which the grandest and most beautiful view is obtained.

"Far below, on the steep side of the mountains up which we had threaded our way, we could see the effects of the autumn frost and sun on the foliage. The colors were in great patches. There were the dark green of the spruce, then the red and green of the oak, further on a long belt of cedar, and patches of the brightest crimson—a mountain shrub—and mingled with the whole, large clumps of yellow quaking-asps.

"Farther away, thirty miles from where we stood, through the center of a dark, dust-colored valley about twenty miles in width, flowed the Gunnison river, and to us, with its fringe of yellow trees, it looked like a winding thread of gold, with an occasional flush of silver, when the sunlight was reflected from some part of it.

"Beyond the river rose the Elk mountains, whose dark shadows and perpetual snows told us they were part of one of the highest ranges in the country. We pushed on through a succession of parks, each surrounded with trees, and generally a mountain stream or lake added to the beauty of the scene.

"We camped in a dark clump of spruce, near us a little stream, and in front a large lake of the coldest and clearest water, fairly alive with trout. At the peep of day we were up and prepared for a tramp before breakfast; there was a splash far off in the lake, the sharp ring of a rifle, a heavy plunge, and a little later V. K. brought in for our breakfast the first deer of the hunt.

"Besides a great many deer, as the result of our rifles, we found in the willows and on the hill-sides grouse as large as turkey hens, on the lakes splendid ducks, and in the streams trout enough to satisfy any number of ravenous appetites.

"One night, by moonlight, we watched the beavers at work. One morning, at sunrise, we were a few feet above the clouds; below us it was snowing; before us, as far as the eye could reach, in great, rolling masses, that were brilliantly white in the morning sun, were the clouds that to us looked like a sea of snow, with here and there a rocky island, as some mountain, taller than its companions, reared its head above the storm.

"The greatest evidence of the former Indian occupants was in the lower part of the country, through which the deer in great numbers pass every spring and fall. There was a V-shaped fence of stone, each arm of the V being a stone fence fully fifteen miles long, the V opening towards the mountains from which the deer came, and the point of the V, instead of being closed, was open for the deer to pass, and in cunningly dug holes would be seated the Indians to kill them. The fence, which had been built entirely by the squaws, was to turn the deer all to this one point, and though it was merely a succession of stone piles, anything that has the appearance of having been made by man is as effectual a barrier to deer as the tallest fence.

"Another cunning device of the Indians is seen wherever there are rocks; when they see a rock about the size of a man's body, they place another about the size of a man's head on top. It is done to accustom the deer to such objects, so that an Indian sitting behind a stone with his head in full view is not likely to frighten them.

"One night, having reached the foot-hills, we camped in a belt of pinyon trees, which, at this time of year, when the nuts are ripe, is the favorite resort of bear. We had killed one that morning. Three of our party spread our blankets together, but the fourth said he would try a night in the hammock, and so went off some distance to the deserted commencement of a cabin. Logs had been piled up about seven feet high, making three sides to the intended cabin, but the front and roof had not been put on. In there he swung his hammock, and, being a cold night, tied himself in, only leaving an opening for his head. And, using his own words, 'I awoke in the night nearly scared to death, for there by my side, eating a stub of candle I had used, or a few feet away eating a piece of venison that hung on the wall, I could all too plainly hear a bear munching, and from the noise I knew it must be a large one. As a boy I had often heard that if you hold your breath the bear would consider you as dead as a door nail, and not bother himself about eating you.

"'Tied in the hammock and unarmed, I was completely at the mercy of the beast if he took the notion, and my only way of getting out was to tip over and slide out, head first.

"'After holding my breath a few seconds, that seemed like ages, I concluded I would get out if it killed me, and out I went. As I gathered myself up I saw the bear was not by me, and therefore supposed he must be on the other side. In about three seconds I was on the top of that wall, and then I saw my bear. One of our mules had wandered over and was standing close by my hammock.

"'The cold night and sharp wind had tingled his ears, and to keep them warm he was shaking his head with a peculiar motion that would double up his ears and make a crunching sound like a bear or other large animal eating.

"'I slept with the boys after that.'"

CHAPTER XXVII

MANUFACTURES AND EARLY SETTLERS

Pueblo

At Pueblo we were entertained with sumptuous hospitality at the residence of Honorable Alva Adams, who, with the enthusiasm of a true Western man, pointed out to us the most attractive features of this flourishing city. In his opinion it is the new Pittsburgh of the West. Here the little giant of the initial narrow gauge of the

C. F. & I. Steel Works, Pueblo

continent, Denver and Rio Grande, turns as it were on a pivot and throws out tracks, arms and branches to every point in the mountains, which has made Pueblo one of the great markets for ore and other supplies, while the Santa Fe with its broad gauge, steel-railed track and elegant equipments places them in dircet communication with the East.

We drove to Bessemer, the town founded and admirably sustained by the "Colorado Coal and Iron Company," where we saw steel rails and other merchantable materials, as nails, spikes, etc., in process of manufacture.

The State Insane Asylum, situated on the outskirts of the city, is one of the most complete buildings in the West for the comfort and care of the afflicted of the race.

The motto over the portals of the Chieftain, "In God we Trust," arrested our attention and impressed us as a rather unique emblem for a newspaper. Editors are generally supposed to rely mainly upon the solid bonanza idea.

We paused for a moment over the grave of Pueblo's first love, "The Old Monarch," a venerable cottonwood of huge dimensions, and read from a card the following:

"The tree that grew here was 380 years old; circumference, 28 ft.; height, 79 ft.; was cut down June 25th, 1883, at the cost of $250."

It was known throughout Colorado as one of the oldest land-marks in the State.

During the Pike's Peak excitement "the old tree" sheltered many a weary traveler. In 1850 thirty-six persons were massacred by the Indians while camping near this spot. Kit Carson, Wild Bill, Buffalo Bill and other noted Indian scouts, have built their camp fires under its wide-spreading and sheltering branches.

The place where the old fort once stood was pointed out to us. We drew upon our imagination in the effort to see a trace of it, for these old forts are interesting, inasmuch as they mark a period in the history of Colorado before its permanent settlement.

Fort Pueblo was the scene of one of the most terrible tragedies ever enacted in the State. On Christmas day, 1854, a number of hunters and trappers in the fort were celebrating the holiday with Mexican whisky of a brand known as "Taos lightning." A band of mountain Utes passing, were invited to participate. They joyously accepted the invitation. Soon they were all furiously drunk, and in the midst of the hilarity that ensued, the Indians murdered every white man in the place. A teamster who had gone that morning to Fort Charles for supplies escaped the terrible fate.

John A. Thatcher is called the founder of the mercantile business in Pueblo. He arrived in Pueblo in 1862 with only one wagonload of merchandise, which he brought across the plains in the primitive fashion of a pioneer, by an ox-team. He rented a rude adobe room, in which the goods were placed on sale, and under his careful guidance the business grew so rapidly, that in 1885, his brother, Mahlon D. Thatcher, joined him as a partner. Within six years the brothers amassed sufficient wealth to venture out as financiers. They established a banking business in connection with their mercantile business. From this bank, within a year, emerged the First National Bank of Pueblo. The institution was wholly under their control, for only a few shares of the stock were held by others.

Mahlon D. Thatcher

In the course of time they established branch banks in various mining districts of Colorado. Gradually they reached out into new realms of enterprise. They promoted railroad construction, also the digging of canals for irrigation, and while building up their own fortune they carried forward the enterprises that developed the resources of the State. They have contributed much toward making Pueblo the city of thrift and enterprise

that it is today. They have the
reputation of being the heaviest
capitalists in the State, and are
widely known as honest, earnest,
progressive men. Apart from
being great financiers, their usefulness as citizens is evidenced in
their homes, where they show genuine hospitality and refinement.

Mrs. M. D. Thatcher

Mrs. Mahlon D. Thatcher has
been prominent in the activities
of women in Pueblo and in the
State. She was the second president of the Colorado Federation
of Women's Clubs, for many years a member of the
Pueblo Wednesday Morning Club and a charter member
of the Pueblo Associated Charities. She is a woman of
distinctive personal attractions and fine intellectual training.

Governor Alva Adams stands pre-eminently, one of
the men needed for the prosperity of the West; a man of
courage, charity, generosity, with a natural desire to aid
the advancement of worthy purposes.

He was just twenty-one years old when he came to
Colorado; had received a fair education in the public
schools of Wisconsin, where he was born and reared, and
was willing to work at anything he could find in the new
country. His first employment was hauling railroad ties
from the mountain forests for use in the construction of
the Denver and Rio Grande line. Within a few weeks
he secured a position with C. W. Sanborn, a lumber and
hardware dealer at Colorado Springs. In the course of
a few months he bought out his employer for about
$4,000, giving his notes for the amount. From that day
he became active in the mercantile business and in the
great work of State-building. In the following year he

opened a store in Pueblo, and soon established branches in the San Juan district. He became interested in politics, and at twenty-six was elected to represent Rio Grande county in the State Legislature. He has been twice elected governor, and his two administrations were characterized by a careful guardianship of the public finances.

Alva Adams

He says: "As governor I held a solemn compact with myself that the State was entitled to the same care and integrity that my hardware store and savings bank called for."

Governor Adams is a man of culture, has traveled extensively and possesses one of the finest libraries in the city. In his social life he is ably assisted by his refined and attractive wife.

Mrs. Adams is interested in the events of today and keeps in the line of progress. Her never-failing, genuine courtesy is the outcome of the great kindness which she feels for all classes and conditions. She is a social favorite and a true friend.

Governor and Mrs. Adams have one son, Alva Blanchard Adams, a young lawyer of Pueblo.

When asked for three hundred words about Pueblo, the governor sent the following:

"If need be, the superiority of Pueblo could be written in three words—climate, transportation, manufacturing. This potential trinity built Palmyra, Bagdad and Damascus in the desert, and it will surely build a great city at the junction of the Arkansas and the Fountain. Nature provides the location where a great city may rise. The Almighty planted the stake and made clear to man the command, 'Here a metropolis shall be.' Water and sunshine and industry are the elements of life—all are in Pueblo in a superlative degree. The Rocky Mountains are a treasure house—all of the passes point to Pueblo. Before the white man came with roads of steel all the trails of trapper, hunter, soldier and Indian led to Pueblo. The ways of least resistance, the easiest roads, all met and crossed at Pueblo. It was the cross-roads of a virgin, primitive, savage land, as it is today the cross-road of the nation. Here is the center of a network of great railroad systems. It is their transfer point of a nation's commerce and travel. Its climate and transportation facilities have made Pueblo the manufacturing center of the West. An unsurpassed if not an unequaled system of public schools, fifty-nine church organizations, our parks, clubs, societies and modest but sincere hospitality of the people makes Pueblo a happy home city for the many thousands of intelligent, prosperous employes of railroads, factories, mills, shops and the hundred industries of every kind.

Mrs. Alva Adams

"Without disparagement of the splendid climate of all Colorado, it is a fact that in mildness, in evenness of temperature, in sunshine, in cure-laden air, in comfort, in healthfulness, in all the attributes of a perfect climate, the average, all-the-year climate of Pueblo surpasses that of any spot within the forty-eight States of the Union. One unexploited resource it is due to humanity to mention: In Pueblo there are wells of magnetic and lithia waters that are the only known panacea for diabetes and kindred complaints. If the curative attributes of Pueblo's climate, air, altitude and waters were known and believed there would come a flood of sufferers surpassing the multitude of faithful that each year migrate to Mecca to say their prayers at the cradle of their prophet and to kiss the black stone of salvation."

The Espinosas

In this city I met Thomas T. Tobin, an old government scout. He was rather uncertain about his age, but from the incidents he cited, his wrinkled visage and mumbled words, I placed him at seventy. But there was not a gray hair in his head, and his eye was clear and sharp. He had just made his first journey on a railway, and was as timid as a child about getting on a street car, but when once fairly seated, he spent hours riding, just to see the city. He declared that he felt much safer on the broad prairies with his horse and rifle than among so many houses, where he was in constant fear of being taken in by sharpers or knocked down by robbers. Yet he is a man of undaunted courage, as the killing of the Espinosas, Colorado's greatest assassins, will show.

The Espinosas were two brutal, ignorant and superstitious Mexicans, accused of horse stealing at first, and who killed one of a posse of soldiers, sent from Fort Garland to their house at Servietta, on the Conejos river, to arrest them. After which they seemed to be under the impression that if they killed a great many Americans and became formidable in their ferocity they would secure a pardon from the governor, and perhaps a commission in the United States army, as sometimes is the result of successful brigandage in Old Mexico.

Men were found dead at one point today, at another tomorrow, and the day following at another, forty or fifty miles or more apart; being invariably shot through the head, and left to lie as they fell, without being robbed of their valuables.

Mystery shrouded it all, for, from their secure hiding places by the roadside, they shot the lone, unsuspecting traveler, and their shot was always certain death; no maimed or wounded ever escaped to inform as to their appearance or whereabouts.

So it continued for a while, and the greatest excitement prevailed, when a company of miners organized to rid the region of this mysterious, unseen terror.

Their rendezvous was at length discovered. Like all cowardly murderers, they fled; the pursuers gained upon them, and finally succeeded in shooting one from his horse, but the leader of the two made his escape.

For a time nothing was heard of him. At last the outlaw addressed a letter in Spanish to Governor Evans, stating, that in revenge for mistreatment he had received from the government, he had killed no less than fifteen Americans. He demanded full pardon for these murders, which, being granted, he would return to his home and be a good citizen; but if the demand was not complied with by the 15th of the coming September the killing would be resumed.

This strange proposition drew no response, and Espinosa resumed hostilities.

Soon afterward a man and woman were traveling through the mountains in a wagon, and when within a short distance of Fort Garland, a military post, they were attacked by this monstrous highwayman. The man escaped, but the woman was carried to the camp of the assassin. In the darkness of the following night she eluded her captor and found her way to the fort, where she told her story, when a party under the guidance of the noted mountaineer, Tom Tobin (who had the reputation of being able to trail grasshoppers through sagebrush), was at once dispatched to arrest or kill the criminal.

Upon reaching the vicinity, Tom ordered his soldiers to halt, while he proceeded quietly on foot, crawling when occasion required it on his hands and knees through the dense undergrowth. While thus cautiously feeling the way, he discovered the bandit's hiding-place, in a dense part of the forest on the mountain side. The bandit, quick to detect the slightest sound, turned his head in a listening attitude, and while thus poised, the scout's bullet did its work, and the career of the assassin was ended. Tobin leaped upon him with the swiftness of a tiger, severed his head from his body, and galloped into Fort Garland with the bloody trophy tied to his saddle's pommel.

Ten years later the Legislature of Colorado ordered a reward of five hundred dollars paid to Mr. Tobin.

Colorado Springs

At Colorado Springs we found another immense hotel, "The Antlers," one of the finest and most picturesque structures in the West. The rush of travel has made these huge establishments necessary in every attractive spot in this country.

The broad avenue and wide streets, shaded by trees, make this "a city beautiful." The Colorado Springs Company was organized in 1871 under the leadership of General W. J. Palmer. A school and a church were the first institutions of the town, which gave Colorado Springs from the very beginning religious and educational advantages. Its artistic, social and musical development have kept pace with its material growth, and it is now called the "Little Lunnon," the "Colorado Athens." A refined

PIKES PEAK AVE, COLORADO SPRINGS

IRVING HOWBERT WINFIELD S STRATTON W. F. SLOCUM

and wealthy population demands improvements and facilities which have made this city famous.

The Colorado Springs park system includes the Garden of the Gods, North Cheyenne canon, the High Drive and Palmer park.

Not far from the residential suburb of Broadmoor is the Stratton home for the poor and aged. W. S. Stratton left the money for this institution, and in all the country there is nothing like this picturesque village, with its red tiled roofs, sheltering aged couples.

Colorado Springs has 32,500 inhabitants; it has opera houses, numerous churches, hospitals, sanitariums, two libraries, two country clubs; men's clubs, one of which has an elegant club building; the state institution for the deaf and blind, the Modern Woodmen sanitarium, the Union Printers' home, all of which prove that it is a live city, even if one can't get a "smile."

Colorado College

The pioneer institution of higher learning is located here. General Palmer laid the foundation in 1874. It passed through a dark and distressing period; in 1888 even the campus was sold for taxes. In that year Dr. William Frederick Slocum accepted the presidency. He entered upon his duties with the enthusiasm born of deep investigation and earnest thought. His noble and cultured wife devoted her tact and wisdom to the service of the college. The enrollment of students today is 700. The college has a faculty of seventy-six members, twenty-seven departments of instruction and seventeen fine buildings. It is co-educational and non-sectarian. Its property is valued at $1,365,540 and it has an endowment fund of $1,043,000. It ranks among the first colleges in the United States.

The Honorable Irving Howbert crossed the plains with an ox-team in 1860, and in 1862 settled in Colorado Springs. During the Civil War he served in the Third Cavalry of Colorado. When peace was declared, he returned at the age of twenty-one and accepted any useful employment that was offered him. He clerked in a general store, was a cowboy, a farmer, a freighter; possessing keen judgment, quick decision and untiring energy, he forged his way to the front, and became a vital factor in the upbuilding of Colorado Springs.

His industry and ability marked him for political favor, and in 1869 he was elected clerk of El Paso county, and re-elected until he served ten years, when he refused to accept the position again. He was then chosen cashier of the First National Bank of Colorado Springs, and in two years was elected president. This institution, which was at that time weak and struggling, he established on a sure foundation. The constant work of protecting, enlarging and upbuilding the interest of the bank for ten years, impaired his health to a degree, that a resignation was necessary.

He was one of the projectors and original incorporators of the Colorado Midland railroad; one of the owners of the Robert E. Lee mine of Leadville, which under his judicious management entered the list of the big producers in that famous district. He was active and conspicuous in the development of Cripple Creek; a promoter and builder of the Colorado Southern and Cripple Creek railroad. His masterful executive ability in directing these enterprises proved him to be a man of genius, skill and determination.

As a Republican he was elected to the State Senate in 1882, and in this position he served the State faithfully; he has also served his party in many State conventions.

Mr. Howbert is a friend and patron of education, for many years on the board of trustees of Colorado College. His private library is one of the finest in the State and around his home life is an atmosphere of culture and refinement. He has written a book on "The Indians of the Pike's Peak Region," which is a valuable contribution to the literature of Colorado.

In the upbuilding of Colorado Springs and the State he stands pre-eminently as one of the men who planned and wrought.

William Jackson Palmer

I went to view the grounds of Glen Eyrie, so-called from the eagles' nest perched in crags. Colorado has many reasons to bless the name of the owner of this magnificent estate.

William Jackson Palmer was brevetted brigadier general at the age of twenty-eight in recognition of heroic service. When he was mustered out of service at the close of the war, he went from the battle field to be secretary of the Kansas Pacific Railroad Company.

Gen. W. J. Palmer

From this position he came to know Colorado. His line ran from Kansas City to Denver, and he knew every mile of it.

In 1869 he conceived the idea of building a road from Denver south to the Rio Grande and Mexico. Colonel W. H. Greenwood, Governor A. C. Hunt, Colonel D. C. Dodge are some of the men who backed General Palmer in the enterprise.

His confidence in the future of this city inspired men of means to subscribe the funds needed for the project. He built the road; the first narrow-gauge in the West, and became its president.

He built lines and branches of railroad to the Rio Grande river and down its course as far south as Santa Fe, New Mexico, all over southwestern Colorado, and extended the main broad-gauge line from Pueblo west, across the Continental range, to Salt Lake City. The Rio Grande and Pacific Company extended this line from Salt Lake City to San Francisco, so that now the Rio Grande road, in connection with the Missouri Pacific, under one management, forms a through trunk railway line from St. Louis, by way of Kansas City, Pueblo and Salt Lake, direct to San Francisco, as the resultant fruit of the foresight and persistent labor of General Palmer, Colorado's great railroad builder.

Brilliant as was General Palmer's war record, it was the constructive work in the time of peace which gives him rank among the nation's greatest citizens.

While building the Rio Grande, the idea of a town grew and took form in his mind, and he became the moving spirit of the company, which owned the first incorporated town, now Colorado Springs. Going farther south, he bought the land south of the Arkansas river opposite Pueblo, and laid out the town of South Pueblo, on the outskirts of which was later built the great steel plant of the Colorado Fuel and Iron Company, covering forty acres and costing $40,000,000.

He made his home in Denver for a while, and then moved to Colorado Springs. A system of public grounds and driveways, at an expenditure of $1,000,000, was General Palmer's donation to the town. He was one of the founders of Colorado College. An individual owned a part of Cheyenne canon, and exacted a toll of twenty-five cents from each one who desired to see the "Seven Falls." To defeat this avarice, General Palmer purchased Cutter mountain and built a trail over it, from which there is a fine view of the falls. He also, in connection with Dr. William A. Bell, built the magnificent Antlers hotel.

His antipathy to publicity was the dominant note in his life. Two years after he gave $100,000 to the Tuskegee Institute the fact became known to the public. Booker T. Washington made reference to it in a report, which was sent over the country, and bitterly repented the oversight, for General Palmer donated the money on the solemn understanding that it was to be silently accepted.

The crowning act of his railroad career, from a philanthropic point of view, was his disbursement of $1,000,000 to the railroad employes, when he retired from the Rio Grande Western. Not only were the forty-four officers of the road remembered, but every employe, from section hand up, received his quota of the disbursements, according to the length of service.

His broad charity, gentleness and courtesy, his aim to improve everything around him, and help those less blessed with the world's goods than himself, made him one of Colorado's best loved citizens.

The day before his death his old friend, Colonel D. C. Dodge of Denver, was hastily summoned. The presence of the colonel, who had stood with him in the great work of railway building, acted as a stimulant upon him; the effect was marvelous. Immediately upon his arrival General Palmer decided on a daring auto ride.

"It is impossible," remonstrated Colonel Dodge, "for the snow of last night has broken the record of thirty-five years, and Glen Eyrie is walled with snow three feet deep; great icicles hang from the eaves of the castle."

"We will ride," said the master of Glen Eyrie. Nothing could stay him; physicians were waved aside; the counsel of friends were silenced. "My old friend, we will ride," he reiterated.

"The car cannot run through the deep drifts," argued Colonel Dodge.

"Nonsense; we shall go," laughed the general.

The chauffeur was called from his lodge and ordered to bring the car around. There was an instant response to the general's command. Men went to work on all sides, clearing the roads. What seemed an impossibility soon shaped itself to the general's requirements. Drifts were cut with shovels, snow plows were put to work, and in a short time the general and Colonel Dodge were making a circuit of Glen Eyrie in a big touring car.

"I now believe that the grip of death was upon him," said Colonel Dodge, "as he rode through this storm, fighting fiercely as in the old days, gritting his teeth in the face of the biting winds, laughing to rout the snow that could not baffle him."

The next day he lapsed into unconsciousness, from which he never rallied, and passed away lulled to a great peace before the spirit left his body.

So passed a philanthropist, a soldier and an empire builder, a man who helped to build a State and helped to save a nation.

He will be remembered for many things, among them, and the most important, the founding at the foot of the Great Peak, Colorado Springs—the beautiful city of homes.

The Cog Road

In 1889 Major John Hurlbut of Colorado Springs conceived the idea of building a railroad from Manitou to the summit of Pike's Peak. Jerome B. Wheeler, Henry Watson and D. H. Moffat endorsed the feasibility of the project, and subscribed for $90,000 worth of stock.

Mr. Hurlbut went to New York to place the remainder of the stock to a half million. While on his way he met Z. G. Simmons of Kenosha, Wisconsin, and through him sold the stock, amounting to $410,000, the purchasers being Z. G. Simmons, Roswell P. Flower of

New York, R. R. Cable, H. H. Porter and David Downs of Chicago.

A company was formed, with Major John Hurlbut president, and the work of grading from Manitou began, for a "rack" railroad on the Swiss Abt system. The trains were running to the half-way station in August, 1890. The first passenger train ran to the summit in 1891.

The exact length of the road is 46,158 feet, nearly eight and three-fourths miles. The altitude of Manitou is 6,600 feet; the summit 14,200; a grade of twenty-five per cent.

This is the highest railroad in the world, and a "trip to the clouds" on the Pike's Peak cog road is the greatest novelty of travel in the Rocky mountains.

In this year of 1915 a motor road to the top of Pike's Peak is in process of construction. A new highway has been built to the celebrated "Cave of the Winds." It climbs Agate mountain by a series of loops, runs along Williams canyon, making a drive that is the delight of motorists.

The Colorado-to-the-Gulf highway and the Pike's Peak Ocean-to-Ocean highway intersect at the foot of Pike's Peak, and good roads connect with the National Lincoln highway and the Santa Fe trail; thus the famous peak that was a "land-mark" to the pioneer is a "motor marker" in this hustling twentieth century.

The Garden of the Gods covers five hundred acres, and contains some of the most remarkable rock formations in the world. The two immense slabs of red sandstone forming the gateway are three hundred feet high. This tract of land at the foot of the historic mountain was deeded to Colorado Springs by the children of the late Charles Elliot Perkins, in compliance with a note found among Mr. Perkins' papers. The terms of the gift specify that this spot shall forever be kept free to the world.

Here are tall cathedral spires, stone giants, gigantic mushrooms and, wonder of wonders, the Balanced rock, poised on a point that looks as if it might be "knocked over with a feather." Surely the gods had a "high old time" in this garden.

Colorado City

The three cities, Colorado Springs, Colorado City and Manitou, are now almost joined together by a continuous settlement.

In 1858 a party from Denver and Auraria went to Pike's Peak to build a town near that land-mark. They organized a company and laid out Colorado City. It was never a mining camp. From the beginning it was intended to be a commercial city. This was the first time "Colorado" had been used to designate a place in this region. It became the sensational nucleus for population, and during the first twelve months over a thousand people settled there.

When Governor Gilpin was authorized in 1861 to organize a territorial government, the first legislature met in Denver September 9 of that year. When the assembly came to locate a seat of government, it was decided to make the town of Colorado City, on the east bank of the Fountain-Qui-Bouille, at the mouth of Camp creek, the capital. This occasioned a great deal of indignation, as Colorado City was at that time but a paper city. None of the capital offices were ever moved there, although the Second Assembly convened there July 7, 1862, elected a speaker and then adjourned to Denver. Today Colorado City, with the Portland and Golden Cycle reduction works, is a point of interest.

The discovery of gold in the Pike's Peak region was reserved for a later day. Now the great peak looks over

the wonderful golden empire of Cripple Creek, which was once an open cattle range. The hills within the really productive area of Cripple Creek were fenced in by Bennett and Myers of Denver, who owned a large part of the territory, devoted exclusively to pasture for cattle. Bob Womack was the mining pioneer of the district. He sank a shaft in Poverty Gulch in 1891, and found good ore. Then began the fame of the great gold camp. W. S. Stratton, once a poor carpenter, made his location July 4, 1891, and became a multi-millionaire.

Manitou

Manitou is connected with Colorado Springs by a branch of the Denver and Rio Grande railway and numerous motor ways. It is situated near the base of Pike's Peak, where mineral springs of iron and soda abound, and is called the Saratoga of the West. These waters are peculiar; some people say they like them. I think they speak truthfully, judging from the crowds that gather around the various springs. The tin cups attached to the curbs of these springs would not supply a fraction of the thirsty souls who rush to these fountains of health. Tin cans, wash pitchers and "little brown jugs" are pressed into service to meet the greedy demand.

The crowded hotels, which are calculated to surprise the tourists at first, cease to excite wonder after one has visited the Garden of the Gods, Cave of the Winds, Glen Eyrie, Rainbow Falls, Pike's Peak and other natural attractions near this place.

A Legend of Manitou

In a time, far back in the past, the Indians of all tribes assembled at Manitou Springs. They knew that the effervescent water contained almost every mineral ingredient beneficial to man. They believed the springs were placed there for a divine purpose, and said the water was good medicine.

Manitou means the "Place of God," or the Great Spirit. From time immemorial, away out upon the plains, and into the mountains, for a distance of a day's journey, in all directions, from Manitou Springs, stakes were driven into the ground, or stones were piled to mark the limits of neutral ground. The tribes of mountains and plains were continually at war with each other. The law was that no battle should be fought, no personal grievance avenged, within the sacred ground of Manitou, and the law was so severe that if any man transgressed in the way of violence against an enemy, the chief of the tribe ordered that the transgressor be at once put to death, and the order was obeyed.

The savages would fight and kill e a c h other even up to the line marked by stakes or piles of stone, but within the sacred precincts of Manitou all was safety and peace. Such is the legend of Manitou.

A CAMPING PARTY

Here we met a camping party who had been some weeks in the mountains and were returning to Denver by way of Manitou. They were dreadfully sunburnt, but happy.

"The only pleasure in camping," said Dick Harwell, his black eyes sparkling with humor, "is the *fun* you can get out of it. Fully equipped with an ample 'grub-box,' a forest of fishing poles, two or three revolvers and shot guns, we felt equal to any emergency, and set out with light hearts and joyful anticipations. The first night out we were lost, having taken the wrong road. While winding about in a dismal canyon, trying to find our way out, night overtook us, and when we pitched our tents it was so dark we could not see an inch from our noses.

The next morning we were aroused by an ear-splitting shriek. A cold, clammy, 'demnition moist' frog had hopped on the forehead of one of the ladies, and, to our consternation, we discovered we had camped by the side of a graveyard. The punster of the crowd remarked that there was a grave side to everything in life.

"Following the narrow road, all up hill and full of boulders, our horses came unaccountably to a dead standstill. We persuaded them in every way, even to firing off our pistols, but they persisted in standing still. There has always existed in my mind a logical connection between stalled teams and swearing; so, requesting the ladies to excuse me, I pitched in.

"It produced the desired effect; away we went, jolting, shaking, rocking, swinging, bumping and oscillating, which threatened to crush every bone in our bodies.

"At length, finding our road again, it led us across a rapid stream. One of the ladies expressed great fear. To comfort her I said I would put my arm around her. At the next crossing, as might have been expected, all the ladies were afraid, but that was too much; I declined embracing the crowd.

"On the bank of this stream stood a man crowned with a stove-pipe hat, his hands neatly encased in kid gloves, fishing. Our driver, a Dutchman, called our attention to this prim fisherman by saying, 'Look, da ist von *soft foot!*'

"The next evening we camped early, and several of us went out for a ramble. Miss L—— and I took a seat on a log by the side of the trail to await the return of our friend, who felt inclined to prospect further.

"Soon we saw him coming, hat in hand and hair flying in the breeze, yelling, 'Run; it's a bear!' I joined in the race, but the lady, with the curiosity peculiar to her sex, stepped out into the trail to get a view of the brute. Obtaining it, she fainted, and there was nothing left for us but to turn and fight the bear. We killed it, because we had to.

"One of our party had a birthday while there," continued Mr. Harwell, "and we gave her a candy-pulling in honor of the event. We cooked the molasses six solid hours, and then had to eat it with a spoon. Like Meg's jelly, 'it wouldn't jell.'

"I had a friend who was mining near the top of Mt. Lincoln. We concluded to go up there and pass a night just to see the sunrise next morning. The night hands had a meal about midnight in the blacksmith shop, and the bellows they used to start a fire at the forge made such an unearthly noise that we were startled wide awake, which resulted in our sleeping too late next morning to witness old Sol's glorious awakening.

"Oh, there is lots of fun in camping, if you can only see it!"

With this profound explosion he seemed pretty well talked out, and we left him.

On the train returning to Denver I was pleased to see Jim Baker, the famous scout and trapper, who had camped on the site of Denver long before Denver was thought of, and had been the companion of Kit Carson, Bent and St. Vrain.

In appearance he was a typical frontiersman—tall and straight as an arrow. Although at the time nearly seventy years old, only his wrinkled visage betrayed his age. There was elasticity in his step and brightness in his eye.

He had spent forty-seven years on the frontier, and I regarded him as a living volume of history.

LANDMARKS KNOCKED AWAY

"My landmarks are all knocked away," said he; "I am very much like the old negro, who said, 'I donno whar

I is, I donno whar I come from, and I donno whar I's goin' to.' He spoke in the frontier dialect, but I will give it in plain English.

"Even the rivers have different names. They were pretty at first, but now there is no beauty in them."

I suggested that the Grand, the Gunnison, the Rio Grande, the Arkansas and the Swan were musical and appropriate.

"Yes," said he, "they have the same names as of old, with the exception of the Gunnison, which was originally called Eagle river.

"The names given in the early days had a distinctive and comprehensive meaning for the frontiersman, and recalled many memories of life on the plains.

"Clear creek was called Vasquez Fork, by which name it ought to be known today, but later arrivals, attracted by its transparent water, and caring nothing for the memory of the old pioneer whose name it bore, called it Clear creek, which has since been discovered to be a misnomer, for it is the muddiest stream in all Christendom, yet it gives tourists something to wonder at and talk about.

"The San Carlos they have corrupted into St. Charles.

"One of the most musical names I ever heard given to a river was El Rio de las Animas, which means 'river of spirits.' The Spaniards christened it thus, because of its deep beauty and stillness. The French traders and trappers called it Purgatoire, but now it is pronounced Picketware, which is a desecration," said the old man with an emphatic shake of his head.

" 'The Fountain' is all that is left of 'La Fontaine qui Bouille,' and the Cache a la Poudre (hiding place of the powder), named from the circumstance that the old French trappers, years before, were accustomed to bury their powder on its banks to conceal it from the Indians, is now called Poudre. The new-comers of the last decade don't appreciate the significance of these names, or in the rush of business haven't time to pronounce them."

Many of the pioneers, like Jim Baker, have lived to see their land-marks knocked away, yet their sympathies are keenly alive for the best welfare of their fellow-men, and their hearts beat responsive to the impulses that throb through the universe of progress. They are proud of the State whose cornerstone they laid,

> "Proud of her mines of silver and gold;
> Proud of her flocks spread over the plains;
> Proud of her sons, patriotic and bold;
> Proud of her fields of golden grain;
> Proud of her mountains and sunny skies;
> Proud of her Statehood, by birthright a peer;
> Midst the stars of the Union she shines, the prize,
> The crowning glory of the hundredth year."

PART X
THE GREAT STATE BUILDING EPOCH

CHAPTER XXVIII
PERSONAL GLIMPSES OF STATE BUILDERS

THE QUEEN CITY OF THE PLAINS

When Colorado became a State, in 1876, Denver had a population of 25,000, a small street car with horse motive power. The Governor's Guard Hall took the place of a theater, and where the union depot now stands was open country. W. N. Byers was running the Rocky Mountain News, while the Tribune, which afterwards became the Republican, was piloted by Herman Beckhurst, with Eugene Field and Rothaker on the editorial staff. The First National Bank had a dingy little office on the corner of Fifteenth and Larimer, and the transfer business of the city was carried on by "Tip" Pearce.

Wolfe Londoner was doing business at his old stand on Fifteenth street, where the pioneers, including George Tritch and Robert Hatten, put in their spare time talking of the old days and regretting that they were gone forever. Lots on Capitol Hill were going begging to anybody who would pay the taxes on them, and business men were lying awake nights to figure out how to meet the exigencies of the hour. All railroad business was at a standstill. In fact, the town was as dead as the proverbial door nail.

The discovery of carbonates at Leadville in 1877 was

flashed across the wires to the uttermost ends of the earth, and people of all nationalities, all classes and conditions, flocked to the great Pike's Peak State, and the boom of 1859 was re-enacted, only a hundred-fold more. A steady stream of supplies for mining poured through the jobbing houses, and Denver became at once a picture of life, color and excitement.

Londoner, it is said, quit telling stories; admitted the days of '59 were back numbers; loaded teams with groceries, started for the city above the clouds, and located a branch store.

The railroad builders, John Evans and David H. Moffat, got busy, and there was a race between the lines as to which would reach the great Eldorado first.

What Leadville has done for Denver is not clearly realized by the people of this time. The wealth of the mines made men rich in a day, and those who had won riches and fame in the "city above the clouds" came one after another to lend Denver of their genius and working energy. Indeed it was the wealth of the mountains that made Denver known everywhere as the "Queen City of the Plains."

H. A. W. Tabor was the father of Leadville. He was there running a general store before the camp reached its high-class boom stage. Two Germans, August Rische and George T. Hook, in the cheerless little town of Fairplay, at the outbreak of the carbonate craze, had a severe attack of the prospecting fever. They hit the trail and never stopped until they landed in Leadville. Then they went to Tabor and asked him for a grubstake—picks, shovels and pans—agreeing to divide by thirds whatever they might find. Tabor, who was always generous, entered into the agreement. They tramped up to the apex of Fryer Hill and began digging. At a depth of twenty-six feet they uncovered a great body of mineral and christened it the "Little Pittsburg."

This was the beginning of H. A. W. Tabor's spectacular career. Rische disposed of his interest to Jerome B. Chaffee and D. H. Moffat for $262,500 and bought a mansion on what is now Capitol Hill in Denver. Tabor sold his interest to Chaffee and Moffat for a million, which was paid him over the counter of the First National Bank in Denver, and with it he bought one-half of the stock of the bank. His income from the Matchless mine was $80,000 to $100,000 per month. Everything he touched seemed to turn to gold; he was the Midas of the camp, and his fame spread over the world. He bought the home of Henry C. Brown, the finest residence in Denver. Then he bought the corner of Curtis and Sixteenth and built on it an elegant opera house.

H. A. W. Tabor

Tabor transformed Denver from a straggling village to a metropolis; his work for the beautifying of the city was pointed out to tourists, who were eager to see and hear about this modern Croesus. He was elected to the United States Senate for a short term to fill a vacancy.

Through a long process of unfortunate investments the whole superstructure of his wealth fell to pieces, and he died a poor man.

He had his faults and weaknesses, but all good citizens esteem him, because he was a powerful factor, working for the general benefit, and the time will come when people pondering over the achievements of heroes in the upbuilding of Colorado will feel that the State owes him a monument.

John C. Mitchell made his money in Leadville, and came to Denver, where he has been a prominent banker for many years. He is a man of generous impulses, always loyal to his friends and associates, and always ready to lend a helping hand whenever needed. He has sound common sense, quick perception, a marvelous grasp of business affairs and an almost intuitive knowledge of men, which is so essential to safe banking. He married a daughter of R. E. Goodell, built an elegant home on the brow of the hill, and the Mitchells are known far and wide for their generous, open-handed hospitality. Mr. Mitchell derives pleasure in smoothing out rough places in the paths of those less fortunate than himself, and his gracious wife is equally generous. Mrs. Mitchell prides herself upon her skill in the culinary art. She has published a cook book, the proceeds of which she

John C. Mitchell

gave to the domestic science department of the Woman's Club. Mrs. Mitchell never lets her left hand know what her right hand is doing, and her right is ever busy with acts of practical charity. Mr. and Mrs. Mitchell have two children, Clark G. Mitchell and Mrs. Henry C. Van Schaack.

William H. James, who for twenty years had lived in the mining districts of Colorado, went to Lake County in 1875. He was elected a member of the constitutional convention from the counties of Park and Lake and was the prime mover of that clause in the constitution which provides that mines shall not be taxed for the period of ten years; he maintained that mining at that time was in its infancy and needed to be encouraged. He later formed a partnership with Edward Eddy in buying and selling ores. In 1878 he was elected mayor of Leadville, an office which he filled to the entire satisfaction of the citizens. During the great strike of the miners in 1880 Leadville was placed under martial law. The State troops were called out to protect the lives and property of the people; Mr. James was appointed brigadier general, and did fine service in quelling the riot. He held an enviable position in the hearts of the people of Leadville and also in Denver, where he made a home and brought up his family. His two children, Mrs. Lewis Lemen and Mr. Harry C. James, reside in Denver. They

William H. James

possess the kind and genial nature of their father, and make many friends.

David May owned a clothing store in Leadville; was elected county treasurer; engaged successfully in mining and established his present great business in Denver.

Dennis Sullivan

Dennis Sullivan began mining in Central. When the gulch ceased to offer a field wide enough for his energies, he went to Leadville, bought several claims on Fryer Hill, and held large interests in the first gas and electric plant. He cleared up several fortunes, retired from business, and was a millionaire at the time of his death, which occurred quite recently.

J. J. Brown, a retired capitalist of Denver, was in the early '80's superintendent of the Maid of Erin. He successfully developed that bonanza which made millions for the owners. He was one of the owners of the Little Jonny, and when the great Ibex Company was formed he secured a substantial block of stock, which has netted him a handsome fortune. His wife has given her time to travel and study. She is philanthropic, and won fame by her heroism in the recent Titanic disaster.

Thomas F. Daly, a man by nature generous and congenial, answered the alluring call to Leadville in 1884. But he failed to find happiness in mining; the insurance business was more to his taste; he was successful in it. In 1894 he came down out of the golden hills, and has followed the insurance business in Denver.

He organized the Capitol Life Insurance Company. By his determination and persistence he has brought it from a beginning of $200,000 assets to over $2,000,000. This is mostly invested in Colorado, of which Mr. Daly is very proud. He is today one of Denver's most active and enthusiastic citizens, and has a natural desire to aid the advancement of every worthy purpose. His frank and openhearted manner inspires friendship.

Thomas F. Daly

Henry Bohm was one of the body of citizens who entered the mining field in the bonanza days—not to mine, but to sell jewels. During his residence in Leadville he made many friends among the prominent men in the state, and these friendships have continued to the present time.

He came to Denver with the rush from Leadville in 1881, and established the Henry Bohm Jewelry Co., which later became the Bohm-Allen Co. His judgment in his line of work is the very best, and he has won the confidence and good will of the people by his honesty and high business standards.

Henry Bohm

Mr. Bohm is a fine, kindly gentleman, and while his business activities draw heavily on his time, he is never too much engaged to ignore his duty as a citizen, and always takes a patriotic interest in every movement for the public welfare.

Judge Luther M. Goddard, another Leadville man, made a home in Denver. He is an able jurist and has served on the bench of the Supreme Court. His honesty and integrity of character i n s p i r e confidence and respect. Mrs. Goddard is a woman of genial, affable manners, a fine musician and a student. She has been president of the Woman's Club, and is still interested in club work.

Luther M. Goddard

O. E. LeFevre, upon his arrival in Denver, established a home in the Highlands, and immediately began the practice of law. He was elected attorney for the Highlands in 1875 and re-elected in 1876. Later he was elected district judge. He made a fortune from the mines at Creede and invested a large part of it in Denver. His elegant home is the center of art, literature and music. He is a lover of books, and his home library is one of the finest in the city. His disposition is sunny and cheerful; his wit is pleasing and his humor kindly. The walls of his residence are adorned with a choice collection of modern French paintings, which reveal his artistic nature. His wife is interested in the charities of Denver. His daughter, Mrs. Harry Bellamy, is a woman of broad education, a pleasing writer, has had fine musical training and often gives her talents in aid of charitable entertainments.

Then there is John M. Maxwell, Phil Golding, Jesse F. McDonald, H. E. Wood—indeed if I had the space I could mention scores of men who, after digging out a fortune in the mountains, helped to make Denver the metropolis of the State.

O. E. Le Fevre

The experiences of these men and women have placed them among the pioneers of the West. They have witnessed and aided the development of a great State, the like of which will never be seen again.

James B. Grant was prominent among the men who helped to unfold the wealth of Leadville, which transformed the face of the State from its look of business gloom to the smiling energy of glad prosperity.

He was born in Alabama in 1848, attended a country school until he was twelve years old. At the age of seventeen he was enrolled in the Southern army. He went to Iowa at the close of the war, and was three years a student in the Agricultural College at Ames. He then went to Cornell University, and from there to the School of Mines at Freiberg, Germany, where he studied metallurgy and kindred branches. His vacations were spent in travel through Europe.

After completing the course in the School of Mines he went to Australia and New Zealand, where he spent six months inspecting the gold mines and stamp mills.

James B. Grant

In 1877 he came to Colorado and mined in Virginia canon. The excitement over the Leadville discoveries led Mr. Grant there. He plunged at once into its busy life, and after making a personal investigation of the ores, he reported to his uncle, Judge Grant, of Davenport, Iowa, that smelting works at Leadville would be a rich investment. Such was the confidence of the judge in his nephew's judgment that he placed $300,000 at his disposal. The nephew pushed the work of construction, and in September, 1878, commenced smelting, which proved remunerative from the start. He bought half a million dollars' worth of ore a month from the Leadville miners. A half interest in the works was sold to Eddy & James.

In the early days of Leadville there was a good deal of friction between the miners and smelting people. The fairness and justice of Mr. Grant were well known, and when the troubles were referred for arbitration, he was selected as umpire to settle the matter. His adjustment of the dispute was accepted as final.

Mr. Henry Head, the friend of Mr. Grant for twenty years, said: "No man could long be associated with Mr. Grant without growing to love him for his genial manner, his very high sense of honor, his clean, moral life and his broad charity for all. While he knew the serious side of life, he had the happy faculty of seeing something funny in nearly all matters, however serious, which made him a most enjoyable companion. When absorbed in a subject, Mr. Grant would often become oblivious to other things, which the following story illustrates:

"One of his earlier ambitions was to have good horses. New Year day, 1880, at his invitation, I joined him in making New Year calls on mutual friends in Leadville. His turn-out, a handsome horse and cutter, proved to be very attractive to people along the street. He was earnestly discussing a question with me while driving down Harrison avenue at a very lively pace. My attention was attracted by violent gestures of persons passing us on both sides. Looking for the cause, I saw one line dragging along on the snow, the governor, blissfully happy, holding the other one. For a time I felt I would be far happier if I were walking. The horse soon answered the call to stop, however, and the line was recovered."

The Grant smelter at Leadville was destroyed by fire, and new works were built at Denver on a larger and better scale, because they determined to enlarge the field of usefulness by treating, in addition to the ores of Leadville, the products of other camps, not only of Colorado, but of Montana, Arizona, Utah and New Mexico.

Mr. Grant was nominated for governor at a Democratic convention in 1882, by acclamation, and was elected by a large majority, the only State officer of his party chosen. He was a favorite with all parties—indeed it was the admiration and love of the people for James B. Grant that made him the first Democratic governor of Colorado. At the exposition in Denver, in 1884, I saw the people lift him and carry him on their shoulders around the grounds.

As chief executive of the State he labored to increase the importance of every industry and to aid in public-spirited and progressive enterprises. His administration was one of the most satisfactory in the history of the State. Governor Grant, having no desire for re-election or ambition for further political preferment, was in a position to act according to his own judgment, regardless of parties or coteries who might wish to influence his actions. It was said of him at that time that "while he was neither a statesman nor a politician, he was what all statesmen and most politicians desire to be—an influence."

He was intensely interested in educational work, and gave freely of his time and influence in the building of our splendid public school system. He served nine years on the board of education and was president of the board for seven years, filling the position with the accuracy and efficiency that was characteristic of his business life.

Mr. Aaron Gove, who was principal of the high school at that time says: "When Governor Grant assumed the duties of his office on the board of education it was promptly suggested to him that as he was connected with the Denver National Bank, it would be proper that that bank be made the depository of the school funds. The funds of the district were deposited with the Colorado National Bank, Mr. William Berger of that bank being treasurer of the board, and, at his death, followed by Mr. Kountze. Mr. Kountze preferred no objection, but Governor Grant assured the board that as the Colorado National Bank had that position, and through a series of years had been always obliging and efficient, he could see no reason for making a change in the treasurership of the board. Furthermore, he assured the board that so long as he was a member, the Denver National Bank would decline to be the custodian of the school funds.

"This illustrates the character of the man. Doubtless, the banks received a material profit from the position, which would have accrued to the Denver National, had the change been made.

"Through Governor Grant's long career as director on the board of education that line of conduct was persistently adhered to by him; nothing whatever that could possibly accrue to a personal advantage was permitted."

It was not only in this country that the record of James B. Grant as a mining engineer and metallurgist was recognized. The record of his searching investigation into the physical condition of the Leadville district was translated into Dutch by General William J. Palmer and submitted to Holland capitalists. The possibilities of the camp, as shown by Mr. Grant's investigation, induced these financiers to buy the bonds of the Denver & Rio Grande railroad's extension from Canon City to Leadville.

When Prince Henry of Prussia visited this country in 1903, Governor Grant was invited to attend the banquet given "captains of industry" by J. Pierpont Morgan in New York.

Mining and assaying engaged Governor Grant's attention, and he became interested in a number of mining companies.

Owing to his activity in the organization of the Denver National Bank, he was made vice-president, which position he held to the day of his death.

He was one of the pillars of the Democratic party in the State from the time he was elected to the important office of governor, but his friends in the Republican party were legion.

The governor was of scholarly attainments, great executive ability, and with it all he was a plain and unpretentious gentleman.

He had faith in the boundless resources of Colorado, and from the beginning of his career he was a zealous advocate and surprising prophet of the industrial development of the State. All through his life can be traced his great love for Colorado and his desire for the well-being of his fellow-man.

He married handsome Mary Goodell, and when he was elected the chief executive of Colorado, she dispensed the hospitality of the governor's home in a way that reflected credit on the State.

Mrs. Grant's early associations in the home of her father, Colonel Goodell, who was always intimate with public life and with her grandfather, Governor Matteson of Illinois, fitted her to occupy the position.

Mrs. James B. Grant

Governor Grant built a palatial residence in Denver on the brow of Capitol Hill, facing the mountains out of which he had dug his fortune. His widow still lives in that home. She is a woman of rare tact and intelligence, deeply interested in club work and everything that stands for the progress of women.

Governor and Mrs. Grant have two sons, Lester and James B., Jr., who are young men of fine promise.

JOHN F. CAMPION

John F. Campion is a strong type of the men who developed the Leadville mines. He said:

"I drove through the mining camps of Colorado in a covered wagon, for three months, and reached Leadville in September, 1879. The mining boom was at its height. I made the acquaintance of a bunch of prospectors who were in the business of making mining locations and selling them as soon as a ten-foot hole was dug. They managed to locate seven or eight claims a week, and I made an arrangement with them to buy the claims at $100 each. One of the peculiarities of this bunch was to get drunk every Saturday after receiving their money. It became my religious duty to go to the police court of the city jail and bail them out on Monday, at which time they usually looked as if they had been shot through a carpet cleaning machine. I sold the claims to J. Whitaker Wright, a famous promoter, and I understood later that he sold the properties in Philadelphia for $10,000 each. He was tried in London

John F. Campion

for fraud, convicted and sentenced to a penal institution for life. In the court room, after the judge had delivered the sentence, he swallowed the fumes of cyanide of potassium from a cigar.

"I heard of a large mass of lead ore at Horse Shoe, which was at the head of Empire Gulch, about twelve miles from Leadville, and immediately secured a number of miners, located my claims, did the assessment work, incorporated a company called the 'Crusader,' and in February, 1880, sold it to a Boston company for $150,000. These were the boom days, when everything was selling and everybody was buying that had money to invest.

"My next mining investment was the Imes, located on Iron Hill. This property was afterwards consolidated with the White Cap Forfeit, Collateral and Norman Bourdman, forming a continuous plat of land extending from the crest of Iron Hill to California Gulch. The property was developed and a large shipment of lead-silver ore taken from it.

"Then I opened up the first downtown property below the carbonate fault. It was called the Elk Consolidated Mining Company. This property produced a large quantity of high-grade ore. The opening of this property caused a great deal of work to be done on adjacent properties, which led to the vast developments that later occurred in what is known as the 'Down-Town' territory.

"Later I secured the right to purchase the Little Jonny and adjacent property on Breece Hill, in the Leadville district. This property is now producing, and has yielded a great many millions of dollars.

"Along with the excitement and the hurrah of a mining camp," continued Mr. Campion, "there are many pathetic things.

"Among the early arrivals in Leadville were Mrs. Hosmer and her daughter. The girl, whose name was

Gertie, was commonly called 'the candy girl.' They established a candy store very close to the Clarendon Hotel, which was the principal hotel at that time. The girl became infatuated with a gambler and ran away with him. Everybody knew her. She was a general favorite with the people. A few months later she returned, broken in health, and her dream of happiness exploded. She lost all interest in the affairs of the world, and appeared to be dying from a broken heart. This girl had a beautiful contralto voice. One evening, a couple of months after she returned, she sent word to several of her friends that she wanted to see them at her house that evening at a certain time. The people invited went to the residence and found the girl emaciated and in a dying condition. She told her guests that she was going to die, and wanted to sing them something. Then in a sweet, strong contralto voice she sang, 'See that My Grave Is Kept Green.' The soul of Gertie Hosmer floated away on the last words of the song."

After accumulating an immense fortune, Mr. Campion built an elegant home in Denver, and has been conspicuously and ably identified with the development of the City and State.

The beet sugar industry in Colorado, with a growth almost as marvelous as Jonah's gourd, is largely due to Mr. John F. Campion.

During the time he was president of the Chamber of Commerce Mr. Campion, with two or three friends, raised a fund to be distributed as prizes throughout the State to farmers raising on an acre tract the best sample of sugar beets. He also employed a man named Holmes to visit the different parts of the State where it was thought sugar beets could be raised, and talk to the farmers, deliver lectures, and in a general way educate them in the sugar beet business. It was suggested that each farmer plant an acre of beets and send his samples to the Agricultural College, where prizes were awarded for the best beets. This was done with the hope that capital would be induced to build sugar mills. It was found impossible to interest capital in the sugar beet business, so Mr. Campion and Mr. Boettcher, Colonel Dodge and J. R. McKinney built the first mill in Colorado, at Grand Junction. This mill was started working, and owing to inexperience a good deal of the sugar went down the Grand river. About 25,000 tons of beets were frozen in the ground, and the company promptly paid for them.

The Great Western Sugar Company, projected by the same syndicate, built the second mill at Loveland, two years later. This mill proved to be a complete success from its inception, and has likely more money to its credit for the size of the mill than any similar mill in the world. A few years later the sugar trust bought the control of both properties, after discovering that it would cost them less money to buy the properties than to "bust" the syndicate that owned them, and started their present construction work of sugar mills, which has led to the building of many more in the State.

In conjunction with Mr. Boettcher, Senator C. J. Hughes and Colonel Dodge, Mr. Campion started the Great Western Packing Company, which has built up a business of millions of dollars yearly. At the inception of this enterprise the packing trust decided they would clean up the outfit, and for years kept sending trainloads of dressed beef into the State of Colorado and adjacent territories, and sold the beef for less than it cost them. For a time the Great Western Packing Company seemed to eat up money; two or three hundred thousand dollars weekly did not cut the slightest figure. One day the trust people came to the conclusion that it would be much cheaper to buy them out than fight them any longer. Swift & Company are now the owners of the property in question.

In conjunction with Mr. Boettcher, Mr. Campion also owns the Big Horn Land and Cattle Company, which has a very large estate and a large number of cattle running thereon. It is located in Jackson County close to the Wyoming line. Some of the finest Hereford cattle in the West have been raised and sold by the concern in question.

In conjunction with Mr. Boettcher, Mr. Campion built a powder and fuse plant, and sent men to Germany to become thoroughly posted in the manufacture of fuse. Later on this plant was sold to the powder trust at a satisfactory price.

While Mr. Campion contributed to the widespread development of Colorado's mineral resources, he has largely participated in developing the other industries of the State. He is a man of masterful executive ability, and has the reputation of being among the heaviest capitalists in Colorado. As a citizen he is generous, patriotic, progressive, and contributes liberally to all enterprises of a religious and philanthropic nature. With a vision of the future, he is today pushing forward great enterprises that will be powerful in shaping the destiny of Colorado.

He was largely the projector of the Colorado Museum of Natural History, which is for the benefit of the city of Denver and the State generally.

Mrs. J. F. Campion

Mrs. Campion is a woman of striking beauty and fine culture. She looks at the world from a broad view-point, and is noted for her work in charitable organizations.

Charles Boettcher

Charles Boettcher was one of the first merchants in Leadville. He established a hardware business in the cloud city and gave his attention to banking, mining and mercantile business, in all of which he was successful. He built the first electric light plant in Leadville, and has been president of that company from its organization.

He made his own way in the world, and became a shrewd observer and judge of local conditions. It was not long before he felt convinced that Denver was destined to become the commercial center of the Rocky Mountain region, and began to make investments in Denver. A few years later he made it his home, and has won a place in the roll of Colorado State builders. He was foremost in starting the sugar beet industry, and helped to steer its course through the trials of early years up to the mammoth accomplishments of the present.

Charles Boettcher

He was largely instrumental in making Denver the great central clearing house of live stock for the Rocky Mountain region.

He was the organizer of the Colorado Portland Cement Company. This industry is contributing to the permanent building of the State, in the culverts and bridges of railroads and highways, in the sidewalks of the cities, in embankments along the streams, in pipes for sewers, in ditch flumes and in the structure of buildings.

Mr. Charles Boettcher, while holding this triple claim to distinction in Colorado's industrial development, is still a young man, and is one of the active and energetic workers along many lines for the upbuilding of the City and State. His son, Mr. Claude Boettcher, is prominent among the younger leaders of public enterprises, and his beautiful and accomplished daughter is a social favorite.

Dr. Lewis Lemen

Dr. Lewis Lemen is a man of striking physical appearance, tall and finely proportioned, with a genial manner that makes him a fine type of the much-loved "family physician." He possesses a rare fund of humor, and enjoys telling stories of his early life in Colorado. He said:

"There is something in eating bacon and stale bread, side by side with a cabin mate, that makes very strong friends. I often think of my early days in Georgetown, and I often go there to look over the old ground and see the old friends. One day in 1873 I was called to see a patient, and had to travel over a winding mountain road. Coming to a place where the road widened, commonly called a turn-out, I stopped to let my horse pant for breath. A moment later Bishop Matz, a local priest, stopped his horse by the side of mine, and while we were talking, Henry Boyer, an undertaker, appeared on the scene. It struck me as a peculiar coincident, and I said in a joking way: 'I wonder if we three are going to the same place.' Upon comparing notes we found that we were going to different places. It was a relief to me, for a doctor dislikes to lose a patient.

"I am a walking advertisement for Colorado's great health-giving climate," continued the doctor. "I arrived in Denver in 1873 and registered at the American house. I was dressed in a light suit and wore a gray plug hat, which in those days was known as the Greeley hat. After breakfast I put on my coat and hat and started out to see what the town looked like. At that time there was a woodyard north of the hotel. I stepped upon the scales and balanced the beam —overcoat, hat and all—at one hundred and thirty-five pounds. Then I started up Sixteenth street and passed a store where a number of men were sitting around the door in the sunshine, and one remarked, 'Poor fellow, he's robbing the graveyard.' At the corner of Fifteenth and Curtis I passed another squad of loungers, and one man, with a motion of his head towards me, said: 'It looks as if he is trying to save funeral expenses.' After I gained my pres-

Dr. L. E. Lemen

ent avoirdupois my friends of those days call me the advertisement for Colorado as a health resort. And there were others, too, who came in the early days, not for gold, but for health—not so much for the cure of disease as for the prevention of the development of disease.

"The merits of Colorado as a sanitarium, especially for those in the early stages of tuberculosis of the lungs, have attracted wide attention. This climatic advantage has been one of the really important elements in the development of the State, for many of the invalids who came here in the early days reached an almost complete recovery from their illness and took an active part in the work of State building."

Dr. Lemen is so well informed in every branch of his profession that he was asked to write a chapter on the medical profession in Smiley's Centennial History of Colorado. He is a public-spirited man, and ranks among the successful men who have made possible the Denver of today. His home in Denver, where he has lived for the past twenty-five years, is one of the most elegant in the city. He is cultured and refined in his tastes and delightfully interesting in conversation. He and his kind, affable wife have a large circle of friends and acquaintances.

Charles S. Thomas

Senator Charles S. Thomas came to Colorado in December, 1871, began the practice of law in Denver and, except in the intervals of his public life, has followed that profession constantly. His objective point when leaving the East was California, but a recent census of Denver, completed the day before his arrival, showing an increase in its population of one hundred per cent in twelve months, followed by the enthusiastic comments of the local press as to immediate future growth, induced him to cast his lot in Colorado.

In 1873 he formed a partnership with Honorable T. M. Patterson, which, broken by a short interval, continued until 1889. A portion of this time Mr. Thomas resided in Leadville. Mr. Thomas was city attorney of Denver in 1875 and 1876; governor of the State in 1899-1900; was elected to the United States Senate in 1912 for the unexpired term of the late Honorable Charles J. Hughes, and was re-elected in 1914 for the succeeding six years.

Mr. Thomas always insists that he is indebted to the counsel, companionship and affection of his wife for whatever success or prominence he may have attained in law, politics or society.

Chas. S. Thomas

Isaac N. Stevens

Isaac Newton Stevens has always been a State builder from the time he came to Colorado, a mere boy.

Early in his career he identified himself with the great commercial and industrial bodies of the State, and no railroad or other enterprise for the benefit or development of the State has been inaugurated that has not had his active support.

Mr. Stevens and the late Earl B. Coe took the initial steps by which sugar beets were introduced into Colorado.

The Great State Building Epoch

They investigated the growing of beets in Nebraska, and determined that the Colorado soil was better adapted to sugar beet growing than was the soil of Nebraska.

They met the practical problem by having themselves placed on a specially created Chamber of Commerce committee, and by inducing John F. Campion to become president of the Chamber of Commerce and give his powerful aid to the enterprise.

They sent to the Agricultural Department at Washington and obtained enough seed for the first year's experiment, and several farmers were induced to plant the seed, and after that first experimental year the growing of sugar beets in Colorado went with a rush.

Isaac N. Stevens

From the inception of the Moffat railroad to the present day Mr. Stevens has been one of its most ardent champions, both as an individual and as proprietor of the Pueblo Chieftain.

In his line of public work Mr. Stevens has owned and edited the Colorado Springs Gazette and the Pueblo Chieftain, and both of these newspapers, under his management, were great powers for public good.

He has written two political novels, "The Liberators" and "An American Suffragette," which have had a large sale in the United States, and both of which have had a marked influence upon American political affairs.

Mr. Stevens has believed that one of the weaknesses

of government in this country was a lack of equipment and training on the part of public officials, and he spent five years in traveling to every section of the globe to study governmental conditions and problems, to the end that he might make his public work more effective.

Mr. Stevens was one of the early men advocates of woman's suffrage. When the question was submitted in Colorado, 1893, Mr. Stevens campaigned the State and raised a considerable portion of the funds for the success of the cause. Since the adoption of suffrage in Colorado Mr. Stevens has campaigned in several eastern States for the woman's cause. He is an able lawyer. As city attorney he displayed fine ability; as a public speaker he is argumentative and forceful; as reader and thinker he keeps himself in touch with the current thought of the time.

John W. Springer

JOHN W. SPRINGER

Mr. John W. Springer came to Denver in 1896, attracted to this glorious climate in the hope of benefiting his wife. His first interest in public affairs was in connection with the late Senator Edward O. Wolcott in making a fight in Colorado for the gold standard.

During the next ten years he built what is known as the "Springer castle," on South Broadway overlooking the city of Denver, and which is surrounded by an estate of 11,000 acres. It is one of the show-places of the entire country.

He became vice-president of the Chamber of Commerce under Mr. John Campion, and vigorously aided in the establishment of the sugar beet industry in this State.

With others he organized the National Live Stock Association, with headquarters in Denver, and was for ten years its active head.

In 1902 he organized the Continental Trust Company, and aided in purchasing the Continental building at Sixteenth and Lawrence streets.

Mr. Springer also aided in organizing the Capitol National Bank, which was afterwards consolidated with the First National Bank of this city.

Mr. Springer also took an enthusiastic part in securing the purchase of the enlargement of the Denver Union Stock Yards and the packing houses, which is one of Denver's greatest assets.

Mr. Springer has aided very many permanent enterprises which are now firmly established in the State of Colorado, notably the Fountain Valley Land and Irrigation Company at Colorado Springs, the Teller Reservoir and Irrigation Company at Pueblo, and the North Platte Canal and Colonization Company, and many others which have been and will be instrumental in bringing thousands of new home-seekers to Colorado. Mr. Springer has always taken the position that Colorado money should be kept at home and that all Colorado enterprises should be heartily supported by the financial interests of the State. Many corporations now doing business in the city of Denver have been supported by him in season and out of season, and his greatest pleasure has been taken in being known as a builder.

Denver's Clubs

The Denver Club owes its existence to the great rush to Denver in 1880. It is a social organization for the business and professional men of the city.

The membership is limited to three hundred resident and two hundred non-resident members. The fine club house, on the corner of Glenarm and Seventeenth, is one of the elegant establishments of its kind west of New York.

The University Club was incorporated January 29, 1891. According to the constitution, "any man shall be eligible to membership in this club who has received from a university or college a degree, to obtain which in regular course at least two years' residence and study are required, or who shall have received an honorary degree from such university or college, or who shall have graduated at the United States Military Academy or at the United States Naval Academy; provided that a candidate who holds an honorary degree only shall be distinguished in art, literature, science or public service; and provided that professional degrees shall entitle to membership only when given by such university or college as shall be designated by the board of directors, and the list of such universities and colleges shall be posted in the rooms of the club."

The Denver Athletic Club was incorporated April 4, 1884. Its objects are as follows:

"That the particular business and objects for which said corporation is formed are to purchase or build and to hold, maintain and operate a gymnasium in the city of Denver, county of Arapahoe, for the amusement, recreation and physical culture of all those who may at any time become members thereof; and also for the purpose of encouraging all proper athletic sports and pastimes of every kind and nature whatsoever."

How Denver Was Made the City of Lights

In 1898 the Denver Consolidated Electric Company and the Denver Consolidated Gas Company were merged

The Great State Building Epoch

in the Denver Gas and Electric Light Company. This new organization brought a commanding personality into Denver's life. Henry L. Doherty was placed at the head of the light company and immediately began a very active and aggressive campaign to give Denver a splendid lighting and power service. Mr. Doherty introduced modern methods in the conduct of this utility and soon made it very apparent that the light company would become an active factor in the upbuilding of the city. He announced that the policy of the organization would be to increase the growth of Denver, and that in doing this work he would not only be helping the prosperity of every citizen, but would also contribute much towards producing dividends for his own company.

Henry L. Doherty

When Mr. Doherty began his work here Denver was poorly illuminated, and he set about to make it the best lighted city in America. One of the first features of this campaign was a movement to build a welcome arch at the Union depot. A number of prominent citizens co-operated with Mr. Doherty in this work, and the result was a magnificent welcome arch, which has since blazed a hearty welcome to every visitor coming within Denver's gates. Following the erection of the welcome arch came a movement to establish the most modern street lighting on Fifteenth, Sixteenth and Seventeenth streets. The lighting of these streets is far ahead of anything of its kind in the country. The popularity of lavish illumination soon spread, and Denver became famous all over the country as "the City of Lights."

The crowning glory of "the City of Lights" was the erection of the Gas and Electric building, which is admitted to be the most artistically illuminated structure in the world. The architects and skilled illuminating engineers collaborated in planning this structure, and the result is an artistic triumph in exterior illumination. The building is studded with 13,000 incandescent lamps of various sizes, giving a total of 200,000 candlepower. It is a splendid monument to Denver enterprise, and has become one of the great show places of the city. The building is built on a deep foundation of granite and concrete, and stands like a night-blooming cereus, a luminous glory to the city, a surprise to tourists, and a splendor before which art must bow its head. It has the simple, majestic architectural lines of the Italian Renaissance, and with its clear, cloud-white surface, ideal for the illumination that suffuses it at night, suggests the product of the jeweler rather than the worker in stone and mortar. Walter Juan Davis, for many years the

Denver Gas & Electric Building

The Great State Building Epoch

Curtis Street—Night View

poet of the Denver Post, dedicated the following poem to the building:

NO NIGHT—ALL LIGHT

With amazement on his face,
Gazing down from some high place,
    Stands the aborigine,
Wondering at all the light,
Muttering the words, "No night"—
    Utterly dumbfounded, he.

Flaming, flaming heaven-high,
What is this that pales the sky,
    Lights up earth and air and all?
Smoking tepee, flickering flame—
What are they since all this came?
    Meaningless, and O, so small!

>   Thus the aborigine;
>   And we others, what say we
>   Of this ever-wondrous thing,
>   Born of mystery and space,
>   Caught and brought from every place,
>   All the earth a-quickening?
>
>   When God said, "Let there be light!"
>   He had read all time aright,
>   And He lit the lambent sun;
>   Now He looks with pleased eyes
>   On the earth—light in the skies—
>   And His royal will is done.

Dr. Pfeiffer's Prophecy

(Dated) Denver, Colo., July 13, 1915.

Within one hundred years Denver will be the capital of the United States, for the same reason that put $750,000,000 in gold in the Denver mint just prior to the present Anglo-Germanic war; and that reason is: safety from foreign attack by water, for it is fifteen hundred miles from the Great Lakes, the Gulf of Mexico and the Pacific ocean. An enemy would have to defeat our army, which could dig itself in for fifteen hundred miles in all directions in a defense of Denver.

Washington, easily captured in 1812, in the next foreign war would soon fall a prey to a hostile fleet equipped with aeroplanes, which, with bombs, in one night could destroy priceless value in the government buildings and cause Congress to adjourn in a hurry.

In Denver the government would also find the finest climate in the temperate zone for the Anglo-Saxon race, and Congress could sit summer and winter, day and night, and work in comfort the year round. Government buildings located around Cheesman park would command a view said by Bayard Taylor to be the finest panorama of mountain scenery in the world.

A capitol located where now is the Catholic cemetery, with a government building in the center of each block all the way around the park, all built of Colorado Yule marble, would form the grandest court of honor ever erected by the hand of man, and it would only be exceeded in beauty and grandeur by the snowy range opposite, whose summit is adorned by the handiwork of God.

CHAPTER XXXVI

A GREATER COLORADO

The Chamber of Commerce and Board of Trade

No part of our nation has achieved so much in so brief a period as Colorado, and Denver, the metropolis of the State, is again building upon new and broader foundations.

The early pioneers began casting about for some means of transportation other than ox teams, and those engaged in commercial trading met and formed a Board of Trade, in order to work together to induce the railroads to extend their lines to Denver. So, in 1867, was organized the first

BOARD OF TRADE OF DENVER

President....................John W. Smith
Vice-Presidents.....John Pierce, Isaac Brinker
Secretary...................Henry C. Leach
Treasurer...................Frank Palmer

Directors:

William M. Clayton	J. H. Morrison
F. Z. Salomon	J. M. Strickler
George Tritch	D. H. Moffat
R. E. Whitsitt	J. S. Brown

In 1884 the Chamber of Commerce was organized on a broader scale than the original Board of Trade, but the two bodies to some extent covered the same field, and to that extent were rivals. The leading members of both organizations felt that a single body could accomplish more for the city than two rival ones, and in 1885 they agreed to consolidate. The result was the present Chamber of Commerce and Board of Trade.

The Great State Building Epoch 513

Mr. Wm. Todd was the treasurer of both bodies prior to the consolidation, and was very active in perfecting the change. He was made treasurer of the consolidated organization.

Since that time every new enterprise tending toward the growth and development of the City and State has been fostered by the Chamber of Commerce.

Through the efforts of the Chamber, during the term of office of John F. Campion, the great sugar beet industry was born. A little later, under the untiring

Birdseye View of Denver

energy of John W. Springer, while president of the Chamber, the Union Stock Yards was made possible.

The Chamber has persistently carried on a campaign of publicity since its organization to exploit the undeveloped resources of the State. It gave its aid to organize the Trans-Mississippi Dry Farming Congress, the National Irrigation Congress and many other enterprises of like character.

The great reclamation project of the Rocky Mountain region was accomplished by the aid of the Chamber through its representatives in Congress. The first headquarters of the enterprise was established in the Chamber of Commerce building on Fourteenth and Lawrence streets.

The Chamber has been instrumental in having the bill passed by Congress forming the Rocky Mountain National Park.

T. B. Stearns

The Chamber made the preparation for the holding of the International Farm Congress and the International Soil Products Exposition in Denver in October, 1915.

Because of the wise and efficient administration of Mr. Thomas B. Stearns, he was re-elected to the position of president. Mr. Stearns is a man of courage and enterprising dash; he has the creative and constructive forces of intellect, united with an unusual capacity for organization. He has given attention to politics without seeking office, has been broadened by extensive reading and by a study of the conditions essential to achieve success in great undertakings.

The Great State Building Epoch

He is ranked with the men who have been foremost in promotion, as well as leaders in the social, political and commercial life of the State.

Mr. Stearns is a director of the United States Chamber of Commerce, which, as its name implies, is by far the most powerful business combination in the United States, and the Denver Chamber will be a strong factor in the work of that organization.

A new organization has recently been launched—the State Chamber of Commerce—with Thomas B. Stearns president, which will be a power in the future development of the State. Every town and hamlet in the State will be represented in the State Chamber, and all matters pertaining to development of any legislation that affects the State in any way will be handled through the State organization. This will insure mutual co-operation from every part of the State, and results are sure to follow.

The secretary, Mr. Thorndike Deland, is energetic and evinces fine ability in the duties of his office.

"The Commercial" is published every Thursday by the Chamber under its able editor, Mr. Johnson. It is a live wire in pushing forward the enterprises of the organization.

The Moffat Tunnel

The Chamber of Commerce, under its energetic and capable president, Mr. Yetter, initiated and pushed forward a scheme for the completion of the Moffat tunnel, as follows:

When Newman Erb, president of the railroad company, asked the people of Denver to take part with him in the construction of this tunnel, which would greatly shorten the distance between Denver and Salt Lake City, there was found to be a charter provision against the issuing of bonds for the assistance of private enterprises, and one which prohibits the maturity of any of the city's obligations being carried to a period of fifty years. To remedy these objections the people of Denver, on the 20th of May, 1913, voted for an amendment to the charter which provides that the city loan its credit for the construction of a tunnel through James Peak.

The contract was then drawn up and signed by Jesse E. Fleming, Charles MacAllister Willcox and Joseph C. Helm, the commissioners on behalf of the city, and Newman Erb for the railroad company.

For the construction of the tunnel a survey was made and an estimation of the cost prepared by three of the most distinguished engineers in the country— J. Vipond Davies of New York, D. W. Brunton and J. Wellington Finch of Denver.

The survey of these men, supplemented by a study of the region made by Professor R. D. George, state geologist, was reported to the commission. The site chosen is at an altitude of 9,100 feet, and involves a tunnel six miles long. They estimated the cost at $4,500,000, of which the city's share would be $3,000,000.

On February 17, 1914, an election was held to vote the bonds. Mrs. Alice Polk Hill was appointed chairman of the woman's committee. She succeeded in arousing the interest of the women in the importance of the tunnel to the City of Denver and the State. A vigorous campaign was made, and the issue carried.

A suit was then brought before Judge George W. Allen of the district court to test the legality of the bonds. Judge Allen, a man with a profound knowledge of the law, who has been on the bench for twenty years, decided the bonds legal. The suit was then carried to the supreme court, where the bonds were decided illegal, and the enterprise turned down.

Judge William H. Gabbert, whose record on the bench has been that of an able and impartial judge, gave a dissenting opinion, setting forth the legality of the bonds. However, the commission, which was appointed by the business organizations of the city, is still at work devising ways and means to build the tunnel, which the majority believe, as shown by the campaign vote, will pour new life into the veins of Denver, and be a lasting monument to the genius of planning and daring of David H. Moffat, "the conquerer of the mountains."

William H. Gabbert

Jesse E. Fleming, the president of the commission, is a man of quick decision, keen judgment and tireless industry. He owes his sucess in life to his inborn capacity for hard work. Whatever the business at hand, he spares himself no amount of labor until he has a thorough knowledge of every phase of it.

In 1893, when the entire country was struggling

Jesse E. Fleming

with financial disaster, Jesse E. Fleming, in spite of the uncompromising conditions, employed workmen and kept on building houses. He helped to give Denver a new lease on life. Because of his faith in the future of the city, and his tenacity in buying real estate, he is called the builder of South Broadway.

He is loyal to his friends, has a full appreciation of the rights of others, and conducts business along the lines of justice and integrity. All movements which tend to the material and social benefit of the State receive his strong support. He is a business man of whom any community might be proud.

Charles MacAllister Willcox is a young man of keen business instincts and rare good judgment. While he is the most approachable of men, he is quick to detect fraud. It would be difficult to impose upon him. He is general manager of the Daniels and Fisher stores, a student of financial conditions, and keeps himself in touch with the current thought of the time. His close application to business is the secret of his success. Always at his post, he gives himself to the routine of his duties, and holds a sure, strong grasp upon the work before him. In his dealings with others his honesty is unquestioned. When once his friendship is given, it can be relied upon in adversity as well as in prosperity, and he is ever ready to help a worthy charity to the extent of his ability.

Charles MacAllister Willcox

He considers the Moffat tunnel a public enterprise which means greater success for the city and also for the individual; hence he looks upon the position of commissioner as a duty in rank or importance with personal interest, and gives it ardent support and willing work.

*Joseph C. Helm is a gentleman in the highest sense of the term. His legal knowledge is profound and his penetrating intellect sees to the heart of a matter at once.

He was elected to the position of supreme judge when only thirty-six years old—the youngest supreme judge that has ever sat upon the bench in Colorado.

He came to Denver from Colorado Springs, built a beautiful residence, and, as he is a home-lover, he spends most of his leisure time there.

He is a man upright in character, with exemplary habits. His kindness of heart has endeared him to many friends. In a quiet way he has been a vital factor in the building of Denver.

LIBRARY

The Denver Library Association was organized in 1876 by a number of public-spirited men, many of them taking life memberships at $50.00 each; and a very good library, reading room and gymnasium was opened on Larimer street between Sixteenth and Seventeenth. It ran about two years and was forced to quit, leaving quite an indebtedness to Mr. Walter S. Cheesman for rent, and to Mr. W. D. Todd, the treasurer, for money advanced. Mr. Todd and Mr. Cheesman do-

Wm. D. Todd

*Recently passed away.

nated the books to the city school board, conditional upon the library being kept open to the public and made the nucleus of a general public library.

M. J. McNamara was a member of the Board of Trade, and in 1884 was one of the committee of three appointed to build the Chamber of Commerce on Fourteenth and Lawrence.

Roger W. Woodbury was president of the Denver Chamber of Commerce in 1885, and Mr. M. J. McNamara was vice-president. One of Mr. Woodbury's early acts was to formulate a plan for a public library, there being no State law under which one could be established and maintained by a municipality. At a meeting of the directors it was voted:

"That a room be set apart in the Chamber of Commerce building for a library, to be known as the Mercantile Library of the City of Denver, under the auspices of the Chamber of Commerce." In order to carry out this plan it was necessary to increase the size of the proposed building, and this was done by adding a fourth story.

It was a unique idea for an organization whose object was to promote the commercial, financial and industrial interests of the city to enter the library field, but the members recognized the necessity for it, and too great praise cannot be given for the work so wisely planned and so well carried out.

Establishing the first free library here remains the crowning act of that organization. It had more than local significance, for it was the first free library between the Missouri river and the Pacific coast.

The committee which had charge during the actual formation of the library was: M. J. McNamara, chairman; Dr. Henry K. Steele, secretary; Chester S. Morey, Fred Z. Salomon, Alfred Butters, David H. Moore and Frank C. Young.

The Great State Building Epoch

In 1886 Mr. McNamara resigned the vice-presidency, and was appointed chairman of the library committee. It was found necessary to raise a fund by popular subscription to establish a public library. Mr. McNamara and Mr. C. S. Morey raised the first money that started the library. To Mr. Charles R. Dudley was given the work of purchasing the first books. The library was opened November, 1886, in the Chamber of Commerce building, under the name of the Mercantile Library of Denver, with 30,000 volumes for circulation. Mr. Dudley, who had ably performed his task, was appointed librarian.

In 1891 the expenses reached a point where the Chamber found it difficult to meet them, and an appeal for assistance was made to the City Council. This resulted in an appropriation of $500 a month, one-half of which was devoted to the purchase of books. During the succeeding seven years the council annually set aside sums varying from $5,000 to $8,000 for the library. In 1893, in recognition of this aid, the name was changed from "The Mercantile" to "The City Library."

In 1897 the General Assembly passed an excellent library law, drawn by members of the library committee, and soon after it was learned that the City Council was willing to act under its provisions. Correspondence between the library committee and the board of education, which had been conducting a free library for nearly a decade in the East Denver High School building, resulted in an agreement that when the necessary ordinance was enacted, each would give its books to the city. The Council passed the ordinance, and the Public Library of the City of Denver came into existence on the 13th of August, 1898.

Because of his untiring energy in the work of creating the Public Library, Mr. McNamara was made honorary member of the Chamber of Commerce. He was a public-spirited man and an active worker in many organizations for the bettering and uplifting of Denver and Colorado, and his early death was a great loss to the community.

The consolidation of the libraries, which took place the following year, made it necessary to secure more ex-

M. J. McNAMARA ■ ROGER W. WOODBURY ■ CHARLES R. DUDLEY

tensive quarters, and a two-story building on two lots was erected on the east corner of Fifteenth street and Court place, under a five years' lease. This was opened to the public on the library's thirteenth birthday.

In January, 1902, the directors bought the ground on which the new building has been erected.

In February, 1902, through the offices of Mr. W. L. Palm, an offer of $200,000 for a building was made by

Mr. Andrew Carnegie, a man who, more than all others combined, has given wisely and lavishly for the upbuilding of that great educational factor—the public library.

Of the $70,000 needed for the building above what Mr. Carnegie gave, $35,000 was furnished by special appropriation. The balance was taken from the book fund. The total expenditure for the ground, building, furniture and fixtures was about $430,000.

The building combines the beauties of the highest types of both Grecian and Roman architecture, and as a perpetual educational factor in the life of Denver it speaks for itself, in a silent, yet eloquent, language.

Chalmers Hadley

The library has an annual appropriation of $65,000. The books have increased to 167,630 volumes. Mr. Chalmers Hadley is now librarian. He is held in high esteem because of his ability, energy and efficiency in directing the affairs of the library.

The enterprises enumerated show that during its thirty years of continuous service to the City and State the Chamber of Commerce has met the needs for which it was organized.

CHAPTER XXX

PIONEER WORK OF TODAY

Present Day Pioneers

The pioneers of the past saw clearly and wrought wisely, and the pioneers of today—men of ability, courage and strong resolve, guided by the knowledge of what has been done—are now engaged in the fascinating work of State building, and planning for other triumphs.

Chester S. Morey

No one can think of Denver men without calling to mind Chester Stephen Morey, at present president of the Great Western Sugar Company, and who has done more to build up the sugar industry of the western States to its present surpassing importance than any other half dozen people. Mr. Morey takes pride in the fact that he is neither a politician nor a reformer, nor does he seek the limelight of publicity. He claims to be nothing but a faithful, hard-working man, who won his rank among the captains of industry by tireless and unceasing efforts. He is now daily seated in a building, as the head of this great sugar corporation, in which he but presses a button to give the world his orders. He credits his success to hard work; he says that his start was due to faithful attention to details in a cellar in a place where he worked as porter.

Mr. Morey was born on a farm in Dane County, Wisconsin, in the year 1847. His birthplace was in what was at the time called "the wilderness of the Northwest," and until he was ten years of age he often went to bed hungry, and went about suffering from cold for want of an overcoat. Poverty made him, when a boy of but nine years of age, one of America's serious little men, and at this early age he took up life's burdens, going to work on his father's farm. He did not fall in love with the occupation of a farmer. Folks lived too far apart, and getting about was too difficult. He was sociable in his yearnings, and the isolation of the country life that all young embryo farmers led caused him to abandon that pursuit, and strike out on lines for himself, in the more congenial surroundings of towns and cities. At this time his chief aim was to obtain an education, and he put by hard-earned pennies to this end.

C. S. Morey

Mr. Morey came to Colorado in 1872. He claims to be the pioneer salesman of the West. As a traveling salesman, which he had before that time taken up, he covered an unusually wide scope of territory—Colorado, New Mexico, Idaho, Utah, Nevada and California. There was little traveling done in those days by train—the stage coaches, a horse or a mule were the traveling facilities of which he was compelled to avail himself. So well did he succeed as a traveling salesman that in 1881 he was taken into the firm of Sprague, Warner & Company as a partner, and he opened a branch of that firm in Denver. A few years later he bought out the Chicago firm's Denver interests, and the C. S. Morey Mercantile Company was substituted for the then famous house of Sprague, Warner & Company. Since that time his interests have been identified with the making of the State's history.

Mr. Morey takes his success in a typical American way. Looking down from great heights makes some men dizzy, but Mr. Morey has kept his head cool. He is the same frank, genial and generous spirit that he was in his very earliest days when he cultivated geniality, frankness and generosity to help along his business as a salesman.

The Denver Club, the Denver Athletic Club and the Country Club all rejoice in Mr. Morey's membership and in the good cheer he scatters about their halls and grounds when he visits them.

As Mr. Morey moves about in Denver one would know that he is on good terms with life. Time has dealt kindly with him, and fortune, which has brought him so many favors, has in no wise spoiled him.

Verner Z. Reed

Mr. Verner Z. Reed, who has been actively engaged in development of various kinds in Colorado and Wyoming for many years, is now chiefly interested in the development of the Salt Creek and other oil fields in Wyoming, which work, in connection with its representative companies, the Midwest Refining Company and the

Midwest Oil Company, occupies a great deal of the time which he devotes to business. Mr. Reed is also interested in the development and construction of irrigation works in Wyoming, as he has been at times past in Colorado. He was one of the pioneers in the Cripple Creek district, and continues to have large interests in that district.

A considerable part of Mr. Reed's time is devoted to matters relating to the charitable institutions of Denver and to matters for the common good.

Mr. Reed has done a great deal of international financing for Colorado and Wyoming enterprises, including the introduction of Cripple Creek mining securities on the London stock market, some sixteen years ago.

Verner Z. Reed

Tyson S. Dines

Honorable Tyson S. Dines is one of the marked and public-spirited men of the State. Since removing to

Colorado some twenty years ago he has been actively associated with many of the State's important public events, and following the death of Winfield S. Stratton, of whose estate he was appointed one of the executors and trustees, he, in conjunction with his co-trustees, commenced the erection of the Stratton Home at Colorado Springs, which has become one of the institutions of that beautiful and thrifty city, and is now in active and successful operation.

T. S. Dines

Mr. Dines was born in Fayette, Missouri, in 1858. He received a collegiate education, and commenced his active life as an educator, in which calling he won substantial fame. Later in life he became a practicing attorney, and is now recognized here in Colorado as one of the most successful of that learned profession. He is the attorney of a number of the great corporations of the State, as well as the trustee of a number of the boards of its different charitable and eleemosynary institutions. He was a member of the Denver school board for two terms, trustee of the State Board for Dependent and Neglected Children under four governors, a trustee of Denver University and of the Agnes Memorial Sanatorium in the suburbs of Denver. Taking it all in all, there are few men in the West of wider and greater activities, or more generally trusted and admired.

LAWRENCE C. PHIPPS

Mr. Lawrence Cowle Phipps, though only a resident of this State for the past fourteen years, has in that time become one of its foremost builders because of the power of statesmanship and quality of public-spiritedness he possesses.

He was born in Amwell Township, Washington County, Pennsylvania, August 13, A. D. 1862, and from the age of five years was reared and educated in Pittsburgh, where he resided until he removed to Colorado. He graduated from high school at the age of sixteen, shortly afterward entering the office of Carnegie Brothers & Company, Ltd., progressing in the steel business with various affiliated companies to the positions of assistant treasurer, treasurer, vice-president and member of the board of managers, until the companies with which he was associated were finally absorbed by the United States Steel Corporation, on April 1, 1901, when he retired from active business.

Lawrence C. Phipps

The fall of that year he brought his family to Denver to reside—being attracted to the State by its unsurpassed climatic conditions—since which time he has become identified with all forward movements in the

City and State, encouraging by gift and service the charity organizations and those for the advancement of the fine arts; while, latterly, his influence as a builder has been felt by both City and State as the head of the Colorado Tax Payers' Protective League in its endeavors to free the City and State of hampering influences and to stimulate a unity of interest and action not only on the part of "the powers that be," but that of each individual citizen, for the ultimate good of all.

Mr. Phipps is primarily identified with the State of Colorado by having built and endowed, in the year 1905, at a cost of $700,000, the Agnes Memorial Sanatorium, an institution located in the suburbs of Denver for the treatment of pulmonary tuberculosis, which has proved a blessing to humanity far beyond the confines of this State.

Next in importance of his activities might be considered his connection with the Denver and Salt Lake railroad, more popularly known as the "Moffat Road," as he has been for some years one of the leading spirits of this enterprise, which embraces two hundred and fifty miles of road, wholly within the State of Colorado, which has done much toward the development of the State in general, having opened up to commerce some of the richest coal and other mineral lands in the United States.

John F. Shafroth

John F. Shafroth came from Fayette, Missouri, to Denver in 1879, and from that time he has been identified with the growth of the City and State, and has been active in projects for the advancement and upbuilding, not only of Colorado, but of the entire West.

During his service in Congress from 1894 to 1904 he urgently championed all measures before that body which looked to the welfare and betterment of the western part of the United States, and actively participated in dealing with questions of national and international import. It was during that period, and under his leadership, that the first agitation for the establishment of national parks in Colorado was started, which was finally culminated in the establishment, not only of the Mesa Verde National Park, but has gone even further and led in the last year to the creation of the Rocky Mountain National Park through united action of the Colorado senators and representatives.

It was while he was in Congress that he delivered a speech on the silver question in defense of the position of the western States of the Union that was considered by many advocates of bimetallism to be absolutely unanswerable.

During his term in Congress he was very eager to uphold the traditions of his State by advocating the cause of the weak and oppressed against the aggressions of the strong.

At the time of both the Boer and Philippine Wars

John F. Shafroth

he earnestly pressed upon Congress, in speeches that were printed by the thousands, and circulated throughout the United States, the duty of the United States to stand by its traditions and uphold truth and justice in their dealings and in the dealings of other nations with a small and numerically inferior people. It was this same love of justice that early in life converted him to the cause of woman suffrage and spurred him on to champion its cause throughout his public life.

Probably the work of Mr. Shafroth which was of more material benefit to the people of Colorado than any other one thing was his action in pushing through the House of Representatives in 1902 the so-called reclamation bill, which has meant so much to the development of the arid lands of the West. It was due to the passage of this bill that the enormous development of irrigable lands in the West received its first tremendous impetus.

The numerous slanders that were at one time cast upon Colorado relative to the men there elected to offices were most emphatically disproved by the action of Mr. Shafroth in voluntarily retiring from Congress on finding that the general election at which he was a candidate for Congress was tainted with fraud.

During his term as governor his efforts were largely directed to bringing about a more democratic form of government and abolishing certain evils that had grown up in the State. The passage of the initiative and referendum, the direct primary, the election of United States senators by direct vote of the people, and the headless ballot law was the culmination of this work. Great strides were also taken in the upbuilding of the State educational institutions, improvement in the State penitentiary and the betterment of the roads of the State.

During his term in the Senate the chief work with which he has been connected was the framing and passage of the federal reserve act of 1913, which is universally declared throughout the country to be a boon to every State and section of the Union. Besides the enormous amount of work undertaken by Mr. Shafroth and the three other senators who were mainly instrumental in framing and passing the so-called banking and currency bill, he was able also to obtain the passage of numerous measures looking to the relief and advancement of the settlers of Colorado. His bill for the relief of desert entrymen and his so-called summer homestead act, looking to a further and greater use of our mountain country, form a part of his work for the betterment and upbuilding of Colorado.

Mrs. John F. Shafroth

Mrs. John F. Shafroth is an unusual woman; while she belongs to numerous organizations, and her influence is felt in all of them, she has no desire to hold office. Her ambition is to keep step in the world of progress. She is interested in all subjects that claim the attention of her husband, and through her finely trained mind she is his constant helper, sharing in his plans and work.

Her education has been broadened by extensive reading and by culture obtained in travel. She is active in club work, enjoys the social side of life, and one of her distinctive traits is her steadfast loyalty to her friends.

Some Present Day Activities

The cornerstone of Colorado was laid of gold and silver, and while she steadily holds her position in the front rank of the producers of the precious metals, she has a rich store of common metals—lead, zinc and copper. Her mineral output includes tungsten, bismuth, vanadium and uranium; other substances, such as sulphur, manganese and graphite, are found in large quantities. Colorado marble is the finest in the country. Colorado is one of the great coal States; her beds of clay

Manufacturers' Association Banquet—Eating Home Products

are of countless variety and vast extent; she has immense bodies of iron ore, of lime, and mountains of building stone.

The distinguishing feature of Colorado's development today is her great variety of industries—mining, agriculture and manufacturing. The vast deposits of coal, iron and stone mineral have been made to pour forth their quota of wealth and enable the establishing of manufactures of almost every description.

The Manufacturers' Association, as its name implies, is strictly an organization composed of manufacturers.

A company has to have its general offices in the State, and manufacture here fifty-one per cent of its products before it is eligible for membership. These restrictions enable the members to handle with success problems which cannot be taken up by other organizations representing diversified lines of business.

The principal purpose of the association is to upbuild and protect the manufacturing industry of the State. Added to that is the work of creating and enlarging a home market for Colorado-made goods. It conducts educational campaigns on the necessity of citizens being loyal to the local interests; it looks after building contracts, inspection of factories by health departments, watches legislation and reaches out in many other directions.

W. J. H. Doran, who was most active in organizing the association, was chosen for its first president, and in April, 1915, he was elected to succeed himself in recognition of the excellent work he had performed.

The Denver Real Estate Exchange, which stimulates interest and activity in real estate investments, is an up-to-date association. The Denver Real Estate Advertiser, ably edited by Halsey M. Rhoads, fosters and maintains a cordial co-operation among the members, and publishes facts and statistics useful to the association and the public.

E. B. Morgan

The Colorado Taxpayers' Protective League, though only about a year old, is a pioneer in its line. About one hundred of our leading citizens, contributing their time and money, are endeavoring to improve the tax conditions and public expenditures of our City and State for the benefit of every taxpayer.

Mr. Edward B. Morgan, chairman of the executive committee of the league, has been appointed by Governor Carlson a member of the Colorado Tax Commission. Mr. Morgan is deeply interested in Colorado and her welfare; he steadfastly adheres to the belief that Denver is destined to become a great city, and proves his faith by making himself one of the leaders in its upbuilding at the present time. Mr. Morgan is convinced that there is a chance for constructive labor on taxation subjects.

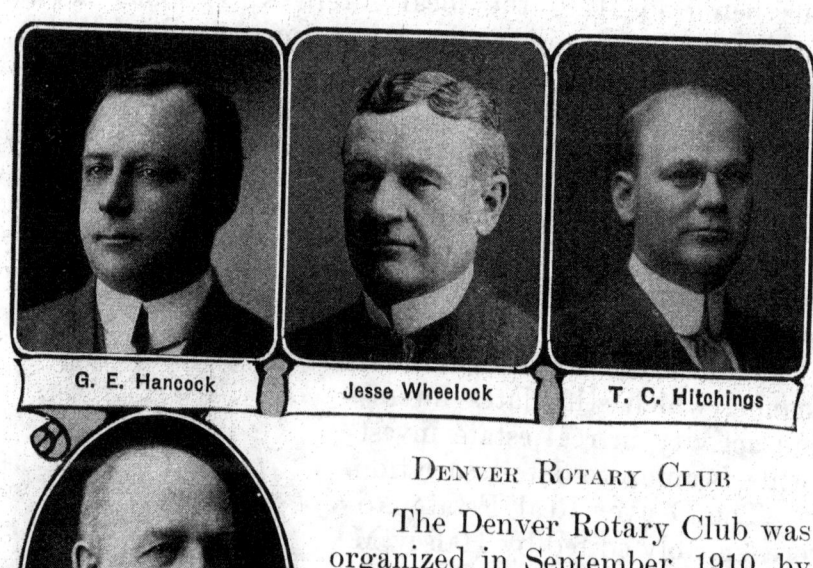

Denver Rotary Club

The Denver Rotary Club was organized in September, 1910, by Gratton E. Hancock. Its charter membership was approximately twenty-five. It has grown to a membership in 1915 of about one hundred and fifty. The accompanying picture shows its four presidents since its organization in Denver.

The idea of rotary clubs originated with Paul P. Harris, an attorney in Chicago, who is known as the "Father of Rotary," and the first club was organized in 1905 in that city. The idea rapidly spread, until at the present time there are one hundred and eighty-six clubs in the United States, Canada and Great Britain, with a total membership of 20,900. These clubs are formed into what is known as the International Association of Rotary Clubs, with international officers and directors.

The unique feature of each club is that only one member is permitted from each line of business or profession. In this respect it is different from all other clubs. Its object is acquaintance and good fellowship among leading men in every line of trade, believing that in this way much good may be done the community in general through the organized efforts of the club as a whole.

Rotary is described as an expression of the faith of the modern man in himself, of his realization that he can be true to himself only when he is true to his neighbor, and no matter how many wheels of contact his own life may impinge, the direction of his turning must be toward kindly judgment, efficient sympathy and neighborliness.

The slogan of the club, "Service, not Self," sums up its ideals and exemplifies, when properly carried out, the aphorism that "he profits most who serves best," which was coined for use in Rotary by one of its first members.

The Colorado Mountain Club is organized to unite the energy, interests and knowledge of the students, explorers and lovers of the mountains of Colorado; to collect and disseminate information regarding them; to stimulate public interest; to encourage the preservation of natural conditions, and to render the mountains accessible.

Governors of Colorado

It has grown since 1912, when it was organized, to a membership of about three hundred, with members all over the United States. Its activities cover a very wide range. It conducts an annual camp in the mountains for two weeks during August, runs a series of week-end excursions of one to three days into the mountains throughout the year, arranges a series of winter public lectures upon natural history and mountaineering subjects, which are very largely attended, and has devoted a great deal of time and money to movements such as the establishment of the Rocky Mountain National Park, the collection of a library, lantern slides and pictorial records of the mountains, the protection of flowers and birds by publicity on that subject, the encouragement of natural history subjects, and the investigation of the Indian and other pioneering history of the State.

Any suitable person interested in the purposes of the organization is entitled to membership, and persons who have climbed a 14,000-foot peak in the State on foot are specially enrolled as "qualified members." The club corresponds and co-operates with all the well-known outdoor clubs of this country. James Grafton Rogers is the president. The work of the special committees is attractive: National Park, Morrison Shafroth; Nature Protection, Mrs. Henry F. Brooks; Library, Miss Ruth G. Rogers; Pictorial, Dr. Wm. H. Crisp; Nomenclature, Miss Harriet W. Vaille; Publicity, Robert B. Rockwell; Peak Registers, Roger W. Toll.

Denver's Mountain Parks

Colorado crowns the supreme altitude of the American continent, and her geographical location, between the north and the south, the east and the west, is of great commercial importance; eventually it will make her the common meeting place and market of exchange. But an advantage greater than that of mineral and agricultural wealth combined is in her climate and scenery.

Colorado is called the "National Sanitarium"—the mecca and pleasure resort of the world.

It was John Brisben Walker who made the first step in the chain of parks and splendid roads that now comprise the mountain parks of Denver by placing the matter before the Chamber of Commerce. A resolution was passed favoring the project.

Lookout Mountain Park Roadway

Mr. Walker took up the subject with the Real Estate Exchange, and a committee was appointed, of which K. A. Pence was the chairman; the Chamber of Commerce appointed a committee, of which Warwick M. Downing was chairman; the Denver Motor Club appointed a committee, with E. E. Sommers as chairman, and all gave efficient help. May 21, 1912, the amendment to the charter was submitted to the people, whereby one-half mill tax was to be levied for mountain parks for a period of five years, and Mr. Pence was the campaign manager. Through his energy and management the people became aroused to the importance of the play-grounds, and the amendment was carried.

The Chamber was instrumental in having the bill passed by Congress, making Estes Park the Rocky Mountain National Park, which will eventually be connected with the Denver mountain parks, forming one great playground at Denver's door.

Estes Park

Joel Estes was the first white settler in that section; he camped there in 1859, and in the following year built his cabin on Fish creek; he and his wife lived there three years before the coming of other white people.

The "back to nature" apostle could not have desired a more simple life than that led by these two pioneers. They lived on wild game, fish, berries, bread, butter and coffee, and came to Denver twice a year to get their mail and sell game or hides. In their honor the park was given the name "Estes."

Joel Estes and Wife

The recently established Rocky Mountain National Park and Estes are situated eighty-five miles northwest of Denver. Enos A. Mills, the noted naturalist, lives in Estes Park, and has given it world-wide fame by his wild life stories. He has devoted his efforts for six years to gain the creation of the Rocky Mountain National Park, and his great desire is to live to see the front range of Colorado's Rockies united in one vast playground for the pleasure seekers and health seekers of the world.

On the Way to Estes Park

Good Roads

This elaborate system of mountain parks makes Denver a touring center, and good roads a necessity. Under the administration of Honorable Thomas J. Ehrhart, State highway commissioner, the Colorado Good Roads Association has accomplished satisfactory results in the construction of good roads in Colorado.

Present plans include 5,840 miles of road, which traverse every valley and connect every county seat and important town in the State.

Mr. Thomas J. Tynan, warden of the Colorado State Penitentiary, says: "The Parkdale-Cotopaxi cut-off is the most important piece of highway construction ever performed in the West, for the reason that it gives the public a fair road from the Kansas line in the east and Denver and Cheyenne in the north to Grand Junction. The work on the Parkdale-Cotopaxi cut-off was commenced by the prisoners of the State Penitentiary in October, 1913, with Captain Charles Baldwin in command.

"It has been the policy of this institution for the last six years to do the heavy and expensive road work throughout the State, especially work that otherwise could not be afforded. This is particularly true in the mountain canyons, where the vast scenic beauties have been opened up for inspection to thousands of tourists.

"While we are doing a great deal of work in the mountains, we have constructed a greater number of miles of roadway in the farming communities. Since the prisoners have been at work on the public highways we have built more than 500 miles of perfect roadway. The prisoners are working simply on the public highways designated by the Highway Commission and surveyed and laid out by them, and the Commission helps the counties in the building of these roads. When the main roads are complete across the State it will mean the construction of thousands of miles of feeder roads from the various mountains and country districts of the State to the main highways. This building of feeder roads has scarcely commenced—it will be going on for years to come."

Motoring in Colorado

The highways are now crossing back and forth through the State, covering it like a spider web. Motoring in Colorado means recreation in its fullest sense. From one end of the State to the other each mile unfurls some new sight—some new thrill of sensation—and during the summer months automobiles may be seen on the streets of the cities and on the roads in the rural sections, bearing license plates from almost every State in the country.

People from all points of the compass are continually dropping in at the Denver Motor Club for information about good roads. Assistant Secretary Ralph P. Benedict says:

"The completion of the Ellwood Pass over the mountains from the San Luis Valley will give a short-cut to Pagosa Springs, Durango, Mesa Verde National Park and the San Juan country. In fact, the automobilist taking in all the wonders between the Rocky Mountain National Park and the Mesa Verde will have to keep going through the entire summer."

The organizations mentioned show how the pioneers of today are directing the building of the splendid State of Colorado and making her the highest example of industrial progress and American civilization. The writers of history in the future will tell what the pioneers of today accomplish.

The End

INDEX

----, Billy 296 Bob 118-119 171 Buckskin Joe 138 Buffalo Bill 455 Cap 335 Daniel 206 Dick 184 359 Marcelina 441 Mike 206 Muzzey 209 211 Old Jim 37 Pat 343 Uncle Dick 32 50 Uncle Samuel 157 Wild Bill 455
ADAMS, 309 Alva 454 457 Alva Blanchard 459 Diadema 225 Gen 308-309 414 Gov 304 458-459 Mrs 458-459
ADRIANCE, Jacob 71 133 Preacher 141
AGASSIZ, Louis 227
AIKENS, James 176
ALDEN, George W 269
ALEXIS, Grand Duke 227
ALLEN, George W 269 516 Henry 154 Judge 269 516
ALLISON, A J 71
ANDREWS, Mr 178 Mrs 177
ARCHER, 196 Col 260 282 290 James 196 282 289-290
ARKINS, 435 John 432

ARTHUR, President 347
ASHLEY, Mrs E M 239
ASTOR, 27
ATKINS, Horace 366
AUSTIN, 246
AYRES, Lee 209-211
BAILEY, A W 225 296 Diadema 225 Joseph L 196 Mrs Dewey C 236 Vice President 146
BAKER, 36-37 Dr 179 James H 179 Jane 36-37 Jim 35-37 215 476 478 Miss 270 Mrs J H 239 Mrs James A 5
BANCROFT, Mrs Frederic J 5
BANKHEAD, Col 216
BARCLAY, 272
BARELA, Senator 180
BARK, G W 155
BARNEY, 222 Mr 63
BARTH, William Moritz 291
BASSETT, 56
BATES, J E 196 Joseph E 283
BAUR, 128 O P 128
BEARD, William H 227

BEATTY, William R 157
BECKHURST, Herman 479
BECKHURTS, Herman 328
BECKWITH, E G 25
BEEBE, F W 332
BELFORD, 348 J B 426
   James 347 James B 347
   James Red-headed
   Rooster Of The Rockies
   347 Mrs James B 367
BELL, James C 180 Mr 289
   William A 467
BELLAMY, Mrs Harry 487
BENEDICT, Mrs J J B 107
   Ralph P 544
BENNET, 61 100 Delegate
   182 H P 56 74 81 83 100
   322 Hiram P 30 241
BENNETT, 472 Horace 274
   Horace W 274
BENT, 25 27 29 218 352
   Charles 29 Col 352-353
   William 28
BENTON, 25 Jessie 24
   Thomas H 24
BERGER, W J 197 William
   490 Wm B 349
BERTHOUD, Capt 337 E L
   332 337
BIERSTADT, 373 Albert 227
BILLINGSGATE, 209
BIRDSALL, Frank C 151
BISSELL, Charles R 71
BLACKBURN, Judge 322

BLAINE, Mr 320 Speaker
   320
BLAKE, 43 C H 55 155
   Charles 49
BLISS, 74-77 148 Edward
   148 Lou 74 Lucien W 71
   Secretary 74
BLOODSWORTH, James
   424
BOETTCHER, Charles 498-
   499 Claude 499 Mr 496-
   497
BOHM, Henry 485 Mr 486
BONAPART, King Of Naples
   42
BOURDMAN, Norman 494
BOUTWELL, Maj 162
BOWEN, L L 102
BOWLES, J C 332
BOWMAN, Mrs 208
BOYD, Jim 384
BOYER, Henry 499
BRADFORD, Allan A 241
   Mary C C 145 239
   Preacher 134 R B 155 R R
   244-245 256 Sam 285 W
   M 134
BREDLINGER, H J 241
BRESSLER, Mr 402
BRIDGER, Jim 29 33-35
BRINKER, Isaac 512
BRNTON, D W 516
BROADWELL, 78-79 281
   James 77 Jim 78

BROCKWAY, John P 417
BROMWELL, H P H 233
BROOKFIELD, Annie A 177
 Mrs 177
BROOKS, Mrs Henry F 539
BROWN, 78 185 291 353
 Abner R 144 Clara 362
 George W 171 H C 109
 185-186 Harry K 107
 Henry C 78 162 184-186
 481 J F 104 109 197 J J
 484 J S 104 109 512 J
 Sidney 291 James H 185
 John Sidney 281 Joseph G
 150 Junius F 105 291 May
 Butler 322 Mr 105-107
 184-185 281 283 Mrs 106-
 107 S E 322
BRUMMEL, Beau 140
BRUSH, J L 270 Jared L 304
 Mr 304
BRYAN, Thomas B 371
BUCHANAN, James 66
 President 99
BUCHER, John J 150
BUCHTEL, Henry A 146
BUCKHOUT, Fannie A 296
BUCKINGHAM, Mayor 322
 R G 322
BUCKLE, 367
BUELL, Sam 343
BULL, J S 175
BURDETT, Bill 187
BURNESS, James M 432

BURNS, Mrs Jj 5
BURRILL, R F 196
BURROUGHS, Ben 342
BURROWS, 319-320
 Congressman 319 J C 319
BUTTERS, Alfred 328 520
BYERS, 35 80-81 148 200 E
 M 94 Mr 73 79-80 147
 Mrs 94-96 Mrs William N
 94 159 W N 72 149 479
 William N 61 115 146 173
 Wm N 269
C, Mrs 205
CABLE, R R 470
CALHOUN, John C 100
CAMERON, Gen 303 R A
 302 312
CAMPBELL, Mrs Richard
 Crawford 327
CAMPION, John 505 John F
 493 495 503 513 Mr 494-
 497 Mrs 498
CANBY, Gen 189
CANNON, Benton 415 Mr
 415
CARLSON, Gov 536
CARNEGIE, Andrew 523 Mr
 523
CARROL, John 424
CARSON, 31 Christopher
 (kit) 30 Kit 23 30-31 33
 35 455 476
CARTER, H J 332
CARTRIGHT, 127

CARTWRIGHT, 141
CASE, F M 283
CASEY, 342-344 Mr 344 P 343 P D 344 Pat 342-343
CASS, Dr 126-127 Joseph B 126 O D 125 127
CASWELL, T B 150
CHAFFEE, 316-318 349 481 Jerome B 241 260 286 297 316 326 329 347 481 Mr 316 321 326 Senator 276
CHAPIN, Russel A 383
CHARLES*II, 366
CHARPIOT, 323
CHASE, Edward 241
CHEESMAN, 260 Mr 257-260 519 W S 186 257 260 Walter 260-261 Walter S 174 260-261 519
CHILCOTT, George M 241 Martha 159 Mrs 159 William 159
CHIVINGTON, 189 Col 137 213-215 395 John M 38 134 189
CHURCH, William 166
CHURCHILL, Isabella 239 John A 46
CLANCY, John 49
CLARK, 11 126 173 297 Austin M 171 C A 332 Clarence J 196 George 224

CLARK (cont.)
George T 224 241 297 400 John M 256 Kate 223 Milton E 171 Mr 267 Mrs 224-225 227 Mrs Fred 225 Nettie 284 Potato 267 Robert M 365 Rufus 267 W A 348
CLARKE, 108 Clarence J 108
CLAYTON, 98 G W 97 George W 98 Thomas S 197 William M 241 512 Wm M 283
CLEMENTS, Judge 185
CLEVELAND, President 116
CLINE, Capt 309
CLOUGH, Henry A 264
CLOUSER, Charles 175-176
COBB, 246 Frank 46 Frank M 40 46
COBERTY, 183
CODY, 250 Bill 250 Buffalo Bill 227 250 W F 227 250 William F (Buffalo Bill) 15
COE, Earl B 502
COLE, 195
COLEMAN, 148
COLFAX, 227 Schuyler 227
COLLIER, D C 141
COLLINS, Mrs Sewell 288
COLUMBUS, 9
COOK, 170 C A 169 Charles A 169 David J 219

COOK (cont.)
  G W 71 Gen 220
COORS, Mrs Grover C 265
CORNFORTH, Mrs Birks 159
CORONADO, 17-18
COSTIGAN, Mrs E P 236
CRANMER, 265 Catherine H 265 George E 265 Martha J 265 Mr 265 W H H 264-265
CREE, Capt 395 John 395
CREIGHTON, Edward 251
CRIPPEN, 89-90 92 Lyman G 89
CRISP, Wm H 539
CROCKER, 222 Freeman B 108 221
CUMMING, Gordon 35
CURTIS, 108 Dell 223 Gen 213 Mr 109 204 407 Mrs 110 Rodney 107 110 194 203 223 Samuel 49
CUSHMAN, Mrs S H 144
CUSTER, 216
CUTHBERT, Mrs 278-279 Mrs Lucius M 278
CUTLER, Mrs L W 159
DAILEY, 148 200 Annie 150 John L 148-149 198 269 Mr 149
DALY, Mr 485 Thomas F 484
DANIELS, 112 228-232 291

DANIELS (cont.)
  422 518 A B 112 283 Alvin B 291 Mr 112 228 230-232 W B 228 231 W C 232
DART, Elizabeth 349
DAVIDSON, William 332
DAVIES, J Vipond 516
DAVIS, C C 194 432 Noah 245 Walter Juan 508
DECATUR, Stephen 323
DECKER, Sarah Platt 236 W S 322 Westbrook S 329
DECORONADO, Francisco Vasquez 16
DEFREES, 338 Wilkes 337
DEITSCH, Isadore 136 270
DELAND, Thorndike 515
DELANO, 241 Milton M 241
DELEON, Ponce 345
DENHAM, 152
DENISON, Mrs Charles 235
DENNIS, Harrison 89
DENVER, J W 48 James W 47
DICKSON, T C 46
DIETERMAN, Henrietta 216
DIGGINGS, Gregory 92
DILL, R G 432
DINES, Mr 528 Tyson S 527
DOBBINS, Al G 150
DODGE, Capt 307 Col 289 468-469 496 D C 282 289 466 468 David C 288

DODGE (cont.)
  Grenville M 282 Nannie O 289
DOHERTY, Henry L 272 507 Mike 223 Mr 272 507
DONAVAN, 124-125 Joe 124 Joseph B 123 Mr 125
DORAN, W J H 535
DORSEY, 89-90
DOUGHERTY, 344 Mike 343
DOUGLAS, Mrs J W 107
DOWNING, Judge 86 Maj 206 208 Warwick M 540
DOWNS, David 470
DOYLE, J B 256
DUDLEY, Charles R 521 J H 49 134 Judson 95 Mr 521
DUGGAN, Martin 424
DYER, Father 137-139
EASTER, John 40
EATON, B H 270 Ben 411 Benjamin H 169 304
ECKHART, 228-229 Mr 230
EDDY, 488 Edward 483
EHRHART, Thomas J 543
ELDREDGE, Mrs C A 5
ELITCH, 159-160 John 159
ELKINS, 319-321 Delegate 319 321 Mr 319 321
ELLIS, Broken Nose Scotty 426 James 426-427 Mary A 176 Mrs 177
ELLSWORTH, 166

ELLSWORTH (cont.)
  L C 108 231 Lewis C 166 Mr 109
ELTURCO, 17-18
EMERY, H D 311
ERB, Newman 515-516
ERNEST, 265 Finis P 265
ESTABROOK, George 224 Mary 175 225 Miss 270 Mollie 270
ESTES, Joel 541
EUBANK, W T 161
EVANS, Gov 109 146 213-214 239 285-286 299 344 461 John 145 193 232 239 257 280 283-286 480 Mr 287 William G 109 286
EWING, John A 429
FAIRCHILD, Mary A 255
FELTON, Judge 445
FERRELL, J M 332
FERRILL, William 150
FETTER, John 164
FIELD, Cyrus W 227 E B 253-254 269 Edward B Jr 255 Eugene 479 Gene 122 152 Martha L 255 Mr 253-254 Mrs 255
FILED, Mr 255
FILLMORE, J H 257 John S 188
FINCH, E V 135 J Wellington 516
FISHER, 228 230-232 422

Index

FISHER (cont.)
  518 G W 131 Mr 231-232
  Mrs 232 Mrs Samuel H
  196 Norton C 188
  Preacher 141 Rev Mr 133
  141 Samuel H 109 196 W
  G 230-231 Woodie 196
FITZGERALD, E 71
FLEISHER, Rabbi 137
FLEMING, 269 Jesse E 516-518
FLOWER, J S 31 Roswell P 469
FORD, 214
FORROSTER, N C 223
FORSYTHE, 216 George A 216
FRAZER, R J 424
FRAZIER, Jesse 444
FREDERIC, John 150
FREMONT, 23-25 30 35
  John C 23 John Charles 23
FRENCH, Adnah 46
FRIEDENTHAL, Sigmond 150
FRIEDMAN, William S 137
FRYER, George 424
FULLER, 14 R R 13
GABBERT, William H 517
GALE, Mrs J S 5
GALLUP, Avery 269 Mrs Avery 225 270
GANTZ, 82 Jacob 82
GARRETSON, Mrs W R 239
GARRISON, 332
GEORGE, Anne 225 R D 516
  Sir 34-35
GIBSON, Mr 148 Thomas 148
GILL, 438 Sam G 437
GILPIN, 100 186 Gov 129
  188 190 193 285 471 Mr
  101 William 99-101 181 239
GODDARD, Mrs Luther M 236
GOLDEN, Thomas 332
GOLDING, Phil 487
GOLDRICK, 141-143 O J
  139-140 150 155
  Professor 142-143
GOLDSMITH, A 136
GOOD, John 113 John E 114-115 John Hasler 115 Mr 114
GOODARD, Luther M 486 Mrs 486
GOODE, Mr 133
GOODELL, Mary 492 R E 482
GORDON, 82-85 James 82
GORE, George 34
GORSLINE, Judge 366
GOSS, 223 Dell 223 Hattie 223 Kate 223
GOVE, Aaron 490
GRAHAM, 45-46 H J 45 William 155

GRANT, Gen 227 Gov 490-492 James B 487 490-491 James B Jr 492 Judge 488 Lester 492 Mary 492 Mr 488-489 491 Mrs 492 President 108 239 316-318 320 324 329 345 347
GREELEY, 12 67 270 302-304 Horace 66 68 302-303 Mr 66-70
GREENLEAF, 48 Mrs L C 225
GREENWOOD, W H 466
GREGORY, 64 89 127 154 266 337-338 John 340 John H 62 337
GRENFELL, Helen M 180
GRUBER, 126 173 C H 171 Mr 173
GUGGENHEIM, Meyer 422 Simon 422
GULCH, Russell 89
GUNNISON, 25 Capt 25-26 John W 25
GUNNSION, 26
GWINN, Senator 247
HADLEY, Chalmers 523
HADLY, W L 328-329
HAGAR, Clarence E 150 Martha 159 Mrs 159
HALE, Alice 277 Horace M 179 President 179
HALL, Charlie 409 Cy 408

HALL (cont.)
Frank 57 227 316 343 345 Gen 345 349 Mr 350 Secretary 216 Sue 227
HALLACK, E F 260
HALLETT, Moses 108 329
HANCOCK, Gen 227 Gratton E 536
HARDIN, Arthur B 164 Fannie D 163 G H 164 Lt 164 Mrs 163-164
HARDING, Mrs T M 239
HARKER, Mollie 225 O H 225
HARRIS, Paul P 537
HARRISON, 79-80 126 Charlie 79 126 President 116
HART, H Martyn 135 Miss 135
HARTMAN, Alonzo 438
HARWELL, Dick 474 Mr 476
HASKELL, T N 196
HASLAM, Pony Bob 250 Robert 250
HASLER, Mrs J E 114
HATTEN, Robert 479
HAYDEN, Professor 227 Thomas 260
HAZEN, W R 227
HEAD, Henry 489 Lafayette 12 30
HEATH, 89

Index

HELM, Joseph C 516 519
HENDERSON, 262 Jack 262 John 150 Mrs J F 159
HENRY, Mr 417 Prince Of Prussia 491 T C 417
HEREFORD, A P 322
HEWITT, Edgar L 7
HILL, 396 Alice Polk 235 269 516 Crawford 279 Mr 276-277 397 Mrs 278-279 N P 166 Nathaniel P 274 Professor 276 Senator 277-279
HITCHINGS, H B 135
HOBBS, 171 256
HOCKADAY, 54 244
HOLLADAY, 126-127 246 Ben 209 245-246
HOLLISTER, Carrie 227 Mrs H L 239 O J 227
HOLMES, Anna Archibald 40 Mrs 40
HOOK, George T 480
HOPKINS, 220 Marshal 220
HORNER, John W 197
HOSKINS, Mr 320
HOSMER, Gertie 495 Mrs 494
HOWARD, Col 194 John 86-87 Judge 86 Mary 87 Mary E 86
HOWBERT, Irving 464 Mr 465
HOWE, Mr 220 Sam 220
HOWLAND, Capt 192 J D 191-192 Jack 192 John D 191
HUBBARD, A W 367 Judge 367
HUEY, William 176
HUGHES, Andrew S 288 Bela M 197 282-283 287 322 328 C J 496 Charles J 502 Gen 288 Georgia 288 Jack 246 Tandy 288
HUNGATE, 202
HUNT, A C 186 256 466 Gov 395
HUNTER, A V 425
HURLBUT, John 469-470 Mr 469
HUSSEY, 171 252 Warren 171 344 354-355
HYNES, Charles F 150
ILIFF, 263 John W 262-263 Mr 263 265 William 400
INDIAN, Black Kettle 217 Chief Douglass 306 309 Chief Johnson 306 Chief Ouray 309 Chief Sapavanaro 309 Chipeta 413 Colorow 309 Douglass 306-307 Ouray 308-309 412-414 Sapavanaro 309 Shavano 309 Slo-a-necka 124 Spotted Horse 205-208
INMAN, 32

IRION, 89-92 John W 88-89
IRWIN, Dick 439 Mr 442
   Richard 440
JACKSON, 62 336 373
   Andrew 191 George 335
   George A 62 332 372
JACOBS, A 136 194
JACOBSON, Col 437 Mrs
   Chas H 236
JAMES, 23 488 Dr 22 Harry
   C 483 Mr 483 William H
   483
JEFFERSON, 19 65 99
   President 18 Thomas 19
JENNINGS, Dr 442
JOHNSON, Andrew 315 Fred
   P 266 Mr 515 President
   315 Theron W 216 W F
   283
JONES, 44 127 141 Jack 44
   245 W W 176
JOSEPHINE, Miss 306-307
KASSLER, George W 171
   186 Mrs George 225
KEATING, Edward J 152
KEENER, F A 109
KEHLER, Father 134-135
   164 J H 134 Mr 134
KELLY, J G 249
KENDRICK, T J 151
KENNEDY, W R 424
KENYON, W R 228
KIMBALL, Mrs Gordon 5
KIME, James 155

KING, 89
KINNA, 43
KIRBY, J C 332
KNOTT, Mrs Franklin Price
   278
KOESTER, August 150
KOUNTZE, 174-175 281
   Augustus 174 Charles B
   174-175 Harold 175
   Herman 174 Luther 108
   174 283 Mary 175 Mollie
   270 Mr 175 490 Mrs C B
   225 Mrs Charles 270
KRATZER, Frank 151
KUYKENDALL, 246-247
   John M 246 340 Judge
   341 Mr 246-247 W L 340
L----, Robert 405
LAMB, H H 144
LANDON, Sam S 150
   Samuel S 150
LANGRISHE, 223 344 Jack
   223 350
LARIMER, Gen 56 William
   49
LAVELLE, Eugene 161
LAWRENCE, 41 C A 56
LEACH, Henry C 512 Mr 263
   Richard E 168
LEE, 362 R E 425 Robert E
   465
LEFEVRE, O E 486
LEHOW, 45 Oscar 44-45
LEITER, L Z 421

LEITSENOUR, Charley 165
LEMEN, Dr 501 Lewis 499
    Mrs Lewis 483
LEONARD, G A 432
LEWIS, 11 George E 152
    John 224 Mrs Thomas A 5
LINCOLN, 251 Abe 187
    President 100 193 239 249
LINDELL, 142
LITTLE, 256
LOGAN, Azel R 150
LONDONER, Mr 121 123
    Wolfe 121 152 479
LONG, 23 Maj 22-23 Mrs
    Elitch 163 Stephen H 22
LORAH, Sam 366
LOVELAND, 333 Mr 333
    337 W A H 146 280-281
    286 332 334
LYTTON, A E 270
MACDONALD, James 332
MACHEBEUF, Bishop 135
    137 139 Joseph P 135
MACMONNIES, 31
MACON, Thomas 446
MAGGARD, Mother 182
MAJORS, 244 247-249 Alex
    250-251 Alexander 247
    Kentucky Christian 251
MALONE, A R 163 Mrs A R
    163
MANSIONS, 272
MARION, 130 C P 155
    Charles P 129

MARRS, 246
MARSH, Professor 444
MARTIN, Charles F 265
MARTINEZ, 246
MARVIN, Grace W 255
MASON, Mrs John 104
MATHERS, Carrie 227 Sue
    227
MATTESON, Gov 492
MATZ, Bishop 499
MAXWELL, John M 487
MAY, David 484
MCAFEE, H H 71
MCCLELLAN, 395 Dr 109
    Mr 394 W G 394
MCCLINTOCK, 181
MCCLURE, 57 George W
    172 Park 245 W P 56-57
MCCLURG, James A 296
    Marcia 296 Mrs Gilbert 5
MCCOOK, 345 E W 260
    Edward 232
MCCORMICK, R R 260
MCCUNE, 122 Alvin 122
    Mrs Alvine 159
MCDEARMON, Mrs 110
MCDONALD, Jesse F 487
MCDOWELL, Mayor 83
    William F 146
MCGAA, 42 46 49 55-56
    Denver 55
MCHUGH, Mrs P J 239 313
MCINTYRE, Gov 304
MCKINLEY, President 116

MCKINNEY, J R 496
MCLAIN, Mrs A H 239
MCLAUGHLIN, 127 394 C H 197 Cyrus H 127 Mrs C H 159
MCLEAN, Samuel 71
MCNAMARA, M J 520 Mr 521
MCNEIL, John L 290 Mr 291-292 Mrs 292-293 Mrs John L 5 292
MCPHEE, Mrs W P 265
MEARS, Mr 412 Otto 328 411
MEEKER, 302-303 306 Mr 302-303 305-306 Mrs 306-307 N C 302 Ralph 310
MERRICK, 148 Jack 147-148 John L 71
MERRITT, Gen 307-308
MICHAEL, Mrs H W 159
MIDDAUGH, 82-83 Mr 85 Shefiff 85 W H 82
MIDDLETON, 246
MIEGE, J B 135
MILLER, John D 40
MILLS, Enos A 541 Mr 397 Sydenham 397 W B 322
MITCHELL, 482 Clark G 483 John C 482 Julius 136 Mr 482-483 Mrs 482-483 Mrs D 159
MOFFAT, 155 286 295-300

MOFFAT (cont.) 481 D H 283 285 298 327 349 469 481 512 David 109 260 295 David H 251 257 260 286 293 295 300 480 517 Fannie A 296 Mr 225 286 299-300 Mrs 225
MOHAMMED, 53
MONK, Mrs Samuel 198
MONROE, James 18
MONTCHAWSON, Baren 35
MOODY, Mr 139
MOONLIGHT, Col 215 Thomas 215
MOORE, 148 David H 146 520 J C 56 241 John C 72 R R 429 Walter 135
MOREY, C S 521 536 Chester S 520 Chester Stephen 524 Mr 524-525 536
MORGAN, Edward B 536 J Pierpont 491 Mr 536
MORRIS, Mrs Peter Randolph 288
MORRISON, J H 512
MORSE, Calvin H 78
MORTZ, August 198
MOSELEY, Mrs R 159
MULLEN, J K 167-169 Mr 169
MURAT, 42 55 Count 69 H 42 Mrs 55 Mrs H 55
MURDSTONE, Miss 440

MYERS, 472
NAPOLEON, 18-19
NELSON, 362
NEWHOUSE, Samuel 422
NICHOLS, 47-48 Charles 46 49 397 David H 178 Mr 176 178
NICHOLSON, Mr 431 Samuel D 430
NOCE, Angelo 150
NOER, Samuel 188
NOLAN, Mr 171
NORRIS, Capt 25
NOTT, Frank W 68
NYE, 43 Bill 152 William 424
O'CONNELL, John B 150
O'CONNOR, George 424
OAKES, 43 D C 30 43 58-59 61 161 Maj 61 161 Mrs 161 Mrs D C 161
ODELL, John M 71
ORAHOOD, Harper M 338
ORMAN, James B 180
OURAY, 30
OWEN, Mr 422-423 425-428 William R 422
PABOR, W E 312
PALM, W L 522
PALMER, Frank 512 Gen 464 467-468 W J 227 286 462 William J 491 William Jackson 466
PATHFINDER, 23-24
PATTERSON, J O 269 Mr 318-319 324-327 T M 7 180 196 241 323-324 426 502 Thomas M 241
PAYNE, Capt 307 Tom 397
PEABODY, 7 Mrs 6-7 Mrs W S 5
PEAK, James 89-90
PEARCE, Tip 479
PEARSE, Julius 197 Mr 197
PENCE, K A 540 Mr 541
PEPPER, 344 Sgt 344
PERCIVAL, Mr 431
PERKINS, Charles Elliot 470 Mr 470
PHIPPS, Lawrence Cowle 529 Mr 530
PICKERELL, Eliza 240
PIERCE, 89 A E 153 155 James F 89 James H 161 John 283 512 Mr 153 156 Tip 246 William H 246
PIKE, 20-23 Zebulon M 20 Zebulon Montgomery 20
PITKIN, Gov 166 305
PLANTER, 227
PLATTE, 119
POLK, Daniel 268-269 Mr 268 President 100
POLLACK, Tom 81
PORTER, 103 H H 470 Henry M 103 185 225 Laura 104 Mr 104 Mrs 104 225 Mrs Henry M 225

PORTER (cont.)
  Mrs Will 110 Ruth 104 W
  E 104
POYNTER, 362
PRICE, 190
PULLMAN, George M 348
PURSLEY, 22 James 22
RALSTON, 352 John 352-353
RANDALL, A J 161 Bishop 139 374-375 449 George M 135
RANKIN, Rev Dr 84
RAVERDY, J B 135
RAY, Sarah 426
REED, James 49 John 397 Mr 527 Verner Z 536
REIGART, John M 323
REYNOLDS, 246 James 397 Jim 394-395 Minnie J 236 Mrs A G 225
RHOADS, Halsey M 150 535 Mrs A G 159
RICH, Mrs C B 5
RICHARDS, D M 232
RICHARDSON, 12 67 133 A D 66 Albert D 133 S 437
RICHE, Jerome 274 Jerome S 166 274 Mr 166 Mrs Jerome 274
RIETHMAN, 118 J J 109
RING, Lydia Maria 143 Miss 143-144
RISCHE, 481 August 480
ROBERTS, H J 297 Mrs Charles E 288
ROBINSON, Helen Ring 234 J 425
ROCKWELL, Robert B 539
ROGERS, Hickory 47 James Grafton 539 Mrs Platt 177 Ruth G 539
ROLLINS, Jennie 225
ROOKER, Mrs S M 55 S M 42
ROOSEVELT, Ex-President 152 President 116
ROTHAKER, 479
ROUNDS, 148 H E 148
ROUTT, 323 Eliza 240 Gov 86 240 322-323 John L 239 321 328
ROWLEY, 89-92 Nathan 89
RUDD, A 87 Anson 445
RUFFNER, Harry 162
RUSSELL, 40-42 64 154 244 247-249 Bill 248 Green 41-42 50 162 J O 42 L J 41 Mrs W C 265 W Green 39-40 42 W H 344 William Green 64
SADLER, Sarah 116
SAFELY, Mrs 177
SAGENDORF, 45 Andrew 44 96 256 Andy 45 Mrs Andrew 159
SAINTVRAIN, Ceran 27 29
SALOMON, F Z 256 260 283

Index

SALOMON (cont.)
  512 Fred 95 Fred Z 136
  520 Mr 95
SANBORN, C W 457
SAUNDERS, James 332
SAYRE, Alfred 322 Elizabeth
  349 Hal 270 349 Hal Sr
  349 Mr 349 Mrs 349
  Robert 349
SCHERRER, Jake 389 391
SCHINNER, Adolph 128
SCHMIDT, Mr 383
SCHOLTZ, 109 Ed B 166
SCHURZ, Secretary 308
SCOTT, Walter 35
SCUDDER, 56 222 Capt 221-222
SEARS, Anne 225 Jasper 225
  Jasper P 169 Jep 170 203
  Mrs 203
SEMPER, Charles S 151 Mr 151
SEWELL, Joseph A 178
SHAFROTH, Congressman 5
  John F 530 Mr 532-533
  Mrs John F 533
SHAKESPEARE, 35
SHEEDY, Dennis 110 Mr 111-113
SHERIDAN, 216
SHERMAN, Gen 215 227
SHOUP, Lt 395
SIBLEY, 189 Henry H 188
SILVERTHORN, Judge 401

SILVERTHORN (cont.)
  Mrs 401
SIMMONS, Z G 469
SIMONTON, 246 Ada 144
  Mr 246
SIMPSON, George 29
SKERRITT, Thomas 218
SLATER, Milo H 191
SLAUGHTER, W M 155
SLOCUM, Mrs William F 5
  William Frederick 464
SLOUGH, John P 189
SMILEY, 11 60 J C 237
SMITH, 42 44 46 55-56 167
  297 349 A J 45 B 332 E L
  322 Eben 349 H P A 47 J
  W 283 John 44 John
  Simpson 42 John W 104
  166-168 185 283 512
  Laura 104 Mr 104 403
  Nannie O 289 O L 151
  Sam 245 Sylvester 297
  Trader 46
SMOKE, 55 Mrs 55
SNEED, Miss 279
SNYDER, President 310 Z X 311
SOLOMON, 68
SOMMERS, E E 540
SOPRIS, Elizabeth Allen 130
  Indiana 130 Irene 130
  Mayor 86 Miss 144 Mr
  130 Mrs 130 Mrs Richard
  159 Richard 128 130

SOPRIS (cont.)
    S T 130 221
SPARKS, Jack 395
SPEER, 201 Robert W 201
SPENGEL, 224
SPRINGER, John W 265 504
    513 Mr 505
STANDLEY, 348 355 Joseph
    348 355
STANSELL, Mr 397
STANTON, I W 332 Irving
    W 332 Mrs Frederick J
    284
STARKS, 79
STEARNS, Mr 514-515
    Thomas B 514-515
STEBBINS, 103
STECK, 245 Amos 108 134
    144 241 245 252 256 Mrs
    202
STEELE, George 80 Gov 72
    102 Henry K 520 Hugh 87
    162 Mr 87-88 Mrs Everett
    225 R W 73 87 101-102
    Robert W 71 73 115
STEVENS, A J 294 Isaac
    Newton 502 Mr 502-504
    Uncle Billy 421
STEWART, A T 231
STOIBER, Mrs E G 5
STONE, 74 76-77 115 Aunty
    313 Dr 74-76 Elizabeth
    313 Judge 116 Lewis 313
    Mrs 313 Sarah 116

STONE (cont.)
    Wilbur F 87 115 182 186
    395
STOUT, 56 E P 44 49 Mr 44
STOWE, Rev Dr 141
STRATTON, Mrs 313 W S
    464 472 Winfield S 528
STRICKLER, J M 512
SULLIVAN, Dennis 355 484
SUMNER, Miss 270
SYMES, G G 196 G S 322
TABOR, 223 426 481
    Augusta 159 Gov 437 H A
    W 424 480-481
TAFT, Ex-President 152 Mrs
    B 5
TALLEYRAND, 19
TAMARACK, 169
TAPPAN, 140-141 Lewis 95
    Lewis N 108 140 Mr 141
TAPPEN, Samuel F 189
TAYLOR, 324 Bayard 227
    324 510 Charles W 418
    Edward T 417 Mrs
    Eugene W 225 R T 424
TELLER, 345 347 H M 180
    329 Henry M 347 416
THATCHER, 355 Joe 348
    359 John A 456 Joseph A
    351 355 Mahlon D 456
    Mr 351-352 355-356 360
    Mrs 355 Mrs M D 239
    Mrs Mahlon D 5 457

Index

THOMAS, Charles S 501 Gov 179 Mr 502
THOMASON, Miss 247 Zachariah 247
THOMPSON, 212
THORNBURG, Maj 306-307 T T 307
THORNE, C R 222
TITSWORTH, Mrs F S 107
TOBIN, Mr 462 Thomas T 460 Tom 462
TODD, Mr 519 W D 109 519 Wm 513
TOLL, Roger W 539
TOTTEN, Oscar B 71
TRAIN, George Francis 282
TRANKLE, Justina 159
TREAT, Charles A 196-197
TRIMBLE, George W 425
TRITCH, George 117 120-121 281 479 512 Mr 120-121
TROUNSTINE, Mr 196 Phil 194
TUPPER, 89-92 Charles 89
TURNER, 171 256
TURPIN, Dick 335-336
TWOMBLY, George 163
TYNAN, Thomas J 543
UPDIKE, Bill 363
UZZELL, Parson 425 Parson Tom 425 Thomas 425
VAILLE, F O 252 Harriet W 539 Mr 253
VANKLEECK, Mrs Henry B 5
VANSCHAACK, Mrs Henry C 483
VILLARD, Henry 66
VINCENT, B T 362 367
VOORHEES, Gus 40
VOORHIES, Mollie 225
VROOM, J B 196
WADDELL, 244 247-249
WADDINGHAM, Wilson 260
WAKELY, Ellsworth 366 Judge 366 Madame 222
WALKER, Deacon 361 John 283 John Brisben 540 Mr 540 Mrs Harold 104
WALL, 246 D K 266 David K 332 Mr 266
WALSH, Thomas F 274 414
WALTHALL, Fannie D 163 Samuel W 163
WARD, Henry 432
WARREN, 252 T H 155
WASHBURN, Hiram 376
WASHINGTON, Booker T 468
WATSON, 336 Henry 469 Jim 335 Joe 439 Mr 440 Mrs 440
WEBSTER, Daniel 24 100
WELLS, E T 364
WELTON, Norman 49
WENTWORTH, Elijah 220

WENTWORTH (cont.)
  Lige 220-221 Old Lige 220
WEST, 334-336 George 332-333 Mr 336
WETHERILL, 3-4
WHEELER, Jerome B 469
WHITEHEAD, Mrs Charles 110
WHITEMAN, Mrs Wilberforce 134
WHITMORE, Mrs J D 236 239
WHITSITT, 56 164 184 Dick 95 Mr 185 R E 49 57 184 188 512 Richard E 56 164
WIDNER, Mrs 177 Mrs L R 177
WIGGINS, 38 Scout 38
WIGGINTON, Mrs W G 224
WILCOX, G W 126
WILLCOX, Charles Macallister 232 516 518
WILLIAMS, 43 A J 49 55 B D 99 Beverly D 71 99 Bill 65 Mrs 332 Parson 65
WILLIAMSON, 395 Ab 394
WILSON, Byrd L 150 James M 117 Joseph C 321 Mr 117-119 President 152
WINDSOR, 272
WINNE, Peter 134
WITTER, 246 256 Daniel 119 260 Ellen C 120 Mrs 227 Mrs Daniel 227
WIXSON, Helen M 8
WOLCOTT, E O 166 326 350 Edward O 504 H R 252 Henry R 166 252 348 Senator 273
WOLFINGER, Leslie 13
WOMACK, Bob 472
WOOD, 80 Carl 79 81 H E 487
WOODBURY, Mr 520 R W 156 Roger W 520
WOODWARD, B F 251-252 Benjamin F 252
WOOLEY, David 176
WOOLWORTH, 155 295 C C 295
WOOTEN, Dick 147
WOOTON, 32-33 50 Dick 29 50 61-62 Mrs 55 R L 29 Richens 50 Richens L 31 50
WRIGHT, J Whitaker 493
WYATT, 61
WYNCOOP, E W 47 Ned 49
YATES, Senator 316
YETTER, Mr 515
YOUNG, Frank C 360 520 Mr 360 362-363
ZELL, Fred 223 Hattie 223
ZERN, Frank 150

www.ingramcontent.com/pod-product-compliance
Lightning Source LLC
Chambersburg PA
CBHW071430300426
44114CB00013B/1378